George Bird Grinnell and the Blackfeet

Blackfoot Lodge Tales
and
Blackfoot Indian Stories

George Bird Grinnell

Introduction
by
Peter N. Jones

Bauu Institute and Press
2011

Library of Congress Cataloging-in-Publication Data

Grinnell, George B.
George Bird Grinnell and the Blackfeet: Blackfoot Lodge Tales and Blackfoot Indian Stories

p.cm

1. Native Americans - Oral Traditions. 2. Blackfeet.

ISBN 13: 978-1-936955-01-5

Bauu Press
Winter Park, Colorado
http://www.bauuinstitute.com

George Bird Grinnell and the Blackfeet

Blackfoot Lodge Tales
and
Blackfoot Indian Stories

George Bird Grinnell

Introduction
by
Peter N. Jones

Bauu Institute and Press
2011

INTRODUCTION

"The noblest work that any man can do is to make life easier for some of his fellows, and in the visible results which follow the stretching out of a hand in help and sympathy to an Indian tribe may be found rich reward and ample encouragement to renewed activity." So wrote George Bird Grinnell in 1899 for an article in *The Atlantic Monthly*. This theme, although it may sound a bit romantic or even neocolonial in today's world, was one that Grinnell deeply believed in, and which is reflected in his life and work. George Bird Grinnell (September 20, 1849 – April 11, 1938) was an American anthropologist, historian, naturalist, and writer who devoted much of his life to documenting and protecting the Plains – and the indigenous people – of the American West. Born in Brooklyn, New York, Grinnell graduated from Yale University with a B.A. in 1870 and a Ph.D. in 1880. Originally specializing in zoology, he became a prominent early conservationist and student of Native American life on the Plains of present-day Montana, Wyoming, North and South Dakota, Kansas, and Nebraska.

Over the course of his life, Grinnell had extensive contact with the terrain, animals and Native Americans of the northern Plains, beginning with his first trip west in 1871. In 1872 "White Wolf", as Grinnell came to be known among the Pawnee, joined Luther North and the Pawnee for their last great buffalo hunt. Later, as a graduate student, he accompanied Lieutenant Colonel George Armstrong Custer's 1874 Black Hills expedition as a naturalist. In 1875, Colonel William Ludlow, who had been part of Custer's Black Hills exploration effort, invited Grinnell to serve as naturalist and mineralogist on an expedition to Montana and the newly established Yellowstone Park. Here he encountered the Gros Ventres (who called him "Gray Clothes") and the Blackfeet (who called him "Fisher Hat"). As a result of this trip, Grinnell prepared an attachment to the expedition's report, in which he documented the poaching of buffalo, deer, elk and antelope for hides in the newly established Park lands. "It is estimated that during the winter of 1874-1875, not less than 3,000 Buffalo and mule deer suffer even more severely than the elk, and the antelope nearly as much," Grinnell wrote in his report. His experience in Yellowstone led Grinnell to pursue conservation efforts and to write the first of many magazine articles dealing with conservation, the protection of the buffalo, justice for Native Americans, and the American West.

Grinnell made hunting trips to the St. Mary Lakes region of the soon to be established Glacier National Park in 1885, 1887 and 1891 in the company of James Willard Schultz, the first professional guide in the region. During the 1885 visit, Grinnell and Schultz while traveling up the Swiftcurrent Valley observed the glacier that now bears his name, along with many other features in the Glacier region.

Grinnell was editor of *Forest and Stream Magazine* from 1876 to 1911, during which time he contributed many articles and essays to that publication, as well as several other magazines and professional publications. Grinnell's books and publications reflect his lifelong study of the northern Plains and the indigenous people and wildlife of the region. His best-known works are on the Cheyenne, including *The Fighting Cheyennes* (1915), and a two-volume work, *The Cheyenne Indians: Their History and Lifeways* (1923), however, it is his work on the Blackfeet that is often underappreciated.

Knowing the Blackfeet as few, perhaps none, have known or know them, Grinnell was the first to record directly from Blackfeet informants the tales that they deemed important. This, in fact, was part of Grinnell's effort to establish an approach that he believed represented a "truer" view and understanding of Native Americans than that represented by his contemporary authors. Grinnell's aim was "truth" and a picture of the "Indian mind" given by the Native himself. In some sense, this approach was nothing new. Henry Schoolcraft in the 1830s relied heavily on stories and myths in his massive study of the Iroquois. H.M. Loomis had done the same for the Micmac and others in his 1884 *The Algonquin Legends of New England*. Grinnell, however, argued that his collections were closer to what informants actually said and were more "true" because the Native was telling his own story. This insistence on the absence of a mediating White "author" is a well-known fiction, but Grinnell's attempt to leave as much of himself out of the narrative adds to the importance of his work today, as it provides a more straightforward telling then the work of his contemporaries. In fact,

Grinnell's friendship with the Blackfeet was more extensive and involved than many of the other Whites in the area during the period and specially those of his contemporary anthropologists and ethnologists. Beginning in 1887, for example, Grinnell began a two year effort to help the Blackfeet deal with starvation and a lack of food supplies resulting from the dealings of a dishonest U.S. Indian agent on the Blackfeet Indian Reservation. Because of his efforts the Blackfeet made him an honorary member of the tribe and gave him the name *Pinut-u-ye-is-tsim-o-kan* or "Fisher Hat." Later, in 1895 Grinnell was appointed by President Cleveland to negotiate a second treaty with the Blackfeet, during which he worked to help secure as favorable a deal as possible under the circumstances for the Blackfeet.

Of the two complete works republished here, *Blackfoot Lodge Tales* was Grinnell's second book, published in 1892, shortly after his return to the East Coast after an extensive stay among the Blackfeet. *Blackfoot Indian Stories* (1914), on the other hand, was published much later in Grinnell's career, and is a continuation of Grinnell's original ethnological style, although with more distance between his time with informants and the field. In both form and content, however, Grinnell's ethnology is founded on narrative, on myth, and story representing the "Indian mind." How much of Grinnell's work involves "unmoderated" story taken down exactly as his informants told him we can never know. The language used can sometimes edge into the romantic when Grinnell paints generalized pictures of Blackfeet life, but he personally would have denied this view of his relation to his informants, in part because of his deep intimacy with many individual tribal members and his expressed concern for tribal welfare over the years.

Not only does the republication of these two complete works provide important sources for those interested in Blackfeet culture, society, and oral traditions at a pivotal point in history, but also for the comparative anthropologist and folklorist. Many of the stories recorded by Grinnell have parallels found among other indigenous groups of the Plains region. The story of the buffalo that ate human flesh until their nature was changed by Old Man, for example, is paralleled in the Kiowa oral tradition of *Sinti*, who in like manner reduced the deer and antelope from dangerous carnivore to timid ruminants. The story of the bad son-in-law who kept all the buffalo hidden under the water and killed one at a time as he wanted is likewise found in the oral traditions of many other tribes, notably in the Cherokee oral tradition of *Kanati*, the owner and lord of the game. *Kutoyis*, the hero born of a clot of blood and grown to strong manhood in four days, has also his parallel among the Cherokees and Sioux in the east and the Omahas on the Plains. Similarly, the "Stories of Old Man" deal with the deeds and feats of *Nápi* (Old Man), who corresponds in many respects to *Nanabozho* of the Ojibwa, *Wisakejak* of the Creek, *Ganoozhigaabe* of the Algonquin, and *Inktonme* of the Assiniboine.

Finally, the chapter on the history and migrations, the social organization and the religion of the Blackfeet, and on their present condition, contains valuable information to be obtained from no other source. Grinnell's passion for detail, for authentic self-representation by Native informants, and his resistance to developing theories about Native life as the basis for analysis, allow his work to continue to be of importance today.

Peter N. Jones
Winter Park, Colorado 2011

BLACKFOOT LODGE TALES

The Story of a Prairie People

BY

GEORGE BIRD GRINNELL

AUTHOR OF "PAWNEE HERO STORIES AND FOLK-TALES"

CHARLES SCRIBNER'S SONS
NEW YORK

CONTENTS

THE STORY OF THE THREE TRIBES.

BLACKFOOT LODGE TALES

We were sitting about the fire in the lodge on Two Medicine. Double Runner, Small Leggings, Mad Wolf, and the Little Blackfoot were smoking and talking, and I was writing in my note-book. As I put aside the book, and reached out my hand for the pipe, Double Runner bent over and picked up a scrap of printed paper, which had fallen to the ground. He looked at it for a moment without speaking, and then, holding it up and calling me by name, said : —

"*Pi-nut-ú-ye is-tsim-okan*, this is education. Here is the difference between you and me, between the Indians and the white people. You know what this means. I do not. If I did know, I should be as smart as you. If all my people knew, the white people would not always get the best of us."

"*Nisah* (elder brother), your words are true. Therefore you ought to see that your children go to school, so that they may get the white man's knowledge. When they are men, they will have to trade with the white people ; and if they know nothing, they can never get rich. The times have changed. It will never again be as it was when you and I were young."

"You say well, *Pi-nut-ú-ye is-tsim-okan*, I have seen the days ; and I know it is so. The old things are passing away, and the children of my children will be like white people. None of them will know how it used to be in their father's days unless they read the things which we have told you, and which you are all the time writing down in your books."

"They are all written down, *Nisah*, the story of the three tribes, Sik-si-kau, Kainah, and Pikúni."

INDIANS AND THEIR STORIES

THE most shameful chapter of American history is that in which is recorded the account of our dealings with the Indians. The story of our government's intercourse with this race is an unbroken narrative of injustice, fraud, and robbery. Our people have disregarded honesty and truth whenever they have come in contact with the Indian, and he has had no rights because he has never had the power to enforce any.

Protests against governmental swindling of these savages have been made again and again, but such remonstrances attract no general attention. Almost every one is ready to acknowledge that in the past the Indians have been shamefully robbed, but it appears to be believed that this no longer takes place. This is a great mistake. We treat them now much as we have always treated them. Within two years, I have been present on a reservation where government commissioners, by means of threats, by bribes given to chiefs, and by casting fraudulently the votes of absentees, succeeded after months of effort in securing votes enough to warrant them in asserting that a tribe of Indians, entirely wild and totally ignorant of farming, had consented to sell their lands, and to settle down each upon 160 acres of the most utterly arid and barren land to be found on the North American continent. The fraud perpetrated on this tribe was as gross as could be practised by one set of men upon another. In a similar way the Southern Utes were recently induced to consent to give up their reservation for another.

Americans are a conscientious people, yet they take no interest in these frauds. They have the Anglo-Saxon spirit of fair play, which sympathizes with weakness, yet no protest is made against the oppression which the Indian suffers. They are generous; a famine in Ireland, Japan, or Russia arouses the sympathy and calls forth the bounty of the nation, yet they give no heed to the distress of the Indians, who are in the very midst of them. They do not realize that Indians are human beings like themselves.

For this state of things there must be a reason, and this reason is to be found, I believe, in the fact that practically no one has any personal knowledge of the Indian race. The few who are acquainted with them are neither writers nor public speakers, and for the most part would find it easier to break a horse than to write a letter. If the general public knows little of this race, those who legislate about them are equally ignorant. From the congressional page who distributes the copies of a pending bill, up through the representatives and senators who vote for it, to the president whose signature makes the measure a law, all are entirely unacquainted with this people or their needs.

Many stories about Indians have been written, some of which are interesting and some, perhaps, true. All, however, have been written by civilized people, and have thus of necessity been misleading. The reason for this is plain. The white person who gives his idea of a story of Indian life inevitably looks at things from the civilized point of view, and assigns to the Indian such motives and feelings as govern the civilized man. But often the feelings which lead an Indian to perform a particular action are not those which would induce a white man to do the same thing, or if they are, the train of reasoning which led up to the Indian's motive is not the reasoning of the white man.

In a volume about the Pawnees,[1] I endeavored to show how Indians think and feel by letting some of them tell their own stories in their own fashion, and thus explain in their own way how they look at the every-day occurrences of their life, what motives govern them, and how they reason.

In the present volume, I treat of another race of Indians in precisely the same way. I give the Blackfoot stories as they have been told to me by the Indians themselves, not elaborating nor adding to them. In all cases except one they were written down as they fell from the lips of the story-teller. Sometimes I have transposed a sentence or two, or have added a few words of explanation ; but the stories as here given are told in the words of the original narrators as nearly as it is possible to render those words into the simplest every-day English. These are Indians' stories, pictures of Indian life drawn by Indian artists, and showing this life from the Indian's point of view. Those who read these stories will have the narratives just as they came to me from the lips of the Indians themselves ; and from the tales they can get a true notion of the real man who is speaking. He is not the Indian of the newspapers, nor of the novel, nor of the Eastern sentimentalist, nor of the Western boomer, but the real Indian as he is in his daily life among his own people, his friends, where he is not embarrassed by the presence of strangers, nor trying to produce effects, but is himself — the true, natural man.

And when you are talking with your Indian friend, as you sit beside him and smoke with him on the bare prairie during a halt in the day's march, or at night lie at length about your lonely camp fire in the mountains, or form one of a circle of feasters in his home lodge, you get very near to nature. Some of the sentiments which he expresses may horrify your civilized mind, but they are not unlike those which your own small boy might utter. The Indian talks of

[1] Pawnee Hero Stories and Folk-Tales.

blood and wounds and death in a commonplace, matter-of-fact way that may startle you. But these things used to be a part of his daily life ; and even to-day you may sometimes hear a dried-up, palsied survivor of the ancient wars cackle out his shrill laugh when he tells as a merry jest, a blood-curdling story of the torture he inflicted on some enemy in the long ago.

I have elsewhere expressed my views on Indian character, the conclusions founded on an acquaintance with this race extending over more than twenty years, during which time I have met many tribes, with some of whom I have lived on terms of the closest intimacy.

The Indian is a man, not very different from his white brother, except that he is undeveloped. In his natural state he is kind and affectionate in his family, is hospitable, honest and straightforward with his fellows, — a true friend. If you are his guest, the best he has is at your disposal ; if the camp is starving, you will still have set before you your share of what food there may be in the lodge. For his friend he will die, if need be. He is glad to perform acts of kindness for those he likes. While travelling in the heats of summer over long, waterless stretches of prairie, I have had an Indian, who saw me suffering from thirst, leave me, without mentioning his errand, and ride thirty miles to fetch me a canteen of cool water.

The Indian is intensely religious. No people pray more earnestly nor more frequently. This is especially true of all Indians of the Plains.

The Indian has the mind and feelings of a child with the stature of a man ; and if this is clearly understood and considered, it will readily account for much of the bad that we hear about him, and for many of the evil traits which are commonly attributed to him. Civilized and educated, the Indian of the better class is not less intelligent than the average white man, and he has every capacity for becoming a good citizen.

This is the view held not only by myself, but by all of the many old frontiersmen that I have known, who have had occasion to live much among Indians, and by most experienced army officers. It was the view held by my friend and schoolmate, the lamented Lieutenant Casey, whose good work in transforming the fierce Northern Cheyennes into United States soldiers is well known among all officers of the army, and whose sad death by an Indian bullet has not yet, I believe, been forgotten by the public.

It is proper that something should be said as to how this book came to be written.

About ten years ago, Mr. J. W. Schultz of Montana, who was then living in the Blackfoot camp, contributed to the columns of the *Forest and Stream*, under the title " Life among the Blackfeet," a series of sketches of that people. These papers seemed to me of unusual interest, and worthy a record in a form more permanent than the columns of a newspaper ; but no opportunity was then presented for filling in the outlines given in them.

Shortly after this, I visited the Pi-kŭn-i tribe of the Blackfeet, and I have spent more or less time in their camps every year since. I have learned to know well all their principal men, besides many of the Bloods and the Blackfeet, and have devoted much time and effort to the work of accumulating from their old men and best warriors the facts bearing on the history, customs, and oral literature of the tribe, which are presented in this volume.

In 1889 my book on the Pawnees was published, and seemed to arouse so much interest in Indian life, from the Indian's standpoint, that I wrote to Mr. Schultz, urging him, as I had often done before, to put his observations in shape for publication, and offered to edit his work, and to see it through the press. Mr. Schultz was unwilling to undertake this task, and begged me to use all the material which I had gathered, and whatever he could supply, in the preparation of a book about the Blackfeet.

A portion of the material contained in these pages was originally made public by Mr. Schultz, and he was thus the discoverer of the literature of the Blackfeet. My own investigations have made me familiar with all the stories here recorded, from original sources, but some of them he first published in the columns of the *Forest and Stream*. For this work he is entitled to great credit, for it is most unusual to find any one living the rough life beyond the frontier, and mingling in daily intercourse with Indians, who has the intelligence to study their traditions, history, and customs, and the industry to reduce his observations to writing.

Besides the invaluable assistance given me by Mr. Schultz, I acknowledge with gratitude the kindly aid of Miss Cora M. Ross, one of the school teachers at the Blackfoot agency, who has furnished me with a version of the story of the origin of the Medicine Lodge ; and of Mrs. Thomas Dawson, who gave me help on the story of the Lost Children. William Jackson, an educated half-breed, who did good service from 1874 to 1879, scouting under Generals Custer and Miles, and William Russell, half-breed, at one time government interpreter at the agency, have both given me valuable assistance. The latter has always placed himself at my service, when I needed an interpreter, while Mr. Jackson has been at great pains to assist me in securing several tales which I might not otherwise have obtained, and has helped me in many ways. The veteran prairie man, Mr. Hugh Monroe, and his son, John Monroe, have also given me much information. Most of the stories I owe to Blackfeet, Bloods, and Piegans of pure race. Some of these men have died within the past few years, among them the kindly and venerable Red Eagle ; Almost-a-Dog, a noble old man who was regarded with respect and affection by Indians and whites ; and that matchless orator, Four Bears. Others, still living, to whom I owe thanks, are Wolf Calf, Big Nose, Heavy Runner, Young Bear Chief, Wolf Tail, Rabid Wolf, Running Rabbit, White Calf, All-are-his-Children, Double Runner, Lone Medicine Person, and many others.

The stories here given cover a wide range of subjects, but are fair examples of the oral literature of the Blackfeet. They deal with religion, the origin of things, the perform- ances of medicine men, the bravery and single-heartedness of warriors.

It will be observed that in more than one case two stories begin in the same way, and for a few paragraphs are told in language which is almost identical. In like manner it is often to be noted that in different stories the same incidents occur. This is all natural enough, when it is remembered that the range of the Indians' experiences is very narrow. The incidents of camp life, of hunting and war excursions, do not offer a very wide variety of conditions ; and of course the stories of the people deal chiefly with matters with which they are familiar. They are based on the every-day life of the narrators.

The reader of these Blackfoot stories will not fail to notice many curious resemblances to tales told among other distant and different peoples. Their similarity to those current among the Ojibwas, and other Eastern Algonquin tribes, is sufficiently obvious and altogether to be expected, nor is it at all remarkable that we should find, among the Blackfeet, tales identical with those told by tribes of different stock far to the south ; but it is a little startling to see in the story of the Worm Pipe a close parallel to the classical myth of Orpheus and Eurydice. In another of the stories is an incident which might have been taken bodily from the Odyssey.

Well-equipped students of general folk-lore will find in these tales much to interest them, and to such may be left the task of commenting on this collection.

STORIES OF ADVENTURE

THE PEACE WITH THE SNAKES

I

In those days there was a Piegan chief named Owl Bear. He was a great chief, very brave and generous. One night he had a dream: he saw many dead bodies of the enemy lying about, scalped, and he knew that he must go to war. So he called out for a feast, and after the people had eaten, he said : —

"I had a strong dream last night. I went to war against the Snakes, and killed many of their warriors. So the signs are good, and I feel that I must go. Let us have a big party now, and I will be the leader. We will start to-morrow night."

Then he told two old men to go out in the camp and shout the news, so that all might know. A big party was made up. Two hundred men, they say, went with this chief to war. The first night they travelled only a little way, for they were not used to walking, and soon got tired.

In the morning the chief got up early and went and made a sacrifice, and when he came back to the others, some said, " Come now, tell us your dream of this night."

"I dreamed good," said Owl Bear. "I had a good dream. We will have good luck."

But many others said they had bad dreams. They saw blood running from their bodies.

Night came, and the party started on, travelling south, and keeping near the foot-hills; and when daylight came, they stopped in thick pine woods and built war lodges.

3

They put up poles as for a lodge, and covered them very thick with pine boughs, so they could build fires and cook, and no one would see the light and smoke; and they all ate some of the food they carried, and then went to sleep.

Again the chief had a good dream, but the others all had bad dreams, and some talked about turning back; but Owl Bear laughed at them, and when night came, all started on. So they travelled for some nights, and all kept dreaming bad except the chief. He always had good dreams. One day after a sleep, a person again asked Owl Bear if he dreamed good. "Yes," he replied. "I have again dreamed of good luck."

"We still dream bad," the person said, "and now some of us are going to turn back. We will go no further, for bad luck is surely ahead." "Go back! go back!" said Owl Bear. "I think you are cowards; I want no cowards with me." They did not speak again. Many of them turned around, and started north, toward home.

Two more days' travel. Owl Bear and his warriors went on, and then another party turned back, for they still had bad dreams. All the men now left with him were his relations. All the others had turned back.

They travelled on, and travelled on, always having bad dreams, until they came close to the Elk River.[1] Then the oldest relation said, "Come, my chief, let us all turn back. We still have bad dreams. We cannot have good luck."

"No," replied Owl Bear, "I will not turn back."

Then they were going to seize him and tie his hands, for they had talked of this before. They thought to tie him and make him go back with them. Then the chief got very angry. He put an arrow on his bow, and said: "Do not touch me. You are my relations; but if any of you try to tie me, I will kill you. Now I am ashamed. My relations are cowards and will turn back. I have told you I have

---

[1] Yellowstone River.

always dreamed good, and that we would have good luck. Now I don't care; I am covered with shame. I am going now to the Snake camp and will give them my body. I am ashamed. Go! go! and when you get home put on women's dresses. You are no longer men."

They said no more. They turned back homeward, and the chief was all alone. His heart was very sad as he travelled on, and he was much ashamed, for his relations had left him.

II

Night was coming on. The sun had set and rain was beginning to fall. Owl Bear looked around for some place where he could sleep dry. Close by he saw a hole in the rocks. He got down on his hands and knees and crept in. Here it was very dark. He could see nothing, so he crept very slowly, feeling as he went. All at once his hand touched something strange. He felt of it. It was a person's foot, and there was a moccasin on it. He stopped, and sat still. Then he felt a little further. Yes, it was a person's leg. He could feel the cowskin legging. Now he did not know what to do. He thought perhaps it was a dead person; and again, he thought it might be one of his relations, who had become ashamed and turned back after him.

Pretty soon he put his hand on the leg again and felt along up. He touched the person's belly. It was warm. He felt of the breast, and could feel it rise and fall as the breath came and went; and the heart was beating fast. Still the person did not move. Maybe he was afraid. Perhaps he thought that was a ghost feeling of him.

Owl Bear now knew this person was not dead. He thought he would try if he could learn who the man was, for he was not afraid. His heart was sad. His people and his relations had left him, and he had made up his mind to give his body to the Snakes. So he began and felt all over

the man, — of his face, hair, robe, leggings, belt, weapons;
and by and by he stopped feeling of him. He could not
tell whether it was one of his people or not.

Pretty soon the strange person sat up and felt all over
Owl Bear; and when he had finished, he took the Piegan's
hand and opened it and held it up, waving it from side to
side, saying by signs, "Who are you?"

Owl Bear put his closed hand against the person's cheek
and rubbed it; he said in signs, "Piegan!" and then he
asked the person who he was. A finger was placed against
his breast and moved across it zigzag. It was the sign for
"Snake."

"*Hai yah!*" thought Owl Bear, "a Snake, my enemy."
For a long time he sat still, thinking. By and by he drew
his knife from his belt and placed it in the Snake's hand,
and signed, "Kill me!" He waited. He thought soon his
heart would be cut. He wanted to die. Why live? His
people had left him.

Then the Snake took Owl Bear's hand and put a knife in
it and motioned that Owl Bear should cut his heart, but the
Piegan would not do it. He lay down, and the Snake lay
down beside him. Maybe they slept. Likely not.

So the night went and morning came. It was light, and
they crawled out of the cave, and talked a long time
together by signs. Owl Bear told the Snake where he
had come from, how his party had dreamed bad and left
him, and that he was going alone to give his body to the
Snakes.

Then the Snake said: "I was going to war, too. I was
going against the Piegans. Now I am done. Are you a
chief?"

"I am the head chief," replied Owl Bear. "I lead. All
the others follow."

"I am the same as you," said the Snake. "I am the
chief. I like you. You are brave. You gave me your knife

to kill you with. How is your heart? Shall the Snakes and the Piegans make peace?"

" Your words are good," replied Owl Bear. "I am glad."

" How many nights will it take you to go home and come back here with your people?" asked the Snake.

Owl Bear thought and counted. " In twenty-five nights," he replied, "the Piegans will camp down by that creek."

" My trail," said the Snake, "goes across the mountains. I will try to be here in twenty-five nights, but I will camp with my people just behind that first mountain. When you get here with the Piegans, come with one of your wives and stay all night with me. In the morning the Snakes will move and put up their lodges beside the Piegans."

"As you say," replied the chief, "so it shall be done." Then they built a fire and cooked some meat and ate together.

" I am ashamed to go home," said Owl Bear. " I have taken no horses, no scalps. Let me cut off your side locks?"

" Take them," said the Snake.

Owl Bear cut off the chief's braids close to his head, and then the Snake cut off the Piegan's braids. Then they exchanged clothes and weapons and started out, the Piegan north, the Snake south.

III

"Owl Bear has come! Owl Bear has come!" the people were shouting.

The warriors rushed to his lodge. *Whish!* how quickly it was filled! Hundreds stood outside, waiting to hear the news.

For a long time the chief did not speak. He was still angry with his people. An old man was talking, telling the news of the camp. Owl Bear did not look at him. He ate some food and rested. Many were in the lodge who had started to war with him. They were now ashamed. They did not speak, either, but kept looking at the fire. After a long time the chief said: "I travelled on alone. I met a Snake. I took his scalp and clothes, and his weapons. See, here is his scalp!" And he held up the two braids of hair.

No one spoke, but the chief saw them nudge each other and smile a little; and soon they went out and said to one another: "What a lie! That is not an enemy's scalp; there is no flesh on it. He has robbed some dead person."

Some one told the chief what they said, but he only laughed and replied: —

"I do not care. They were too much afraid even to go on and rob a dead person. They should wear women's dresses."

Near sunset, Owl Bear called for a horse, and rode all through camp so every one could hear, shouting out: "Listen! listen! To-morrow we move camp. We travel south. The Piegans and Snakes are going to make peace. If any one refuses to go, I will kill him. All must go."

Then an old medicine man came up to him and said: "*Kyi*, Owl Bear! listen to me. Why talk like this? You know we are not afraid of the Snakes. Have we not fought them and driven them out of this country? Do you think we are afraid to go and meet them? No. We will go and make peace with them as you say, and if they want to fight, we will fight. Now you are angry with those who started to war with you. Don't be angry. Dreams belong to the Sun. He gave them to us, so that we can see ahead and know what will happen. The Piegans are not cowards. Their dreams told them to turn back. So do not be angry with them any more."

"There is truth in what you say, old man," replied Owl Bear; "I will take your words."

IV

In those days the Piegans were a great tribe. When they travelled, if you were with the head ones, you could not see the last ones, they were so far back. They had more horses than they could count, so they used fresh horses every day and travelled very fast. On the twenty-fourth day they reached the place where Owl Bear had told the Snake they would camp, and put up their lodges along the creek. Soon some young men came in, and said they had seen some fresh horse trails up toward the mountain.

" It must be the Snakes," said the chief; " they have already arrived, although there is yet one night." So he called one of his wives, and getting on their horses they set out to find the Snake camp. They took the trail up over the mountain, and soon came in sight of the lodges. It was a big camp. Every open place in the valley was covered with lodges, and the hills were dotted with horses ; for the Snakes had a great many more horses than the Piegans.

Some of the Snakes saw the Piegans coming, and they ran to the chief, saying: " Two strangers are in sight, coming this way. What shall be done?"

" Do not harm them," replied the chief. " They are friends of mine. I have been expecting them." Then the Snakes wondered, for the chief had told them nothing about his war trip.

Now when Owl Bear had come to the camp, he asked in signs for the chief's lodge, and they pointed him to one in the middle. It was small and old. The Piegan got off his horse, and the Snake chief came out and hugged him and kissed him, and said: " I am glad you have come to-day to my lodge. So are my people. You are tired. Enter my lodge and we will eat." So they went inside and many of the Snakes came in, and they had a great feast.

Then the Snake chief told his people how he had met

the Piegan, and how brave he was, and that now they were
going to make a great peace ; and he sent some men to tell
the people, so that they would be ready to move camp in
the morning. Evening came. Everywhere people were
shouting out for feasts, and the chief took Owl Bear to
them. It was very late when they returned. Then the
Snake had one of his wives make a bed at the back of the
lodge ; and when it was ready he said : " Now, my friend,
there is your bed. This is now your lodge ; also the
woman who made the bed, she is now your wife ; also
everything in this lodge is yours. The parfleches, saddles,
food, robes, bowls, everything is yours. I give them to you
because you are my friend and a brave man."

"You give me too much," replied Owl Bear. "I am
ashamed, but I take your words. I have nothing with me
but one wife. She is yours."

Next morning camp was broken early. The horses were
driven in, and the Snake chief gave Owl Bear his whole
band, — two hundred head, all large, powerful horses.

All were now ready, and the chiefs started ahead. Close
behind them were all the warriors, hundreds and hundreds,
and last came the women and children, and the young men
driving the loose horses. As they came in sight of the
Piegan camp, all the warriors started out to meet them,
dressed in their war costumes and singing the great war
song. There was no wind, and the sound came across the
valley and up the hill like the noise of thunder. Then the
Snakes began to sing, and thus the two parties advanced.
At last they met. The Piegans turned and rode beside
them, and so they came to the camp. Then they got off
their horses and kissed each other. Every Piegan asked a
Snake into his lodge to eat and rest, and the Snake women
put up their lodges beside the Piegan lodges. So the great
peace was made.

In Owl Bear's lodge there was a great feast, and when

they had finished he said to his people : " Here is the man whose scalp I took. Did I say I killed him? No. I gave him my knife and told him to kill me. He would not do it ; and he gave me his knife, but I would not kill him. So we talked together what we should do, and now we have made peace. And now (turning to the Snake) this is your lodge, also all the things in it. My horses, too, I give you. All are yours."

So it was. The Piegan took the Snake's wife, lodge, and horses, and the Snake took the Piegan's, and they camped side by side. All the people camped together, and feasted each other and made presents. So the peace was made.

V

For many days they camped side by side. The young men kept hunting, and the women were always busy drying meat and tanning robes and cowskins. Buffalo were always close, and after a while the people had all the meat and robes they could carry. Then, one day, the Snake chief said to Owl Bear: " Now, my friend, we have camped a long time together, and I am glad we have made peace. We have dug a hole in the ground, and in it we have put our anger and covered it up, so there is no more war between us. And now I think it time to go. To-morrow morning the Snakes break camp and go back south."

" Your words are good," replied Owl Bear. " I too am glad we have made this peace. You say you must go south, and I feel lonesome. I would like you to go with us so we could camp together a long time, but as you say, so it shall be done. To-morrow you will start south. I too shall break camp, for I would be lonesome here without you ; and the Piegans will start in the home direction."

The lodges were being taken down and packed. The men sat about the fireplaces, taking a last smoke together.

They were now great friends. Many Snakes had married Piegan women, and many Piegans had married Snake women. At last all was ready. The great chiefs mounted their horses and started out, and soon both parties were strung out on the trail.

Some young men, however, stayed behind to gamble a while. It was yet early in the morning, and by riding fast it would not take them long to catch up with their camps. All day they kept playing; and sometimes the Piegans would win, and sometimes the Snakes.

It was now almost sunset. "Let us have one horse race," they said, "and we will stop." Each side had a good horse, and they ran their best; but they came in so close together it could not be told who won. The Snakes claimed that their horse won, and the Piegans would not allow it. So they got angry and began to quarrel, and pretty soon they began to fight and to shoot at each other, and some were killed.

Since that time the Snakes and Piegans have never been at peace.

THE LOST WOMAN

I

A LONG time ago the Blackfeet were camped on Backfat Creek. There was in the camp a man who had but one wife, and he thought a great deal of her. He never wanted to have two wives. As time passed they had a child, a little girl. Along toward the end of the summer, this man's wife wanted to get some berries, and she asked her husband to take her to a certain place where berries grew, so that she could get some. The man said to his wife: "At this time of the year, I do not like to go to that place to pick berries. There are always Snake or Crow war parties travelling about there." The woman wanted very much to go, and she coaxed her husband about it a great deal; and at last he said he would go, and they started, and many women followed them.

When they came to where the berries grew, the man said to his wife: "There are the berries down in that ravine. You may go down there and pick them, and I will go up on this hill and stand guard. If I see any one coming, I will call out to you, and you must all get on your horses and run." So the women went down to pick berries.

The man went up on the hill and sat down and looked over the country. After a little time, he looked down into another ravine not far off, and saw that it was full of horsemen coming. They started to gallop up towards him, and he called out in a loud voice, "Run, run, the enemy is rushing on us." The women started to run, and he jumped on his

13

horse and followed them. The enemy rushed after them, and he drew his bow and arrows, and got ready to fight and defend the women. After they had gone a little way, the enemy had gained so much that they were shooting at the Blackfeet with their arrows, and the man was riding back and forth behind the women, and whipping up the horses, now of one, now of another, to make them go faster. The enemy kept getting closer, and at last they were so near that they were beginning to thrust at him with their lances, and he was dodging them and throwing himself down, now on one side of his horse, and then on the other.

At length he found that he could no longer defend all the women, so he made up his mind to leave those that had the slowest horses to the mercy of the enemy, while he would go on with those that had the faster ones. When he found that he must leave the women, he was excited and rode on ahead; but as he passed, he heard some one call out to him, "Don't leave me," and he looked to one side, and saw that he was leaving his wife. When he heard his wife call out thus to him, he said to her: "There is no life for me here. You are a fine-looking woman. They will not kill you, but there is no life for me." She answered: " No, take pity on me. Do not leave me. My horse is giving out. Let us both get on one horse and then, if we are caught, we will die together." When he heard this, his heart was touched and he said : "No, wife, I will not leave you. Run up beside my horse and jump on behind me." The enemy were now so near that they had killed or captured some of the women, and they had come up close enough to the man so that they got ready to hit at him with their war clubs. His horse was now wounded in places with arrows, but it was a good, strong, fast horse.

His wife rode up close to him, and jumped on his horse behind him. When he started to run with her, the enemy had come up on either side of him, and some were behind him, but they were afraid to shoot their arrows for fear of hitting their own people, so they struck at the man with their war clubs. But they did not want to kill the woman, and they did not hurt him. They reached out with their hands to try to pull the woman off the horse; but she had put her arms around her husband and held on tight, and they could not get her off, but they tore her clothing off her. As she held her husband, he could not use his arrows, and could not fight to defend himself. His horse was now going very slowly, and all the enemy had caught up to them, and were all around them.

The man said to his wife: " Never mind, let them take you: they will not kill you. You are too handsome a woman for them to kill you." His wife said, " No, it is no harm for us both to die together." When he saw that his wife would not get off the horse and that he could not fight, he said to her: " Here, look out! You are crowding me on to the neck of the horse. Sit further back." He began to edge himself back, and at last, when he got his wife pretty far back on the horse, he gave a great push and shoved her off behind. When she fell off, his horse had more speed and began to run away from the enemy, and he would shoot back his arrows; and now, when they would ride up to strike him with their hatchets, he would shoot them and kill them, and they began to be afraid of him, and to edge away from him. His horse was very long-winded; and now, as he was drawing away from the enemy, there were only two who were yet able to keep up with him. The rest were being left behind, and they stopped, and went back to where the others had killed or captured the women; and now only two men were pursuing.

After a little while, the Blackfoot jumped off his horse to fight on foot, and the two enemies rode up on either side of him, but a long way off, and jumped off their horses. When he saw the two on either side of him, he took a sheaf of arrows in his hand and began to rush, first toward the one on the right, and then toward the one on the left. As he

did this, he saw that one of the men, when he ran toward him
and threatened to shoot, would draw away from him, while
the other would stand still. Then he knew that one of them
was a coward and the other a brave man. But all the time
they were closing in on him. When he saw that they were
closing in on him, he made a rush at the brave man. This
one was shooting arrows all the time ; but the Blackfoot did
not shoot until he got close to him, and then he shot an
arrow into him and ran up to him and hit him with his stone
axe and killed him. Then he turned to the cowardly one
and ran at him. The man turned to run, but the Blackfoot
caught him and hit him with his axe and killed him.

After he had killed them, he scalped them and took their
arrows, their horses, and the stone knives that they had.
Then he went home, and when he rode into the camp he was
crying over the loss of his wife. When he came to his lodge
and got off his horse, his friends went up to him and asked
what was the matter. He told them how all the women
had been killed, and how he had been pursued by two enemies,
and had fought with them and killed them both, and he
showed them the arrows and the horses and the scalps. He
told the women's relations that they had all been killed ; and all
were in great sorrow, and crying over the loss of their friends.

The next morning they held a council, and it was decided
that a party should go out and see where the battle had been,
and find out what had become of the women. When they
got to the place, they found all the women there dead, except
this man's wife. Her they could not find. They also found
the two Indians that the man had said that he had killed,
and, besides, many others that he had killed when he was running away.

II

When he got back to the camp, this Blackfoot picked up
his child and put it on his back, and walked round the camp

mourning and crying, and the child crying, for four days and four nights, until he was exhausted and worn out, and then he fell asleep. When the rest of the people saw him walking about mourning, and that he would not eat nor drink, their hearts were very sore, and they felt very sorry for him and for the child, for he was a man greatly thought of by the people.

While he lay there asleep, the chief of the camp came to him and woke him, and said: "Well, friend, what have you decided on? What is your mind? What are you going to do?" The man answered: "My child is lonely. It will not eat. It is crying for its mother. It will not notice any one. I am going to look for my wife." The chief said, "I cannot say anything." He went about to all the lodges and told the people that this man was going away to seek his wife.

Now there was in the camp a strong medicine man, who was not married and would not marry at all. He had said, "When I had my dream, it told me that I must never have a wife." The man who had lost his wife had a very beautiful sister, who had never married. She was very proud and very handsome. Many men had wanted to marry her, but she would not have anything to do with any man. The medicine man secretly loved this handsome girl, the sister of the poor man. When he heard of this poor man's misfortune, the medicine man was in great sorrow, and cried over it. He sent word to the poor man, saying: "Go and tell this man that I have promised never to take a wife, but that if he will give me his beautiful sister, he need not go to look for his wife. I will send my secret helper in search of her."

When the young girl heard what this medicine man had said, she sent word to him, saying, "Yes, if you bring my brother's wife home, and I see her sitting here by his side, I will marry you, but not before." But she did not mean what she said. She intended to deceive him in some way, and not to marry him at all. When the girl sent this message to him, the medicine man sent for her and her brother to come to his lodge. When they had come, he spoke to the poor man and said, " If I bring your wife here, are you willing to give me your sister for my wife?" The poor man answered, "Yes." But the young girl kept quiet in his presence, and had nothing to say. Then the medicine man said to them : " Go. To-night in the middle of the night you will hear me sing." He sent everybody out of his lodge, and said to the people : " I will close the door of my lodge, and I do not want any one to come in to-night, nor to look through the door. A spirit will come to me to-night." He made the people know, by a sign put out before the door of his lodge, that no one must enter it, until such time as he was through making his medicine. Then he built a fire, and began to get out all his medicine. He unwrapped his bundle and took out his pipe and his rattles and his other things. After a time, the fire burned down until it was only coals and his lodge was dark, and on the fire he threw sweet-scented herbs, sweet grass, and sweet pine, so as to draw his dream-helper to him.

Now in the middle of the night he was in the lodge sing-ing, when suddenly the people heard a strange voice in the lodge say : " Well, my chief, I have come. What is it?" The medicine man said, " I want you to help me." The voice said, "Yes, I know it, and I know what you want me to do." The medicine man asked, "What is it?" The voice said, " You want me to go and get a woman." The medicine man answered : "That is what I want. I want you to go and get a woman — the lost woman." The voice said to him, " Did I not tell you never to call me, unless you were in great need of my help?" The medicine man an-swered, "Yes, but that girl that was never going to be married is going to be given to me through your help." Then the voice said, " Oh !" and it was silent for a little while. Then it went on and said : " Well, we have a good

teeling for you, and you have been a long time not married ;
so we will help you to get that girl, and you will have her.
Yes, we have great pity on you. We will go and look for
this woman, and will try to find her, but I cannot promise
you that we will bring her ; but we will try. We will go, and
in four nights I will be back here again at this same time,
and I think that I can bring the woman ; but I will not
promise. While I am gone, I will let you know how I get on.
Now I am going away." And then the people heard in the
lodge a sound like a strong wind, and nothing more. He
was gone.

Some people went and told the sister what the medicine
man and the voice had been saying, and the girl was very
down-hearted, and cried over the idea that she must be
married, and that she had been forced into it in this way.

III

When the dream person went away, he came late at night
to the camp of the Snakes, the enemy. The woman who
had been captured was always crying over the loss of her
man and her child. She had another husband now. The
man who had captured her had taken her for his wife. As
she was lying there, in her husband's lodge, crying for sorrow for her loss, the dream person came to her. Her husband was asleep. The dream-helper touched her and
pushed her a little, and she looked up and saw a person
standing by her side ; but she did not know who it was.
The person whispered in her ear, "Get up, I want to take
you home." She began to edge away from her husband,
and at length got up, and all the time the person was moving
toward the door. She followed him out, and saw him walk
away from the lodge, and she went after. The person kept
ahead, and the woman followed him, and they went away,
travelling very fast. After they had travelled some distance,

she called out to the dream person to stop, for she was getting tired. Then the person stopped, and when he saw the woman sitting, he would sit down, but he would not talk to her.

As they travelled on, the woman, when she got tired, would sit down, and because she was very tired, she would fall asleep; and when she awoke and looked up, she always saw the person walking away from her, and she would get up and follow him. When day came, the shape would be far ahead of her, but at night it would keep closer. When she spoke to this person, the woman would call him "young man." At one time she said to him, " Young man, my moccasins are all worn out, and my feet are getting very sore, and I am very tired and hungry." When she had said this, she sat down and fell asleep, and as she was falling asleep, she saw the person going away from her. He went back to the lodge of the medicine man.

During this night the camp heard the medicine man singing his song, and they knew that the dream person must be back again, or that his chief must be calling him. The medicine man had unwrapped his bundle, and had taken out all his things, and again had a fire of coals, on which he burned sweet pine and sweet grass. Those who were listening heard a voice say : " Well, my chief, I am back again, and I am here to tell you something. I am bringing the woman you sent me after. She is very hungry and has no moccasins. Get me those things, and I will take them back to her." The medicine man went out of the lodge, and called to the poor man, who was mourning for his wife, that he wanted to see him. The man came, carrying the child on his back, to hear what the medicine man had to say. He said to him: " Get some moccasins and something to eat for your wife. I want to send them to her. She is coming." The poor man went to his sister, and told her to give him some moccasins and some pemmican. She made a bundle of these things, and the man took them to the medicine man, who gave them to the dream person; and again he disappeared out of the lodge like a wind.

IV

When the woman awoke in the morning and started to get up, she hit her face against a bundle lying by her, and when she opened it, she found in it moccasins and some pemmican; and she put on the moccasins and ate, and while she was putting on the moccasins and eating, she looked over to where she had last seen the person, and he was sitting there with his back toward her. She could never see his face. When she had finished eating, he got up and went on, and she rose and followed. They went on, and the woman thought, " Now I have travelled two days and two nights with this young man, and I wonder what kind of a man he is. He seems to take no notice of me." So she made up her mind to walk fast and to try to overtake him, and see what sort of a man he was. She started to do so, but however fast she walked, it made no difference. She could not overtake him. Whether she walked fast, or whether she walked slow, he was always the same distance from her. They travelled on until night, and then she lay down again and fell asleep. She dreamed that the young man had left her again.

The dream person had really left her, and had gone back to the medicine man's lodge, and said to him: " Well, my chief, I am back again. I am bringing the woman. You must tell this poor man to get on his horse, and ride back toward Milk River (the Teton). Let him go in among the high hills on this side of the Muddy, and let him wait there until daylight, and look toward the hills of Milk River; and after the sun is up a little way, he will see a band of antelope running toward him, along the trail that

the Blackfeet travel. It will be his wife who has frightened
these antelope. Let him wait there for a while, and he will
see a person coming. This will be his wife. Then let him
go to meet her, for she has no moccasins. She will be glad
to see him, for she is crying all the time."

The medicine man told the poor man this, and he got on
his horse and started, as he had been told. He could not
believe that it was true. But he went. At last he got to
the place, and a little while after the sun had risen, as he was
lying on a hill looking toward the hills of the Milk River, he
saw a band of antelope running toward him, as he had been
told he would see. He lay there for a long time, but saw
nothing else come in sight; and finally he got angry and
thought that what had been told him was a lie, and he got
up to mount his horse and ride back. Just then he saw, away
down, far off on the prairie, a small black speck, but he did
not think it was moving, it was so far off, — barely to be seen.
He thought maybe it was a rock. He lay down again and
took sight on the speck by a straw of grass in front of him,
and looked for a long time, and after a while he saw the speck
pass the straw, and then he knew it was something. He got
on his horse and started to ride up and find out what it was,
riding way around it, through the hills and ravines, so that
he would not be seen. He rode up in a ravine behind it,
pretty near to it, and then he could see it was a person on
foot. He got out his bow and arrows and held them ready
to use, and then started to ride up to it. He rode toward
the person, and at last he got near enough to see that it was
his wife. When he saw this, he could not help crying; and
as he rode up, the woman looked back, and knew first the
horse, and then her husband, and she was so glad that she
fell down and knew nothing.

After she had come to herself and they had talked together,
they got on the horse and rode off toward camp. When he
came over the hill in sight of camp, all the people began to

say, " Here comes the man "; and at last they could see from a distance that he had some one on the horse behind him, and they knew that it must be his wife, and they were glad to see him bringing her back, for he was a man thought a great deal of, and everybody liked him and liked his wife and the way he was kind to her.

Then the handsome girl was given to the medicine man and became his wife.

ADVENTURES OF BULL TURNS ROUND

I

ONCE the camp moved, but one lodge stayed. It belonged to Wolf Tail; and Wolf Tail's younger brother, Bull Turns Round, lived with him. Now their father loved both his sons, but he loved the younger one most, and when he went away with the big camp, he said to Wolf Tail: "Take care of your young brother; he is not yet a strong person. Watch him that nothing befall him."

One day Wolf Tail was out hunting, and Bull Turns Round sat in front of the lodge making arrows, and a beautiful strange bird lit on the ground before him. Then cried one of Wolf Tail's wives, "Oh, brother, shoot that little bird." "Don't bother me, sister," he replied, " I am making arrows." Again the woman said, " Oh, brother, shoot that bird for me." Then Bull Turns Round fitted an arrow to his bow and shot the bird, and the woman went and picked it up and stroked her face with it, and her face swelled up so big that her eyes and nose could not be seen. But when Bull Turns Round had shot the bird, he went off hunting and did not know what had happened to the woman's face.

Now when Wolf Tail came home and saw his wife's face, he said, " What is the matter?" and his wife replied : " Your brother has pounded me so that I cannot see. Go now and kill him." But Wolf Tail said, " No, I love my brother; I cannot kill him." Then his wife cried and said: " I know you do not love me ; you are glad your brother has beaten me. If you loved me, you would go and kill him."

24

Then Wolf Tail went out and looked for his brother, and when he had found him, he said: "Come, let us get some feathers. I know where there is an eagle's nest;" and he took him to a high cliff, which overhung the river, and on the edge of this cliff was a dead tree, in the top of which the eagles had built their nest. Then said Wolf Tail, "Climb up, brother, and kill the eagles;" and when Bull Turns Round had climbed nearly to the top, Wolf Tail called out, "I am going to push the tree over the cliff, and you will be killed."

"Oh, brother! oh, brother! pity me; do not kill me," said Bull Turns Round.

"Why did you beat my wife's face so?" said Wolf Tail.

"I didn't," cried the boy; "I don't know what you are talking about."

"You lie," said Wolf Tail, and he pushed the tree over the cliff. He looked over and saw his brother fall into the water, and he did not come up again. Then Wolf Tail went home and took down his lodge, and went to the main camp. When his father saw him coming with only his wives, he said to him, "Where is your young brother?" And Wolf Tail replied: "He went hunting and did not come back. We waited four days for him. I think the bears must have killed him."

II

Now when Bull Turns Round fell into the river, he was stunned, and the water carried him a long way down the stream and finally lodged him on a sand shoal. Near this shoal was a lodge of Under Water People (*Sū'-yē-tŭp'-pi*), an old man, his wife, and two daughters. This old man was very rich: he had great flocks of geese, swans, ducks, and other water-fowl, and a big herd of buffalo which were tame. These buffalo always fed near by, and the old man called them every evening to come and drink. But he and his

family ate none of these. Their only food was the blood-
sucker.[1]

Now the old man's daughters were swimming about in the
evening, and they found Bull Turns Round lying on the shoal,
dead, and they went home and told their father, and begged
him to bring the person to life, and give him to them for a husband. " Go, my daughters," he said, " and make four sweat
lodges, and I will bring the person." He went and got Bull
Turns Round, and when the sweat lodges were finished, the
old man took him into one of them, and when he had sprinkled
water on the hot rocks, he scraped a great quantity of sand
off Bull Turns Round. Then he took him into another lodge
and did the same thing, and when he had taken him into the
fourth sweat lodge and scraped all the sand off him, Bull
Turns Round came to life, and the old man led him out and
gave him to his daughters. And the old man gave his son-in-
law a new lodge and bows and arrows, and many good presents.

Then the women cooked some bloodsuckers, and gave
them to their husband, but when he smelled of them he
could not eat, and he threw them in the fire. Then his
wives asked him what he would eat. " Buffalo," he replied,
" is the only meat for men."

" Oh, father ! " cried the girls, running to the old man's
lodge, " our husband will not eat our food. He says buffalo
is the only meat for men."

"Go then, my daughters," said the old man, "and tell
your husband to kill a buffalo, but do not take nor break any
bones, for I will make it alive again." Then the old man
called the buffalo to come and drink, and Bull Turns Round
shot a fat cow and took all the meat. And when he had
roasted the tongue, he gave each of his wives a small piece
of it, and they liked it, and they roasted and ate plenty of
the meat.

[1] Blackfoot — *Est'-stŭk-ki*, suck-bite; from *Est-ah-tope*, suck, and *I-sik-
stŭk-ki*, bite.

III

One day Bull Turns Round went to the old man and said, " I mourn for my father."

"How did you come to be dead on the sand shoal?" asked the old man. Then Bull Turns Round told what his brother had done to him.

"Take this piece of sinew," said the old man. " Go and see your father. When you throw this sinew on the fire, your brother and his wife will roll, and twist up and die." Then the old man gave him a herd of buffalo, and many dogs to pack the lodge, and other things ; and Bull Turns Round took his wives, and went to find his father.

One day, just after sunset, they came in sight of the big camp, and they went and pitched the lodge on the top of a very high butte ; and the buffalo fed close by, and there were so many of them that they covered the whole hill.

Now the people were starving, and some had died, for they had no buffalo. In the morning, early, a man arose whose son had starved to death, and when he went out and saw this lodge on the top of the hill, and all the buffalo feeding by it, he cried out in a loud voice ; and the people all came out and looked at it, and they were afraid, for they thought it was *Stōn'-i-tăp-i.*[1] Then said the man whose son had died : " I am no longer glad to live. I will go up to this lodge, and find out what this is." Now when he said this, all the men grasped their bows and arrows and followed him, and when they went up the hill, the buffalo just moved out of their path and kept on feeding ; and just as they came to the lodge, Bull Turns Round came out, and all the people said, "Here is the one whom we thought the bears had killed." Wolf Tail ran up, and said, " Oh, brother, you are not dead. You went to get feathers, but we thought you had

[1] There is no word in English which corresponds to this. It is used when speaking of things wonderful or supernatural.

been killed." Then Bull Turns Round called his brother into the lodge, and he threw the sinew on the fire ; and Wolf Tail, and his wife, who was standing outside, twisted up and died.

Then Bull Turns Round told his father all that had happened to him ; and when he learned that the people were starving, he filled his mouth with feathers and blew them out, and the buffalo ran off in every direction, and he said to the people, " There is food, go chase it." Then the people were very glad, and they came each one and gave him a present. They gave him war shirts, bows and arrows, shields, spears, white robes, and many curious things.

KŪT-O'-YIS

LONG ago, down where Two Medicine and Badger Creeks come together, there lived an old man. He had but one wife and two daughters. One day there came to his camp a young man who was very brave and a great hunter. The old man said : " Ah ! I will have this young man to help me. I will give him my daughters for wives." So he gave him his daughters. He also gave this son-in-law all his wealth, keeping for himself only a little lodge, in which he lived with his old wife. The son-in-law lived in a lodge that was big and fine.

At first the son-in-law was very good to the old people. Whenever he killed anything, he gave them part of the meat, and furnished plenty of robes and skins for their bedding and clothing. But after a while he began to be very mean to them.

Now the son-in-law kept the buffalo hidden under a big log jam in the river. Whenever he wanted to kill anything, he would have the old man go to help him ; and the old man would stamp on the log jam and frighten the buffalo, and when they ran out, the young man would shoot one or two, never killing wastefully. But often he gave the old people nothing to eat, and they were hungry all the time, and began to grow thin and weak.

One morning, the young man called his father-in-law to go down to the log jam and hunt with him. They started, and the young man killed a fat buffalo cow. Then he said to the old man, " Hurry back now, and tell your children to get the

dogs and carry this meat home, then you can have something to eat." And the old man did as he had been ordered,
thinking to himself : " Now, at last, my son-in-law has taken
pity on me. He will give me part of this meat." When he
returned with the dogs, they skinned the cow, cut up the
meat and packed it on the dog travois, and went home. Then
the young man had his wives unload it, and told his father-
in-law to go home. He did not give him even a piece of
liver. Neither would the older daughter give her parents
anything to eat, but the younger took pity on the old people
and stole a piece of meat, and when she got a chance threw
it into the lodge to the old people. The son-in-law told his
wives not to give the old people anything to eat. The only
way they got food was when the younger woman would throw
them a piece of meat unseen by her husband and sister.

Another morning, the son-in-law got up early, and went
and kicked on the old man's lodge to wake him, and called
him to get up and help him, to go and pound on the log
jam to drive out the buffalo, so that he could kill some.
When the old man pounded on the jam, a buffalo ran out,
and the son-in-law shot it, but only wounded it. It ran
away, but at last fell down and died. The old man followed
it, and came to where it had lost a big clot of blood from
its wound. When he came to where this clot of blood was
lying on the ground, he stumbled and fell, and spilled his
arrows out of his quiver ; and while he was picking them up,
he picked up also the clot of blood, and hid it in his quiver.
" What are you picking up?" called out the son-in-law.
" Nothing," said the old man ; " I just fell down and spilled
my arrows, and am putting them back." " Curse you, old
man," said the son-in-law, " you are lazy and useless. Go
back and tell your children to come with the dogs and get
this dead buffalo." He also took away his bow and arrows
from the old man.

The old man went home and told his daughters, and then

went over to his own lodge, and said to his wife : " Hurry now, and put the kettle on the fire. I have brought home something from the butchering." " Ah ! " said the old woman, "has our son-in-law been generous, and given us something nice?" " No," answered the old man ; " hurry up and put the kettle on." When the water began to boil, the old man tipped his quiver up over the kettle, and immediately there came from the pot a noise as of a child crying, as if it were being hurt, burnt or scalded. They looked in the kettle, and saw there a little boy, and they quickly took it out of the water. They were very much surprised. The old woman made a lashing to put the child in, and then they talked about it. They decided that if the son-in-law knew that it was a boy, he would kill it, so they resolved to tell their daughters that the baby was a girl. Then he would be glad, for he would think that after a while he would have it for a wife. They named the child Küt-o′-yis (Clot of Blood).

The son-in-law and his wives came home, and after a while he heard the child crying. He told his youngest wife to go and find out whether that baby was a boy or a girl ; if it was a boy, to tell them to kill it. She came back and told them that it was a girl. He did not believe this, and sent his oldest wife to find out the truth of the matter. When she came back and told him the same thing, he believed that it was really a girl. Then he was glad, for he thought that when the child had grown up he would have another wife. He said to his youngest wife, " Take some pemmican over to your mother ; not much, just enough so that there will be plenty of milk for the child."

Now on the fourth day the child spoke, and said, " Lash me in turn to each one of these lodge poles, and when I get to the last one, I will fall out of my lashing and be grown up." The old woman did so, and as she lashed him to each lodge pole he could be seen to grow, and finally when they lashed him to the last pole, he was a man. After Kŭt-o'-yis had looked about the inside of the lodge, he looked out through a hole in the lodge covering, and then, turning round, he said to the old people : " How is it there is nothing to eat in this lodge? I see plenty of food over by the other lodge." " Hush up," said the old woman, " you will be heard. That is our son-in-law. He does not give us anything at all to eat." " Well," said Kŭt-o'-yis, " where is your pis'kun?" The old woman said, " It is down by the river. We pound on it and the buffalo come out."

Then the old man told him how his son-in-law abused him. " He has taken my weapons from me, and even my dogs · and for many days we have had nothing to eat, except now and then a small piece of meat our daughter steals for us "

" Father," said Kŭt-o'-yis, " have you no arrows?" " No, my son," he replied ; " but I have yet four stone points."

" Go out then and get some wood," said Kŭt-o'-yis. " We will make a bow and arrows. In the morning we will go down and kill something to eat."

Early in the morning Kŭt-o'-yis woke the old man, and said, " Come, we will go down now and kill when the buffalo come out." When they had reached the river, the old man said : " Here is the place to stand and shoot. I will go down and drive them out." As he pounded on the jam, a rat cow ran out, and Kŭt-o'-yis killed it.

Meantime the son-in-law had gone out, and as usual knocked on the old man's lodge, and called to him to get up and go down to help him kill. The old woman called to him that her husband had already gone down. This made the son-in-law very angry. He said : "I have a good mind to kill you right now, old woman. I guess I will by and by."

The son-in-law went on down to the jam, and as he drew near, he saw the old man bending over, skinning a buffalo. " Old man," said he, " stand up and look all around you. Look well, for it will be your last look." Now when he had seen the son-in-law coming, Kŭt-o'-yis had lain down and hidden himself behind the buffalo's carcass. He told the old man to say to his son-in-law, " You had better take your last look, for I am going to kill you, right now." The old man said this. " Ah !" said the son-in-law, "you make me angrier still, by talking back to me." He put an arrow to his bow and shot at the old man, but did not hit him. Kŭt-o'-yis told the old man to pick up the arrow and shoot it back at him, and he did so. Now they shot at each other four times, and then the old man said to Kŭt-o'-yis : "I am afraid now. Get up and help me." So Kŭt-o'-yis got up on his feet and said : " Here, what are you doing? I think you have been badly treating this old man for a long time."

Then the son-in-law smiled pleasantly, for he was afraid of Kŭt-o'-yis. " Oh, no," he said, " no one thinks more of this old man than I do. I have always taken great pity on him."

Then Kŭt-o'-yis said : "You lie. I am going to kill you now." He shot him four times, and the man died. Then Kŭt-o'-yis told the old man to go and bring down the daughter who had acted badly toward him. He did so, and Kŭt-o'-yis killed her. Then he went up to the lodges and said to the younger woman, " Perhaps you loved your husband." "Yes," she said, " I love him." So he killed her, too. Then he said to the old people : " Go over there now, and live in that lodge. There is plenty there to eat, and when it is gone I will kill more. As for myself, I will make a journey around about. Where are there any people? In what direction?" " Well," said the old man, " up above here on Badger Creek and Two Medicine, where the pis'kun is, there are some people."

Kŭt-o'-yis went up to where the pis'kun was, and saw there many lodges of people. In the centre of the camp was a large lodge, with a figure of a bear painted on it. He did not go into this lodge, but went into a very small one near by, where two old women lived ; and when he went in, he asked

them for something to eat.   They set before him some lean
dried meat and some belly fat.   "How is this?" he asked.
"Here is a pis'kun with plenty of fat meat and back fat. Why
do you not give me some of that?"   "Hush," said the old
women.   "In that big lodge near by, lives a big bear and
his wives and children.   He takes all those nice things and
leaves us nothing.   He is the chief of this place."

Early in the morning, Kŭt-o'-yis told the old women to
get their dog travois, and harness it, and go over to the
pis'kun, and that he was going to kill for them some fat
meat.   He reached there just about the time the buffalo
were being driven in, and shot a cow, which looked very
scabby, but was really very fat.   Then he helped the old
women to butcher, and when they had taken the meat to
camp, he said to them, "Now take all the choice fat
pieces, and hang them up so that those who live in the bear
lodge will notice them."

They did this, and pretty soon the old chief bear said to
his children: "Go out now, and look around.   The people
have finished killing by this time.   See where the nicest
pieces are, and bring in some nice back fat."   A young
bear went out of the lodge, stood up and looked around,
and when it saw this meat close by, at the old women's
lodge, it went over and began to pull it down.   "Hold on
there," said Kŭt-o'-yis.   "What are you doing here, taking
the old women's meat?" and he hit him over the head with
a stick that he had.   The young bear ran home crying, and
said to his father, "A young man has hit me on the head."
Then all the bears, the father and mother, and uncles and
aunts, and all the relations, were very angry, and all rushed
out toward the old women's lodge.

Kŭt-o'-yis killed them all, except one little child bear, a
female, which escaped.   "Well," said Kŭt-o'-yis, "you can
go and breed bears, so there will be more."

Then said Kŭt-o'-yis to the old women: "Now, grandmothers, where are there any more people? I want to travel around and see them." The old women said : "The nearest ones are at the point of rocks (on Sun River) There is a pis'kun there." So Kŭt-o'-yis travelled off toward this place, and when he reached the camp, he entered an old woman's lodge.

The old woman set before him a plate of bad food. "How is this?" he asked. "Have you nothing better than this to set before a stranger? You have a pis'kun down there, and must get plenty of fat meat. Give me some pemmican." "We cannot do that," the old woman replied, "because there is a big snake here, who is chief of the camp. He not only takes the best pieces, but often he eats a handsome young woman, when he sees one." When Kŭt-o'-yis heard this he was angry, and went over and entered the snake's lodge. The women were cooking up some sarvis berries. He picked up the dish, and ate the berries, and threw the dish out of the door. Then he went over to where the snake was lying asleep, pricked him with his knife, and said : "Here, get up. I have come to see you." This made the snake angry. He partly raised himself up and began to rattle, when Kŭt-o'-yis cut him into pieces with his knife. Then he turned around and killed all his wives and children, except one little female snake, which escaped by crawling into a crack in the rocks. "Oh, well," said Kŭt-o'-yis, "you can go and breed young snakes, so there will be more. The people will not be afraid of little snakes." Kŭt-o'-yis said to the old woman, "Now you go into this snake's lodge and take it for yourself, and everything that is in it."

Then he asked them where there were some more people. They told him that there were some people down the river, and some up in the mountains. But they said : "Do not go there, for it is bad, because Ai-sin'-o-ko-ki (Wind Sucker) lives there. He will kill you." It pleased Kŭt-o'-yis to know that there was such a person, and he went to the mountains. When he got to the place where Wind Sucker lived, he looked into his mouth, and could see many dead people there, — some skeletons and some just dead. He went in, and there he saw a fearful sight. The ground was white as snow with the bones of those who had died. There were bodies with flesh on them; some were just dead, and some still living. He spoke to a living person, and asked, "What is that hanging down above us?" The person answered that it was Wind Sucker's heart. Then said Kŭt-o'-yis: "You who still draw a little breath, try to shake your heads (in time to the song), and those who are still able to move, get up and dance. Take courage now, we are going to have the ghost dance." So Kŭt-o'-yis bound his knife, point upward, to the top of his head and began to dance, singing the ghost song, and all the others danced with him; and as he danced up and down, the point of the knife cut Wind Sucker's heart and killed him. Kŭt-o'-yis took his knife and cut through Wind Sucker's ribs, and freed those who were able to crawl out, and said to those who could still travel to go and tell their people that they should come here for the ones who were still alive but unable to walk.

Then he asked some of these people: "Where are there any other people? I want to visit all the people." They said to him: "There is a camp to the westward up the river, but you must not take the left-hand trail going up, because on that trail lives a woman, a handsome woman, who invites men to wrestle with her and then kills them. You must avoid her." This was what Kŭt-o'-yis was looking for. This was his business in the world, to kill off all the bad things. So he asked the people just where this woman lived, and asked where it was best to go to avoid her. He did this, because he did not wish the people to know that he wanted to meet her.

He started on his way, and at length saw this woman standing by the trail. She called out to him, "Come here, young man, come here ; I want to wrestle with you." "No," replied the young man, "I am in a hurry. I cannot stop." But the woman called again, "No, no, come now and wrestle once with me." When she had called him four times, Kŭt-o'-yis went up to her. Now on the ground, where this woman wrestled with people, she had placed many broken and sharp flints, partly hiding them by the grass. They seized each other, and began to wrestle over these broken flints, but Kŭt-o'-yis looked at the ground and did not step on them. He watched his chance, and suddenly gave the woman a wrench, and threw her down on a large sharp flint, which cut her in two ; and the parts of her body fell asunder.

Then Kŭt-o'-yis went on, and after a while came to where a woman kept a sliding place ; and at the far end of it there was a rope, which would trip people up, and when they were tripped, they would fall over a high cliff into deep water, where a great fish would eat them. When this woman saw him coming, she cried out, "Come over here, young man, and slide with me." "No," he replied, "I am in a hurry." She kept calling him, and when she had called the fourth time, he went over to slide with her. "This sliding," said the woman, "is a very pleasant pastime." "Ah !" said Kŭt-o'-yis, "I will look at it." He looked at the place, and, looking carefully, he saw the hidden rope. So he started to slide, and took out his knife, and when he reached the rope, which the woman had raised, he cut it, and when it parted, the woman fell over backward into the water, and was eaten up by the big fish.

Again he went on, and after a while he came to a big camp. This was the place of a man-eater. Kŭt-o'-yis called a little girl he saw near by, and said to her : "Child, I am going into that lodge to let that man-eater kill and eat me.

Watch close, therefore, and when you can get hold of one of my bones, take it out and call all the dogs, and when they have all come up to you, throw it down and cry out, 'Kŭt-o'-yis, the dogs are eating your bones!'"

Then Kŭt-o'-yis entered the lodge, and when the man-eater saw him, he cried out, "*O'ki, O'ki*," and seemed glad to see him, for he was a fat young man. The man-eater took a large knife, and went up to Kŭt-o'-yis, and cut his throat, and put him into a great stone kettle to cook. When the meat was cooked, he drew the kettle from the fire, and ate the body, limb by limb, until it was all eaten up.

Then the little girl, who was watching, came up to him, and said, "Pity me, man-eater, my mother is hungry and asks you for those bones." So the old man bunched them up together and handed them to her. She took them out, and called all the dogs to her, and threw the bones down to the dogs, crying out, "Look out, Kŭt-o'-yis; the dogs are eating you!" and when she said that, Kŭt-o'-yis arose from the pile of bones.

Again he went into the lodge, and when the man-eater saw him, he cried out, "How, how, how! the fat young man has survived," and seemed surprised. Again he took his knife and cut Kŭt-o'-yis' throat, and threw him into the kettle. Again, when the meat was cooked, he ate it up, and again the little girl asked for the bones, which he gave her; and, taking them out, she threw them to the dogs, crying, "Kŭt-o'-yis, the dogs are eating you!" and Kŭt-o'-yis again arose from the bones.

When the man-eater had cooked him four times, he again went into the lodge, and, seizing the man-eater, he threw him into the boiling kettle, and his wives and children too, and boiled them to death.

The man-eater was the seventh and last of the bad animals and people who were destroyed by Kŭt-o'-yis.

THE BAD WIFE

I

THERE was once a man who had but one wife. He was not a chief, but a very brave warrior. He was rich, too, so he could have had plenty of wives if he wished ; but he loved his wife very much, and did not want any more. He was very good to this woman. She always wore the best clothes that could be found. If any other woman had a fine buckskin dress, or something very pretty, the man would buy it for her.

It was summer. The berries were ripe, and the woman kept saying to her husband, "Let us go and pick some berries for winter." "No," replied the man. "It is dangerous now. The enemy is travelling all around." But still the woman kept teasing him to go. So one day he told her to get ready. Some other women went, too. They all went on horseback, for the berries were a long way from camp. When they got to the place, the man told the women to keep near their horses all the time. He would go up on a butte near by and watch. "Be careful," he said. "Keep by your horses, and if you see me signal, throw away your berries, get on your horses and ride towards camp as fast as you can."

They had not picked many berries before the man saw a war party coming. He signalled the women, and got on his horse and rode towards them. It happened that this man and his wife both had good horses, but the others, all old women, rode slow old travois horses, and the enemy

39

soon overtook and killed them. Many kept on after the
two on good horses, and after a while the woman's horse
began to get tired ; so she asked her husband to let her ride
on his horse with him. The woman got up behind him, and
they went on again. The horse was a very powerful one,
and for a while went very fast ; but two persons make a heavy
load, and soon the enemy began to gain on them. The
man was now in a bad plight ; the enemy were overtaking
him, and the woman holding him bound his arms so that he
could not use his bow.

"Get off," he said to her. "The enemy will not kill you.
You are too young and pretty. Some one of them will take
you, and I will get a big party of our people and rescue
you."

"No, no," cried the woman ; "let us die here together."

"Why die?" cried the man. "We are yet young, and may
live a long time together. If you don't get off, they will
soon catch us and kill me, and then they will take you anyhow. Get off, and in only a short time I will get you back."

"No, no," again cried the woman ; "I will die here with
you."

"Crazy person!" cried the man, and with a quick jerk he
threw the woman off.

As he said, the enemy did not kill her. The first one
who came up counted *coup* and took her. The man, now
that his horse was lightened, easily ran away from the war
party, and got safe to camp.

II

Then there was great mourning. The relatives of the old
women who had been killed, cut their hair and cried.
The man, too, cut off his hair and mourned. He knew
that his wife was not killed, but he felt very badly because
he was separated from her. He painted himself black, and

walked all through the camp, crying. His wife had many
relations, and some of them went to the man and said:
"We pity you very much. We mourn, too, for our sister.
But come. Take courage. We will go with you, and try
to get her back."

"It is good," replied the man. "I feel as if I should die,
stopping uselessly here. Let us start soon."

That evening they got ready, and at daylight started out
on foot. There were seven of them in all. The husband,
five middle-aged men, the woman's relations, and a young
man, her own young brother. He was a very pretty boy.
His hair was longer than any other person's in camp.

They soon found the trail of the war party, and followed
it for some days. At last they came to the Big River,[1] and
there, on the other side, they saw many lodges. They crept
down a coulée into the valley, and hid in a small piece of
timber just opposite the camp. Toward evening the man
said: "*Kyi*, my brothers. To-night I will swim across and
look all through the camp for my wife. If I do not find her,
I will cache and look again to-morrow evening. But if I do
not return before daylight of the second night, then you will
know I am killed. Then you will do as you think best.
Maybe you will want to take revenge. Maybe you will go
right back home. That will be as your hearts feel."

As soon as it was dark, he swam across the river and went
all about through the camp, peeping in through the doorways
of the lodges, but he did not see his wife. Still, he knew
she must be there. He had followed the trail of the party
to this place. They had not killed her on the way. He
kept looking in at the lodges until it was late, and the people
let the fires go out and went to bed. Then the man went
down to where the women got their water from the river.
Everywhere along the stream was a cut bank, but in one
place a path of steps had been made down to the water's

[1] Missouri River.

edge. Near this path, he dug a hole in the bank and crawled into it, closing up the entrance, except one small hole, through which he could look, and watch the people who came to the river.

As soon as it was daylight, the women began to come for water. *Tum, tum, tum, tum*, he could hear their footsteps as they came down the path, and he looked eagerly at every one. All day long the people came and went, — the young and old ; and the children played about near him. He saw many strange people that day. It was now almost sunset, and he began to think that he would not see his wife there. *Tum, tum, tum, tum*, another woman came down the steps, and stopped at the water's edge. Her dress was strange, but he thought he knew the form. She turned her head and looked down the river, and he saw her face. It was his wife. He pushed away the dirt, crawled out, went to her and kissed her. "*Kyi*," he said, " hurry, and let us swim across the river. Five of your relations and your own young brother are waiting for us in that piece of timber."

"Wait," replied his wife. "These people have given me a great many pretty things. Let me go back. When it is night I will gather them up, steal a horse, and cross over to you."

"No, no," cried the man. "Let the pretty things go ; come, let us cross at once."

"Pity me," said the woman. "Let me go and get my things. I will surely come to-night. I speak the truth."

"How do you speak the truth?"[1] asked her husband.

"That my relations there across the river may be safe and live long, I speak the truth."

"Go then," said the man, "and get your things. I will cross the river now." He went up on the bank and walked down the river, keeping his face hidden. No one noticed him, or if they did, they thought he belonged to the camp.

---

[1] Blackfoot — *Tsa-ki-an-ist-o-man-i?*   *i.e.,* How you like truth ?

As soon as he had passed the first bend, he swam across the river, and soon joined his relations.

"I have seen my wife," he said to them. "She will come over as soon as it is dark. I let her go back to get some things that were given her."

"You are crazy," said one of the men, "very crazy. She already loves this new man she has, or she would not have wanted to go back."

"Stop that," said the husband; "do not talk bad of her. She will surely come."

III

The woman went back to her lodge with the water, and, sitting down near the fireplace, she began to act very strangely. She took up pieces of charred wood, dirt, and ashes in her hands and ate them, and made queer noises.

"What is it?" asked the man who had taken her for a wife. "What is the matter with you?" He spoke in signs.

The woman also spoke in signs. She answered him: "The Sun told me that there are seven persons across the river in that piece of timber. Five of them are middle-aged, another is a young boy with very long hair, another is a man who mourns. His hair is cut short."

The Snake did not know what to do, so he called in some chiefs and old men to advise with him. They thought that the woman might be very strong medicine. At all events, it would be a good thing to go and look. So the news was shouted out, and in a short time all the warriors had mounted their best horses, and started across the river. It was then almost dark, so they surrounded the piece of timber, and waited for morning to begin the search.

"*Kyi*," said one of the woman's relations to her husband. "Did I not speak the truth? You see now what that woman has done for us."

At daylight the poor husband strung his bow, took a handful of arrows from his quiver, and said : "This is my fault. I have brought you to this. It is right that I should die first," and he started to go out of the timber.

"Wait," said the eldest relative. "It shall not be so. I am the first to go. I cannot stay back to see my brother die. You shall go out last." So he jumped out of the brush, and began shooting his arrows, but was soon killed.

"My brother is too far on the road alone,"[1] cried another relation, and he jumped out and fought, too. What use, one against so many? The Snakes soon had his scalp.

So they went out, one after another, and at last the husband was alone. He rushed out very brave, and shot his arrows as fast as he could. "Hold !" cried the Snake man to his people. "Do not kill him ; catch him. This is the one my wife said to bring back alive. See ! his hair is cut short." So, when the man had shot away all his arrows, they seized and tied him, and, taking the scalps of the others, returned to camp.

They took the prisoner into the lodge where his wife was. His hands were tied behind his back, and they tied his feet, too. He could not move.

As soon as the man saw his wife, he cried. He was not afraid. He did not care now how soon he died. He cried because he was thinking of all the trouble and death this woman had caused. "What have I done to you," he asked his wife, "that you should treat me this way? Did I not always use you well? I never struck you. I never made you work hard."

"What does he say?" asked the Snake man.

"He says," replied the woman, "that when you are done smoking, you must knock the ashes and fire out of your pipe on his breast."

---

[1] Meaning that his brother's spirit, or shadow, was travelling alone the road to the Sand Hills, and that he must overtake him.

The Snake was not a bad-hearted man, but he thought
now that this woman had strong medicine, that she had Sun
power; so he thought that everything must be done as she
said. When the man had finished smoking, he emptied the
pipe on the Piegan's breast, and the fire burned him badly.

Then the poor man cried again, not from the pain, but to
think what a bad heart this woman had. Again he spoke
to her. "You cannot be a person," he said. "I think you
are some fearful animal, changed to look like a woman."

"What is he saying now?" asked the Snake.

"He wants some boiling water poured on his head," replied the woman.

"It shall be as he says," said the Snake; and he had his
women heat some water. When it was ready, one of them
poured a little of it here and there on the captive's head
and shoulders. Wherever the hot water touched, the hair
came out and the skin peeled off. The pain was so bad
that the Piegan nearly fainted. When he revived, he said to
his wife: "Pity me. I have suffered enough. Let them kill
me now. Let me hurry to join those who are already travelling to the Sand Hills."

The woman turned to the Snake chief, and said, "The
man says that he wants you to give him to the Sun."

"It is good," said the Snake. "To-morrow we move
camp. Before we leave here, we will give him to the Sun."

There was an old woman in this camp who lived all alone,
in a little lodge of her own. She had some friends and
relations, but she said she liked to live by herself. She had
heard that a Piegan had been captured, and went to the
lodge where he was. When she saw them pour the boiling
water on him, she cried and felt badly. This old woman
had a very good heart. She went home and lay down by
her dog, and kept crying, she felt so sorry for this poor man.
Pretty soon she heard people shouting out the orders of the
chief. They said: "Listen! listen! To-morrow we move

camp.   Get ready now and pack up everything.   Before we go, the Piegan man will be given to the Sun."

Then the old woman knew what to do.   She tied a piece of buckskin around her dog's mouth, so he could not bark, and then she took him way out in the timber and tied him where he could not be seen.   She also filled a small sack with pemmican, dried meat, and berries, and put it near the dog.

In the morning the people rose early.   They smoothed a cotton-wood tree, by taking off the bark, and painted it black.   Then they stood the Piegan up against it, and fastened him there with a great many ropes.   When they had tied him so he could not move, they painted his face black, and the chief Snake made a prayer, and gave him to the Sun.

Every one was now busy getting ready to move camp. This old woman had lost her dog, and kept calling out for him and looking all around.   "*Tsis'-i!*" she cried.   "*Tsis'-i!* Come here.   Knock the dog on the head !¹   Wait till I find him, and I'll break his neck."

The people were now all packed up, and some had already started on the trail.   "Don't wait for me," the old woman said.   "Go on, I'll look again for my dog, and catch up with you."

When all were gone, the old woman went and untied her dog, and then, going up to where the Piegan was tied, she cut the ropes, and he was free.   But already the man was very weak, and he fell down on the ground.   She rubbed his limbs, and pretty soon he felt better.   The old woman was so sorry for him that she cried again, and kissed him. Then the man cried, too.   He was so glad that some one pitied him.   By and by he ate some of the food the old woman had given him, and felt strong again.   He said to her in signs : " I am not done.   I shall go back home now,

¹A Blackfoot curse.

but I will come again. I will bring all the Piegans with me, and we will have revenge."

" You say well," signed the old woman.

" Help me," again said the man. " If, on the road you are travelling, this camp should separate, mark the trail my wife takes with a stick. You, too, follow the party she goes with, and always put your lodge at the far end of the village. When I return with my people, I will enter your lodge, and tell you what to do."

" I take your speech," replied the old woman. "As you say, so it shall be." Then she kissed him again, and started on after her people. The man went to the river, swam across, and started for the North.

IV

Why are the people crying? Why is all this mourning? Ah! the poor man has returned home, and told how those who went with him were killed. He has told them the whole story. They are getting ready for war. Every one able to fight is going with this man back to the Snakes. Only a few will be left to guard the camp. The mother of that bad woman is going, too. She has sharpened her axe, and told what she will do when she sees her daughter. All are ready. The best horses have been caught up and saddled, and the war party has started, — hundreds and hundreds of warriors. They are strung out over the prairie as far as you can see.

When they got to the Missouri River, the poor man showed them where the lodge in which they had tortured him had stood. He took them to see the tree, where he had been bound. The black paint was still on it.

From here, they went slowly. Some young men were sent far ahead to scout. The second day, they came back to the main body, and said they had found a camping place just deserted, and that there the trail forked. The poor man then went ahead, and at the forks he found a willow twig stuck in the ground, pointing to the left hand trail. When the others came up, he said to them : "Take care of my horse now, and travel slowly. I will go ahead on foot and find the camp. It must be close. I will go and see that old woman, and find out how things are."

Some men did not want him to do this ; they said that the old woman might tell about him, and then they could not surprise the camp.

"No," replied the man. "It will not be so. That old woman is almost the same as my mother. I know she will help us."

He went ahead carefully, and near sunset saw the camp. When it was dark, he crept near it and entered the old woman's lodge. She had placed it behind, and a little way off from, the others. When he went in the old woman was asleep, but the fire was still burning a little. He touched her, and she jumped up and started to scream ; but he put his hand on her mouth, and when she saw who it was she laughed and kissed him. "The Piegans have come," he told her. "We are going to have revenge on this camp to-night. Is my wife here?"

"Still here," replied the old woman. "She is chief now. They think her medicine very strong."

"Tell your friends and relations," said the Piegan, " that you have had a dream, and that they must move into the brush yonder. Have them stay there with you, and they will not be hurt. I am going now to get my people."

It was very late in the night. Most of the Snakes were in bed and asleep. All at once the camp was surrounded with warriors, shouting the war cry and shooting, stabbing, and knocking people on the head as fast as they came out of the lodges.

That Piegan woman cried out : " Don't hurt me. I am a Piegan. Are any of my people here ? "

" Many of your relations are here," some one said. "They will protect you."

Some young men seized and tied her, as her husband had said to do. They had hard work to keep her mother from killing her. *"Hai yah!"* the old woman cried. " There is my Snake woman daughter. Let me split her head open."

The fight was soon over. The Piegans killed the people almost as fast as they came out of their lodges. Some few escaped in the darkness. When the fight was over, the young warriors gathered up a great pile of lodge poles and brush, and set fire to it. Then the poor man tore the dress off his bad wife, tied the scalp of her dead Snake man around her neck, and told her to dance the scalp dance in the fire. She cried and hung back, calling out for pity. The people only laughed and pushed her into the fire. She would run through it, and then those on the other side would push her back. So they kept her running through the fire, until she fell down and died.

The old Snake woman had come out of the brush with her relations. Because she had been so good, the Piegans gave her, and those with her, one-half of all the horses and valuable things they had taken. "*Kyi!*" said the Piegan chief. " That is all for you, because you helped this poor man. To-morrow morning we start back North. If your heart is that way, go too and live with us." So these Snakes joined the Piegans and lived with them until they died, and their children married with the Piegans, and at last they were no longer Snake people.[1]

[1] When the Hudson's Bay Company first established a fort at Edmonton, a daughter of one of these Snakes married a white employee of the company, named, in Blackfoot, *O-wai*, Egg.

THE LOST CHILDREN

ONCE a camp of people stopped on the bank of a river. There were but a few lodges of them. One day the little children in the camp crossed the river to play on the other side. For some time they stayed near the bank, and then they went up over a little hill, and found a bed of sand and gravel; and there they played for a long time.

There were eleven of these children. Two of them were daughters of the chief of the camp, and the smaller of these wanted the best of everything. If any child found a pretty stone, she would try to take it for herself. The other children did not like this, and they began to tease the little girl, and to take her things away from her. Then she got angry and began to cry, and the more she cried, the more the children teased her; so at last she and her sister left the others, and went back to the camp.

When they got there, they told their father what the other children had done to them, and this made the chief very angry. He thought for a little while, and then got up and went out of the lodge, and called aloud, so that everybody might hear, saying: "Listen! listen! Your children have teased my child and made her cry. Now we will move away, and leave them behind. If they come back before we get started, they shall be killed. If they follow us and overtake the camp, they shall be killed. If the father and mother of any one of them take them into their lodge, I will kill that father and mother. Hurry now, hurry and

50

pack up, so that we can go. Everybody tear down the lodges, as quickly as you can."

When the people heard this, they felt very sorry, but they had to do as the chief said; so they tore down the lodges, and quickly packed the dog travois, and started off. They packed in such a hurry that they left many little things lying in camp, — knives and awls, bone needles and moccasins.

The little children played about in the sand for a long time, but at last they began to get hungry; and one little girl said to the others, " I will go back to the camp, and get some dried meat and bring it here, so that we may eat." And she started to go to the camp. When she came to the top of the hill and looked across the river, she saw that there were no lodges there, and did not know what to think of it. She called down to the children, and said, "The camp has gone "; but they did not believe her, and went on playing. She kept on calling, and at last some of them came to her, and then all, and saw that it was as she had said. They went down to the river, and crossed it, and went to where the lodges had stood. When they got there, they saw on the ground the things that had been left out in packing; and as each child saw and knew something that had belonged to its own parents, it cried and sang a little song, saying: "Mother, here is your bone needle; why did you leave your children?" "Father, here is your arrow; why did you leave your children?" It was very mournful, and they all cried.

There was among them a little girl who had on her back her baby brother, whom she loved dearly. He was very young, a nursing child, and already he was hungry and beginning to fret. This little girl said to the others: "We do not know why they have gone, but we know they have gone. We must follow the trail of the camp, and try to catch up with them." So the children started to follow the camp. They travelled on all day; and just at night they saw, near the trail, a little lodge. They had heard the people talk of a bad old woman who killed and ate persons, and some of the children thought that this old woman might live here; and they were afraid to go to the lodge. Others said: "Perhaps some person lives here who has a good heart. We are very tired and very hungry and have nothing to eat and no place to keep warm. Let us go to this lodge."

They went to it; and when they went in, they saw sitting by the fire an old woman. She spoke kindly to them, and asked them where they were travelling; and they told her that the camp had moved on and left them, and that they were trying to find their people, that they had nothing to eat, and were tired and hungry. The old woman fed them, and told them to sleep here to-night, and to-morrow they could go on and find their people. "The camp," she said, "passed here to-day when the sun was low. They have not gone far. To-morrow you will overtake them." She spread some robes on the ground and said: "Now lie here and sleep. Lie side by side with your heads toward the fire, and when morning comes, you can go on your journey." The children lay down and soon slept.

In the middle of the night, the old woman got up, and built a big fire, and put on it a big stone kettle, full of water. Then she took a big knife, and, commencing at one end of the row, began to cut off the heads of the children, and to throw them into the pot. The little girl with the baby brother lay at the other end of the row, and while the old woman was doing this, she awoke and saw what was taking place. When the old woman came near to her, she jumped up and began to beg that she would not kill her. "I am strong," she said. "I will work hard for you. I can bring your wood and water, and tan your skins. Do not kill my little brother and me. Take pity on us and save us alive.

Everybody has left us, but do you have pity. You shall see how quickly I will work, how you will always have plenty of wood. I can work quickly and well." The old woman thought for a little while, then she said : "Well, I will let you live for a time, anyhow. You shall sleep safely to-night."

The next day, early, the little girl took her brother on her back, and went out and gathered a big pile of wood, and brought it to the lodge before the old woman was awake. When she got up, she called to the girl, "Go to the river and get a bucket of water." The girl put her brother on her back, and took the bucket to go. The old woman said to her : "Why do you carry that child every-where? Leave him here." The girl said : "Not so. He is always with me, and if I leave him he will cry and make a great noise, and you will not like that." The old woman grumbled, but the girl went on down to the river.

When she got there, just as she was going to fill her bucket, she saw standing by her a great bull. It was a mountain buffalo, one of those who live in the timber ; and the long hair of its head was all full of pine needles and sticks and branches, and matted together. (It was a *Su'ye-stü'mik*, a water bull.) When the girl saw him, she prayed him to take her across the river, and so to save her and her little brother from the bad old woman. The bull said, " I will take you across, but first you must take some of the sticks out of my head." The girl begged him to start at once ; but the bull said, " No, first take the sticks out of my head." The girl began to do it, but before she had done much, she heard the old woman calling to her to bring the water. The girl called back, " I am trying to get the water clear," and went on fixing the buffalo's head. The old woman called again, saying, " Hurry, hurry with that water." The girl answered, " Wait, I am washing my little brother." Pretty soon the old woman called out, " If you don't bring that water, I will kill you and your brother." By this time the girl had most of the sticks out of the bull's head, and he told her to get on his back, and went into the water and swam with her across the river. As he reached the other bank, the girl could see the old woman coming from her lodge down to the river with a big stick in her hand.

When the bull reached the bank, the girl jumped off his back and started off on the trail of the camp. The bull swam back again to the other side of the river, and there stood the old woman. This bull was a sort of servant of the old woman. She said to him: "Why did you take those children across the river? Take me on your back now and carry me across quickly, so that I can catch them." The bull said, " First take these sticks out of my head." "No," said the old woman; "first take me across, then I will take the sticks out." The bull repeated, "First take the sticks out of my head, then I will take you across." This made the old woman very mad, and she hit him with the stick she had in her hand; but when she saw that he would not go, she began to pull the sticks out of his head very roughly, tearing out great handfuls of hair, and every moment ordering him to go, and threatening what she would do to him when she got back. At last the bull took her on his back, and began to swim across with her, but he did not swim fast enough to please her, so she began to pound him with her club to make him go faster; and when the bull got to the middle of the river, he rolled over on his side, and the old woman slipped off, and was carried down the river and drowned.

The girl followed the trail of the camp for several days, feeding on berries and roots that she dug; and at last one night after dark she overtook the camp. She went into the lodge of an old woman, who was camped off at one side, and the old woman pitied her and gave her some food, and told her where her father's lodge was. The girl went to it, but when she went in, her parents would not receive her.

She had tried to overtake them for the sake of her little brother, who was growing thin and weak because he had not nursed ; and now her mother was afraid to have her stay with them. She even went and told the chief that her children had come back. Now when the chief heard that these two children had come back, he was angry ; and he ordered that the next day they should be tied to a post in the camp, and that the people should move on and leave them here. " Then," he said, " they cannot follow us."

The old woman who had pitied the children, when she heard what the chief had ordered, made up a bundle of dried meat, and hid it in the grass near the camp. Then she called her dog to her, — a little curly dog. She said to the dog : —

" Now listen. To-morrow when we are ready to start, I will call you to come to me, but you must pay no attention to what I say. Run off, and pretend to be chasing squirrels. I will try to catch you, and if I do so, I will pretend to whip you ; but do not follow me. Stay behind, and when the camp has passed out of sight, chew off the strings that bind those children ; and when you have done this, show them where I have hidden that food. Then you can follow the camp and catch up to us." The dog stood before the old woman, and listened to all that she said, turning his head from side to side, as if paying close attention.

Next morning it was done as the chief had said. The children were tied to the tree with raw hide strings, and the people tore down all the lodges and moved off. The old woman called her dog to follow her, but he was digging at a gopher hole and would not come. Then she went up to him and struck at him hard with her whip, but he dodged and ran away, and then stood looking at her. Then the old woman got very mad and cursed him, but he paid no attention ; and finally she left him, and followed the camp. When the people had all passed out of sight, the dog went to the children, and gnawed the strings which tied them, until he had bitten them through.   So the children were free.

Then the dog was glad, and danced about and barked and ran round and round.   Pretty soon he came up to the little girl, and looked up in her face, and then started away, trotting.   Every little while he would stop and look back.   The girl thought he wanted her to follow him.   She did so, and he took her to where the bundle of dried meat was, and showed it to her.   Then, when he had done this, he jumped up on her, and licked the baby's face, and then started off, running as hard as he could along the trail of the camp, never stopping to look back.   The girl did not follow him. She now knew that it was no use to go to the camp again. Their parents would not receive them, and the chief would perhaps order them to be killed.

She went on her way, carrying her little brother and the bundle of dried meat.   She travelled for many days, and at last came to a place where she thought she would stop. Here she built a little lodge of poles and brush, and stayed there.   One night she had a dream, and an old woman came to her in the dream, and said to her, "To-morrow take your little brother, and tie him to one of the lodge poles, and the next day tie him to another, and so every day tie him to one of the poles, until you have gone all around the lodge and have tied him to each pole.   Then you will be helped, and will no more have bad luck."

When the girl awoke in the morning, she remembered what the dream had told her, and she bound her little brother to one of the lodge poles ; and each day after this she tied him to one of the poles.   Each day he grew larger, until, when she had gone all around the lodge, he was grown to be a fine young man.

Now the girl was glad, and proud of her young brother who was so large and noble-looking.   He was quiet, not speaking much, and sometimes for days he would not say anything. He seemed to be thinking all the time. One morning he told the girl that he had a dream and that he wished her to help him build a pis'kun. She was afraid to ask him about the dream, for she thought if she asked questions he might not like it. So she just said she was ready to do what he wished. They built the pis'kun, and when it was finished, the boy said to his sister: "The buffalo are to come to us, and you are not to see them. When the time comes, you are to cover your head and to hold your face close to the ground; and do not lift your head nor look, until I throw a piece of kidney to you." The girl said, "It shall be as you say."

When the time came, the boy told her where to go; and she went to the place, a little way from the lodge, not far from the corral, and sat down on the ground, and covered her head, holding her face close to the earth. After she had sat there a little while, she heard the sound of animals running, and she was excited and curious, and raised her head to look; but all she saw was her brother, standing near, looking at her. Before he could speak, she said to him: "I thought I heard buffalo coming, and because I was anxious for food, I forgot my promise and looked. Forgive me this time, and I will try again." Again she bent her face to the ground, and covered her head.

Soon she heard again the sound of animals running, at first a long way off, and then coming nearer and nearer, until at last they seemed close, and she thought they were going to run over her. She sprang up in fright and looked about, but there was nothing to be seen but her brother, looking sadly at her. She went close to him and said: "Pity me. I was afraid, for I thought the buffalo were going to run over me." He said: "This is the last time. If again you look, we will starve; but if you do not look, we will always have plenty, and will never be without meat." The girl looked at him, and said, "I will try hard this time, and even if those animals run right over me, I will not look until you throw the kidney to me." Again she covered her head, pressing her face against the earth and putting her hands against her ears, so that she might not hear. Suddenly, sooner than she thought, she felt the blow from the meat thrown at her, and, springing up, she seized the kidney and began to eat it. Not far away was her brother, bending over a fat cow ; and, going up to him, she helped him with the butchering. After that was done, she kindled a fire and cooked the best parts of the meat, and they ate and were satisfied.

The boy became a great hunter. He made fine arrows that went faster than a bird could fly, and when he was hunting, he watched all the animals and all the birds, and learned their ways, and how to imitate them when they called. While he was hunting, the girl dressed buffalo hides and the skins of deer and other animals. She made a fine new lodge, and the boy painted it with figures of all the birds and the animals he had killed.

One day, when the girl was bringing water, she saw a little way off a person coming. When she went in the lodge, she told her brother, and he went out to meet the stranger. He found that he was friendly and was hunting, but had had bad luck and killed nothing. He was starving and in despair, when he saw this lone lodge and made up his mind to go to it. As he came near it, he began to be afraid, and to wonder if the people who lived there were enemies or ghosts ; but he thought, " I may as well die here as starve," so he went boldly to it. The strange person was very much surprised to see this handsome young man with the kind face, who could speak his own language. The boy took him into the lodge, and the girl put food before him. After he had eaten, he told his story, saying that the game had left them, and that many of his people were dying of hunger. As he talked, the girl listened ; and at last she remembered the man, and knew that he belonged to her camp.

She asked him questions, and he talked about all the people in the camp, and even spoke of the old woman who owned the dog. The boy advised the stranger, after he had rested, to return to his camp, and tell the people to move up to this place, that here they would find plenty of game. After he had gone, the boy and his sister talked of these things. The girl had often told him what she had suffered, what the chief had said and done, and how their own parents had turned against her, and that the only person whose heart had been good to her was this old woman. As the young man heard all this again, he was angry at his parents and the chief, but he felt great kindness for the old woman and her dog. When he learned that those bad people were living, he made up his mind that they should suffer and die.

When the strange person reached his own camp, he told the people how well he had been treated by these two persons, and that they wished him to bring the whole camp to where they were, and that there they should have plenty. This made great joy in the camp, and all got ready to move. When they reached the lost children's camp, they found everything as the stranger had said. The brother gave a feast; and to those whom he liked he gave many presents, but to the old woman and the dog he gave the best presents of all. To the chief nothing at all was given, and this made him very much ashamed. To the parents no food was given, but the boy tied a bone to the lodge poles above the fire, and told the parents to eat from it without touching it with their hands. They were very hungry, and tried to eat from this bone; and as they were stretching out their necks to reach it — for it was above them — the boy cut off their heads with his knife. This frightened all the people, the chief most of all; but the boy told them how it all was, and how he and his sister had survived.

When he had finished speaking, the chief said he was sorry for what he had done, and he proposed to his people that this young man should be made their chief. They were glad to do this. The boy was made the chief, and lived long to rule the people in that camp.

MIK–A'PI—RED OLD MAN

I

IT was in the valley of "It fell on them "[1] Creek, near the mountains, that the Pikŭn'i were camped when Mik-a'pi went to war. It was far back, in the days of stone knives, long before the white people had come. This was the way it happened.

Early in the morning a band of buffalo were seen in the foot-hills of the mountains, and some hunters went out to get meat. Carefully they crawled along up the coulées and drew near to the herd; and, when they had come close to them, they began to shoot, and their arrows pierced many fat cows. But even while they were thus shooting, they were surprised by a war party of Snakes, and they began to run back toward the camp. There was one hunter, named Fox-eye, who was very brave. He called to the others to stop, saying: "They are many and we are few, but the Snakes are not brave. Let us stop and fight them." But the other hunters would not listen. "We have no shields," they said, "nor our war medicine. There are many of the enemy. Why should we foolishly die?"

They hurried on to camp, but Fox-eye would not turn back. He drew his arrows from the quiver, and prepared to fight. But, even as he placed an arrow, a Snake had

[1] Armells Creek in Northern Montana is called *Et-tsis-ki-ots-op*, "It fell on them." A long time ago a number of Blackfeet women were digging in a bank near this creek for the red clay which they use for paint, when the bank gave way and fell on them, burying and killing them.

crawled up by his side, unseen.   In the still air, the Piegan
heard the sharp twang of a bow string, but, before he could
turn his head, the long, fine-pointed arrow pierced him
through and through.   The bow and arrows dropped from
his hands, he swayed, and then fell forward on the grass,
dead.   But now the warriors came pouring from the camp
to aid him.   Too late !   The Snakes quickly scalped their
fallen enemy, scattered up the mountain, and were lost to
sight.

Now Fox-eye had two wives, and their father and mother
and all their near relations were dead.   All Fox-eye's relatives, too, had long since gone to the Sand Hills.[1]   So these
poor widows had no one to avenge them, and they mourned
deeply for the husband so suddenly taken from them.
Through the long days they sat on a near hill and mourned,
and their mourning was very sad.

There was a young warrior named Mik-a'pi.   Every morning he was awakened by the crying of these poor widows,
and through the day his heart was touched by their wailing.
Even when he went to rest, their mournful cries reached
him through the darkness, and he could not sleep.   So he
sent his mother to them.   "Tell them," he said, "that I
wish to speak to them."   When they had entered, they sat
close by the door-way, and covered their heads.

"*Kyi !*" said Mik-a'pi.   "For days and nights I have
heard your mourning, and I too have silently mourned.   My
heart has been very sad.   Your husband was my near friend,
and now he is dead and no relations are left to avenge him.
So now, I say, I will take the load from your hearts.   I will
avenge him.   I will go to war and take many scalps, and
when I return, they shall be yours.   You shall paint your
faces black, and we will all rejoice that Fox-eye is avenged."

When the people heard that Mik-a'pi was going to war,

[1] Sand Hills: the shadow land; place of ghosts; the Blackfoot future
world.

many warriors wished to join him, but he refused them ; and
when he had taken a medicine sweat, and got a medicine-
pipe man to make medicine for him during his absence, he
started from the camp one evening, just after sunset. It is
only the foolish warrior who travels in the day ; for other
war parties may be out, or some camp-watcher sitting on a
hill may see him from far off, and lay plans to destroy him.
Mik-a'pi was not one of these. He was brave but cautious,
and he had strong medicine. Some say that he was related
to the ghosts, and that they helped him. Having now
started to war against the Snakes, he travelled in hidden
places, and at sunrise would climb a hill and look carefully
in all directions, and during the long day would lie there,
and watch, and take short sleeps.

Now, when Mik-a'pi had come to the Great Falls (of the
Missouri), a heavy rain set in ; and, seeing a hole in the
rocks, he crawled in and lay down in the farther end to
sleep. The rain did not cease, and when night came he
could not travel because of the darkness and storm ; so
he lay down to sleep again. But soon he heard something
coming into the cave toward him, and then he felt a hand
laid on his breast, and he put out his hand and touched
a person. Then Mik-a'pi put the palm of his hand on
the person's breast and jerked it to and fro, and then he
touched the person with the point of his finger, which, in
the sign language, means, " Who are you ? "

The strange person then took Mik-a'pi's hand, and made
him feel of his own right hand. The thumb and all the fingers were closed except the forefinger, which was extended ;
and when Mik-a'pi touched it the person moved his hand
forward with a zigzag motion, which means "Snake." Then
Mik-a'pi was glad. Here had come to him one of the tribe
he was seeking. But he thought it best to wait for daylight
before attacking him. So, when the Snake in signs asked
him who he was, he replied, by making the sign for paddling

a canoe, that he was a Pend d'Oreille, or River person. For he knew that the Snakes and the Pend d'Oreilles were at peace.

Then they both lay down to sleep, but Mik-a'pi did not sleep. Through the long night he watched for the first dim light, so that he might kill his enemy. The Snake slept soundly ; and just at daybreak Mik-a'pi quietly strung his bow, fitted an arrow, and, taking aim, sent the thin shaft through his enemy's heart. The Snake quivered, half rose up, and with a groan fell back dead. Then Mik-a'pi took his scalp and his bow and arrows, and also his bundle of moccasins ; and as daylight had come, he went out of the cave and looked all about. No one was in sight. Probably the Snake, like himself, had gone alone to war. But, ever cautious, he travelled only a short distance, and waited for night before going on. The rain had ceased and the day was warm. He took a piece of dried meat and back fat from his pouch and ate them, and, after drinking from the river, he climbed up on a high rock wall and slept.

Now in his dream he fought with a strange people, and was wounded. He felt blood trickling from his wounds, and when he awoke, he knew that he had been warned to turn back. The signs also were bad. He saw an eagle rising with a snake, which dropped from its claws and escaped. The setting sun, too, was painted,[1] — a sure warning to people that danger is near. But, in spite of all these things, Mik-a'pi determined to go on. He thought of the poor widows mourning and waiting for revenge. He thought of the glad welcome of the people, if he should return with many scalps ; and he thought also of two young sisters, whom he wanted to marry. Surely, if he could return and bring the proofs of brave deeds, their parents would be glad to give them to him.

[1] Sun dogs.

II

It was nearly night. The sun had already disappeared behind the sharp-pointed gray peaks. In the fading light the far-stretching prairie was turning dark. In a valley, sparsely timbered with quaking aspens and cotton-woods, stood a large camp. For a long distance up and down the river rose the smoke of many lodges. Seated on a little hill overlooking the valley, was a single person. With his robe drawn tightly around him, he sat there motionless, looking down on the prairie and valley below.

Slowly and silently something was crawling through the grass toward him. But he heard nothing. Still he gazed eastward, seeking to discover any enemy who might be approaching. Still the dark object crawled slowly onward. Now it was so close to him that it could almost touch him. The person thought he heard a sound, and started to turn round. Too late! Too late! A strong arm grasped him about the neck and covered his mouth. A long jagged knife was thrust into his breast again and again, and he died without a cry. Strange that in all that great camp no one should have seen him killed!

Still extended on the ground, the dark figure removed the scalp. Slowly he crawled back down the hill, and was lost in the gathering darkness. It was Mik-a'pi, and he had another Snake scalp tied to his belt. His heart was glad, yet he was not satisfied. Some nights had passed since the bad signs had warned him, yet he had succeeded. "One more," he said. "One more scalp I must have, and then I will go back." So he went far up on the mountain, and hid in some thick pines and slept. When daylight came, he could see smoke rise as the women started their fires. He also saw many people rush up on the hill, where the dead watcher lay. He was too far off to hear their angry shouts

and mournful cries, but he sung to himself a song of war and
was happy.

Once more the sun went to his lodge behind the mountains, and as darkness came Mik-a'pi slowly descended the
mountain and approached the camp.   This was the time of
danger.   Behind each bush, or hidden in a bunch of the tall
rye grass, some person might be watching to warn the camp
of an approaching enemy.   Slowly and like a snake, he
crawled around the outskirts of the camp, listening and looking.   He heard a cough and saw a movement of a bush.
There was a Snake.   Could he kill him and yet escape?
He was close to him now.   So he sat and waited, consider-
ing how to act.   For a long time he sat there waiting.   The
moon rose and travelled high in the sky.   The Seven Persons[1] slowly swung around, and pointed downward.   It was
the middle of the night.   Then the person in the bush stood
up and stretched out his arms and yawned, for he was tired
of watching, and thought that no danger was near; but as
he stood thus, an arrow pierced his breast.   He gave a loud
yell and tried to run, but another arrow struck him and
he fell.

At the sound the warriors rushed forth from the lodges
and the outskirts of the camp; but as they came, Mik-a'pi
tore the scalp from his fallen enemy, and started to run
toward the river.   Close behind him followed the Snakes.
Arrows whizzed about him.   One pierced his arm.   He
plucked it out.   Another struck his leg, and he fell.   Then a
great shout arose from the Snakes.   Their enemy was down.
Now they would be revenged for two lately taken lives.   But
where Mik-a'pi fell was the verge of a high rock wall; below
rushed the deep river, and even as they shouted, he rolled
from the wall, and disappeared in the dark water far below.
In vain they searched the shores and bars.   They did not
find him.

[1] The constellation of the Great Bear.

Mĭk-a'pi had sunk deep in the water. The current was swift, and when at last he rose to the surface, he was far below his pursuers. The arrow in his leg pained him, and with difficulty he crawled out on a sand-bar. Luckily the arrow was lance-shaped instead of barbed, so he managed to draw it out. Near by on the bar was a dry pine log, lodged there by the high spring water. This he managed to roll into the stream ; and, partly resting on it, he again drifted down with the current. All night he floated down the river, and when morning came he was far from the camp of the Snakes. Benumbed with cold and stiff from the arrow wounds, he was glad to crawl out on the bank, and lie down in the warm sunshine. Soon he slept.

III

The sun was already in the middle when he awoke. His wounds were swollen and painful; yet he hobbled on for a time, until the pain became so great he could go no further, and he sat down, tired and discouraged.

"True the signs," he said. " How crazy I was to go against them ! Useless now my bravery, for here I must stay and die. The widows will still mourn ; and in their old age who will take care of my father and my mother? Pity me now, oh Sun ! Help me, oh great Above Medicine Person ! Look down on your wounded and suffering child. Help me to survive ! "

What was that crackling in the brush near by? Was it the Snakes on his trail? Mik-a'pi strung his bow and drew out his arrows. No ; it was not a Snake. It was a bear. There he stood, a big grizzly bear, looking down at the wounded man. " What does my brother here ? " he said. " Why does he pray to survive ? "

"Look at my leg," said Mik-a'pi, " swollen and sore. Look at my wounded arm. I can hardly draw the bow.

Far the home of my people, and my strength is gone. Surely here I must die, for I cannot travel and I have no food."

"Now courage, my brother," said the bear. "Now not faint heart, my brother, for I will help you, and you shall survive."

When he had said this, he lifted Mik-a'pi and carried him to a place of thick mud; and here he took great handfuls[1] of the mud and plastered the wounds, and he sung a medicine song while putting on the mud. Then he carried Mik-a'pi to a place where were many sarvis berries, and broke off great branches of the fruit, and gave them to him, saying, "Eat, my brother, eat!" and he broke off more branches, full of large ripe berries, for him; but already Mik-a'pi was satisfied and could eat no more. Then said the bear, "Lie down, now, on my back, and hold tight by my hair, and we will travel on." And when Mik-a'pi had got on and was ready, he started off on a long swinging trot.

All through the night he travelled on without stopping. When morning came, they rested awhile, and ate more berries; and again the bear plastered his wounds with mud. In this way they travelled on, until, on the fourth day, they came close to the lodges of the Pikŭn'i; and the people saw them coming and wondered.

"Get off, my brother, get off," said the bear. "There are your people. I must leave you." And without another word, he turned and went off up the mountain.

All the people came out to meet the warrior, and they carried him to the lodge of his father. He untied the three scalps from his belt and gave them to the widows, saying: "You are revenged. I wipe away your tears." And every one rejoiced. All his female relations went through the camp, shouting his name and singing, and every one prepared for the scalp dance.

[1] The bear's paws are called *O-kits-iks*, the term also for a person's hands. The animal itself is regarded as almost human.

First came the widows. Their faces were painted black, and they carried the scalps tied on poles. Then came the medicine men, with their medicine pipes unwrapped; then the bands of the *I-kun-uh'-kah-tsi*, all dressed in war costume; then came the old men; and last the women and children. They all sang the war song and danced. They went all through the village in single file, stopping here and there to dance, and Mik-a'pi sat outside the lodge, and saw all the people dance by him. He forgot his pain and was proud, and although he could not dance, he sang with them.

Soon they made the Medicine Lodge, and, first of all the warriors, Mik-a'pi was chosen to cut the raw-hide which binds the poles, and as he cut the strands, he counted the *coups* he had made. He told of the enemies he had killed, and all the people shouted his name and praised him. The father of those two young sisters gave them to him. He was glad to have such a son-in-law. Long lived Mik-a'pi. Of all the great chiefs who have lived and died, he was the greatest. He did many other great and daring things. It must be true, as the old men have said, that he was helped by the ghosts, for no one can do such things without help from those fearful and unknown persons.

HEAVY COLLAR AND THE GHOST WOMAN

THE Blood camp was on Old Man's River, where Fort McLeod now stands. A party of seven men started to war toward the Cypress Hills. Heavy Collar was the leader. They went around the Cypress Mountains, but found no enemies and started back toward their camp. On their homeward way, Heavy Collar used to take the lead. He would go out far ahead on the high hills, and look over the country, acting as scout for the party. At length they came to the south branch of the Saskatchewan River, above Seven Persons' Creek. In those days there were many war parties about, and this party travelled concealed as much as possible in the coulées and low places.

As they were following up the river, they saw at a distance three old bulls lying down close to a cut bank. Heavy Collar left his party, and went out to kill one of these bulls, and when he had come close to them, he shot one and killed it right there. He cut it up, and, as he was hungry, he went down into a ravine below him, to roast a piece of meat; for he had left his party a long way behind, and night was now coming on. As he was roasting the meat, he thought, — for he was very tired, — "It is a pity I did not bring one of my young men with me. He could go up on that hill and get some hair from that bull's head, and I could wipe out my gun." While he sat there thinking this, and talking to himself, a bunch of this hair came over him through the air, and fell on the ground right in front of him. When this hap-

70

pened, it frightened him a little ; for he thought that perhaps some of his enemies were close by, and had thrown the bunch of hair at him. After a little while, he took the hair, and cleaned his gun and loaded it, and then sat and watched for a time. He was uneasy, and at length decided that he would go on further up the river, to see what he could discover. He went on, up the stream, until he came to the mouth of the St. Mary's River. It was now very late in the night, and he was very tired, so he crept into a large bunch of rye-grass to hide and sleep for the night.

The summer before this, the Blackfeet (*Sik-si-kau*) had been camped on this bottom, and a woman had been killed in this same patch of rye-grass where Heavy Collar had lain down to rest. He did not know this, but still he seemed to be troubled that night. He could not sleep. He could always hear something, but what it was he could not make out. He tried to go to sleep, but as soon as he dozed off he kept thinking he heard something in the distance. He spent the night there, and in the morning when it became light, there he saw right beside him the skeleton of the woman who had been killed the summer before.

That morning he went on, following up the stream to Belly River. All day long as he was travelling, he kept thinking about his having slept by this woman's bones. It troubled him. He could not forget it. At the same time he was very tired, because he had walked so far and had slept so little. As night came on, he crossed over to an island, and determined to camp for the night. At the upper end of the island was a large tree that had drifted down and lodged, and in a fork of this tree he built his fire, and got in a crotch of one of the forks, and sat with his back to the fire, warming himself, but all the time he was thinking about the woman he had slept beside the night before. As he sat there, all at once he heard over beyond the tree, on the other side of the fire, a sound as if something were being dragged toward him along the ground. It sounded as if a piece of a lodge were being dragged over the grass. It came closer and closer.

Heavy Collar was scared. He was afraid to turn his head and look back to see what it was that was coming. He heard the noise come up to the tree in which his fire was built, and then it stopped, and all at once he heard some one whistling a tune. He turned around and looked toward the sound, and there, sitting on the other fork of the tree, right opposite to him, was the pile of bones by which he had slept, only now all together in the shape of a skeleton. This ghost had on it a lodge covering. The string, which is tied to the pole, was fastened about the ghost's neck ; the wings of the lodge stood out on either side of its head, and behind it the lodge could be seen, stretched out and fading away into the darkness. The ghost sat on the old dead limb and whistled its tune, and as it whistled, it swung its legs in time to the tune.

When Heavy Collar saw this, his heart almost melted away. At length he mustered up courage, and said : " Oh ghost, go away, and do not trouble me. I am very tired ; I want to rest." The ghost paid no attention to him, but kept on whistling, swinging its legs in time to the tune. Four times he prayed to her, saying : " Oh ghost, take pity on me ! Go away and leave me alone. I am tired ; I want to rest." The more he prayed, the more the ghost whistled and seemed pleased, swinging her legs, and turning her head from side to side, sometimes looking down at him, and sometimes up at the stars, and all the time whistling.

When he saw that she took no notice of what he said, Heavy Collar got angry at heart, and said, " Well, ghost, you do not listen to my prayers, and I shall have to shoot you to drive you away." With that he seized his gun, and throwing it to his shoulder, shot right at the ghost. When he shot at her, she fell over backward into the darkness, screaming out : " Oh Heavy Collar, you have shot me, you have killed me ! You dog, Heavy Collar ! there is no place on this earth where you can go that I will not find you ; no place where you can hide that I will not come."

As she fell back and said this, Heavy Collar sprang to his feet, and ran away as fast as he could. She called after him : " I have been killed once, and now you are trying to kill me again. Oh Heavy Collar ! " As he ran away, he could still hear her angry words following him, until at last they died away in the distance. He ran all night long, and whenever he stopped to breathe and listen, he seemed to hear in the distance the echoes of her voice. All he could hear was, " Oh Heavy Collar ! " and then he would rush away again. He ran until he was all tired out, and by this time it was daylight. He was now quite a long way below Fort McLeod. He was very sleepy, but dared not lie down, for he remembered that the ghost had said that she would follow him. He kept walking on for some time, and then sat down to rest, and at once fell asleep.

Before he had left his party, Heavy Collar had said to his young men : " Now remember, if any one of us should get separated from the party, let him always travel to the Belly River Buttes. There will be our meeting-place." When their leader did not return to them, the party started across the country and went toward the Belly River Buttes. Heavy Collar had followed the river up, and had gone a long distance out of his way ; and when he awoke from his sleep, he too started straight for the Belly River Buttes, as he had said he would.

When his party reached the Buttes, one of them went up on top of the hill to watch. After a time, as he looked down the river, he saw two persons coming, and as they came nearer, he saw that one of them was Heavy Collar, and by his side was a woman. The watcher called up the rest of the party, and said to them : " Here comes our chief. He has had luck. He is bringing a woman with him. If he brings her into camp, we will take her away from him." And they all laughed. They supposed that he had captured her. They went down to the camp, and sat about the fire, looking at the two people coming, and laughing among themselves at the idea of their chief bringing in a woman. When the two persons had come close, they could see that Heavy Collar was walking fast, and the woman would walk by his side a little way, trying to keep up, and then would fall behind, and then trot along to catch up to him again. Just before the pair reached camp there was a deep ravine that they had to cross. They went down into this side by side, and then Heavy Collar came up out of it alone, and came on into the camp.

When he got there, all the young men began to laugh at him and to call out, "Heavy Collar, where is your woman?" He looked at them for a moment, and then said: "Why, I have no woman. I do not understand what you are talking about." One of them said: "Oh, he has hidden her in that ravine. He was afraid to bring her into camp." Another said, "Where did you capture her, and what tribe does she belong to?" Heavy Collar looked from one to another, and said: "I think you are all crazy. I have taken no woman. What do you mean?" The young man said: "Why, that woman that you had with you just now: where did you get her, and where did you leave her? Is she down in the coulée? We all saw her, and it is no use to deny that she was with you. Come now, where is she?" When they said this, Heavy Collar's heart grew very heavy, for he knew that it must have been the ghost woman; and he told them the story. Some of the young men could not believe this, and they ran down to the ravine, where they had last seen the woman. There they saw in the soft dirt the tracks made by Heavy Collar, when he went down into the ravine, but there were no other tracks near his, where

they had seen the woman walking.   When they found that
it was a ghost that had come along with Heavy Collar, they
resolved to go back to their main camp.   The party had
been out so long that their moccasins were all worn out, and
some of them were footsore, so that they could not travel
fast, but at last they came to the cut banks, and there found
their camp — seven lodges.

That night, after they had reached camp, they were
inviting each other to feasts.   It was getting pretty late in
the night, and the moon was shining brightly, when one of
the Bloods called out for Heavy Collar to come and eat
with him.   Heavy Collar shouted, "Yes, I will be there
pretty soon."   He got up and went out of the lodge, and
went a little way from it, and sat down.   While he was
sitting there, a big bear walked out of the brush close to
him.   Heavy Collar felt around him for a stone to throw at
the bear, so as to scare it away, for he thought it had not
seen him.   As he was feeling about, his hand came upon a
piece of bone, and he threw this over at the bear, and hit it.
Then the bear spoke, and said: "Well, well, well, Heavy
Collar; you have killed me once, and now here you are
hitting me.   Where is there a place in this world where you
can hide from me?   I will find you, I don't care where
you may go."   When Heavy Collar heard this, he knew it
was the ghost woman, and he jumped up and ran toward his
lodge, calling out, "Run, run! a ghost bear is upon us!"

All the people in the camp ran to his lodge, so that it
was crowded full of people.   There was a big fire in the
lodge, and the wind was blowing hard from the west.   Men,
women, and children were huddled together in the lodge,
and were very much afraid of the ghost.   They could hear
her walking toward the lodge, grumbling, and saying: "I will
kill all these dogs.   Not one of them shall get away."   The
sounds kept coming closer and closer, until they were right
at the lodge door.   Then she said, "I will smoke you to

death." And as she said this, she moved the poles, so that the wings of the lodge turned toward the west, and the wind could blow in freely through the smoke hole. All this time she was threatening terrible things against them. The lodge began to get full of smoke, and the children were crying, and all were in great distress — almost suffocating. So they said, "Let us lift one man up here inside, and let him try to fix the ears, so that the lodge will get clear of smoke." They raised a man up, and he was standing on the shoulders of the others, and, blinded and half strangled by the smoke, was trying to turn the wings. While he was doing this, the ghost suddenly hit the lodge a blow, and said, "*Un!*" and this scared the people who were holding the man, and they jumped and let him go, and he fell down. Then the people were in despair, and said, "It is no use; she is resolved to smoke us to death." All the time the smoke was getting thicker in the lodge.

Heavy Collar said: "Is it possible that she can destroy us? Is there no one here who has some strong dream power that can overcome this ghost?"

His mother said: "I will try to do something. I am older than any of you, and I will see what I can do." So she got down her medicine bundle and painted herself, and got out a pipe and filled it and lighted it, and stuck the stem out through the lodge door, and sat there and began to pray to the ghost woman. She said: "Oh ghost, take pity on us, and go away. We have never wronged you, but you are troubling us and frightening our children. Accept what I offer you, and leave us alone."

A voice came from behind the lodge and said: "No, no, no; you dogs, I will not listen to you. Every one of you must die."

The old woman repeated her prayer: "Ghost, take pity on us. Accept this smoke and go away."

Then the ghost said: "How can you expect me to smoke,

when I am way back here? Bring that pipe out here. I have no long bill to reach round the lodge." So the old woman went out of the lodge door, and reached out the stem of the pipe as far as she could reach around toward the back of the lodge. The ghost said : " No, I do not wish to go around there to where you have that pipe. If you want me to smoke it, you must bring it here." The old woman went around the lodge toward her, and the ghost woman began to back away, and said, " No, I do not smoke that kind of a pipe." And when the ghost started away, the old woman followed her, and she could not help herself.

She called out, " Oh my children, the ghost is carrying me off ! " Heavy Collar rushed out, and called to the others, " Come, and help me take my mother from the ghost." He grasped his mother about the waist and held her, and another man took him by the waist, and another him, until they were all strung out, one behind the other, and all following the old woman, who was following the ghost woman, who was walking away.

All at once the old woman let go of the pipe, and fell over dead. The ghost disappeared, and they were troubled no more by the ghost woman.

THE WOLF-MAN

THERE was once a man who had two bad wives. They had no shame. The man thought if he moved away where there were no other people, he might teach these women to become good, so he moved his lodge away off on the prairie. Near where they camped was a high butte, and every evening about sundown, the man would go up on top of it, and look all over the country to see where the buffalo were feed· ing, and if any enemies were approaching. There was a buffalo skull on the hill, which he used to sit on.

"This is very lonesome," said one woman to the other, one day. "We have no one to talk with nor to visit."

"Let us kill our husband," said the other. "Then we will go back to our relations and have a good time."

Early in the morning, the man went out to hunt, and as soon as he was out of sight, his wives went up on top of the butte. There they dug a deep pit, and covered it over with light sticks, grass, and dirt, and placed the buffalo skull on top.

In the afternoon they saw their husband coming home, loaded down with meat he had killed. So they hurried to cook for him. After eating, he went up on the butte and sat down on the skull. The slender sticks gave way, and he fell into the pit. His wives were watching him, and when they saw him disappear, they took down the lodge, packed everything on the dog travois, and moved off, going toward the main camp. When they got near it, so that the people could hear them, they began to cry and mourn.

78

"Why is this?" they were asked. "Why are you mourning? Where is your husband?"

"He is dead," they replied. "Five days ago he went out to hunt, and he never came back." And they cried and mourned again.

When the man fell into the pit, he was hurt. After a while he tried to get out, but he was so badly bruised he could not climb up. A wolf, travelling along, came to the pit and saw him, and pitied him. *Ah-h-w-o-o-o-o! Ah-h-w-o-o-o-o!* he howled, and when the other wolves heard him they all came running to see what was the matter. There came also many coyotes, badgers, and kit-foxes.

"In this hole," said the wolf, "is my find. Here is a fallen-in man. Let us dig him out, and we will have him for our brother."

They all thought the wolf spoke well, and began to dig. In a little while they had a hole close to the man. Then the wolf who found him said, "Hold on; I want to speak a few words to you." All the animals listening, he continued, "We will all have this man for our brother, but I found him so I think he ought to live with us big wolves." All the others said that this was well; so the wolf went into the hole, and tearing down the rest of the dirt, dragged the almost dead man out. They gave him a kidney to eat, and when he was able to walk a little, the big wolves took him to their home. Here there was a very old blind wolf, who had powerful medicine. He cured the man, and made his head and hands look like those of a wolf. The rest of his body was not changed.

In those days the people used to make holes in the pis'-kun walls and set snares, and when wolves and other animals came to steal meat, they were caught by the neck. One night the wolves all went down to the pis'kun to steal meat, and when they got close to it, the man-wolf said: "Stand here a little while. I will go down and fix the places, so you will not be caught." He went on and sprung all the snares; then he went back and called the wolves and others, — the coyotes, badgers, and foxes, — and they all went in the pis'kun and feasted, and took meat to carry home.

In the morning the people were surprised to find the meat gone, and their nooses all drawn out. They wondered how it could have been done. For many nights the nooses were drawn and the meat stolen; but once, when the wolves went there to steal, they found only the meat of a scabby bull, and the man-wolf was angry, and cried out: "Bad-you-give-us-o-o-o! Bad-you-give-us-o-o-o-o!"

The people heard him, and said: "It is a man-wolf who has done all this. We will catch him." So they put pemmican and nice back fat in the pis'kun, and many hid close by. After dark the wolves came again, and when the man-wolf saw the good food, he ran to it and began eating. Then the people all rushed in and caught him with ropes and took him to a lodge. When they got inside to the light of the fire, they knew at once who it was. They said, "This is the man who was lost."

"No," said the man, "I was not lost. My wives tried to kill me. They dug a deep hole, and I fell into it, and I was hurt so badly that I could not get out; but the wolves took pity on me and helped me, or I would have died there."

When the people heard this, they were angry, and they told the man to do something.

"You say well," he replied. "I give those women to the *I-kun-uh'-kah-tsi;* they know what to do."

After that night the two women were never seen again.

THE FAST RUNNERS

ONCE, long ago, the antelope and the deer met on the prairie. At this time both of them had galls and both dew claws. They began to talk together, and each was telling the other what he could do. Each one told how fast he could run, and before long they were disputing as to which could run the faster. Neither would allow that the other could beat him, so they agreed that they would have a race to decide which was the swifter, and they bet their galls on the race. When they ran, the antelope proved the faster runner, and beat the deer and took his gall.

Then the deer said : " Yes, you have beaten me on the prairie, but that is not where I live. I only go out there sometimes to feed, or when I am travelling around. We ought to have another race in the timber. That is my home, and there I can run faster than you can."

The antelope felt very big because he had beaten the deer in the race, and he thought wherever they might be, he could run faster than the deer. So he agreed to race in the timber, and on this race they bet their dew claws.

They ran through the thick timber, among the brush and over fallen logs, and this time the antelope ran slowly, because he was not used to this kind of travelling, and the deer easily beat him, and took his dew claws.

Since then the deer has had no gall, and the antelope no dew claws.

[NOTE. A version of the first portion of this story is current among the Pawnees, and has been printed in Pawnee Hero Stories and Folk Tales.]

TWO WAR TRAILS

I

MANY years ago there lived in the Blood camp a boy named Screech Owl (A'-tsi-tsi). He was rather a lonely boy, and did not care to go with other boys. He liked better to be by himself. Often he would go off alone, and stay out all night away from the camp. He used to pray to all kinds of birds and animals that he saw, and ask them to take pity on him and help him, saying that he wanted to be a warrior. He never used paint. He was a fine looking young man, and he thought it was foolish to use paint to make oneself good looking.

When Screech Owl was about fourteen years old, a large party of Blackfeet were starting to war against the Crees and the Assinaboines. The young man said to his father : "Father, with this war party many of my cousins are going. I think that now I am old enough to go to war, and I would like to join them." His father said, "My son, I am willing ; you may go." So he joined the party.

His father gave his son his own war horse, a black horse with a white spot on its side — a very fast horse. He offered him arms, but the boy refused them all, except a little trapping axe. He said, "I think this hatchet will be all that I shall need." Just as they were about to start, his father gave the boy his own war headdress. This was not a war bonnet, but a plume made of small feathers, the feathers of thunder birds, for the thunder bird was his father's medicine. He said to the boy, "Now, my son, when you

82

go into battle, put this plume in your head, and wear it as I have worn it."

The party started and travelled north-east, and at length they came to where Fort Pitt now stands, on the Saskatchewan River. When they had got down below Fort Pitt, they saw three riders, going out hunting. These men had not seen the war party. The Blackfeet started around the men, so as to head them off when they should run. When they saw the men, the Screech Owl got off his horse, and took off all his clothes, and put on his father's war plume, and began to ride around, singing his father's war song. The older warriors were getting ready for the attack, and when they saw this young boy acting in this way, they thought he was making fun of the older men, and they said: "Here, look at this boy! Has he no shame? He had better stay behind." When they got on their horses, they told him to stay behind, and they charged the Crees. But the boy, instead of staying behind, charged with them, and took the lead, for he had the best horse of all. He, a boy, was leading the war party, and still singing his war song.

The three Crees began to run, and the boy kept gaining on them. They did not want to separate, they kept together; and as the boy was getting closer and closer, the last one turned in his saddle and shot at the Screech Owl, but missed him. As the Cree fired, the boy whipped up his horse, and rode up beside the Cree and struck him with his little trapping axe, and knocked him off his horse. He paid no attention to the man that he had struck, but rode on to the next Cree. As he came up with him, the Cree raised his gun and fired, but just as he did so, the Blackfoot dropped down on the other side of his horse, and the ball passed over him. He straightened up on his horse, rode up by the Cree, and as he passed, knocked him off his horse with his axe. When he knocked the second Cree off his horse, the Blackfeet, who were following, whooped in triumph and to encourage him, shouting, "*A-wah-heh'*" (Take courage). The boy was still singing his father's war song.

By this time, the main body of the Blackfeet were catching up with him. He whipped his horse on both sides, and rode on after the third Cree, who was also whipping his horse as hard as he could, and trying to get away. Meantime, some of the Blackfeet had stopped to count *coup* on and scalp the two dead Crees, and to catch the two ponies. Screech Owl at last got near to the third Cree, who kept aiming his gun at him. The boy did not want to get too close, until the Cree had fired his gun, but he was gaining a little, and all the time was throwing himself from side to side on his horse, so as to make it harder for the Cree to hit him. When he had nearly overtaken the enemy, the Cree turned, raised his gun and fired ; but the boy had thrown himself down behind his horse, and again the ball passed over him. He raised himself up on his horse, and rushed on the Cree, and struck him in the side of the body with his axe, and then again, and with the second blow, he knocked him off his horse.

The boy rode on a little further, stopped, and jumped off his horse, while the rest of the Blackfeet had come up and were killing the fallen man. He stood off to one side and watched them count *coup* on and scalp the dead.

The Blackfeet were much surprised at what the young man had done. After a little while, the leader decided that they would go back to the camp from which they had come. When he had returned from this war journey this young man's name was changed from A'-tsi-tsi to E-kūs'-kini (Low Horn). This was his first war path.

From that time on the name of E-kūs'-kini was often heard as that of one doing some great deed.

II

E-kūs'-kini started on his last war trail from the Black-foot crossing (*Su-yoh-pah'-wah-ku*). He led a party of six Sarcees. He was the seventh man.

On the second day out, they came to the Red Deer's River. When they reached this river, they found it very high, so they built a raft to cross on. They camped on the other side. In crossing, most of their powder got wet. The next morning, when they awoke, E-kūs'-kini said: "Well, trouble is coming for us. We had better go back from here. We started on a wrong day. I saw in my sleep our bodies lying on the prairie, dead." Some of the young men said: "Oh well, we have started, we had better go on. Perhaps it is only a mistake. Let us go on and try to take some horses anyhow." E-kūs'-kini said: "Yes, that is very true. To go home is all foolishness; but remember that it is by your wish that we are going on." He wanted to go back, not on his own account, but for the sake of his young men — to save his followers.

From there they went on and made another camp, and the next morning he said to his young men: "Now I am sure. I have seen it for certain. Trouble is before us." They camped two nights at this place and dried some of their powder, but most of it was caked and spoilt. He said to his young men: "Here, let us use some sense about this. We have no ammunition. We cannot defend our-selves. Let us turn back from here." So they started across the country for their camp.

They crossed the Red Deer's River, and there camped again. The next morning E-kūs'-kini said: "I feel very uneasy to-day. Two of you go ahead on the trail and keep a close lookout. I am afraid that to-day we are going to see our enemy." Two of the young men went ahead, and when they had climbed to the top of a ridge and looked

over it on to Sarvis Berry (Saskatoon) Creek, they came back
and told E-kūs'-kini that they had seen a large camp of
people over there, and that they thought it was the Piegans,
Bloods, Blackfeet, and Sarcees, who had all moved over
there together. Saskatoon Creek was about twenty miles
from the Blackfoot camp. He said : " No, it cannot be our
people. They said nothing about moving over here ; it must
be a war party. It is only a few days since we left, and there
was then no talk of their leaving that camp. It cannot be
they." The two young men said : "Yes, they are our
people. There are too many of them for a war party. We
think that the whole camp is there." They discussed this
for some little time, E-kūs'-kini insisting that it could not be
the Blackfoot camp, while the young men felt sure that it
was. These two men said, " Well, we are going on into the
camp now." Low Horn said : "Well, you may go. Tell
my father that I will come into the camp to-night. I do
not like to go in in the daytime, when I am not bringing
back anything with me."

It was now late in the afternoon, and the two young men
went ahead toward the camp, travelling on slowly. A little
after sundown, they came down the hill on to the flat of the
river, and saw there the camp. They walked down toward it,
to the edge of the stream, and there met two women, who had
come down after water. The men spoke to them in Sarcee,
and said, " Where is the Sarcee camp?" The women did
not understand them, so they spoke again, and asked the
same question in Blackfoot. Then these two women called
out in the Cree language, "Here are two Blackfeet, who
have come here and are talking to us." When these men
heard the women talk Cree, and saw what a mistake they
had made, they turned and ran away up the creek. They
ran up above camp a short distance, to a place where a few
willow bushes were hanging over the stream, and pushing
through these, they hid under the bank, and the willows above

concealed them. The people in the camp came rushing out, and men ran up the creek, and down, and looked everywhere for the two enemies, but could find nothing of them.

Now when these people were running in all directions, hunting for these two men, E-kūs'-kini was coming down the valley slowly with the four other Sarcees. He saw some Indians coming toward him, and supposed that they were some of his own people, coming to meet him, with horses for him to ride. At length, when they were close to him, and E-kūs'-kini could see that they were the enemy, and were taking the covers off their guns, he jumped to one side and stood alone and began to sing his war song. He called out, " Children of the Crees, if you have come to try my manhood, do your best." In a moment or two he was surrounded, and they were shooting at him from all directions. He called out again, " People, you can't kill me here, but I will take my body to your camp, and there you shall kill me." So he advanced, fighting his way toward the Cree camp, but before he started, he killed two of the Crees there. His enemies kept coming up and clustering about him : some were on foot and some on horseback. They were thick about him on all sides, and they could not shoot much at him, for fear of killing their own people on the other side.

One of the Sarcees fell. E-kūs'-kini said to his men, " A-wah-heh' " (Take courage). "These people cannot kill us here. Where that patch of choke-cherry brush is, in the very centre of their camp, we will go and take our stand." Another Sarcee fell, and now there were only three of them. E-kūs'-kini said to his remaining men : " Go straight to that patch of brush, and I will fight the enemy off in front and at the sides, and so will keep the way open for you. These people cannot kill us here. There are too many of their own people. If we can get to that brush, we will hurt them badly." All this time they were killing enemies, fighting

bravely, and singing their war songs. At last they gained
the patch of brush, and then with their knives they began to
dig holes in the ground, and to throw up a shelter.

In the Cree camp was Kŏm-in'-ă-kūs (Round), the chief
of the Crees, who could talk Blackfoot well. He called out :
" E-kūs'-kini, there is a little ravine running out of that
brush patch, which puts into the hills. Crawl out through
that, and try to get away. It is not guarded." E-kūs'-kini
replied : " No, Children of the Crees, I will not go. You
must remember that it is E-kūs'-kini that you are fighting
with — a man who has done much harm to your people. I
am glad that I am here. I am sorry for only one thing ;
that is, that my ammunition is going to run out. To-morrow
you may kill me."

All night long the fight was kept up, the enemy shooting
all the time, and all night long E-kūs'-kini sang his death
song. Kŏm-in'-ă-kūs called to him several times : " E-kūs'-
kini, you had better do what I tell you. Try to get away."
But he shouted back, "No," and laughed at them. He
said : " You have killed all my men. I am here alone, but
you cannot kill me." Kŏm-in'-ă-kūs, the chief, said : "Well,
if you are there at daylight in the morning, I will go into
that brush and will catch you with my hands. I will be the
man who will put an end to you." E-kūs'-kini said : "Kŏm-
in'-ă-kūs, do not try to do that. If you do, you shall surely
die." The patch of brush in which he had hidden had
now been all shot away, cut off by the bullets of the enemy.

When day came, E-kūs'-kini called out : " Eh, Kŏm-in'-ă-
kūs, it is broad daylight now. I have run out of ammunition. I have not another grain of powder in my horn.
Now come and take me in your hands, as you said you
would." Kŏm-in'-ă-kūs answered : " Yes, I said that I was
the one who was going to catch you this morning. Now I
am coming."

He took off all his clothes, and alone rushed for the

breastworks. E-kūs'-kini's ammunition was all gone, but he still had one load in his gun, and his dagger. Kŏm-in'-ă-kūs came on with his gun at his shoulder, and E-kūs'-kini sat there with his gun in his hand, looking at the man who was coming toward him with the cocked gun pointed at him. He was singing his death song. As Kŏm-in'-ă-kūs got up close, and just as he was about to fire, E-kūs'-kini threw up his gun and fired, and the ball knocked off the Cree chief's forefinger, and going on, entered his right eye and came out at the temple, knocking the eye out. Kŏm-in'-ă-kūs went down, and his gun flew a long way.

When Kŏm-in'-ă-kūs fell, the whole camp shouted the war whoop, and cried out, "This is his last shot," and they all charged on him. They knew that he had no more ammunition.

The head warrior of the Crees was named Bunch of Lodges. He was the first man to jump inside the breastworks. As he sprang inside, E-kūs'-kini met him, and thrust his dagger through him, and killed him on the spot. Then, as the enemy threw themselves on him, and he began to feel the knives stuck into him from all sides, he gave a war whoop and laughed, and said, "Only now I begin to think that I am fighting." All the time he was cutting and stabbing, jumping backward and forward, and all the time laughing. When he was dead, there were fifteen dead Crees lying about the earthworks. E-kūs'-kini's body was cut into small pieces and scattered all over the country, so that he might not come to life again.

III

That morning, before it was daylight, the two Sarcees who had hidden in the willows left their hiding-place and made their way to the Blackfoot camp. When they got there, they told that when they had left the Cree camp E-kūs'-

kini was surrounded, and the firing was terrible. When E-kūs'-kini's father heard this, he got on his horse and rode through the camp, calling out : " My boy is surrounded ; let us turn out and go to help him. I have no doubt they are many tens to one, but he is powerful, and he may be fighting yet." No time was lost in getting ready, and soon a large party started for the Cree camp. When they came to the battle-ground, the camp had been moved a long time. The old man looked about, trying to gather up his son's body, but it was found only in small pieces, and not more than half of it could be gathered up.

After the fight was over, the Crees started on down to go to their own country. One day six Crees were travelling along on foot, scouting far ahead. As they were going down into a little ravine, a grizzly bear jumped up in front of them and ran after them. The bear overtook, and tore up, five of them, one after another. The sixth got away, and came home to camp. The Crees and the Blackfeet believe that this was the spirit of E-kūs'-kini, for thus he comes back. They think that he is still on the earth, but in a different shape.

E-kūs'-kini was killed about forty years ago. When he was killed, he was still a boy, not married, only about twenty-four years old.

STORIES OF ANCIENT TIMES

SCARFACE

I

In the earliest times there was no war. All the tribes were at peace. In those days there was a man who had a daughter, a very beautiful girl. Many young men wanted to marry her, but every time she was asked, she only shook her head and said she did not want a husband.

"How is this?" asked her father. "Some of these young men are rich, handsome, and brave."

"Why should I marry?" replied the girl. "I have a rich father and mother. Our lodge is good. The parfleches are never empty. There are plenty of tanned robes and soft furs for winter. Why worry me, then?"

The Raven Bearers held a dance; they all dressed carefully and wore their ornaments, and each one tried to dance the best. Afterwards some of them asked for this girl, but still she said no. Then the Bulls, the Kit-foxes, and others of the *I-kun-uh'-kah-tsi* held their dances, and all those who were rich, many great warriors, asked this man for his daughter, but to every one of them she said no. Then her father was angry, and said : "Why, now, this way? All the best men have asked for you, and still you say no. I believe you have a secret lover."

"Ah!" said her mother. "What shame for us should a child be born and our daughter still unmarried!" "Father! mother!" replied the girl, "pity me. I have no secret lover,

93

but now hear the truth. That Above Person, the Sun, told me, 'Do not marry any of those men, for you are mine; thus you shall be happy, and live to great age'; and again he said, 'Take heed. You must not marry. You are mine.'"

"Ah!" replied her father. "It must always be as he says." And they talked no more about it.

There was a poor young man, very poor. His father, mother, all his relations, had gone to the Sand Hills. He had no lodge, no wife to tan his robes or sew his moccasins. He stopped in one lodge to-day, and to-morrow he ate and slept in another; thus he lived. He was a good-looking young man, except that on his cheek he had a scar, and his clothes were always old and poor.

After those dances some of the young men met this poor Scarface, and they laughed at him, and said: "Why don't you ask that girl to marry you? You are so rich and handsome!" Scarface did not laugh; he replied: "Ah! I will do as you say. I will go and ask her." All the young men thought this was funny. They laughed a great deal. But Scarface went down by the river. He waited by the river, where the women came to get water, and by and by the girl came along. "Girl," he said, "wait. I want to speak with you. Not as a designing person do I ask you, but openly where the Sun looks down, and all may see."

"Speak then," said the girl.

"I have seen the days," continued the young man "You have refused those who are young, and rich, and brave. Now, to-day, they laughed and said to me, 'Why do you not ask her?' I am poor, very poor. I have no lodge, no food, no clothes, no robes and warm furs. I have no relations; all have gone to the Sand Hills; yet, now, to-day, I ask you, take pity, be my wife."

The girl hid her face in her robe and brushed the ground with the point of her moccasin, back and forth, back and forth; for she was thinking. After a time she said: "True.

I have refused all those rich young men, yet now the poor one asks me, and I am glad. I will be your wife, and my people will be happy. You are poor, but it does not matter. My father will give you dogs. My mother will make us a lodge. My people will give us robes and furs. You will be poor no longer."

Then the young man was happy, and he started to kiss her, but she held him back, and said: "Wait! The Sun has spoken to me. He says I may not marry; that I belong to him. He says if I listen to him, I shall live to great age. But now I say: Go to the Sun. Tell him, 'She whom you spoke with heeds your words. She has never done wrong, but now she wants to marry. I want her for my wife.' Ask him to take that scar from your face. That will be his sign. I will know he is pleased. But if he refuses, or if you fail to find his lodge, then do not return to me."

"Oh!" cried the young man, "at first your words were good. I was glad. But now it is dark. My heart is dead. Where is that far-off lodge? where the trail, which no one yet has travelled?"

"Take courage, take courage!" said the girl; and she went to her lodge.

II

Scarface was very sad. He sat down and covered his head with his robe and tried to think what to do. After a while he got up, and went to an old woman who had been kind to him. "Pity me," he said. "I am very poor. I am going away now on a long journey. Make me some moccasins."

"Where are you going?" asked the old woman. "There is no war; we are very peaceful here."

"I do not know where I shall go," replied Scarface. "I am in trouble, but I cannot tell you now what it is."

So the old woman made him some moccasins, seven pairs,

with parfleche soles, and also she gave him a sack of food, — pemmican of berries, pounded meat, and dried back fat ; for this old woman had a good heart.   She liked the young man.

All alone, and with a sad heart, he climbed the bluffs and stopped to take a last look at the camp.   He wondered if he would ever see his sweetheart and the people again.   "*Hai'. yu !*   Pity me, O Sun," he prayed, and turning, he started to find the trail.

For many days he travelled on, over great prairies, along timbered rivers and among the mountains, and every day his sack of food grew lighter ; but he saved it as much as he could, and ate berries, and roots, and sometimes he killed an animal of some kind.   One night he stopped by the home of a wolf.   "*Hai-yah !*" said that one ; "what is my brother doing so far from home?"

"Ah !" replied Scarface, "I seek the place where the Sun lives ; I am sent to speak with him."

"I have travelled far," said the wolf.   "I know all the prairies, the valleys, and the mountains, but I have never seen the Sun's home.   Wait ; I know one who is very wise. Ask the bear.   He may tell you."

The next day the man travelled on again, stopping now and then to pick a few berries, and when night came he arrived at the bear's lodge.

"Where is your home?" asked the bear.   "Why are you travelling alone, my brother?"

"Help me !   Pity me !" replied the young man ; "because of her words [1] I seek the Sun.   I go to ask him for her."

"I know not where he stops," replied the bear.   "I have travelled by many rivers, and I know the mountains, yet I have never seen his lodge.   There is some one beyond, that striped-face, who is very smart.   Go and ask him."

The badger was in his hole.   Stooping over, the young

[1] A Blackfoot often talks of what this or that person said, without mentioning names.

man shouted : "Oh, cunning striped-face ! Oh, generous animal ! I wish to speak with you."

"What do you want ? " said the badger, poking his head out of the hole.

"I want to find the Sun's home," replied Scarface. " I want to speak with him."

" I do not know where he lives," replied the badger. " I never travel very far. Over there in the timber is a wolverine. He is always travelling around, and is of much knowledge. Maybe he can tell you."

Then Scarface went to the woods and looked all around for the wolverine, but could not find him. So he sat down to rest. " *Hai'-yu ! Hai'-yu !* " he cried. " Wolverine, take pity on me. My food is gone, my moccasins worn out. Now I must die."

"What is it, my brother ? " he heard, and looking around, he saw the animal sitting near.

" She whom I would marry," said Scarface, " belongs to the Sun ; I am trying to find where he lives, to ask him for her."

" Ah ! " said the wolverine. " I know where he lives. Wait ; it is nearly night. To-morrow I will show you the trail to the big water. He lives on the other side of it."

Early in the morning, the wolverine showed him the trail, and Scarface followed it until he came to the water's edge. He looked out over it, and his heart almost stopped. Never before had any one seen such a big water. The other side could not be seen, and there was no end to it. Scarface sat down on the shore. His food was all gone, his moccasins worn out. His heart was sick. " I cannot cross this big water," he said. " I cannot return to the people. Here, by this water, I shall die."

Not so. His Helpers were there. Two swans came swimming up to the shore. " Why have you come here ? " they asked him. " What are you doing ? It is very far to the place where your people live."

"I am here," replied Scarface, "to die. Far away, in my country, is a beautiful girl. I want to marry her, but she belongs to the Sun. So I started to find him and ask for her. I have travelled many days. My food is gone. I cannot go back. I cannot cross this big water, so I am going to die."

"No," said the swans; "it shall not be so. Across this water is the home of that Above Person. Get on our backs, and we will take you there."

Scarface quickly arose. He felt strong again. He waded out into the water and lay down on the swans' backs, and they started off. Very deep and black is that fearful water. Strange people live there, mighty animals which often seize and drown a person. The swans carried him safely, and took him to the other side. Here was a broad hard trail leading back from the water's edge.

"*Kyi*," said the swans. "You are now close to the Sun's lodge. Follow that trail, and you will soon see it."

III

Scarface started up the trail, and pretty soon he came to some beautiful things, lying in it. There was a war shirt, a shield, and a bow and arrows. He had never seen such pretty weapons; but he did not touch them. He walked carefully around them, and travelled on. A little way further on, he met a young man, the handsomest person he had ever seen. His hair was very long, and he wore clothing made of strange skins. His moccasins were sewn with bright colored feathers. The young man said to him, "Did you see some weapons lying on the trail?"

"Yes," replied Scarface; "I saw them."

"But did you not touch them?" asked the young man.

"No; I thought some one had left them there, so I did not take them."

"You are not a thief," said the young man. "What is your name?"

"Scarface."

"Where are you going?"

"To the Sun."

"My name," said the young man, "is A-pi-su'-ahts.[1] The Sun is my father; come, I will take you to our lodge. My father is not now at home, but he will come in at night."

Soon they came to the lodge. It was very large and handsome; strange medicine animals were painted on it. Behind, on a tripod, were strange weapons and beautiful clothes — the Sun's. Scarface was ashamed to go in, but Morning Star said, "Do not be afraid, my friend; we are glad you have come."

They entered. One person was sitting there, Ko-ko-mik'-e-is,[2] the Sun's wife, Morning Star's mother. She spoke to Scarface kindly, and gave him something to eat. "Why have you come so far from your people?" she asked.

Then Scarface told her about the beautiful girl he wanted to marry. "She belongs to the Sun," he said. "I have come to ask him for her."

When it was time for the Sun to come home, the Moon hid Scarface under a pile of robes. As soon as the Sun got to the doorway, he stopped, and said, "I smell a person."

"Yes, father," said Morning Star; "a good young man has come to see you. I know he is good, for he found some of my things on the trail and did not touch them."

Then Scarface came out from under the robes, and the Sun entered and sat down. "I am glad you have come to our lodge," he said. "Stay with us as long as you think best. My son is lonesome sometimes; be his friend."

The next day the Moon called Scarface out of the lodge, and said to him: "Go with Morning Star where you please, but never hunt near that big water; do not let him go there.

[1] Early Riser, *i.e.* The Morning Star.   [2] Night red light, the Moon.

It is the home of great birds which have long sharp bills ; they kill people. I have had many sons, but these birds have killed them all. Morning Star is the only one left."

So Scarface stayed there a long time and hunted with Morning Star. One day they came near the water, and saw the big birds.

" Come," said Morning Star ; " let us go and kill those birds."

" No, no ! " replied Scarface ; " we must not go there. Those are very terrible birds ; they will kill us."

Morning Star would not listen. He ran towards the water, and Scarface followed. He knew that he must kill the birds and save the boy. If not, the Sun would be angry and might kill him. He ran ahead and met the birds, which were coming towards him to fight, and killed every one of them with his spear : not one was left. Then the young men cut off their heads, and carried them home. Morning Star's mother was glad when they told her what they had done, and showed her the birds' heads. She cried, and called Scarface " my son." When the Sun came home at night, she told him about it, and he too was glad. " My son," he said to Scarface, " I will not forget what you have this day done for me. Tell me now, what can I do for you ? "

"*Hai'-yu*," replied Scarface. "*Hai'-yu*, pity me. I am here to ask you for that girl. I want to marry her. I asked her, and she was glad ; but she says you own her, that you told her not to marry."

" What you say is true," said the Sun. " I have watched the days, so I know it. Now, then, I give her to you ; she is yours. I am glad she has been wise. I know she has never done wrong. The Sun pities good women. They shall live a long time. So shall their husbands and children. Now you will soon go home. Let me tell you something. Be wise and listen : I am the only chief. Everything is mine. I made the earth, the mountains, prairies, rivers, and forests. I made the people and all the animals. This is why I say I alone am the chief. I can never die. True, the winter makes me old and weak, but every summer I grow young again."

Then said the Sun: "What one of all animals is smartest? The raven is, for he always finds food. He is never hungry. Which one of all the animals is most *Nat-o'-ye*[1]? The buffalo is. Of all animals, I like him best. He is for the people. He is your food and your shelter. What part of his body is sacred? The tongue is. That is mine. What else is sacred? Berries are. They are mine too. Come with me and see the world." He took Scarface to the edge of the sky, and they looked down and saw it. It is round and flat, and all around the edge is the jumping-off place [or walls straight down]. Then said the Sun: "When any man is sick or in danger, his wife may promise to build me a lodge, if he recovers. If the woman is pure and true, then I will be pleased and help the man. But if she is bad, if she lies, then I will be angry. You shall build the lodge like the world, round, with walls, but first you must build a sweat house of a hundred sticks. It shall be like the sky [a hemisphere], and half of it shall be painted red. That is me. The other half you will paint black. That is the night."

Further said the Sun: "Which is the best, the heart or the brain? The brain is. The heart often lies, the brain never." Then he told Scarface everything about making the Medicine Lodge, and when he had finished, he rubbed a powerful medicine on his face, and the scar disappeared. Then he gave him two raven feathers, saying: "These are the sign for the girl, that I give her to you. They must always be worn by the husband of the woman who builds a Medicine Lodge."

[1] This word may be translated as "of the Sun," "having Sun power," or more properly, something sacred.

The young man was now ready to return home. Morning Star and the Sun gave him many beautiful presents. The Moon cried and kissed him, and called him "my son." Then the Sun showed him the short trail. It was the Wolf Road (Milky Way). He followed it, and soon reached the ground.

IV

It was a very hot day. All the lodge skins were raised, and the people sat in the shade. There was a chief, a very generous man, and all day long people kept coming to his lodge to feast and smoke with him. Early in the morning this chief saw a person sitting out on a butte near by, close wrapped in his robe. The chief's friends came and went, the sun reached the middle, and passed on, down towards the mountains. Still this person did not move. When it was almost night, the chief said: "Why does that person sit there so long? The heat has been strong, but he has never eaten nor drunk. He may be a stranger; go and ask him in."

So some young men went up to him, and said: "Why do you sit here in the great heat all day? Come to the shade of the lodges. The chief asks you to feast with him."

Then the person arose and threw off his robe, and they were surprised. He wore beautiful clothes. His bow, shield, and other weapons were of strange make. But they knew his face, although the scar was gone, and they ran ahead, shouting, "The scarface poor young man has come. He is poor no longer. The scar on his face is gone."

All the people rushed out to see him. "Where have you been?" they asked. "Where did you get all these pretty things?" He did not answer. There in the crowd stood that young woman; and taking the two raven feathers from his head, he gave them to her, and said: "The trail was very long, and I nearly died, but by those Helpers, I found his lodge. He is glad. He sends these feathers to you. They are the sign."

Great was her gladness then. They were married, and made the first Medicine Lodge, as the Sun had said. The Sun was glad. He gave them great age. They were never sick. When they were very old, one morning, their children said: "Awake! Rise and eat." They did not move. In the night, in sleep, without pain, their shadows had departed for the Sand Hills.

ORIGIN OF THE I-KUN-UH'-KAH-TSI [1]

I

THE BULL BAND

THE people had built a great pis'kun, very high and strong, so that no buffalo could escape ; but somehow the buffalo would not jump over the cliff. When driven toward it, they would run nearly to the edge, and then, swerving to the right or left, they would go down the sloping hills and cross the valley in safety. So the people were hungry, and began to starve.

One morning, early, a young woman went to get water, and she saw a herd of buffalo feeding on the prairie, right on the edge of the cliff above the pis'kun. "Oh!" she cried out, "if you will only jump off into the pis'kun, I will marry one of you." This she said for fun, not meaning it, and great was her wonder when she saw the buffalo come jumping, tumbling, falling over the cliff.

Now the young woman was scared, for a big bull with one bound cleared the pis'kun walls and came toward her. "Come," he said, taking hold of her arm. "No, no!" she replied pulling back. "But you said if the buffalo would jump over, you would marry one ; see, the pis'kun is filled." And without more talk he led her up over the bluff, and out on to the prairie.

[1] An account of the *I-kun-uh'-kah-tsi*, with a list of its different bands or societies and their duties, will be found in the chapter on Social Organization.

104

When the people had finished killing the buffalo and cutting up the meat, they missed this young woman, and her
relations were very sad, because they could not find her.
Then her father took his bow and quiver, and said, " I will
go and find her." And he went up over the bluff and out
on the prairie.

After he had travelled some distance he came to a wallow,
and a little way off saw a herd of buffalo. While sitting by
the wallow, — for he was tired — and thinking what he should
do, a magpie came and lit near him. "Ha ! *Ma-me-at'-si-
kim-i*," he said, " you are a beautiful bird ; help me. Look
everywhere as you travel about, and if you see my daughter,
tell her, ' Your father waits by the wallow.' " The magpie
flew over by the herd of buffalo, and seeing the young
woman, he lit on the ground near her, and commenced
picking around, turning his head this way and that way,
and, when close to her, he said, " Your father waits by the
wallow." " Sh-h-h ! sh-h-h !" replied the girl, in a whisper,
looking around scared, for her bull husband was sleeping
near by. "Don't speak so loud. Go back and tell him to
wait."

" Your daughter is over there with the buffalo. She says
' wait !' " said the magpie, when he had flown back to the
man.

By and by the bull awoke, and said to his wife, " Go
and get me some water." Then the woman was glad, and
taking a horn from his head she went to the wallow. " Oh,
why did you come?" she said to her father. " You will
surely be killed."

" I came to take my daughter home ; come, let us hurry."

" No, no !" she replied ; " not now. They would chase us
and kill us. Wait till he sleeps again, and I will try to get
away," and, filling the horn with water, she went back.

The bull drank a swallow of the water. " Ha !" said he,
" a person is close by here."

" No one," replied the woman ; but her heart rose up.

The bull drank a little more, and then he stood up and bellowed, " *Bu-u-u! m-m-ah-oo!* " Oh, fearful sound ! Up rose the bulls, raised their short tails and shook them, tossed their great heads, and bellowed back. Then they pawed the dirt, rushed about here and there, and coming to the wallow, found that poor man. There they trampled him with their great hoofs, hooked him and trampled him again, and soon not even a small piece of his body could be seen.

Then his daughter cried, "*Oh ! ah ! Ni'-nah-ah ! Oh ! ah ! Ni'-nah-ah !*" (My father ! My father !) " Ah ! " said her bull husband, " you mourn for your father. You see now how it is with us. We have seen our mothers, fathers, many of our relations, hurled over the rocky walls, and killed for food by your people. But I will pity you. I will give you one chance. If you can bring your father to life, you and he can go back to your people."

Then the woman said to the magpie: " Pity me. Help me now ; go and seek in the trampled mud ; try and find a little piece of my father's body, and bring it to me."

The magpie flew to the place. He looked in every hole, and tore up the mud with his sharp nose. At last he found something white ; he picked the mud from around it, and then pulling hard, he brought out a joint of the backbone, and flew with it back to the woman.

She placed it on the ground, covered it with her robe, and then sang. Removing the robe, there lay her father's body as if just dead. Once more she covered it with the robe and sang, and when she took away the robe, he was breathing, and then he stood up. The buffalo were surprised ; the magpie was glad, and flew round and round, making a great noise.

" We have seen strange things this day," said her bull husband. " He whom we trampled to death, even into small pieces, is alive again. The people's medicine is very strong. Now, before you go, we will teach you our dance and our song. You must not forget them."[1] When the dance was over, the bull said : "Go now to your home, and do not forget what you have seen. Teach it to the people. The medicine shall be a bull's head and a robe. All the persons who are to be 'Bulls' shall wear them when they dance."

Great was the joy of the people, when the man returned with his daughter. He called a council of the chiefs, and told them all that had happened. Then the chiefs chose certain young men, and this man taught them the dance and song of the bulls, and told them what the medicine should be. This was the beginning of the *I-kun-uh'-kah-tsi*.

II

THE OTHER BANDS

For a long time the buffalo had not been seen. The pis'kun was useless, and the hunters could find no food for the people. Then a man who had two wives, a daughter, and two sons, said : "I shall not stop here to die. To-morrow we will move toward the mountains, where we shall perhaps find deer and elk, sheep and antelope, or, if not, at least we shall find plenty of beaver and birds. Thus we shall survive."

When morning came, they packed the travois, lashed them on the dogs, and then moved out. It was yet winter, and they travelled slowly. They were weak, and could go but a little way in a day. The fourth night came, and they sat in their lodge, very tired and hungry. No one spoke, for those who are hungry do not care for words. Suddenly

[1] Here the narrator repeated the song and showed the dance. As is fitting to the dance of such great beasts, the air is slow and solemn, and the step ponderous and deliberate.

the dogs began to bark, and soon, pushing aside the door-curtain, a young man entered.

"*O'kyĭ!*" said the old man, and he motioned the stranger to a sitting-place.

They looked at this person with surprise and fear, for there was a black wind[1] which had melted the snow, and covered the prairie with water, yet this person's leggings and moccasins were dry. They sat in silence a long time.

Then said he : "Why is this? Why do you not give me some food?"

"Ah!" replied the old man, "you behold those who are truly poor. We have no food. For many days the buffalo did not come in sight, and we shot deer and other animals which people eat, and when all these had been killed, we began to starve. Then said I, 'We will not stay here to starve to death'; and we started for the mountains. This is the fourth night of our travels."

"Ah!" said the young man. "Then your travels are ended. Close by here, we are camped by our pis'kun. Many buffalo have been run in, and our parfleches are filled with dried meat. Wait; I will go and bring you some."

As soon as he went out, they began to talk about this strange person. They were very much afraid of him, and did not know what to do. The children began to cry, and the women were trying to quiet them, when the young man returned, bringing some meat and three *pis-tsi-ko'-an.*[2]

"*Kyi!*" said he. "To-morrow move over to our lodges. Do not be afraid. No matter what strange things you see, do not fear. All will be your friends. Now, one thing I caution you about. In this be careful. If you should find an arrow lying about, in the pis'kun, or outside, no matter where, do not touch it; neither you, nor your wives nor children." Having said this, he went out.

Then the old man took his pipe and smoked and prayed,

---

[1] The "chinook."   [2] Unborn buffalo calves.

saying : " Hear now, Sun ! Listen, Above People. Listen, Under Water People. Now you have taken pity. Now you have given us food. We are going to those strange ones, who walk through water with dry moccasins. Protect us among those to-be-feared people. Let us survive. Man, woman, child, give us long life ; give us long life !"

Once more the smell of roasting meat. The children played. They talked and laughed who had so long been silent. They ate plenty and lay down and slept.

Early in the morning, as soon as the sun rose, they took down their lodge, packed up, and started for the strange camp. They found it was a wonderful place. There by the pis'kun, and far up and down the valley were the lodges of meat-eaters. They could not see them all, but close by they saw the lodges of the Bear band, the Fox band, and the Badger band. The father of the young man who had given them meat was chief of the Wolf band, and by that band they pitched their lodge. Ah ! That was a happy place. Food there was plenty. All day people shouted out for feasts, and everywhere was heard the sound of drums and song and dancing.

The new-comers went to the pis'kun for meat, and one of the children found an arrow lying on the ground. It was a beautiful arrow, the stone point long and sharp, the shaft round and straight. All around the people were busy ; no one was looking. The boy picked up the arrow and hid it under his robe. Then there was a fearful noise. All the animals howled and growled, and ran toward him. But the chief Wolf said : " Hold ! We will let him go this time ; for he is young yet, and not of good sense." So they let him go.

When night came, some one shouted out for a feast, say-ing : "*Wo'-ka-hit ! Wo'-ka-hit ! Mah-kwe'-i-ke-tum-ok-ah-wah-hit. Ke-tŭk'-ka-pŭk'-si-pim.*" ("Listen ! Listen ! Wolf, you are to feast. Enter with your friend.") "We are asked," said the chief Wolf to his new friend, and together they went to the lodge.

Within, the fire burned brightly, and many men were already there, the old and wise of the Raven band. Hanging behind the seats were the writings[1] of many deeds. Food was placed before them, — pemmican of berries and dried back fat ; and when they had eaten, a pipe was lighted. Then spoke the Raven chief: " Now, Wolf, I am going to give our new friend a present. What say you?"

" It is as you say," replied the Wolf. " Our new friend will be glad."

Then the Raven chief took from the long parfleche sack a slender stick, beautifully dressed with many colored feathers ; and on the end of it was fastened the skin of a raven, head, wings, feet, and all. " We," he said, " are the *Mas-to-pah'-ta-kiks* (Raven carriers, or those who bear the Raven). Of all the above animals, of all the flyers, where is one so smart? None. The Raven's eyes are sharp. His wings are strong. He is a great hunter and never hungry. Far, far off on the prairie he sees his food, and deep hidden in the pines it does not escape his eye. Now the song and the dance."

When he had finished singing and dancing, he gave the stick to the man, and said : "Take it with you, and when you have returned to your people, you shall say : Now there are already the Bulls, and he who is the Raven chief says : 'There shall be more, there shall be the *I-kun-uh'-kah-tsi*, so that the people may survive, and of them shall be the Raven carriers.' You will call a council of the chiefs and wise old men, and they will choose the persons. Teach them the song and the dance, and give them the medicine. It shall be theirs forever."

Soon they heard another person shouting for a feast, and, going, they entered the lodge of the *Sin'-o-pah* chief. Here,

---

[1] That is, the painting on cowskin of the various battles and adventures in which the owner of the lodge had taken part.

too, were the old men assembled.   After they had eaten of
that set before them, the chief said : "Those among whom
you are newly arrived are generous.   They do not look at
their possessions, but give to the stranger and pity the poor.
The Kit-fox is a little animal, but what one is smarter?
None.   His hair is like the dead prairie grass.   His eyes are
sharp, his feet noiseless, his brain cunning.   His ears receive
the far-off sound.   Here is our medicine, take it."   And he
gave the stick.   It was long, crooked at one end, wound
with fur, and tied here and there to it were eagle feathers.
At the end was a fox's skin.   Again the chief said : "Hear
our song.   Do not forget it ; and the dance, too, you must
remember.   When you get home, teach them to the
people."

Again they heard the feast shout, and he who called was
the Bear chief.   Now when they had smoked, the chief
said : "What say you, friend Wolf ?   Shall we give our new
friend something?"

"As you say," replied the Wolf.   "It is yours to give."

Then said the Bear : "There are many animals, and some
of them are powerful.   But the Bear is the strongest and
bravest of all.   He fears nothing, and is always ready to
fight."   Then he put on a necklace of bear claws, a belt of
bear fur, and around his head a band of the fur ; and sang
and danced.   When he had finished, he gave them to the
man, saying : "Teach the people our song and dance, and
give them this medicine.   It is powerful."

It was now very late.   The Seven Persons had arrived at
midnight, yet again they heard the feast shout from the far
end of camp.   In this lodge the men were painted with
streaks of red and their hair was all brushed to one side.
After the feast the chief said : "We are different from all the
others here.   We are called the *Mŭt'-siks*.[1]   We are death.
We know not fear.   Even if our enemies are in number like

[1] Brave, courageous.

the grass, we do not turn away, but fight and conquer.
Bows are good weapons.   Spears are better, but our weapon
is the knife."   Then the chief sang and danced, and afterwards he gave the Wolf's friend the medicine.   It was a
long knife, and many scalps were tied on the handle.
"This," he said, "is for the *I-kun-uh'-kah-tsi.*"

Once more they were called to a feast and entered the
Badger chief's lodge.   He taught the man the Badger
song and dance and gave him the medicine.   It was a large
rattle, ornamented with beaver claws and bright feathers.
They smoked two pipes in the Badger's lodge, and then went
home and slept.

Early next day, the man and his family took down their
lodge, and prepared to move camp.   Many women came
and made them presents of dried meat, pemmican, and
berries.   They were given so much they could not take it
all with them.   It was many days before they joined the
main camp, for the people, too, had moved to the south after
buffalo.   As soon as the lodge was pitched, the man called
all the chiefs to come and feast, and he told them all he had
seen, and showed them the medicines.   The chiefs chose
certain young men for the different bands, and this man
taught them the songs and dances, and gave each band
their medicine.

ORIGIN OF THE MEDICINE PIPE

THUNDER — you have heard him, he is everywhere. He roars in the mountains, he shouts far out on the prairie. He strikes the high rocks, and they fall to pieces. He hits a tree, and it is broken in slivers. He strikes the people, and they die. He is bad. He does not like the towering cliff, the standing tree, or living man. He likes to strike and crush them to the ground. Yes! yes! Of all he is most powerful; he is the one most strong. But I have not told you the worst: he sometimes steals women.

Long ago, almost in the beginning, a man and his wife were sitting in their lodge, when Thunder came and struck them. The man was not killed. At first he was as if dead, but after a while he lived again, and rising looked about him. His wife was not there. "Oh, well," he thought, "she has gone to get some water or wood," and he sat a while; but when the sun had under-disappeared, he went out and inquired about her of the people. No one had seen her. He searched throughout the camp, but did not find her. Then he knew that Thunder had stolen her, and he went out on the hills alone and mourned.

When morning came, he rose and wandered far away, and he asked all the animals he met if they knew where Thunder lived. They laughed, and would not answer. The Wolf said: "Do you think we would seek the home of the only one we fear? He is our only danger. From all others we can run away; but from him there is no running. He strikes, and there we lie. Turn back! go home! Do not look for

the dwelling-place of that dreadful one." But the man kept
on, and travelled far away. Now he came to a lodge, — a
queer lodge, for it was made of stone; just like any other
lodge, only it was made of stone. Here lived the Raven
chief. The man entered.

"Welcome, my friend," said the chief of Ravens. "Sit
down, sit down." And food was placed before him.

Then, when he had finished eating, the Raven said, "Why
have you come?"

"Thunder has stolen my wife," replied the man. "I seek
his dwelling-place that I may find her."

"Would you dare enter the lodge of that dreadful person?" asked the Raven. "He lives close by here. His
lodge is of stone, like this; and hanging there, within, are
eyes, — the eyes of those he has killed or stolen. He has
taken out their eyes and hung them in his lodge. Now, then,
dare you enter there?"

"No," replied the man. "I am afraid. What man could
look at such dreadful things and live?"

"No person can," said the Raven. "There is but one
old Thunder fears. There is but one he cannot kill. It is I,
it is the Ravens. Now I will give you medicine, and he
shall not harm you. You shall enter there, and seek among
those eyes your wife's; and if you find them, tell that
Thunder why you came, and make him give them to you.
Here, now, is a raven's wing. Just point it at him, and he
will start back quick; but if that fail, take this. It is an
arrow, and the shaft is made of elk-horn. Take this, I say,
and shoot it through the lodge."

"Why make a fool of me?" the poor man asked. "My
heart is sad. I am crying." And he covered his head with
his robe, and wept.

"Oh," said the Raven, "you do not believe me. Come
out, come out, and I will make you believe." When they

stood outside, the Raven asked, "Is the home of your people far?"

"A great distance," said the man.

"Can you tell how many days you have travelled?"

"No," he replied, "my heart is sad. I did not count the days. The berries have grown and ripened since I left."

"Can you see your camp from here?" asked the Raven.

The man did not speak. Then the Raven rubbed some medicine on his eyes and said, "Look!" The man looked, and saw the camp. It was close. He saw the people. He saw the smoke rising from the lodges.

"Now you will believe," said the Raven. "Take now the arrow and the wing, and go and get your wife."

So the man took these things, and went to the Thunder's lodge. He entered and sat down by the door-way. The Thunder sat within and looked at him with awful eyes. But the man looked above, and saw those many pairs of eyes. Among them were those of his wife.

"Why have you come?" said the Thunder in a fearful voice.

"I seek my wife," the man replied, "whom you have stolen. There hang her eyes."

"No man can enter my lodge and live," said the Thunder; and he rose to strike him. Then the man pointed the raven wing at the Thunder, and he fell back on his couch and shivered. But he soon recovered, and rose again. Then the man fitted the elk-horn arrow to his bow, and shot it through the lodge of rock; right through that lodge of rock it pierced a jagged hole, and let the sunlight in.

"Hold," said the Thunder. "Stop; you are the stronger. Yours the great medicine. You shall have your wife. Take down her eyes." Then the man cut the string that held them, and immediately his wife stood beside him.

"Now," said the Thunder, "you know me. I am of great power. I live here in summer, but when winter comes, I go far south. I go south with the birds. Here is my pipe. It is medicine. Take it, and keep it. Now, when I first come in the spring, you shall fill and light this pipe, and you shall pray to me, you and the people. For I bring the rain which makes the berries large and ripe. I bring the rain which makes all things grow, and for this you shall pray to me, you and all the people."

Thus the people got the first medicine pipe. It was long ago.

THE BEAVER MEDICINE

THIS story goes back many years, to a time before the Indians went to war against each other. Then there was peace among all the tribes. They met, and did not kill each other. They had no guns and they had no horses. When two tribes met, the head chiefs would take each a stick and touch each other. Each had counted a *coup* on the other, and they then went back to their camps. It was more a friendly than a hostile ceremony.

Oftentimes, when a party of young men had gone to a strange camp, and had done this to those whom they had visited, they would come back to their homes and would tell the girls whom they loved that they had counted a *coup* on this certain tribe of people. After the return of such a party, the young women would have a dance. Each one would wear clothing like that of the man she loved, and as she danced, she would count a *coup*, saying that she herself had done the deed which her young lover had really done. Such was the custom of the people.

There was a chief in a camp who had three wives, all very pretty women. He used to say to these women, whenever a dance was called : " Why do not you go out and dance too? Perhaps you have some one in the camp that you love, and for whom you would like to count a *coup*." Then the women would say, " No, we do not wish to join the dance ; we have no lovers."

There was in the camp a poor young man, whose name was Ápi-kŭnni. He had no relations, and no one to tan

117

robes or furs for him, and he was always badly clad and in
rags.   Whenever he got some clothing, he wore it as long
as it would hold together.   This young man loved the
youngest wife of the chief, and she loved him.   But her
parents were not rich, and they could not give her to Ápi-
kŭnni, and when the chief wanted her for a wife, they gave
her to him.   Sometimes Ápi-kŭnni and this girl used to
meet and talk together, and he used to caution her, saying,
"Now be careful that you do not tell any one that you see
me."   She would say, "No, there is no danger; I will not
let it be known."

One evening, a dance was called for the young women to
dance, and the chief said to his wives: "Now, women, you
had better go to this dance.   If any of you have persons
whom you love, you might as well go and dance for them."
Two of them said: "No, we will not go.   There is no one
that we love."   But the third said, "Well, I think I will go
and dance."   The chief said to her, "Well, go then; your
lover will surely dress you up for the dance."

The girl went to where Ápi-kŭnni was living in an old
woman's lodge, very poorly furnished, and told him what
she was going to do, and asked him to dress her for the
dance.   He said to her: "Oh, you have wronged me by
coming here, and by going to the dance.   I told you to
keep it a secret."   The girl said: "Well, never mind; no
one will know your dress.   Fix me up, and I will go and join
the dance anyway."   "Why," said Ápi-kŭnni, "I never have
been to war.   I have never counted any *coups*.   You will go
and dance and will have nothing to say.   The people will
laugh at you."   But when he found that the girl wanted to
go, he painted her forehead with red clay, and tied a goose skin,
which he had, about her head, and lent her his badly tanned
robe, which in spots was hard like a parfleche.   He said to
her, "If you will go to the dance, say, when it comes your
turn to speak, that when the water in the creeks gets warm,

you are going to war, and are going to count a *coup* on some people."

The woman went to the dance, and joined in it. All the people were laughing at her on account of her strange dress, — a goose skin around her head, and a badly tanned robe about her. The people in the dance asked her: "Well, what are you dancing for? What can you tell?" The woman said, "I am dancing here to-day, and when the water in the streams gets warm next spring, I am going to war; and then I will tell you what I have done to any people." The chief was standing present, and when he learned who it was that his young wife loved, he was much ashamed and went to his lodge.

When the dance was over, this young woman went to the lodge of the poor young man to give back his dress to him. Now, while she had been gone, Ápi-künni had been thinking over all these things, and he was very much ashamed. He took his robe and his goose skin and went away. He was so ashamed that he went away at once, travelling off over the prairie, not caring where he went, and crying all the time. As he wandered away, he came to a lake, and at the foot of this lake was a beaver dam, and by the dam a beaver house. He walked out on the dam and on to the beaver house. There he stopped and sat down, and in his shame cried the rest of the day, and at last he fell asleep on the beaver house.

While he slept, he dreamed that a beaver came to him — a very large beaver — and said: "My poor young man, come into my house. I pity you, and will give you something that will help you." So Ápi-künni got up, and followed the beaver into the house. When he was in the house, he awoke, and saw sitting opposite him a large white beaver, almost as big as a man. He thought to himself, "This must be the chief of all the beavers, white because very old." The beaver was singing a song. It was a very strange song, and he sang it a long time. Then he said to Ápi-kŭnni, "My son, why are you mourning?" and the young man told him everything that had happened, and how he had been shamed. Then the beaver said: "My son, stay here this winter with me. I will provide for you. When the time comes, and you have learned our songs and our ways, I will let you go. For a time make this your home." So Ápi-kŭnni stayed there with the beaver, and the beaver taught him many strange things. All this happened in the fall.

Now the chief in the camp missed this poor young man, and he asked the people where he had gone. No one knew. They said that the last that had been seen of him he was travelling toward the lake where the beaver dam was.

Ápi-kŭnni had a friend, another poor young man named Wolf Tail, and after a while, Wolf Tail started out to look for his friend. He went toward this lake, looking everywhere, and calling out his name. When he came to the beaver house, he kicked on the top and called, "Oh, my brother, are you here?" Ápi-kŭnni answered him, and said: "Yes, I am here. I was brought in while I was asleep, and I cannot give you the secret of the door, for I do not know it myself." Wolf Tail said to him, "Brother, when the weather gets warm a party is going to start from camp to war." Ápi-kŭnni said: "Go home and try to get together all the moccasins you can, but do not tell them that I am here. I am ashamed to go back to the camp. When the party starts, come this way and bring me the moccasins, and we two will start from here." He also said: "I am very thin. The beaver food here does not agree with me. We are living on the bark of willows." Wolf Tail went back to the camp and gathered together all the moccasins that he could, as he had been asked to do.

When the spring came, and the grass began to start, the war party set out. At this time the beaver talked to Ápi-kŭnni a long time, and told him many things. He dived down into the water, and brought up a long stick of aspen wood, cut off from it a piece as long as a man's arm, trimmed the twigs off it, and gave it to the young man. "Keep this," the beaver said, "and when you go to war take it with you." The beaver also gave him a little sack of medicine, and told him what he must do.

When the party started out, Wolf Tail came to the beaver house, bringing the moccasins, and his friend came out of the house. They started in the direction the party had taken and travelled with them, but off to one side. When they stopped at night, the two young men camped by themselves.

They travelled for many days, until they came to Bow River, and found that it was very high. On the other side of the river, they saw the lodges of a camp. In this camp a man was making a speech, and Ápi-kŭnni said to his friend, "Oh, my brother, I am going to kill that man to-day, so that my sweetheart may count *coup* on him." These two were at a little distance from the main party, above them on the river. The people in the camp had seen the Blackfeet, and some had come down to the river. When Ápi-kŭnni had said this to Wolf Tail, he took his clothes off and began to sing the song the beaver had taught him. This was the song : —

> I am like an island,
> For on an island I got my power.
> In battle I live
> While people fall away from me.

While he sang this, he had in his hand the stick which the beaver had given him. This was his only weapon.

He ran to the bank, jumped in and dived, and came up in the middle of the river, and started to swim across. The rest of the Blackfeet saw one of their number swimming across the river, and they said to each other : "Who is that?

Why did not some one stop him?" While he was swimming across, the man who had been making the speech saw him and went down to meet him. He said: "Who can this man be, swimming across the river? He is a stranger. I will go down and meet him, and kill him." As the boy was getting close to the shore, the man waded out in the stream up to his waist, and raised his knife to stab the swimmer. When Ápi-kŭnni got near him, he dived under the water and came up close to the man, and thrust the beaver stick through his body, and the man fell down in the water and died. Ápi-kŭnni caught the body, and dived under the water with it, and came up on the other side where he had left his friend. Then all the Blackfeet set up the war whoop, for they were glad, and they could hear a great crying in the camp. The people there were sorry for the man who was killed.

People in those days never killed one another, and this was the first man ever killed in war.

They dragged the man up on the bank, and Ápi-kŭnni said to his brother, "Cut off those long hairs on the head." The young man did as he was told. He scalped him and counted *coup* on him; and from that time forth, people, when they went to war, killed one another and scalped the dead enemy, as this poor young man had done. Two others of the main party came to the place, and counted *coup* on the dead body, making four who had counted *coup*. From there, the whole party turned about and went back to the village whence they had come.

When they came in sight of the lodges, they sat down in a row facing the camp. The man who had killed the enemy was sitting far in front of the others. Behind him sat his friend, and behind Wolf Tail, sat the two who had counted *coup* on the body. So these four were strung out in front of the others. The chief of the camp was told that some people were sitting on a hill near by, and when he had gone out and looked, he said: "There is some one sitting way in front. Let somebody go out and see about it." A young man ran out to where he could see, and when he had looked, he ran back and said to the chief, "Why, that man in front is the poor young man."

The old chief looked around, and said: "Where is that young woman, my wife? Go and find her." They went to look for her, and found her out gathering rosebuds, for while the young man whom she loved was away, she used to go out and gather rosebuds and dry them for him. When they found her, she had her bosom full of them. When she came to the lodge, the chief said to her: "There is the man you love, who has come. Go and meet him." She made ready quickly and ran out and met him. He said: "Give her that hair of the dead man. Here is his knife. There is the coat he had on, when I killed him. Take these things back to the camp, and tell the people who made fun of you that this is what you promised them at the time of that dance."

The whole party then got up and walked to the camp. The woman took the scalp, knife and coat to the lodge, and gave them to her husband. The chief invited Ápi-künni to come to his lodge to visit him. He said: "I see that you have been to war, and that you have done more than any of us have ever done. This is a reason why you should be a chief. Now take my lodge and this woman, and live here. Take my place and rule these people. My two wives will be your servants." When Ápi-künni heard this, and saw the young woman sitting there in the lodge, he could not speak. Something seemed to rise up in his throat and choke him.

So this young man lived in the camp and was known as their chief.

After a time, he called his people together in council and told them of the strange things the beaver had taught him, and the power that the beaver had given him. He said:

"This will be a benefit to us while we are a people now, and afterward it will be handed down to our children, and if we follow the words of the beaver we will be lucky. This seed the beaver gave me, and told me to plant it every year. When we ask help from the beaver, we will smoke this plant."

This plant was the Indian tobacco, and it is from the beaver that the Blackfeet got it. Many strange things were taught this man by the beaver, which were handed down and are followed till to-day.

THE BUFFALO ROCK

A SMALL stone, which is usually a fossil shell of some kind, is known by the Blackfeet as I-nis'-kim, the buffalo stone. This object is strong medicine, and, as indicated in some of these stories, gives its possessor great power with buffalo. The stone is found on the prairie, and the person who succeeds in obtaining one is regarded as very fortunate. Sometimes a man, who is riding along on the prairie, will hear a peculiar faint chirp, such as a little bird might utter. The sound he knows is made by a buffalo rock. He stops and searches on the ground for the rock, and if he cannot find it, marks the place and very likely returns next day, either alone or with others from the camp, to look for it again. If it is found, there is great rejoicing. How the first buffalo rock was obtained, and its power made known, is told in the following story.

Long ago, in the winter time, the buffalo suddenly disappeared. The snow was so deep that the people could not move in search of them, for in those days they had no horses. So the hunters killed deer, elk, and other small game along the river bottoms, and when these were all killed off or driven away, the people began to starve.

One day, a young married man killed a jack-rabbit. He was so hungry that he ran home as fast as he could, and told one of his wives to hurry and get some water to cook it. While the young woman was going along the path to the river, she heard a beautiful song. It sounded close by, but she looked all around and could see no one.

125

The song seemed to come from a cotton-wood tree near the path. Looking closely at this tree she saw a queer rock jammed in a fork, where the tree was split, and with it a few hairs from a buffalo, which had rubbed there. The woman was frightened and dared not pass the tree. Pretty soon the singing stopped, and the I-nis'-kim [buffalo rock] spoke to the woman and said: "Take me to your lodge, and when it is dark, call in the people and teach them the song you have just heard. Pray, too, that you may not starve, and that the buffalo may come back. Do this, and when day comes, your hearts will be glad."

The woman went on and got some water, and when she came back, took the rock and gave it to her husband, telling him about the song and what the rock had said. As soon as it was dark, the man called the chiefs and old men to his lodge, and his wife taught them this song. They prayed, too, as the rock had said should be done. Before long, they heard a noise far off. It was the tramp of a great herd of buffalo coming. Then they knew that the rock was very powerful, and, ever since that, the people have taken care of it and prayed to it.

[NOTE.— I-nis'-kims are usually small *Ammonites*, or sections of *Baculites*, or sometimes merely oddly shaped nodules of flint. It is said of them that if an I-nis'-kim is wrapped up and left undisturbed for a long time, it will have young ones; two small stones similar in shape to the original one will be found in the package with it.]

ORIGIN OF THE WORM PIPE

THERE was once a man who was very fond of his wife. After they had been married for some time they had a child, a boy. After that, the woman got sick, and did not get well. The young man did not wish to take a second woman. He loved his wife so much. The woman grew worse and worse. Doctoring did not seem to do her any good. At last she died. The man used to take his baby on his back and travel out, walking over the hills crying. He kept away from the camp. After some time, he said to the little child : "My little boy, you will have to go and live with your grandmother. I am going to try and find your mother, and bring her back." He took the baby to his mother's lodge, and asked her to take care of it, and left it with her. Then he started off, not knowing where he was going nor what he was going to do.

He travelled toward the Sand Hills. The fourth night out he had a dream. He dreamed that he went into a little lodge, in which lived an old woman. This old woman said to him, "Why are you here, my son?" He said : "I am mourning day and night, crying all the while. My little son, who is the only one left me, also mourns." "Well," said the old woman, "for whom are you mourning?" He said : "I am mourning for my wife. She died some time ago. I am looking for her." "Oh!" said the old woman, "I saw her. She passed this way. I myself am not powerful medicine, but over by that far butte lives another old woman. Go to her, and she will give you power to enable

127

you to continue your journey. You could not go there by yourself without help. Beyond the next butte from her lodge, you will find the camp of the ghosts."

The next morning he awoke and went on to the next butte. It took him a long day to get there, but he found no lodge there, so he lay down and went to sleep. Again he dreamed. In his dream, he saw a little lodge, and an old woman came to the door-way and called him. He went in, and she said to him: "My son, you are very poor. I know why you have come this way. You are seeking your wife, who is now in the ghost country. It is a very hard thing for you to get there. You may not be able to get your wife back, but I have great power, and I will do all I can for you. If you do exactly as I tell you, you may succeed." She then spoke to him with wise words, telling him what he should do. Also she gave him a bundle of medicine, which would help him on his journey.

Then she said: "You stay here for a while, and I will go over there [to the ghosts' camp], and try to bring some of your relations; and if I am able to bring them back, you may return with them, but on the way you must shut your eyes. If you should open them and look about you, you would die. Then you would never come back. When you get to the camp, you will pass by a big lodge, and they will say to you, 'Where are you going, and who told you to come here?' You will reply, 'My grandmother, who is standing out here with me, told me to come.' They will try to scare you. They will make fearful noises, and you will see strange and terrible things; but do not be afraid."

Then the old woman went away, and after a time came back with one of the man's relations. He went with this relation to the ghosts' camp. When they came to the big lodge, some one called out and asked the man what he was doing, and he answered as the old woman had told him to do. As he passed on through the camp, the ghosts tried to scare him with all kinds of fearful sights and sounds, but he kept up a brave heart.

He came to another lodge, and the man who owned it came out, and asked him where he was going. He said: "I am looking for my dead wife. I mourn for her so much that I cannot rest. My little boy, too, keeps crying for his mother. They have offered to give me other wives, but I do not want them. I want the one for whom I am searching."

The ghost said to him: "It is a fearful thing that you have come here. It is very likely that you will never go away. There never was a person here before." The ghost asked him to come into the lodge, and he went.

Now this chief ghost said to him: "You will stay here four nights, and you will see your wife; but you must be very careful or you will never go back. You will die right here."

Then the chief went outside and called out for a feast, inviting this man's father-in-law and other relations, who were in the camp, saying, "Your son-in-law invites you to a feast," as if to say that their son-in-law was dead, and had become a ghost, and had arrived at the ghost camp.

Now when these invited people, the relations and some of the principal men of the camp, had reached the lodge, they did not like to go in. They called out, "There is a person here." It seems as if there was something about him that they could not bear the smell of. The ghost chief burned sweet pine in the fire, which took away this smell, and the people came in and sat down. Then the host said to them: " Now pity this son-in-law of yours. He is seeking his wife. Neither the great distance nor the fearful sights that he has seen here have weakened his heart. You can see for yourselves he is tender-hearted. He not only mourns for his wife, but mourns because his little boy is now alone with no mother; so pity him and give him back his wife."

The ghosts consulted among themselves, and one said to the person, "Yes, you will stay here four nights; then we will give you a medicine pipe, the Worm Pipe, and we will give you back your wife, and you may return to your home."

Now, after the third night, the chief ghost called together all the people, and they came, the man's wife with them. One of them came beating a drum; and following him was another ghost, who carried the Worm Pipe, which they gave to him.

Then said the chief ghost: "Now, be very careful. To-morrow you and your wife will start on your homeward journey. Your wife will carry the medicine pipe, and some of your relations are going along with you for four days. During this time, you must not open your eyes, or you will return here and be a ghost forever. You see that your wife is not now a person; but in the middle of the fourth day you will be told to look, and when you have opened your eyes, you will see that your wife has become a person, and that your ghost relations have disappeared."

His father-in-law spoke to him before he went away, and said: "When you get near home, you must not go at once into the camp. Let some of your relations know that you have arrived, and ask them to build a sweat house for you. Go into this sweat house and wash your body thoroughly, leaving no part of it, however small, uncleansed; for if you do you will be nothing [will die]. There is something about us ghosts difficult to remove. It is only by a thorough sweat that you can remove it. Take care, now, that you do as I tell you. Do not whip your wife, nor strike her with a knife, nor hit her with fire; for if you do, she will vanish before your eyes and return to the Sand Hills."

Now they left the ghost country to go home, and on the fourth day, the wife said to her husband, "Open your eyes." He looked about him and saw that those who had been with them had vanished, but he found that they were standing in front of the old woman's lodge by the butte. She came out and said : " Here, give me back those mysterious medicines of mine, which enabled you to accomplish your purpose." He returned them to her, and became then fully a person once more.

Now, when they drew near to the camp, the woman went on ahead, and sat down on a butte. Then some curious persons came out to see who it might be. As they approached, the woman called out to them : " Do not come any nearer. Go tell my mother and my relations to put up a lodge for us, a little way from camp, and to build a sweat house near by it." When this had been done, the man and his wife went in and took a thorough sweat, and then they went into the lodge, and burned sweet grass and purified their clothing and the Worm Pipe ; and then their relations and friends came in to see them. The man told them where he had been, and how he had managed to get back his wife, and that the pipe hanging over the door-way was a medicine pipe, the Worm Pipe, presented to him by his ghost father-in-law. That is how the people came to possess the Worm Pipe. This pipe belongs to that band of the Piegans known as *Esk'-sin-i-tŭp'piks*, the Worm People.

Not long after this, in the night, this man told his wife to do something ; and when she did not begin at once, he picked up a brand from the fire, not that he intended to strike her with it, but he made as if he would hit her, when all at once she vanished, and was never seen again.

THE GHOSTS' BUFFALO

A LONG time ago there were four Blackfeet, who went to war against the Crees. They travelled a long way, and at last their horses gave out, and they started back toward their homes. As they were going along they came to the Sand Hills; and while they were passing through them, they saw in the sand a fresh travois trail, where people had been travelling.

One of the men said: "Let us follow this trail until we come up with some of our people. Then we will camp with them." They followed the trail for a long way, and at length one of the Blackfeet, named E-kūs'-kini, — a very powerful person, — said to the others: "Why follow this longer? It is just nothing." The others said: "Not so. These are our people. We will go on and camp with them." They went on, and toward evening, one of them found a stone maul and a dog travois. He said: "Look at these things. I know this maul and this travois. They belonged to my mother, who died. They were buried with her. This is strange." He took the things. When night overtook the men, they camped.

Early in the morning, they heard, all about them, sounds as if a camp of people were there. They heard a young man shouting a sort of war cry, as young men do; women chopping wood; a man calling for a feast, asking people to come to his lodge and smoke, — all the different sounds of the camp. They looked about, but could see nothing; and then they were frightened and covered their heads with their robes. At last they took courage, and started to look around and see what they could learn about this strange thing. For a little while they saw nothing, but pretty soon one of them said: "Look over there. See that pis'kun. Let us go over and look at it." As they were going toward it, one of them picked up a stone pointed arrow. He said: "Look at this. It belonged to my father. This is his place." They started to go on toward the pis'kun, but suddenly they could see no pis'kun. It had disappeared all at once.

A little while after this, one of them spoke up, and said: "Look over there. There is my father running buffalo. There! he has killed. Let us go over to him." They all looked where this man pointed, and they could see a person on a white horse, running buffalo. While they were looking, the person killed the buffalo, and got off his horse to butcher it. They started to go over toward him, and saw him at work butchering, and saw him turn the buffalo over on its back; but before they got to the place where he was, the person got on his horse and rode off, and when they got to where he had been skinning the buffalo, they saw lying on the ground only a dead mouse. There was no buffalo there. By the side of the mouse was a buffalo chip, and lying on it was an arrow painted red. The man said: "That is my father's arrow. That is the way he painted them." He took it up in his hands; and when he held it in his hands, he saw that it was not an arrow but a blade of spear grass. Then he laid it down, and it was an arrow again.

Another Blackfoot found a buffalo rock, I-nis'-kim.

Some time after this, the men got home to their camp. The man who had taken the maul and the dog travois, when he got home and smelled the smoke from the fire, died, and so did his horse. It seems that the shadow of the person who owned the things was angry at him and followed him home.

Two others of these Blackfeet have since died, killed in war ; but E-kūs'-kini is alive yet.   He took a stone and an iron arrow point that had belonged to his father, and always carried them about with him.   That is why he has lived so long. The man who took the stone arrow point found near the pis'kun, which had belonged to his father, took it home with him.   This was his medicine.   After that he was badly wounded in two fights, but he was not killed ; he got well.

The one who took the buffalo rock, I-nis'-kim, it afterward made strong to call the buffalo into the pis'kun.   He would take the rock and put it in his lodge close to the fire, where he could look at it, and would pray over it and make medicine.   Sometimes he would ask for a hundred buffalo to jump into the pis'kun, and the next day a hundred would jump in.   He was powerful.

STORIES OF OLD MAN

THE BLACKFOOT GENESIS

ALL animals of the Plains at one time heard and knew him, and all birds of the air heard and knew him. All things that he had made understood him, when he spoke to them, — the birds, the animals, and the people.

Old Man was travelling about, south of here, making the people. He came from the south, travelling north, making animals and birds as he passed along. He made the mountains, prairies, timber, and brush first. So he went along, travelling northward, making things as he went, putting rivers here and there, and falls on them, putting red paint here and there in the ground, — fixing up the world as we see it to-day. He made the Milk River (the Teton) and crossed it, and, being tired, went up on a little hill and lay down to rest. As he lay on his back, stretched out on the ground, with arms extended, he marked himself out with stones, — the shape of his body, head, legs, arms, and everything. There you can see those rocks to-day. After he had rested, he went on northward, and stumbled over a knoll and fell down on his knees. Then he said, "You are a bad thing to be stumbling against"; so he raised up two large buttes there, and named them the Knees, and they are called so to this day. He went on further north, and with some of the rocks he carried with him he built the Sweet Grass Hills.

Old Man covered the plains with grass for the animals to feed on. He marked off a piece of ground, and in it he made to grow all kinds of roots and berries,   camas, wild carrots, wild turnips, sweet-root, bitter-root, sarvis berries, bull berries, cherries, plums, and rosebuds. He put trees in the ground. He put all kinds of animals on the ground. When he made the bighorn with its big head and horns, he made it out on the prairie. It did not seem to travel easily on the prairie; it was awkward and could not go fast. So he took it by one of its horns, and led it up into the mountains, and turned it loose; and it skipped about among the rocks, and went up fearful places with ease. So he said, "This is the place that suits you; this is what you are fitted for, the rocks and the mountains." While he was in the mountains, he made the antelope out of dirt, and turned it loose, to see how it would go. It ran so fast that it fell over some rocks and hurt itself. He saw that this would not do, and took the antelope down on the prairie, and turned it loose; and it ran away fast and gracefully, and he said, "This is what you are suited to."

One day Old Man determined that he would make a woman and a child; so he formed them both — the woman and the child, her son — of clay. After he had moulded the clay in human shape, he said to the clay, "You must be people," and then he covered it up and left it, and went away. The next morning he went to the place and took the covering off, and saw that the clay shapes had changed a little. The second morning there was still more change, and the third still more. The fourth morning he went to the place, took the covering off, looked at the images, and told them to rise and walk; and they did so. They walked down to the river with their Maker, and then he told them that his name was *Na'pi*, Old Man.

As they were standing by the river, the woman said to him, "How is it? will we always live, will there be no end to it?" He said: "I have never thought of that. We will have to decide it. I will take this buffalo chip and throw it in the river. If it floats, when people die, in four days they will become alive again; they will die for only four days. But if it sinks, there will be an end to them." He threw the chip into the river, and it floated. The woman turned and picked up a stone, and said: "No, I will throw this stone in the river; if it floats we will always live, if it sinks people must die, that they may always be sorry for each other."[1] The woman threw the stone into the water, and it sank. "There," said Old Man, "you have chosen. There will be an end to them."

It was not many nights after, that the woman's child died, and she cried a great deal for it. She said to Old Man: "Let us change this. The law that you first made, let that be a law." He said: "Not so. What is made law must be law. We will undo nothing that we have done. The child is dead, but it cannot be changed. People will have to die."

That is how we came to be people. It is he who made us.

The first people were poor and naked, and did not know how to get a living. Old Man showed them the roots and berries, and told them that they could eat them; that in a certain month of the year they could peel the bark off some trees and eat it, that it was good. He told the people that the animals should be their food, and gave them to the people, saying, "These are your herds." He said: "All these little animals that live in the ground — rats, squirrels, skunks, beavers — are good to eat. You need not fear to eat of their flesh." He made all the birds that fly, and told the people that there was no harm in their flesh, that it could be eaten. The first people that he created he used to take about through the timber and swamps and over the prairies, and show them the different plants. Of a certain plant he would say, "The root of this plant, if gathered in a certain month of the year, is good for a certain sickness." So they learned the power of all herbs.

[1] That is, that their friends who survive may always remember them.

In those days there were buffalo. Now the people had no arms, but those black animals with long beards were armed ; and once, as the people were moving about, the buffalo saw them, and ran after them, and hooked them, and killed and ate them. One day, as the Maker of the people was travelling over the country, he saw some of his children, that he had made, lying dead, torn to pieces and partly eaten by the buffalo. When he saw this he was very sad. He said : "This will not do. I will change this. The people shall eat the buffalo."

He went to some of the people who were left, and said to them, "How is it that you people do nothing to these animals that are killing you?" The people said : "What can we do? We have no way to kill these animals, while they are armed and can kill us." Then said the Maker : "That is not hard. I will make you a weapon that will kill these animals." So he went out, and cut some sarvis berry shoots, and brought them in, and peeled the bark off them. He took a larger piece of wood, and flattened it, and tied a string to it, and made a bow. Now, as he was the master of all birds and could do with them as he wished, he went out and caught one, and took feathers from its wing, and split them, and tied them to the shaft of wood. He tied four feathers along the shaft, and tried the arrow at a mark, and found that it did not fly well. He took these feathers off, and put on three ; and when he tried it again, he found that it was good. He went out and began to break sharp pieces off the stones. He tried them, and found that the black flint stones made the best arrow points, and some white flints. Then he taught the people how to use these things.

Then he said : "The next time you go out, take these things with you, and use them as I tell you, and do not run from these animals. When they run at you, as soon as they get pretty close, shoot the arrows at them, as I have taught you ; and you will see that they will run from you or will run in a circle around you."

Now, as people became plenty, one day three men went out on to the plain to see the buffalo, but they had no arms. They saw the animals, but when the buffalo saw the men, they ran after them and killed two of them, but one got away.   One day after this, the people went on a little hill to look about, and the buffalo saw them, and said, "*Saiyah*, there is some more of our food," and they rushed on them. This time the people did not run.   They began to shoot at the buffalo with the bows and arrows *Na'pi* had given them, and the buffalo began to fall ; but in the fight a person was killed.

At this time these people had flint knives given them, and they cut up the bodies of the dead buffalo.   It is not healthful to eat the meat raw, so Old Man gathered soft dry rotten driftwood and made punk of it, and then got a piece of hard wood, and drilled a hole in it with an arrow point, and gave them a pointed piece of hard wood, and taught them how to make a fire with fire sticks, and to cook the flesh of these animals and eat it.

They got a kind of stone that was in the land, and then took another harder stone and worked one upon the other, and hollowed out the softer one, and made a kettle of it. This was the fashion of their dishes.

Also Old Man said to the people : " Now, if you are overcome, you may go and sleep, and get power.   Something will come to you in your dream, that will help you.   Whatever these animals tell you to do, you must obey them, as they appear to you in your sleep.   Be guided by them.   If anybody wants help, if you are alone and travelling, and cry aloud for help, your prayer will be answered.   It may be by the eagles, perhaps by the buffalo, or by the bears. Whatever animal answers your prayer, you must listen to him."

That was how the first people got through the world, by the power of their dreams.

After this, Old Man kept on, travelling north. Many of the animals that he had made followed him as he went. The animals understood him when he spoke to them, and he used them as his servants. When he got to the north point of the Porcupine Mountains, there he made some more mud images of people, and blew breath upon them, and they became people. He made men and women. They asked him, "What are we to eat?" He made many images of clay, in the form of buffalo. Then he blew breath on these, and they stood up; and when he made signs to them, they started to run. Then he said to the people, "Those are your food." They said to him, "Well, now, we have those animals; how are we to kill them?" "I will show you," he said. He took them to the cliff, and made them build rock piles like this, $>$; and he made the people hide behind these piles of rock, and said, "When I lead the buffalo this way, as I bring them opposite to you, rise up."

After he had told them how to act, he started on toward a herd of buffalo. He began to call them, and the buffalo started to run toward him, and they followed him until they were inside the lines. Then he dropped back; and as the people rose up, the buffalo ran in a straight line and jumped over the cliff. He told the people to go and take the flesh of those animals. They tried to tear the limbs apart, but they could not. They tried to bite pieces out, and could not. So Old Man went to the edge of the cliff, and broke some pieces of stone with sharp edges, and told them to cut the flesh with these. When they had taken the skins from these animals, they set up some poles and put the hides on them, and so made a shelter to sleep under. There were some of these buffalo that went over the cliff that were not dead. Their legs were broken, but they were still alive.

The people cut strips of green hide, and tied stones in the middle, and made large mauls, and broke in the skulls of the buffalo, and killed them.

After he had taught those people these things, he started off again, travelling north, until he came to where Bow and Elbow rivers meet.   There he made some more people, and taught them the same things.   From here he again went on northward.   When he had come nearly to the Red Deer's River, he reached the hill where the Old Man sleeps. There he lay down and rested himself.   The form of his body is to be seen there yet.

When he awoke from his sleep, he travelled further north-ward and came to a fine high hill.   He climbed to the top of it, and there sat down to rest.   He looked over the country below him, and it pleased him.   Before him the hill was steep, and he said to himself, " Well, this is a fine place for sliding ; I will have some fun," and he began to slide down the hill.   The marks where he slid down are to be seen yet, and the place is known to all people as the " Old Man's Sliding Ground."

This is as far as the Blackfeet followed Old Man.   The Crees know what he did further north.

In later times once, *Na'pi* said, " Here I will mark you off a piece of ground," and he did so.[1]   Then he said : "There is your land, and it is full of all kinds of animals, and many things grow in this land.   Let no other people come into it.   This is for you five tribes (Blackfeet, Bloods, Piegans, Gros Ventres, Sarcees).   When people come to cross the line, take your bows and arrows, your lances and

[1] The boundaries of this land are given as running east from a point in the summit of the Rocky Mountains west of Fort Edmonton, taking in the country to the east and south, including the Porcupine Hills, Cypress Moun-tains, and Little Rocky Mountains, down to the mouth of the Yellowstone on the Missouri; then west to the head of the Yellowstone, and across the Rocky Mountains to the Beaverhead ; thence to the summit of the Rocky Mountains and north along them to the starting-point.

your battle axes, and give them battle and keep them out. If they gain a footing, trouble will come to you."

Our forefathers gave battle to all people who came to cross these lines, and kept them out. Of late years we have let our friends, the white people, come in, and you know the result. We, his children, have failed to obey his laws.

THE DOG AND THE STICK

THIS happened long ago. In those days the people were hungry. No buffalo nor antelope were seen on the prairie. The deer and the elk trails were covered with grass and leaves; not even a rabbit could be found in the brush. Then the people prayed, saying: "Oh, Old Man, help us now, or we shall die. The buffalo and deer are gone. Uselessly we kindle the morning fires; useless are our arrows; our knives stick fast in the sheaths."

Then Old Man started out to find the game, and he took with him a young man, the son of a chief. For many days they travelled the prairies and ate nothing but berries and roots. One day they climbed a high ridge, and when they had reached the top, they saw, far off by a stream, a single lodge.

"What kind of a person can it be," said the young man, "who camps there all alone, far from friends?"

"That," said Old Man, "is the one who has hidden all the buffalo and deer from the people. He has a wife and a little son."

Then they went close to the lodge, and Old Man changed himself into a little dog, and he said, "That is I." Then the young man changed himself into a root-digger,[1] and he said, "That is I."

Now the little boy, playing about, found the dog, and he carried it to his father, saying, "Look! See what a pretty little dog I have found."

---

[1] A carved and painted stick about three feet long, shaped like a sacking needle, used by women to unearth roots.

145

"Throw it away," said his father; "it is not a dog." And the little boy cried, but his father made him carry the dog away. Then the boy found the root-digger; and, again picking up the dog, he carried them both to the lodge, saying, "Look, mother! see the pretty root-digger I have found!"

"Throw tnem both away," said his father; "that is not a stick, that is not a dog."

"I want that stick," said the woman; "let our son have the little dog."

"Very well," said her husband, "but remember, if trouble comes, you bring it on yourself and on our son." Then he sent his wife and son off to pick berries; and when they were out of sight, he went out and killed a buffalo cow, and brought the meat into the lodge and covered it up, and the bones, skin and offal he threw in the creek. When his wife returned, he gave her some of the meat to roast; and while they were eating, the little boy fed the dog three times, and when he gave it more, his father took the meat away, saying, "That is not a dog, you shall not feed it more."

In the night, when all were asleep, Old Man and the young man arose in their right shapes, and ate of the meat. "You were right," said the young man; "this is surely the person who has hidden the buffalo from us." "Wait," said Old Man; and when they had finished eating, they changed themselves back into the stick and the dog.

In the morning the man sent his wife and son to dig roots, and the woman took the stick with her. The dog followed the little boy. Now, as they travelled along in search of roots, they came near a cave, and at its mouth stood a buffalo cow. Then the dog ran into the cave, and the stick, slipping from the woman's hand, followed, gliding along like a snake. In this cave they found all the buffalo and other game, and they began to drive them out; and soon the prairie

was covered with buffalo and deer. Never before were seen
so many.

Pretty soon the man came running up, and he said to his
wife, " Who now drives out my animals?" and she replied,
"The dog and the stick are now in there."   " Did I not tell
you," said he, "that those were not what they looked like?
See now the trouble you have brought upon us," and he put
an arrow on his bow and waited for them to come out.
But they were cunning, for when the last animal — a big
bull — was about to go out, the stick grasped him by the
hair under his neck, and coiled up in it, and the dog held
on by the hair beneath, until they were far out on the prairie,
when they changed into their true shapes, and drove the
buffalo toward camp.

When the people saw the buffalo coming, they drove
a big band of them to the pis'kun; but just as the leaders
were about to jump off, a raven came and flapped its
wings in front of them and croaked, and they turned off
another way.   Every time a band of buffalo was driven near
the pis'kun, this raven frightened them away.   Then Old
Man knew that the raven was the one who had kept the
buffalo cached.

So he went and changed himself into a beaver, and lay
stretched out on the bank of the river, as if dead; and the
raven, which was very hungry, flew down and began to pick at
him.   Then Old Man caught it by the legs and ran with it
to camp, and all the chiefs came together to decide what
should be done with it.   Some said to kill it, but Old Man
said, " No! I will punish it," and he tied it over the lodge,
right in the smoke hole.

As the days went by, the raven grew poor and weak, and
his eyes were blurred with the thick smoke, and he cried
continually to Old Man to pity him.   One day Old Man
untied him, and told him to take his right shape, saying:
"Why have you tried to fool Old Man?   Look at me!   I

cannot die. Look at me! Of all peoples and tribes I am the chief. I cannot die. I made the mountains. They are standing yet. I made the prairies and the rocks. You see them yet. Go home, then, to your wife and your child, and when you are hungry hunt like any one else, or you shall die."

THE BEARS

Now Old Man was walking along, and far off he saw many wolves; and when he came closer, he saw there the chief of the wolves, a very old one, and sitting around him were all his children.

Old Man said, " Pity me, Wolf Chief; make me into a wolf, that I may live your way and catch deer and everything that runs fast."

" Come near then," said the Wolf Chief, " that I may rub your body with my hands, so that hair will cover you."

" Hold," said Old Man; " do not cover my body with hair. On my head, arms, and legs only, put hair."

When the Chief Wolf had done so, he said to Old Man: "You shall have three companions to help you, one is a very swift runner, another a good runner, and the last is not very fast. Take them with you now, and others of my younger children who are learning to hunt, but do not go where the wind blows; keep in the shelter, or the young ones will freeze to death." Then they went hunting, and Old Man led them on the high buttes, where it was very cold.

At night, they lay down to sleep, and Old Man nearly froze; and he said to the wolves, "Cover me with your tails." So all the wolves lay down around him, and covered his body with their tails, and he soon got warm and slept. Before long he awoke and said angrily, "Take off those tails," and the wolves moved away; but after a little time he again became cold, and cried out, " Oh my young brothers, cover me with your tails or I shall freeze." So they lay down by him again and covered his body with their tails.

When it was daylight, they all rose and hunted. They saw some moose, and, chasing them, killed three. Now, when they were about to eat, the Chief Wolf came along with many of his children, and one wolf said, " Let us make pemmican of those moose " ; and every one was glad. Then said the one who made pemmican, " No one must look, everybody shut his eyes, while I make the pemmican " ; but Old Man looked, and the pemmican-maker threw a round bone and hit him on the nose, and it hurt. Then Old Man said, " Let me make the pemmican." So all the wolves shut their eyes, and Old Man took the round bone and killed the wolf who had hit him. Then the Chief Wolf was angry, and he said, " Why did you kill your brother? " " I didn't mean to," replied Old Man. " He looked and I threw the round bone at him, but I only meant to hurt him a little." Then said the Chief Wolf: " You cannot live with us any longer. Take one of your companions, and go off by yourselves and hunt." So Old Man took the swift runner, and they went and lived by themselves a long time ; and they killed all the elk, and deer, and antelope, and moose they wanted.

One morning they awoke, and Old Man said : " Oh my young brother, I have had a bad dream. Hereafter, when you chase anything, if it jumps a stream, you must not follow it. Even a little spring you must not jump." And the wolf promised not to jump over water.

Now one day the wolf was chasing a moose, and it ran on to an island. The stream about it was very small ; so the wolf thought : " This is such a little stream that I must jump it. That moose is very tired, and I don't think it will leave the island." So he jumped on to the island, and as soon as he entered the brush, a bear caught him, for the island was the home of the Chief Bear and his two brothers.

Old Man waited a long time for the wolf to come back, and then went to look for him. He asked all the birds he met if they had seen him, but they all said they had not.

At last he saw a kingfisher, who was sitting on a limb overhanging the water. " Why do you sit there, my young brother?" said Old Man. " Because," replied the king-fisher, "the Chief Bear and his brothers have killed your wolf; they have eaten the meat and thrown the fat into the river, and whenever I see a piece come floating along, I fly down and get it." Then said Old Man, " Do the Bear Chief and his brothers often come out? and where do they live?" " They come out every morning to play," said the kingfisher; " and they live upon that island."

Old Man went up there and saw their tracks on the sand, where they had been playing, and he turned himself into a rotten tree. By and by the bears came out, and when they saw the tree, the Chief Bear said: " Look at that rotten tree. It is Old Man. Go, brothers, and see if it is not." So the two brothers went over to the tree, and clawed it; and they said, " No, brother, it is only a tree." Then the Chief Bear went over and clawed and bit the tree, and although it hurt Old Man, he never moved. Then the Bear Chief was sure it was only a tree, and he began to play with his brothers. Now while they were playing, and all were on their backs, Old Man leaned over and shot an arrow into each one of them; and they cried out loudly and ran back on the island. Then Old Man changed into himself, and walked down along the river. Pretty soon he saw a frog jumping along, and every time it jumped it would say, "*Ni'-nah O-kyai'-yu!*" And sometimes it would stop and sing:—

"*Ni'-nah O-kyai'-yu! Ni'-nah O-kyai'-yu!*
Chief Bear! Chief Bear!
Nap'-i I-nit'-si-wah Ni'-nah O-kyai'-yu!"
Old Man kill him Chief Bear!

"What do you say?" cried Old Man. The frog repeated what he had said.

"Ah!" exclaimed Old Man, "tell me all about it."

"The Chief Bear and his brothers," replied the frog, "were playing on the sand, when Old Man shot arrows into them. They are not dead, but the arrows are very near their hearts; if you should shove ever so little on them, the points would cut their hearts. I am going after medicine now to cure them."

Then Old Man killed the frog and skinned her, and put the hide on himself and swam back to the island, and hopped up toward the bears, crying at every step, "*Ni'-nah O-kyai'-yu !*" just as the frog had done.

"Hurry," cried the Chief Bear.

"Yes," replied Old Man, and he went up and shoved the arrow into his heart.

"I cured him; he is asleep now," he cried, and he went up and shoved the arrow into the biggest brother's heart. "I cured them; they are asleep now"; and he went up and shoved the arrow into the other bear's heart. Then he built a big fire and skinned the bears, and tried out the fat and poured it into a hollow in the ground; and he called all the animals to come and roll in it, that they might be fat. And all the animals came and rolled in it. The bears came first and rolled in it, that is the reason they get so fat. Last of all came the rabbits, and the grease was almost all gone; but they filled their paws with it and rubbed it on their backs and between their hind legs. That is the reason why rabbits have two such large layers of fat on their backs, and that is what makes them so fat between the hind legs.

[NOTE. — The four preceding stories show the serious side of Old Man's character. Those which follow represent him as malicious, foolish, and impotent.]

THE WONDERFUL BIRD

ONE day, as Old Man was walking about in the woods, he saw something very queer. A bird was sitting on the limb of a tree making a strange noise, and every time it made this noise, its eyes would go out of its head and fasten on the tree; then it would make another kind of a noise, and its eyes would come back to their places.

"Little Brother," cried Old Man, "teach me how to do that."

"If I show you how to do that," replied the bird, "you must not let your eyes go out of your head more than three times a day. If you do, you will be sorry."

"Just as you say, Little Brother. The trick is yours, and I will listen to you."

When the bird had taught Old Man how to do it, he was very glad, and did it three times right away. Then he stopped. "That bird has no sense," he said. "Why did he tell me to do it only three times? I will do it again, anyhow." So he made his eyes go out a fourth time; but now he could not call them back. Then he called to the bird, "Oh Little Brother, come help me get back my eyes." The little bird did not answer him. It had flown away. Then Old Man felt all over the trees with his hands, but he could not find his eyes; and he wandered about for a long time, crying and calling the animals to help him.

A wolf had much fun with him. The wolf had found a dead buffalo, and taking a piece of the meat which smelled bad, he would hold it close to Old Man. "I smell

something dead," Old Man would say. " I wish I could
find it ; I am nearly starved to death." And he would feel
all around for it.   Once, when the wolf was doing this, Old
Man caught him, and, plucking out one of his eyes, he put it
in his own head.   Then he could see, and was able to find his
own eyes ; but he could never again do the trick the little
bird had taught him.

THE RACE

Once Old Man was travelling around, when he heard some very queer singing. He had never heard anything like this before, and looked all around to see who it was. At last he saw it was the cottontail rabbits, singing and making medicine. They had built a fire, and got a lot of hot ashes, and they would lie down in these ashes and sing while one covered them up. They would stay there only a short time though, for the ashes were very hot.

" Little Brothers," said Old Man, " that is very wonderful, how you lie in those hot ashes and coals without burning. I wish you would teach me how to do it."

"Come on, Old Man," said the rabbits, "we will show you how to do it. You must sing our song, and only stay in the ashes a short time." So Old Man began to sing, and he lay down, and they covered him with coals and ashes, and they did not burn him at all.

"That is very nice," he said. " You have powerful medicine. Now I want to know it all, so you lie down and let me cover you up."

So the rabbits all lay down in the ashes, and Old Man covered them up, and then he put the whole fire over them. One old rabbit got out, and Old Man was about to put her back when she said, " Pity me, my children are about to be born."

"All right," replied Old Man. " I will let you go, so there will be some more rabbits ; but I will roast these nicely and have a feast." And he put more wood on the fire. When the rabbits were cooked, he cut some red willow brush and laid them on it to cool. The grease soaked into these branches, so, even to-day if you hold red willow over a fire, you will see the grease on the bark. You can see, too, that ever since, the rabbits have a burnt place on their backs, where the one that got away was singed.

Old Man sat down, and was waiting for the rabbits to cool a little, when a coyote came along, limping very badly. "Pity me, Old Man," he said, "you have lots of cooked rabbits; give me one of them."

"Go away," exclaimed Old Man. "If you are too lazy to catch your food, I will not help you."

"My leg is broken," said the coyote. "I can't catch anything, and I am starving. Just give me half a rabbit."

"I don't care if you die," replied Old Man. "I worked hard to cook all these rabbits, and I will not give any away. But I will tell you what we will do. We will run a race to that butte, way out there, and if you beat me you can have a rabbit."

"All right," said the coyote. So they started. Old Man ran very fast, and the coyote limped along behind, but close to him, until they got near to the butte. Then the coyote turned round and ran back very fast, for he was not lame at all. It took Old Man a long time to go back, and just before he got to the fire, the coyote swallowed the last rabbit, and trotted off over the prairie.

THE BAD WEAPONS

ONCE Old Man was fording a river, when the current carried him down stream, and he lost his weapons. He was very hungry, so he took the first wood he could find, and made a bow and arrows, and a handle for his knife and spear. When he had finished them, he started up a mountain. Pretty soon he saw a bear digging roots, and he thought he would have some fun, so he hid behind a log and called out, "No-tail animal, what are you doing?" The bear looked up, but, seeing no one, kept on digging.

Then Old Man called out again, "Hi! you dirt-eater!" and then he dodged back out of sight. Then the bear sat up again, and this time he saw Old Man and ran after him.

Old Man began shooting arrows at him, but the points only stuck in the skin, for the shafts were rotten and snapped off. Then he threw his spear, but that too was rotten, and broke. He tried to stab the bear, but his knife handle was also rotten and broke, so he turned and ran; and the bear pursued him. As he ran, he looked about for some weapon, but there was none, not even a rock. He called out to the animals to help him, but none came. His breath was almost gone, and the bear was very close to him, when he saw a bull's horn lying on the ground. He picked it up, placed it on his head, and, turning around, bellowed so loudly that the bear was scared and ran away.

THE ELK

Old Man was very hungry. He had been a long time without food, and was thinking how he could get something to eat, when he saw a band of elk on a ridge. So he went up to them and said, "Oh, my brothers, I am lonesome because I have no one to follow me."

"Go on, Old Man," said the elk, "we will follow you." Old Man led them about a long time, and when it was dark, he came near a high-cut bank. He ran around to one side where there was a slope, and he went down and then stood right under the steep bluff, and called out, "Come on, that is a nice jump, you will laugh."

So the elk jumped off, all but one cow, and were killed.

"Come on," said Old Man, "they have all jumped but you, it is nice."

"Take pity on me," replied the cow. "My child is about to be born, and I am very heavy. I am afraid to jump."

"Go on, then," answered Old Man; "go and live; then there will be plenty of elk again some day."

Now Old Man built a fire and cooked some ribs, and then he skinned all the elk, cut up the meat to dry, and hung the tongues up on a pole.

Next day he went off, and did not come back until night, when he was very hungry again. "I'll roast some ribs," he said, "and a tongue, and I'll stuff a marrow gut and cook that. I guess that will be enough for to-night." But when he got to the place, the meat was all gone. The wolves had eaten it. "I was smart to hang up those tongues," he said, "or I would not have had anything to eat." But the tongues were all hollow. The mice had eaten the meat out, leaving only the skin. So Old Man starved again.

158

OLD MAN DOCTORS

A PIS'KUN had been built, and many buffalo had been run in and killed. The camp was full of meat. Great sheets of it hung in the lodges and on the racks outside; and now the women, having cut up all the meat, were working on the hides, preparing some for robes, and scraping the hair from others, to make leather.

About this time, Old Man came along. He had come from far and was very tired, so he entered the first lodge he came to and sat down. Now this lodge belonged to three old women. Their husbands had died or been killed in war, and they had no relations to help them, so they were very poor. After Old Man had rested a little, they set a dish of food before him. It was dried bull meat, very tough, and some pieces of belly fat.

"*Hai'-yah ho !*" cried Old Man, after he had tasted a piece. "You treat me badly. A whole pis'kun of fat buffalo just killed; the camp red with meat, and here these old women give me tough bull meat and belly fat to eat. Hurry now ! roast me some ribs and a piece of back fat."

"Alas !" exclaimed one old woman. "We have no good food. All our helpers are dead, and we take what others leave. Bulls and poor cows are all the people leave us."

"Ah !" said Old Man, "how poor ! you are very poor. Take courage now. I will help you. To-morrow they will run another band into the pis'kun. I will be there. I will kill the fattest cow, and you can have it all."

Then the old women were glad. They talked to one

159

another, saying, "Very good heart, Old Man. He helps the poor. Now we will live. We will have marrow guts and liver. We will have paunch and fat kidneys."

Old Man said nothing more. He ate the tough meat and belly fat, and rolled up in his robe and went to sleep.

Morning came. The people climbed the bluffs and went out on to the prairie, where they hid behind the piles of rock and bushes, which reached far out from the cliff in lines which were always further and further apart. After a while, he who leads the buffalo was seen coming, bringing a large band after him. Soon they were inside the lines. The people began to rise up behind them, shouting and waving their robes. Now they reached the edge of the bluff. The leaders tried to stop and turn, but those behind kept pushing on, and nearly the whole band dashed down over the rocks, only a few of the last ones turning aside and escaping.

The lodges were now deserted. All the people were gone to the pis'kun to kill the buffalo and butcher them. Where was Old Man? Did he take his bow and arrows and go to the pis'kun to kill a fat cow for the poor old women? No. He was sneaking around, lifting the door-ways of the lodges and looking in. Bad person, Old Man. In the chief's lodge he saw a little child, a girl, asleep. Outside was a buffalo's gall, and taking a long stick he dipped the end of it in the gall; and then, reaching carefully into the lodge, he drew it across the lips of the child asleep. Then he threw the stick away, and went in and sat down. Soon the girl awoke and began to cry. The gall was very bitter and burned her lips.

"Pity me, Old Man," she said. "Take this fearful thing from my lips."

"I do not doctor unless I am paid," he replied. Then said the girl: "See all my father's weapons hanging there.

His shield, war head-dress, scalps, and knife. Cure me now, and I will give you some of them."

" I have more of such things than I want," he replied. (What a liar ! he had none at all.)

Again said the girl, " Pity me, help me now, and I will give you my father's white buffalo robe."

" I have plenty of white robes," replied Old Man. (Again he lied, for he never had one.)

" Old Man," again said the girl, " in this lodge lives a widow woman, my father's relation. Remove this fearful thing from my lips, and I will have my father give her to you."

" Now you speak well," replied Old Man. " I am a little glad. I have many wives " (he had none), " but I would just as soon have another one."

So he went close to the child and pretended to doctor her, but instead of that, he killed her and ran out. He went to the old women's lodge, and wrapped a strip of cowskin about his head, and commenced to groan, as if he was very sick.

Now the people began to come from the pis'kun, carrying great loads of meat. This dead girl's mother came, and when she saw her child lying dead, and blood on the ground, she ran back crying out : " My daughter has been killed ! My daughter has been killed ! "

Then all the people began to shout out and run around, and the warriors and young men looked in the lodges, and up and down the creek in the brush, but they could find no one who might have killed the child.

Then said the father of the dead girl : " Now, to-day, we will find out who killed this child. Every man in this camp — every young man, every old man — must come and jump across the creek ; and if any one does not jump across, if he falls in the water, that man is the one who did the killing."

All heard this, and they began to gather at the creek, one behind another; and the women and children went to look on, for they wanted to see the person who had killed the little child. Now they were ready. They were about to jump, when some one cried out, "Old Man is not here."

"True," said the chief, looking around, "Old Man is not here." And he sent two young men to bring him.

"Old Man!" they cried out, when they came to the lodge, "a child has been killed. We have all got to jump to find out who did it. The chief has sent for you. You will have to jump, too."

"*Ki'-yo!*" exclaimed the old women. "Old Man is very sick. Go off, and let him alone. He is so sick he could not kill meat for us to-day."

"It can't be helped," the young men replied. "The chief says every one must jump."

So Old Man went out toward the creek very slowly, and very much scared. He did not know what to do. As he was going along he saw a *ni'-po-mŭk-i*,[1] and he said: "Oh my little brother, pity me. Give me some of your power to jump the creek, and here is my necklace. See how pretty it is. I will give it to you."

So they traded; Old Man took some of the bird's power, and the bird took Old Man's necklace and put it on.

Now they jump. *Wo'-ka-hi!* they jump way across and far on to the ground. Now they jump; another! another! another! Now it comes Old Man's turn. He runs, he jumps, he goes high, and strikes the ground far beyond any other person's jump. Now comes the *ni'-po-mŭk-i*. "*Wo'-ka-hi!*" the men shout. "*Ki'-yo!*" cry the women, "the bird has fallen in the creek." The warriors are running to kill him. "Wait! Hold on!" cries the bird. "Let me speak a few words. Every one knows I am a good jumper. I can jump further than any one; but Old Man asked me for some of

---

[1] The chickadee.

my power, and I gave it to him, and he gave me this necklace. It is very heavy and pulled me down. That is why I
fell into the creek."

Then the people began to shout and talk again, some saying to kill the bird, and some not, when Old Man shouted
out : "Wait, listen to me. What's the use of quarrelling or
killing anybody? Let us go back, and I will doctor the child
alive."

Good words. The people were glad. So they went back,
and got ready for the doctoring. First, Old Man ordered
a large fire built in the lodge where the dead girl was lying.
Two old men were placed at the back of the lodge, facing
each other. They had spears, which they held above their
heads and were to thrust back and forth at each other in
time to the singing. Near the door-way were placed two
old women, facing each other. Each one held a *puk'-sah-
tchis,*[1] — a maul, — with which she was to beat time to the
singing. The other seats in the lodge were taken by people
who were to sing. Now Old Man hung a big roll of belly
fat close over the fire, so that the hot grease began to drip,
and everything was ready, and the singing began. This
was Old Man's song : —

Ahk-sa'-kē-wah,   Ahk-sa'-kē-wah,   Ahk-sa'-kē-wah, etc.
I don't care,   I don't care,   I don't care.

And so they sung for a long time, the old men jabbing their
spears at each other, and the old women pretending to hit
each other with their mauls.

After a while they rested, and Old Man said : " Now I
want every one to shut their eyes. No one can look. I am
going to begin the real doctoring." So the people shut

[1] A round or oblong stone, to which a handle was bound by rawhide
thongs, used for breaking marrow bones, etc.

their eyes, and the singing began again. Then Old Man took the dripping hot fat from the fire, gave it a mighty swing around the circle in front of the people's faces, jumped out the door-way, and ran off. Every one was burned. The two old men wounded each other with their spears. The old women knocked each other on the head with their mauls. The people cried and groaned, wiped their burned faces, and rushed out the door; but Old Man was gone. They saw him no more.

THE ROCK

ONCE Old Man was travelling, and becoming tired he sat down on a rock to rest. After a while he started to go on, and because the sun was hot he threw his robe over the rock, saying: " Here, I give you my robe, because you are poor and have let me rest on you. Always keep it."

He had not gone very far, when it began to rain, and meeting a coyote he said: " Little brother, run back to that rock, and ask him to lend me his robe. We will cover ourselves with it and keep dry." So the coyote ran back to the rock, but returned without the robe. " Where is the robe? " asked Old Man. " *Sai-yah !* " replied the coyote. " The rock said you gave him the robe, and he was going to keep it."

Then Old Man was very angry, and went back to the rock and jerked the robe off it, saying: " I only wanted to borrow this robe until the rain was over, but now that you have acted so mean about it, I will keep it. You don't need a robe anyhow. You have been out in the rain and snow all your life, and it will not hurt you to live so always."

With the coyote he went off into a coulée, and sat down. The rain was falling, and they covered themselves with the robe and were very comfortable. Pretty soon they heard a loud noise, and Old Man told the coyote to go up on the hill and see what it was. Soon he came running back, saying, " Run ! run ! the big rock is coming " ; and they both ran away as fast as they could. The coyote tried to crawl into a badger hole, but it was too small for him and he stuck fast, and before he could get out, the rock rolled over him and crushed his hind parts. Old Man was scared, and as he ran he threw off his robe and what clothes he could, so that he might run faster. The rock kept gaining on him all the time.

Not far off was a band of buffalo bulls, and Old Man cried out to them, saying, " Oh my brothers, help me, help me. Stop that rock." The bulls ran and tried to stop it, but it crushed their heads. Some deer and antelope tried to help Old Man, but they were killed, too. A lot of rattlesnakes formed themselves into a lariat, and tried to catch it ; but those at the noose end were all cut to pieces. The rock was now close to Old Man, so close that it began to hit his heels ; and he was about to give up, when he saw a flock of bull bats circling over his head. " Oh my little brothers," he cried, " help me. I am almost dead." Then the bull bats flew down, one after another, against the rock ; and every time one of them hit it he chipped off a piece, and at last one hit it fair in the middle and broke it into two pieces.

Then Old Man was very glad. He went to where there was a nest of bull bats, and made the young ones' mouths very wide and pinched off their bills, to make them pretty and queer looking. That is the reason they look so to-day.

THE THEFT FROM THE SUN

ONCE Old Man was travelling around, when he came to the Sun's lodge, and the Sun asked him to stay a while. Old Man was very glad to do so.

One day the meat was all gone, and the Sun said, "*Kyi!* Old Man, what say you if we go and kill some deer?"

"You speak well," replied Old Man. "I like deer meat."

The Sun took down a bag and pulled out a beautiful pair of leggings. They were embroidered with porcupine quills and bright feathers. "These," said the Sun, "are my hunting leggings. They are great medicine. All I have to do is to put them on and walk around a patch of brush, when the leggings set it on fire and drive the deer out so that I can shoot them."

"*Hai-yah!*" exclaimed Old Man. "How wonderful!" He made up his mind he would have those leggings, if he had to steal them.

They went out to hunt, and the first patch of brush they came to, the Sun set on fire with his hunting leggings. A lot of white-tail deer ran out, and they each shot one.

That night, when they went to bed, the Sun pulled off his leggings and placed them to one side. Old Man saw where he put them, and in the middle of the night, when every one was asleep, he stole them and went off. He travelled a long time, until he had gone far and was very tired, and then, making a pillow of the leggings, lay down and slept. In the morning, he heard some one talking. The Sun was saying, "Old Man, why are my leggings under your head?" He looked around, and saw he was in the Sun's lodge, and thought he must have wandered around and got lost, and returned there.   Again the Sun spoke and said, "What are you doing with my leggings?" "Oh," replied Old Man, "I couldn't find anything for a pillow, so I just put these under my head."

Night came again, and again Old Man stole the leggings and ran off. This time he did not walk at all; he just kept running until pretty near morning, and then lay down and slept. You see what a fool he was. He did not know that the whole world is the Sun's lodge.   He did not know that, no matter how far he ran, he could not get out of the Sun's sight. When morning came, he found himself still in the Sun's lodge. But this time the Sun said : "Old Man, since you like my leggings so much, I will give them to you. Keep them." Then Old Man was very glad and went away.

One day his food was all gone, so he put on the medicine leggings and set fire to a piece of brush. He was just going to kill some deer that were running out, when he saw that the fire was getting close to him. He ran away as fast as he could, but the fire gained on him and began to burn his legs. His leggings were all on fire. He came to a river and jumped in, and pulled off the leggings as soon as he could. They were burned to pieces.

Perhaps the Sun did this to him because he tried to steal the leggings.

THE FOX

ONE day Old Man went out hunting and took the fox with him. They hunted for several days, but killed nothing. It was nice warm weather in the late fall. After they had become very hungry, as they were going along one day, Old Man went up over a ridge and on the other side he saw four big buffalo bulls lying down ; but there was no way by which they could get near them. He dodged back out of sight and told the fox what he had seen, and they thought for a long time, to see if there was no way by which these bulls might be killed.

At last Old Man said to the fox : "My little brother, I can think of only one way to get these bulls. This is my plan, if you agree to it. I will pluck all the fur off you except one tuft on the end of your tail. Then you go over the hill and walk up and down in sight of the bulls, and you will seem so funny to them that they will laugh themselves to death."

The fox did not like to do this, but he could think of nothing better, so he agreed to what Old Man proposed. Old Man plucked him perfectly bare, except the end of his tail, and the fox went over the ridge and walked up and down. When he had come close to the bulls, he played around and walked on his hind legs and went through all sorts of antics. When the bulls first saw him, they got up on their feet, and looked at him. They did not know what to make of him. Then they began to laugh, and the more they looked at him, the more they laughed, until at last one

169

by one they fell down exhausted and died. Then Old Man came over the hill, and went down to the bulls, and began to butcher them. By this time it had grown a little colder.

"Ah, little brother," said Old Man to the fox, "you did splendidly. I do not wonder that the bulls laughed themselves to death. I nearly died myself as I watched you from the hill. You looked very funny." While he was saying this, he was working away skinning off the hides and getting the meat ready to carry to camp, all the time talking to the fox, who stood about, his back humped up and his teeth chattering with the cold. Now a wind sprang up from the north and a few snowflakes were flying in the air. It was growing colder and colder. Old Man kept on talking, and every now and then he would say something to the fox, who was sitting behind him perfectly still, with his jaw shoved out and his teeth shining.

At last Old Man had the bulls all skinned and the meat cut up, and as he rose up he said : "It is getting pretty cold, isn't it ? Well, we do not care for the cold. We have got all our winter's meat, and we will have nothing to do but feast and dance and sing until spring." The fox made no answer. Then Old Man got angry, and called out : "Why don't you answer me ? Don't you hear me talking to you ?" The fox said nothing. Then Old Man was mad, and he said, "Can't you speak ?" and stepped up to the fox and gave him a push with his foot, and the fox fell over. He was dead, frozen stiff with the cold.

OLD MAN AND THE LYNX

OLD MAN was travelling round over the prairie, when he saw a lot of prairie-dogs sitting in a circle. They had built a fire, and were sitting around it. Old Man went toward them, and when he got near them, he began to cry, and said, "Let me, too, sit by that fire." The prairie-dogs said: "All right, Old Man. Don't cry. Come and sit by the fire." Old Man sat down, and saw that the prairie-dogs were playing a game. They would put one of their number in the fire and cover him up with the hot ashes; and then, after he had been there a little while, he would say *sk, sk*, and they would push the ashes off him, and pull him out.

Old Man said, "Teach me how to do that"; and they told him what to do, and put him in the fire, and covered him up with the ashes, and after a little while he said *sk, sk*, like a prairie-dog, and they pulled him out again. Then he did it to the prairie-dogs. At first he put them in one at a time, but there were many of them, and pretty soon he got tired, and said, "Come, I will put you all in at once." They said, "Very well, Old Man," and all got in the ashes; but just as Old Man was about to cover them up, one of them, a female heavy with young, said, "Do not cover me up; the heat may hurt my children, which are about to be born." Old Man said: "Very well. If you do not want to be covered up, you can sit over by the fire and watch the rest." Then he covered up all the others.

At length the prairie-dogs said *sk, sk*, but Old Man did not sweep the ashes off and pull them out of the fire. He

171

let them stay there and die. The old she one ran off to a hole and, as she went down in it, said *sk, sk.* Old Man chased her, but he got to the hole too late to catch her. So he said : " Oh, well, you can go. There will be more prairie-dogs by and by."

When the prairie-dogs were roasted, Old Man cut a lot of red willow brush to lay them on, and then sat down and began to eat. He ate until he was full, and then felt sleepy. He said to his nose : " I am going to sleep now. Watch for me and wake me up in case anything comes near." Then Old Man slept. Pretty soon his nose snored, and he woke up and said, " What is it ? " The nose said, " A raven is flying over there." Old Man said, " That is nothing," and went to sleep again. Soon his nose snored again. Old Man said, " What is it now ? " The nose said, " There is a coyote over there, coming this way." Old Man said, " A coyote is nothing," and again went to sleep. Presently his nose snored again, but Old Man did not wake up. Again it snored, and called out, " Wake up, a bob-cat is coming." Old Man paid no attention. He slept on.

The bob-cat crept up to where the fire was, and ate up all the roast prairie-dogs, and then went off and lay down on a flat rock, and went to sleep. All this time the nose kept trying to wake Old Man up, and at last he awoke, and the nose said : " A bob-cat is over there on that flat rock. He has eaten all your food." Then Old Man called out loud, he was so angry. He went softly over to where the bob-cat lay, and seized it, before it could wake up to bite or scratch him. The bob-cat cried out, " Hold on, let me speak a word or two." But Old Man would not listen ; he said, " I will teach you to steal my food." He pulled off the lynx's tail, pounded his head against the rock so as to make his face flat, pulled him out long, so as to make him small-bellied, and then threw him away into the brush. As he went sneaking off, Old Man said, " There, that is the way you bob-cats shall always be." That is the reason the lynxes look so to-day.

Old Man went back to the fire, and looked at the red willow sticks where his food had been, and it made him mad at his nose. He said, "You fool, why did you not wake me?" He took the willow sticks and thrust them in the coals, and when they took fire, he burned his nose. This pained him greatly, and he ran up on a hill and held his nose to the wind, and called on it to blow hard and cool him. A hard wind came, and it blew him away down to Birch Creek. As he was flying along, he caught at the weeds and brush to try to stop himself, but nothing was strong enough to hold him. At last he seized a birch tree. He held on to this, and it did not give way. Although the wind whipped him about, this way and that, and tumbled him up and down, the tree held him. He kept calling to the wind to blow gently, and finally it listened to him and went down.

So he said: "This is a beautiful tree. It has kept me from being blown away and knocked all to pieces. I will ornament it and it shall always be like that." So he gashed it across with his stone knife, as you see it to-day.

THE STORY OF THE THREE TRIBES

THE PAST AND THE PRESENT

FIFTY years ago the name Blackfoot was one of terrible meaning to the white traveller who passed across that desolate buffalo-trodden waste which lay to the north of the Yellowstone River and east of the Rocky Mountains. This was the Blackfoot land, the undisputed home of a people which is said to have numbered in one of its tribes — the Pi-kŭn'-i — 8000 lodges, or 40,000 persons. Besides these, there were the Blackfeet and the Bloods, three tribes of one nation, speaking the same language, having the same customs, and holding the same religious faith.

But this land had not always been the home of the Blackfeet. Long ago, before the coming of the white men, they had lived in another country far to the north and east, about Lesser Slave Lake, ranging between Peace River and the Saskatchewan, and having for their neighbors on the north the Beaver Indians. Then the Blackfeet were a timber people. It is said that about two hundred years ago the Chippeweyans from the east invaded this country and drove them south and west. Whether or no this is true, it is quite certain that not many generations back the Blackfeet lived on the North Saskatchewan River and to the north of that stream.[1] Gradually working their way westward, they at length reached the Rocky Mountains, and, finding game abundant, remained there until they obtained horses, in the very earliest years of the present century. When they

[1] For a more extended account of this migration, see *American Anthropologist*, April, 1892, p. 153.

secured horses and guns, they took courage and began to venture out on to the plains and to go to war. From this time on, the Blackfeet made constant war on their neighbors to the south, and in a few years controlled the whole country between the Saskatchewan on the north and the Yellowstone on the south.

It was, indeed, a glorious country which the Blackfeet had wrested from their southern enemies. Here nature has reared great mountains and spread out broad prairies. Along the western border of this region, the Rocky Mountains lift their snow-clad peaks above the clouds. Here and there, from north to south, and from east to west, lie minor ranges, black with pine forests if seen near at hand, or in the distance mere gray silhouettes against a sky of blue. Between these mountain ranges lies everywhere the great prairie ; a monotonous waste to the stranger's eye, but not without its charm. It is brown and bare ; for, except during a few short weeks in spring, the sparse bunch-grass is sear and yellow, and the silver gray of the wormwood lends an added dreariness to the landscape. Yet this seemingly desert waste has a beauty of its own. At intervals it is marked with green winding river valleys, and everywhere it is gashed with deep ravines, their sides painted in strange colors of red and gray and brown, and their perpendicular walls crowned with fantastic columns and figures of stone or clay, carved out by the winds and the rains of ages. Here and there, rising out of the plain, are curious sharp ridges, or square-topped buttes with vertical sides, sometimes bare, and sometimes dotted with pines, — short, sturdy trees, whose gnarled trunks and thick, knotted branches have been twisted and wrung into curious forms by the winds which blow unceasingly, hour after hour, day after day, and month after month, over mountain range and prairie, through gorge and coulée.

These prairies now seem bare of life, but it was not

always so.   Not very long ago, they were trodden by mul-
titudinous herds of buffalo and antelope; then, along the
wooded river valleys and on the pine-clad slopes of the
mountains, elk, deer, and wild sheep fed in great numbers.
They are all gone now.   The winter's wind still whistles
over Montana prairies, but nature's shaggy-headed wild
cattle no longer feel its biting blasts.   Where once the
scorching breath of summer stirred only the short stems of
the buffalo-grass, it now billows the fields of the white man's
grain.   Half-hidden by the scanty herbage, a few bleached
skeletons alone remain to tell us of the buffalo; and the
broad, deep trails, over which the dark herds passed by
thousands, are now grass-grown and fast disappearing under
the effacing hand of time.   The buffalo have disappeared,
and the fate of the buffalo has almost overtaken the Blackfeet.

As known to the whites, the Blackfeet were true prairie
Indians, seldom venturing into the mountains, except when
they crossed them to war with the Kutenais, the Flatheads,
or the Snakes.   They subsisted almost wholly on the flesh
of the buffalo.   They were hardy, untiring, brave, ferocious.
Swift to move, whether on foot or horseback, they made
long journeys to war, and with telling force struck their
enemies.   They had conquered and driven out from the
territory which they occupied the tribes who once inhabited
it, and maintained a desultory and successful warfare against
all invaders, fighting with the Crees on the north, the
Assinaboines on the east, the Crows on the south, and the
Snakes, Kalispels, and Kutenais on the southwest and
west.   In those days the Blackfeet were rich and powerful.
The buffalo fed and clothed them, and they needed nothing
beyond what nature supplied.   This was their time of success and happiness.

Crowded into a little corner of the great territory which
they once dominated, and holding this corner by an uncer-

tain tenure, a few Blackfeet still exist, the pitiful remnant of a once mighty people. Huddled together about their agencies, they are facing the problem before them, striving, helplessly but bravely, to accommodate themselves to the new order of things; trying in the face of adverse surroundings to wrench themselves loose from their accustomed ways of life; to give up inherited habits and form new ones; to break away from all that is natural to them, from all that they have been taught — to reverse their whole mode of existence. They are striving to earn their living, as the white man earns his, by toil. The struggle is hard and slow, and in carrying it on they are wasting away and growing fewer in numbers. But though unused to labor, ignorant of agriculture, unacquainted with tools or seeds or soils, knowing nothing of the ways of life in permanent houses or of the laws of health, scantily fed, often utterly discouraged by failure, they are still making a noble fight for existence.

Only within a few years — since the buffalo disappeared — has this change been going on; so recently has it come that the old order and the new meet face to face. In the trees along the river valleys, still quietly resting on their aërial sepulchres, sleep the forms of the ancient hunter-warrior who conquered and held this broad land; while, not far away, Blackfoot farmers now rudely cultivate their little crops, and gather scanty harvests from narrow fields.

It is the meeting of the past and the present, of savagery and civilization. The issue cannot be doubtful. Old methods must pass away. The Blackfeet will become civilized, but at a terrible cost. To me there is an interest, profound and pathetic, in watching the progress of the struggle.

DAILY LIFE AND CUSTOMS

INDIANS are usually represented as being a silent, sullen race, seldom speaking, and never laughing nor joking. However true this may be in regard to some tribes, it certainly was not the case with most of those who lived upon the great Plains. These people were generally talkative, merry, and light-hearted; they delighted in fun, and were a race of jokers. It is true that, in the presence of strangers, they were grave, silent, and reserved, but this is nothing more than the shyness and embarrassment felt by a child in the presence of strangers. As the Indian becomes acquainted, this reserve wears off; he is at his ease again and appears in his true colors, a light-hearted child. Certainly the Blackfeet never were a taciturn and gloomy people. Before the disappearance of the buffalo, they were happy and cheerful. Why should they not have been? Food and clothing were to be had for the killing and tanning. All fur animals were abundant, and thus the people were rich. Meat, really the only food they cared for, was plenty and cost nothing. Their robes and furs were exchanged with the traders for bright-colored blankets and finery. So they wanted nothing.

It is but nine years since the buffalo disappeared from the land. Only nine years have passed since these people gave up that wild, free life which was natural to them, and ah! how dear! Let us go back in memory to those happy days and see how they passed the time.

The sun is just rising. Thin columns of smoke are creeping from the smoke holes of the lodges, and ascending in the still morning air. Everywhere the women are busy, carrying water and wood, and preparing the simple meal. And now we see the men come out, and start for the river. Some are followed by their children; some are even carrying those too small to walk. They have reached the water's edge. Off drop their blankets, and with a plunge and a shivering *ah-h-h* they dash into the icy waters. Winter and summer, storm or shine, this was their daily custom. They said it made them tough and healthy, and enabled them to endure the bitter cold while hunting on the bare bleak prairie. By the time they have returned to the lodges, the women have prepared the early meal. A dish of boiled meat — some three or four pounds — is set before each man; the children are served as much as they can eat, and the wives take the rest. The horses are now seen coming in, hundreds and thousands of them, driven by boys and young men who started out after them at daylight. If buffalo are close at hand, and it has been decided to make a run, each hunter catches his favorite buffalo horse, and they all start out together; they are followed by women, on the travois or pack horses, who will do most of the butchering, and transport the meat and hides to camp. If there is no band of buffalo near by, they go off, singly or by twos and threes, to still-hunt scattering buffalo, or deer, or elk, or such other game as may be found. The women remaining in camp are not idle. All day long they tan robes, dry meat, sew moccasins, and perform a thousand and one other tasks. The young men who have stayed at home carefully comb and braid their hair, paint their faces, and, if the weather is pleasant, ride or walk around the camp so that the young women may look at them and see how pretty they are.

Feasting began early in the morning, and will be carried on far into the night. A man who gives a feast has his wives cook the choicest food they have, and when all is ready, he goes outside the lodge and shouts the invitation, calling out each guest's name three times, saying that he is invited to eat, and concludes by announcing that a certain number of pipes — generally three — will be smoked. The guests having assembled, each one is served with a dish of food. Be the quantity large or small, it is all that he will get. If he does not eat it all, he may carry home what remains. The host does not eat with his guests. He cuts up some tobacco, and carefully mixes it with *l'herbe*, and when all have finished eating, he fills and lights a pipe, which is smoked and passed from one to another, beginning with the first man on his left. When the last person on the left of the host has smoked, the pipe is passed back around the circle to the one on the right of the door, and smoked to the left again. The guests do not all talk at once. When a person begins to speak, he expects every one to listen, and is never interrupted. During the day the topics for conversation are about the hunting, war, stories of strange adventures, besides a good deal of good-natured joking and chaffing. When the third and last pipeful of tobacco has been smoked, the host ostentatiously knocks out the ashes and says "*Kyi*," whereupon all the guests rise and file out. Seldom a day passed but each lodge-owner in camp gave from one to three feasts. In fact almost all a man did, when in camp, was to go from one of these gatherings to another.

A favorite pastime in the day was gambling with a small wheel called *it-se'-wah*. This wheel was about four inches in diameter, and had five spokes, on which were strung different-colored beads, made of bone or horn. A level, smooth piece of ground was selected, at each end of which was placed a log. At each end of the course were two men, who gambled against each other. A crowd always surrounded them, betting on the sides. The wheel was rolled along the course, and each man at the end whence it started, darted an arrow at it. The cast was made just before the wheel reached the log at the opposite end of the track, and points were counted according as the arrow passed between the spokes, or when the wheel, stopped by the log, was in contact with the arrow, the position and nearness of the different beads to the arrow representing a certain number of points. The player who first scored ten points won. It was a very difficult game, and one had to be very skilful to win.

Another popular game was what with more southern tribes is called " hands " ; it is like " Button, button, who's got the button ? " Two small, oblong bones were used, one of which had a black ring around it. Those who participated in this game, numbering from two to a dozen, were divided into two equal parties, ranged on either side of the lodge. Wagers were made, each person betting with the one directly opposite him. Then a man took the bones, and, by skilfully moving his hands and changing the objects from one to the other, sought to make it impossible for the person opposite him to decide which hand held the marked one. Ten points were the game, counted by sticks, and the side which first got the number took the stakes. A song always accompanied this game, a weird, unearthly air, — if it can be so called, — but when heard at a little distance, very pleasant and soothing. At first a scarcely audible murmur, like the gentle soughing of an evening breeze, it gradually increased in volume and reached a very high pitch, sank quickly to a low bass sound, rose and fell, and gradually died away, to be again repeated. The person concealing the bones swayed his body, arms, and hands in time to the air, and went through all manner of graceful and intricate movements for the purpose of confusing the guesser. The stakes were sometimes very high, two or three horses or more, and men have been known to lose everything they possessed, even to their clothing.

The children, at least the boys, played about and did as

they pleased. Not so with the girls. Their duties began
at a very early age. They carried wood and water for their
mothers, sewed moccasins, and as soon as they were strong
enough, were taught to tan robes and furs, make lodges,
travois, and do all other woman's — and so menial — work.
The boys played at mimic warfare, hunted around in the
brush with their bows and arrows, made mud images of
animals, and in summer spent about half their time in the
water. In winter, they spun tops on the ice, slid down hill
on a contrivance made of buffalo ribs, and hunted rabbits.

Shortly after noon, the hunters began to return, bringing
in deer, antelope, buffalo, elk, occasionally bear, and, sometimes, beaver which they had trapped. The camp began to
be more lively. In all directions persons could be heard
shouting out invitations to feasts. Here a man was lying
back on his couch singing and drumming ; there a group of
young men were holding a war dance ; everywhere the
people were eating, singing, talking, and joking. As the
light faded from the western sky and darkness spread over
the camp, the noise and laughter increased. In many
lodges, the people held social dances, the women, dressed in
their best gowns, ranged on one side, the men on the other ;
all sung, and three or four drummers furnished an accom-
paniment ; the music was lively if somewhat jerky. At
intervals the people rose and danced, the "step" being
a bending of the knees and swinging of the body, the
women holding their arms and hands in various graceful
positions.

With the night came the rehearsal of the wondrous doings
of the gods. These tales may not be told in the daytime.
Old Man would not like that, and would cause any one who
narrated them while it was light to become blind. All
Indians are natural orators, but some far exceed others in
their powers of expression. Their attitudes, gestures, and
signs are so suggestive that they alone would enable one to

understand the stories they relate.   I have seen these story-
tellers so much in earnest, so entirely carried away by the
tale they were relating, that they fairly trembled with excitement.   They held their little audiences spell-bound.
The women dropped their half-sewn moccasin from their
listless hands, and the men let the pipe go out.   These
stories for the most part were about the ancient gods and
their miraculous doings.   They were generally related by
the old men, warriors who had seen their best days.   Many
of them are recorded in this book.   They are the explanations of the phenomena of life, and contain many a moral
for the instruction of youth.

The *I-kŭn-ŭh'-kah-tsi* contributed not a little to the entertainment of every-day life.   Frequent dances were held by
the different bands of the society, and the whole camp
always turned out to see them.   The animal-head masks,
brightly painted bodies, and queer performances were dear
to the Indian heart.

Such was the every-day life of the Blackfeet in the buffalo
days.   When the camp moved, the women packed up their
possessions, tore down the lodges, and loaded everything on
the backs of the ponies or on the travois.   Meantime the
chiefs had started on, and the soldiers — the Brave band of
the *I-kun-uh'-kah-tsi* — followed after them.   After these
leaders had gone a short distance, a halt was made to allow
the column to close up.   The women, children, horses, and
dogs of the camp marched in a disorderly, straggling fashion,
often strung out in a line a mile or two long.   Many of the
men rode at a considerable distance ahead, and on each side
of the marching column, hunting for any game that might
be found, or looking over the country for signs of enemies.

Before the Blackfeet obtained horses in the very first
years of the present century, and when their only beasts of
burden were dogs, their possessions were transported by
these animals or on men's backs.   We may imagine that in

those days the journeys made were short ones, the camp travelling but a few miles.

In moving the camp in ancient days, the heaviest and bulkiest things to be transported were the lodges. These were sometimes very large, often consisting of thirty cow-skins, and, when set up, containing two or three fires like this ⟋* * *⟍ or in ground plan like this (* * *). The skins of these large lodges were sewn together in strips, of which there would be sometimes as many as four ; and, when the lodge was set up, these strips were pinned together as the front of a common lodge is pinned to-day. The dogs carried the provisions, tools, and utensils, sometimes the lodge strips, if these were small enough, or anything that was heavy, and yet could be packed in small compass ; for since dogs are small animals, and low standing, they cannot carry bulky burdens. Still, some of the dogs were large enough to carry a load of one hundred pounds. Dogs also hauled the travois, on which were bundles and sometimes babies. This was not always a safe means of transportation for infants, as is indicated by an incident related by John Monroe's mother as having occurred in her father's time. The camp, on foot of course, was crossing a strip of open prairie lying between two pieces of timber, when a herd of buffalo, stampeding, rushed through the marching column. The loaded dogs rushed after the buffalo, dragging the travois after them and scattering their loads over the prairie. Among the lost chattels were two babies, dropped off some-where in the long grass, which were never found.

There were certain special customs and beliefs which were a part of the every-day life of the people.

In passing the pipe when smoking, it goes from the host, who takes the first smoke, to the left, passing from hand to hand to the door. It may not be passed across the door to the man on the other side, but must come back, — no one smoking, — pass the host, and go round to the man across the door from the last smoker. This man smokes and passes it to the one on his left, and so it goes on until it reaches the host again. A person entering a lodge where people are smoking must not pass in front of them, that is, between the smokers and the fire.

A solemn form of affirmation, the equivalent of the civilized oath, is connected with smoking, which, as is well known, is with many tribes of Indians a sacred ceremony. If a man sitting in a lodge tells his companions some very improbable story, something that they find it very hard to believe, and they want to test him, to see if he is really telling the truth, the pipe is given to a medicine man, who paints the stem red and prays over it, asking that if the man's story is true he may have long life, but if it is false his life may end in a short time. The pipe is then filled and lighted, and passed to the man, who has seen and overheard what has been done and said. The medicine man says to him : " Accept this pipe, but remember that, if you smoke, your story must be as sure as that there is a hole through this pipe, and as straight as the hole through this stem. So your life shall be long and you shall survive, but if you have spoken falsely your days are counted." The man may refuse the pipe, saying, " I have told you the truth ; it is useless to smoke this pipe." If he declines to smoke, no one believes what he has said ; he is looked upon as having lied. If, however, he takes the pipe and smokes, every one believes him. It is the most solemn form of oath. The Blackfoot pipes are usually made of black or green slate or sandstone.

The Blackfeet do not whip their children, but still they are not without some training. Children must be taught, or they will not know anything ; if they do not know anything, they will have no sense ; and if they have no sense they will not know how to act. They are instructed in manners, as well as in other more general and more important matters.

If a number of boys were in a lodge where older people

were sitting, very likely the young people would be talking and laughing about their own concerns, and making so much noise that the elders could say nothing. If this continued too long, one of the older men would be likely to get up and go out and get a long stick and bring it in with him. When he had seated himself, he would hold it up, so that the children could see it and would repeat a cautionary formula, "I will give you gum!" This was a warning to them to make less noise, and was always heeded — for a time. After a little, however, the boys might forget and begin to chatter again, and presently the man, without further warning, would reach over and rap one of them on the head with the stick, when quiet would again be had for a time.

In the same way, in winter, when the lodge was full of old and young people, and through lack of attention the fire died down, some older person would call out, "Look out for the skunk!" which would be a warning to the boys to put some sticks on the fire. If this was not done at once, the man who had called out might throw a stick of wood across the lodge into the group of children, hitting and hurting one or more of them. It was taught also that, if, when young and old were in the lodge and the fire had burned low, an older person were to lay the unburned ends of the sticks upon the fire, all the children in the lodge would have the scab, or itch. So, at the call "Look out for the scab!" some child would always jump to the fire, and lay up the sticks.

There were various ways of teaching and training the children. Men would make long speeches to groups of boys, playing in the camps, telling them what they ought to do to be successful in life. They would point out to them that to accomplish anything they must be brave and untiring in war; that long life was not desirable; that the old people always had a hard time, were given the worst side of the lodge and generally neglected; that when the camp was moved they suffered from cold; that their sight was dim, so that they could not see far; that their teeth were gone, so that they could not chew their food.   Only discomfort and misery await the old.   Much better, while the body is strong and in its prime, while the sight is clear, the teeth sound, and the hair still black and long, to die in battle fighting bravely. The example of successful warriors would be held up to them, and the boys urged to emulate their brave deeds. To such advice some boys would listen, while others would not heed it.

The girls also were instructed.   All Indians like to see women more or less sober and serious-minded, not giggling all the time, not silly.   A Blackfoot man who had two or three girls would, as they grew large, often talk to them and give them good advice.   After watching them, and taking the measure of their characters, he would one day get a buffalo's front foot and ornament it fantastically with feathers.   When the time came, he would call one of his daughters to him and say to her: "Now I wish you to stand here in front of me and look me straight in the eye without laughing.   No matter what I may do, do not laugh." Then he would sing a funny song, shaking the foot in the girl's face in time to the song, and looking her steadily in the eye.   Very likely before he had finished, she would begin to giggle.   If she did this, the father would stop singing and tell her to finish laughing ; and when she was serious again, he would again warn her not to laugh, and then would repeat his song.   This time perhaps she would not laugh while he was singing.   He would go through with this same performance before all his daughters.   To such as seemed to have the steadiest characters, he would give good advice. He would talk to each girl of the duties of a woman's life and warn her against the dangers which she might expect to meet.

At the time of the Medicine Lodge, he would take her to the lodge and point out to her the Medicine Lodge woman.

He would say : "There is a good woman. She has built this Medicine Lodge, and is greatly honored and respected by all the people. Once she was a girl just like you ; and you, if you are good and live a pure life, may some day be as great as she is now. Remember this, and try to live a worthy life."

At the time of the Medicine Lodge, the boys in the camp also gathered to see the young men count their *coups*. A man would get up, holding in one hand a bundle of small sticks, and, taking one stick from the bundle, he would recount some brave deed, throwing away a stick as he completed the narrative of each *coup*, until the sticks were all gone, when he sat down, and another man stood up to begin his recital. As the boys saw and heard all this, and saw how respected those men were who had done the most and bravest things, they said to themselves, "That man was once a boy like us, and we, if we have strong hearts, may do as much as he has done." So even the very small boys used often to steal off from the camp, and follow war parties. Often they went without the knowledge of their parents, and poorly provided, without food or extra moccasins. They would get to the enemy's camp, watch the ways of the young men, and so learn about going to war, how to act when on the war trail so as to be successful. Also they came to know the country.

The Blackfeet men often went off by themselves to fast and dream for power. By no means every one did this, and, of those who attempted it, only a few endured to the end, — that is, fasted the whole four days, — and obtained the help sought. The attempt was not usually made by young boys before they had gone on their first war journey. It was often undertaken by men who were quite mature. Those who underwent this suffering were obliged to abstain from food or drink for four days and four nights, resting for two nights on the right side, and for two nights on the left. It

was deemed essential that the place to which a man re-
sorted for this purpose should be unfrequented, where few
or no persons had walked; and it must also be a place that
tried the nerve, where there was some danger.   Such situa-
tions were mountain peaks; or narrow ledges on cut cliffs,
where a careless movement might cause a man to fall to his
death on the rocks below; or islands in lakes, which could
only be reached by means of a raft, and where there was
danger that a person might be seized and carried off by the
Sū'-yē tŭp'-pi, or Under Water People; or places where the
dead had been buried, and where there was much danger
from ghosts.   Or a man might lie in a well-worn buffalo trail,
where the animals were frequently passing, and so he might
be trodden on by a travelling band of buffalo; or he might
choose a locality where bears were abundant and dangerous.
Wherever he went, the man built himself a little lodge of
brush, moss, and leaves, to keep off the rain; and, after
making his prayers to the sun and singing his sacred songs,
he crept into the hut and began his fast.   He was not allowed to take any covering with him, nor to roof over his
shelter with skins.   He always had with him a pipe, and
this lay by him, filled, so that, when the spirit, or dream, came,
it could smoke.   They did not appeal to any special class
of helpers, but prayed to all alike.   Often by the end of the
fourth day, a secret helper — usually, but by no means always,
in the form of some animal — appeared to the man in a dream,
and talked with him, advising him, marking out his course
through life, and giving him its power.   There were some,
however, on whom the power would not work, and a much
greater number who gave up the fast, discouraged, before the
prescribed time had been completed, either not being able
to endure the lack of food and water, or being frightened
by the strangeness or loneliness of their surroundings, or by
something that they thought they saw or heard.   It was no
disgrace to fail, nor was the failure necessarily known, for

the seeker after power did not always, nor perhaps often, tell any one what he was going to do.

Three modes of burial were practised by the Blackfeet. They buried their dead on platforms placed in trees, on platforms in lodges, and on the ground in lodges. If a man dies in a lodge, it is never used again. The people would be afraid of the man's ghost. The lodge is often used to wrap the body in, or perhaps the man may be buried in it.

As soon as a person is dead, be it man, woman, or child, the body is immediately prepared for burial, by the nearest female relations. Until recently, the corpse was wrapped in a number of robes, then in a lodge covering, laced with rawhide ropes, and placed on a platform of lodge poles, arranged on the branches of some convenient tree. Some times the outer wrapping — the lodge covering — was omitted. If the deceased was a man, his weapons, and often his medicine, were buried with him. With women a few cooking utensils and implements for tanning robes were placed on the scaffolds. When a man was buried on a platform in a lodge, the platform was usually suspended from the lodge poles.

Sometimes, when a great chief or noted warrior died, his lodge would be moved some little distance from the camp, and set up in a patch of brush. It would be carefully pegged down all around, and stones piled on the edges to make it additionally firm. For still greater security, a rope fastened to the lodge poles, where they come together at the smoke hole, came down, and was securely tied to a peg in the ground in the centre of the lodge, where the fireplace would ordinarily be. Then the beds were made up all around the lodge, and on one of them was placed the corpse, lying as if asleep. The man's weapons, pipe, war clothing, and medicine were placed near him, and the door then closed. No one ever again entered such a lodge. Outside the lodge, a number of his horses, often twenty or more, were killed, so

that he might have plenty to ride on his journey to the
Sand Hills, and to use after arriving there.   If a man had a
favorite horse, he might order it to be killed at his grave, and
his order was always carried out.   In ancient times, it is
said, dogs were killed at the grave.

Women mourn for deceased relations by cutting their hair
short.   For the loss of a husband or son (but not a daughter),
they not only cut their hair, but often take off one or more
joints of their fingers, and always scarify the calves of their
legs.   Besides this, for a month or so, they daily repair to
some place near camp, generally a hill or little rise of ground,
and there cry and lament, calling the name of the deceased
over and over again.   This may be called a chant or song,
for there is a certain tune to it.   It is in a minor key and
very doleful.   Any one hearing it for the first time, even
though wholly unacquainted with Indian customs, would at
once know that it was a mourning song, or at least was the
utterance of one in deep distress.   There is no fixed period
for the length of time one must mourn.   Some keep up this
daily lament for a few weeks only, and others much longer.
I once came across an old wrinkled woman, who was
crouched in the sage brush, crying and lamenting for some
one, as if her heart would break.   On inquiring if any one
had lately died, I was told she was mourning for a son she
had lost more than twenty years before.

Men mourn by cutting a little of their hair, going without
leggings, and for the loss of a son, sometimes scarify their
legs.   This last, however, is never done for the loss of a wife,
daughter, or any relative except a son.

Many Blackfeet change their names every season.   Whenever a Blackfoot counts a new *coup*, he is entitled to a new
name.   A Blackfoot will never tell his name if he can avoid
it.   He believes that if he should speak his name, he would
be unfortunate in all his undertakings.

It was considered a gross breach of propriety for a man to meet his mother-in-law, and if by any mischance he did so, or what was worse, if he spoke to her, she demanded a very heavy payment, which he was obliged to make. The mother-in-law was equally anxious to avoid meeting or speaking to her son-in-law.

HOW THE BLACKFOOT LIVED

THE primitive clothing of the Blackfeet was made of the dressed skins of certain animals. Women seldom wore a head covering. Men, however, in winter generally used a cap made of the skin of some small animal, such as the antelope, wolf, badger, or coyote. As the skin from the head of these animals often formed part of the cap, the ears being left on, it made a very odd-looking head-dress. Sometimes a cap was made of the skin of some large bird, such as the sage-hen, duck, owl, or swan.

The ancient dress of the women was a shirt of cowskin, with long sleeves tied at the wrist, a skirt reaching half-way from knees to ankles, and leggings tied above the knees, with sometimes a supporting string running from the belt to the leggings. In more modern times, this was modified, and a woman's dress consisted of a gown or smock, reaching from the neck to below the knees. There were no sleeves, the armholes being provided with top coverings, a sort of cape or flap, which reached to the elbows. Leggings were of course still worn. They reached to the knee, and were generally made, as was the gown, of the tanned skins of elk, deer, sheep, or antelope. Moccasins for winter use were made of buffalo robe, and of tanned buffalo cowskin for summer wear. The latter were always made with parfleche soles, which greatly increased their durability, and were often ornamented over the instep or toes with a three-pronged figure, worked in porcupine quills or beads, the three prongs representing, it is said, the three divisions or tribes of the

196

nation. The men wore a shirt, breech-clout, leggings which reached to the thighs, and moccasins. In winter both men and women wore a robe of tanned buffalo skin, and sometimes of beaver. In summer a lighter robe was worn, made of cowskin or buckskin, from which the hair had been removed. Both sexes wore belts, which supported and confined the clothing, and to which were attached knife-sheaths and other useful articles.

Necklaces and ear-rings were worn by all, and were made of shells, bone, wood, and the teeth and claws of animals. Elk tushes were highly prized, and were used for ornamenting women's dresses. A gown profusely decorated with them was worth two good horses. Eagle feathers were used by the men to make head-dresses and to ornament shields and also weapons. Small bunches of owl or grouse feathers were sometimes tied to the scalp locks. It is doubtful if the women ever took particular care of their hair. The men, however, spent a great deal of time brushing, braiding, and ornamenting their scalp locks. Their hair was usually worn in two braids, one on each side of the head. Less frequently, four braids were made, one behind and in front of each ear. Sometimes, the hair of the forehead was cut off square, and brushed straight up ; and not infrequently it was made into a huge topknot and wound with otter fur. Often a slender lock, wound with brass wire or braided, hung down from one side of the forehead over the face.

As a rule, the men are tall, straight, and well formed. Their features are regular, the eyes being large and well set, and the nose generally moderately large, straight, and thin. Their chests are splendidly developed. The women are quite tall for their sex, but, as a rule, not so good-looking as the men. Their hands are large, coarse, and knotted by hard labor ; and they early become wrinkled and careworn. They generally have splendid constitutions. I have known them to resume work a day after childbirth ; and once, when travelling, I knew a woman to halt, give birth to a child, and catch up with the camp inside of four hours.

As a rule, children are hardy and vigorous. They are allowed to do about as they please from the time they are able to walk. I have often seen them playing in winter in the snow, and spinning tops on the ice, barefooted and half-naked. Under such conditions, those which have feeble constitutions soon die. Only the hardiest reach maturity and old age.

It is said that very long ago the people made houses of mud, sticks, and stones. It is not known what was their size or shape, and no traces of them are known to have been found. For a very long time, the lodge seems to have been their only dwelling. In ancient times, before they had knives of metal, stones were used to hold down the edges of the lodge, to keep it from being blown away. These varied in size from six inches to a foot or more in diameter. Everywhere on the prairie, one may now see circles of these stones, and, within these circles, the smaller ones, which surrounded the fireplace. Some of them have lain so long that only the tops now project above the turf, and undoubtedly many of them are buried out of sight.

Lodges were always made of tanned cowskin, nicely cut and sewn together, so as to form an almost perfect cone. At the top were two large flaps, called ears, which were kept extended or closed, according to the direction and strength of the wind, to create a draft and keep the lodge free from smoke. The lodge covering was supported by light, straight pine or spruce poles, about eighteen of which were required. Twelve cowskins made a lodge about fourteen feet in diameter at the base, and ten feet high. I have heard of a modern one which contained forty skins. It was over thirty feet in diameter, and was so heavy that the skins were sewn in two pieces which buttoned together.

An average-sized dwelling of this kind contained eighteen

skins and was about sixteen feet in diameter. The lower edge of the lodge proper was fastened, by wooden pegs, to within an inch or two of the ground. Inside, a lining, made of brightly painted cowskin, reached from the ground to a height of five or six feet. An air space of the thickness of the lodge poles — two or three inches — was thus left between the lining and the lodge covering, and the cold air, rushing up through it from the outside, made a draft, which aided the ears in freeing the lodge of smoke. The door was three or four feet high and was covered by a flap of skin, which hung down on the outside. Thus made, with plenty of buffalo robes for seats and bedding, and a good stock of firewood, a lodge was very comfortable, even in the coldest weather.

It was not uncommon to decorate the outside of the lodge with buffalo tails and brightly painted pictures of animals. Inside, the space around was partitioned off into couches, or seats, each about six feet in length. At the foot and head of every couch, a mat, made of straight, peeled willow twigs, fastened side by side, was suspended on a tripod at an angle of forty-five degrees, so that between the couches spaces were left like an inverted V, thus $\wedge$, making convenient places to store articles which were not in use. The owner of the lodge always occupied the seat or couch at the back of the lodge, directly opposite the door-way, the places on his right being occupied by his wives and daughters; though sometimes a Blackfoot had so many wives that they occupied the whole lodge. The places on his left were reserved for his sons and visitors. When a visitor entered a lodge, he was assigned a seat according to his rank, — the nearer to the host, the greater the honor.

Bows were generally made of ash wood, which grows east of the mountains toward the Sand Hills. When for any reason they could not obtain ash, they used the wood of the choke-cherry tree, but this had not strength nor spring enough to be of much service. I have been told also that sometimes they used hazle wood for bows.

Arrows were made of shoots of the sarvis berry wood, which was straight, very heavy, and not brittle. They were smoothed and straightened by a stone implement. The grooves were made by pushing the shafts through a rib or other flat bone in which had been made a hole, circular except for one or two projections on the inside. These projections worked out the groove. The object of these grooves is said to have been to allow the blood to flow freely. Each man marked his arrows by painting them, or by some special combination of colored feathers. The arrow heads were of two kinds, — barbed slender points for war, and barbless for hunting. Knives were originally made of stone, as were also war clubs, mauls, and some of the scrapers for fleshing and graining hides. Some of the flint knives were long, others short. A stick was fitted to them, forming a wooden handle. The handles of mauls and war clubs were usually made of green sticks fitted as closely as possible into a groove made in the stone, the whole being bound together by a covering of hide put on green, tightly fitted and strongly sewed. This, as it shrunk in drying, bound the different parts of the implement together in the strongest possible manner. Short, heavy spears were used, the points being of stone or bone, barbed.

I have heard no explanation among the Blackfeet of the origin of fire. In ancient times, it was obtained by means of fire sticks, as described elsewhere. The starting of the spark with these sticks is said to have been hard work. At almost their first meeting with the whites, they obtained flints and steels, and learned how to use them.

In ancient times, — in the days of fire sticks and even later, within the memory of men now living, — fire used to be carried from place to place in a " fire horn." This was a buffalo horn slung by a string over the shoulder like a powder horn. The horn was lined with moist, rotten wood, and the open end had a wooden stopper or plug fitted to it. On leaving camp in the morning, the man who carried the horn took from the fire a small live coal and put it in the horn, and on this coal placed a piece of punk, and then plugged up the horn with the stopper. The punk smouldered in this almost air-tight chamber, and, in the course of two or three hours, the man looked at it, and if it was nearly consumed, put another piece of punk in the horn. The first young men who reached the appointed camping ground would gather two or three large piles of wood in different places, and as soon as some one who carried a fire horn reached camp, he turned out his spark at one of these piles of wood, and a little blowing and nursing gave a blaze which started the fire. The other fires were kindled from this first one, and when the women reached camp and had put the lodges up, they went to these fires, and got coals with which to start those in their lodges. This custom of borrowing coals persisted up to the last days of the buffalo, and indeed may even be noticed still.

The punk here mentioned is a fungus, which grows on the birch tree. The Indians used to gather this in large quantities and dry it. It was very abundant at the Touchwood Hills (whence the name) on Beaver Creek, a tributary of the Saskatchewan from the south.

The Blackfeet made buckets, cups, basins, and dishes from the lining of the buffalo's paunch. This was torn off in large pieces, and was stretched over a flattened willow or cherry hoop at the bottom and top. These hoops were sometimes inside and sometimes outside the bucket or dish. In the latter case, the hoop at the bottom was often sewed to the paunch, which came down over it, double on the outside, the needle holes being pitched with gum or tallow. The hoop at the upper edge was also sewed to the paunch, and a rawhide bail passed under it, to carry it by.

These buckets were shaped somewhat like our wooden ones, and were of different sizes, some of them holding four or five gallons. They were more or less flexible, and when carried in a pack, they could be flattened down like a crush hat, and so took up but little room. If set on the ground when full, they would stand up for a while, but as they soon softened and fell down, they were usually hung up by the bail on a little tripod. Cups were made in the same way as buckets, but on a smaller scale and without the bail. Of course, nothing hot could be placed in these vessels.

It is doubtful if the Blackfeet ever made any pottery or basket ware. They, however, made bowls and kettles of stone. There is an ancient children's song which consists of a series of questions asked an elk, and its replies to the same. In one place, the questioner sings, "Elk, what is your bowl (or dish)?" and the elk answers, "*Ok-wi-tok-so-ka*," stone bowl. On this point, Wolf Calf, a very old man, states that in early days the Blackfeet sometimes boiled their meat in a stone bowl made out of a hard clayey rock.[1] Choosing a fragment of the right size and shape, they would pound it with another heavier rock, dealing light blows until a hollow had been made in the top. This hollow was made deeper by pounding and grinding; and when it was deep enough, they put water in it, and set it on the fire, and the water would boil. These pots were strong and would last a long time. I do not remember that any other tribe of Plains Indians made such stone bowls or mortars, though, of course, they were commonly made, and in singular perfection, by the Pacific Coast tribes; and I have known of rare cases in which basalt mortars and small soapstone ollas have been found on the central plateau of the continent in southern Wyoming. These articles, however, had no doubt been obtained by trade from Western tribes.

Serviceable ladles and spoons were made of wood and of

[1] See The Blackfoot Genesis, p. 141.

buffalo and mountain sheep horn. Basins or flat dishes were sometimes made of mountain sheep horn, boiled, split, and flattened, and also of split buffalo horn, fitted and sewn together with sinew, making a flaring, saucer-shaped dish. These were used as plates or eating dishes. Of course, they leaked a little, for the joints were not tight. Wooden bowls and dishes were made from knots and protuberances of trees, dug out and smoothed by fire and the knife or by the latter alone.

It is not known that these people ever made spears, hooks, or other implements for capturing fish. They appear never to have used boats of any kind, not even "bull boats." Their highest idea of navigation was to lash together a few sticks or logs, on which to transport their possessions across a river.

Red, brown, yellow, and white paints were made by burning clays of these colors, which were then pulverized and mixed with a little grease. Black paint was made of charred wood.

Bags and sacks were made of parfleche, usually ornamented with buckskin fringe, and painted with various designs in bright colors. Figures having sharp angles are most common.

The diet of the Blackfeet was more varied than one would think. Large quantities of sarvis berries (*Amelanchier alnifolia*) were gathered whenever there was a crop (which occurs every other year), dried, and stored for future use. These were gathered by women, who collected the branches laden with ripe fruit, and beat them over a robe spread upon the ground. Choke-cherries were also gathered when ripe, and pounded up, stones and all. A bushel of the fruit, after being pounded up and dried, was reduced to a very small quantity. This food was sometimes eaten by itself, but more often was used to flavor soups and to mix with pemmican. Bull berries (*Shepherdia argentea*) were a favorite fruit, and were gathered in large quantities, as was also the white berry of the red willow. This last is an exceedingly bitter, acrid fruit, and to the taste of most white men wholly unpleasant and repugnant. The Blackfeet, however, are very fond of it; perhaps because it contains some property necessary to the nourishment of the body, which is lacking in their every-day food.

The camas root, which grows abundantly in certain localities on the east slope of the Rockies, was also dug, cooked, and dried. The bulbs were roasted in pits, as by the Indians on the west side of the Rocky Mountains, the Kalispels, and others. It is gathered while in the bloom — June 15 to July 15. A large pit is dug in which a hot fire is built, the bottom being first lined with flat stones. After keeping up this fire for several hours, until the stones and earth are thoroughly heated, the coals and ashes are removed. The pit is then lined with grass, and is filled almost to the top with camas bulbs. Over these, grass is laid, then twigs, and then earth to a depth of four inches. On this a fire is built, which is kept up for from one to three days, according to the quantity of the bulbs in the pit.

When the pit is opened, the small children gather about it to suck the syrup, which has collected on the twigs and grass, and which is very sweet. The fresh-roasted camas tastes something like a roasted chestnut, with a little of the flavor of the sweet potato. After being cooked, the roots are spread out in the sun to dry, and are then put in sacks to be stored away. Sometimes a few are pounded up with sarvis berries, and dried.

Bitter-root is gathered, dried, and boiled with a little sugar. It is a slender root, an inch or two long and as thick as a goose quill, white in color, and looking like short lengths of spaghetti. It is very starchy.

In the spring, a certain root called *mats* was eaten in great quantities. This plant was known to the early French employees of the Hudson's Bay and American Fur Companies as *pomme blanche* (*Psoralea esculenta*).

All parts of such animals as the buffalo, elk, deer, etc., were eaten, save only the lungs, gall, and one or two other organs. A favorite way of eating the paunch or stomach was in the raw state. Liver, too, was sometimes eaten raw. The unborn calf of a fresh-killed animal, especially buffalo, was considered a great delicacy. The meat of this, when boiled, is white, tasteless, and insipid. The small intestines of the buffalo were sometimes dried, but more often were stuffed with long, thin strips of meat. During the stuffing process, the entrail was turned inside out, thus confining with the meat the sweet white fat that covers the intestine. The next step was to roast it a little, after which the ends were tied to prevent the escape of the juices, and it was thoroughly boiled in water. This is a very great delicacy, and when properly prepared is equally appreciated by whites and Indians.

As a rule, there were but two ways of cooking meat, — boiling and roasting. If roasted, it was thoroughly cooked ; but if boiled, it was only left in the water long enough to lose the red color, say five or ten minutes. Before they got kettles from the whites, the Blackfeet often boiled meat in a green hide. A hole was dug in the ground, and the skin, flesh side up, was laid in it, being supported about the edges of the hole by pegs. The meat and water having been placed in this hollow, red-hot stones were dropped in the water until it became hot and the meat was cooked.

In time of plenty, great quantities of dried meat were prepared for use when fresh meat could not be obtained. In making dried meat, the thicker parts of an animal were cut in large, thin sheets and hung in the sun to dry. If the weather was not fine, the meat was often hung up on lines or scaffolds in the upper part of the lodge. When properly cured and if of good quality, the sheets were about one-fourth of an inch thick and very brittle. The back fat of the buffalo was also dried, and eaten with the meat as we eat butter with bread. Pemmican was made of the flesh of the buffalo. The meat was dried in the usual way ; and, for this use, only lean meat, such as the hams, loin, and shoulders, was chosen. When the time came for making the pemmican, two large fires were built of dry quaking aspen wood, and these were allowed to burn down to red coals. The old women brought the dried meat to these fires, and the sheets of meat were thrown on the coals of one of them, allowed to heat through, turned to keep them from burning, and then thrown on the flesh side of a dry hide, that lay on the ground near by. After a time, the roasting of this dried meat caused a smoke to rise from the fire in use, which gave the meat a bitter taste, if cooked in it. They then turned to the other fire, and used that until the first one had burned clear again. After enough of the roasted meat had been thrown on the hide, it was flailed out with sticks, and being very brittle was easily broken up, and made small. It was constantly stirred and pounded until it was all fine. Meantime, the tallow of the buffalo had been melted in a large kettle, and the pemmican bags prepared. These were made of bull's hide, and were in two pieces, cut oblong, and with the corners rounded off. Two such pieces sewed together made a bag which would hold one hundred pounds. The pounded meat and tallow — the latter just beginning to cool — were put in a trough made of bull's hide, a wooden spade being used to stir the mixture. After it was thoroughly mixed, it was shovelled into one of the sacks, held open, and rammed down and packed tight with a big stick, every effort being made to expel all the air. When the bag was full and packed as tight as possible, it was sewn up. It was then put on the ground, and the women jumped on it to make it still more tight and solid. It was then laid away in the sun to cool and dry. It usually took the meat of two cows to make a bag of one hundred pounds ; a very large bull might make a sack of from eighty to one hundred pounds.

A much finer grade of pemmican was made from the choicest parts of the buffalo with marrow fat. To this dried berries and pounded choke-cherries were added, making a delicious food, which was extremely nutritious. Pemmican was eaten either dry as it came from the sack, or stewed with water.

In the spring, the people had great feasts of the eggs of ducks and other water-fowl. A large quantity having been gathered, a hole was dug in the ground, and a little water put in it. At short intervals above the water, platforms of sticks were built, on which the eggs were laid. A smaller hole was dug at one side of the large hole, slanting into the bottom of it. When all was ready, the top of the larger hole was covered with mud, laid upon cross sticks, and red-hot stones were dropped into the slant, when they rolled down into the water, heating it, and so cooking the eggs by steam.

Fish were seldom eaten by these people in early days, but now they seem very fond of them. Turtles, frogs, and lizards are considered creatures of evil, and are never eaten. Dogs, considered a great delicacy by the Crees, Gros Ventres, Sioux, Assinaboines, and other surrounding tribes, were never eaten by the Blackfeet. No religious motive is assigned for this abstinence. I once heard a Piegan say that it was wrong to eat dogs. "They are our true friends," he said. "Men say they are our friends and then turn against us, but our dogs are always true. They mourn when we are absent, and are always glad when we return. They keep watch for us in the night when we sleep. So pity the poor dogs."

Snakes, grasshoppers, worms, and other insects were never eaten. Salt was an unknown condiment. Many are now very fond of it, but I know a number, especially old people, who never eat it.

SOCIAL ORGANIZATION

THE social organization of the Blackfeet is very simple. The three tribes acknowledged a blood relationship with each other, and, while distinct, still considered themselves a nation. In this confederation, it was understood that there should be no war against each other. However, between 1860 and 1870, when the whiskey trade was in its height, the three tribes were several times at swords' points on account of drunken brawls. Once, about sixty or seventy years ago, the Bloods and Piegans had a quarrel so serious that men were killed on both sides and horses stolen; yet this was hardly a real war, for only a part of each tribe was involved, and the trouble was not of long duration.

Each one of the Blackfoot tribes is subdivided into gentes, a gens being a body of consanguineal kindred in the male line. It is noteworthy that the Blackfeet, although Algonquins, have this system of subdivision, and it may be that among them the gentes are of comparatively recent date. No special duties are assigned to any one gens, nor has any gens, so far as I know, any special " medicine " or " totem."

Below is a list of the gentes of each tribe.

BLACKFEET (*Sik'-si-kau*)

Gentes:

Puh-ksi-nah'-mah-yiks	Flat Bows.
Mo-tah'-tos-iks	Many Medicines.
Siks-in'-o-kaks	Black Elks.
E'-mi-tah-pahk-sai-yiks	Dogs Naked.
Sai'-yiks	Liars.

208

Ai-sik'-stŭk-iks	Biters.
Tsin-ik-tsis'-tso-yiks	Early Finished Eating.
Ap'-i-kai-yiks	Skunks.

BLOODS (*Kai'-nah*)

Siks-in'-o-kaks	Black Elks.
Ah-kwo'-nis-tsists	Many Lodge Poles.
Ap-ut'-o-si-kai-nah	North Bloods.
Is-tsi'-kai-nah	Woods Bloods.
In-uhk'-so-yi-stam-iks	Long Tail Lodge Poles.
Nit'-ik-skiks	Lone Fighters.
Siks-ah'-pun-iks	Blackblood.
Ah-kaik'-sum-iks	
I-sis'-o-kas-im-iks	Hair Shirts.
Ah-kai'-po-kaks	Many Children.
Sak-si-nah'-mah-yiks	Short Bows.
Ap'-i-kai-yiks	Skunks.
Ahk-o'-tash-iks	Many Horses.

PIEGANS (*Pi-kŭn'-ĭ*)

Ah'-pai-tup-iks	Blood People.
Ah-kai-yi-ko-ka'-kin-iks	White Breasts.
Ki'yis	Dried Meat.
Sik-ut'-si-pum-aiks	Black Patched Moccasins.
Sik-o-pok'-si-maiks	Blackfat Roasters.
Tsin-ik-sis'-tso-yiks	Early Finished Eating.
Kut'-ai-im-iks	They Don't Laugh.
I'-pok-si-maiks	Fat Roasters.
Sik'-o-kĭt-sim-iks	Black Doors.
Ni-taw'-yiks	Lone Eaters.
Ap'-i-kai-yiks	Skunks.
Mi-ah-wah'-pĭt-siks	Seldom Lonesome.
Nit'-ak-os-kit-si-pup-iks	Obstinate.
Nit'-ik-skiks	Lone Fighters.
I-nuks'-iks	Small Robes.
Mi-aw'-kin-ai-yiks	Big Topknots.
Esk'-sin-ai-tŭp-iks	Worm People.
I-nuk-si'-kah-ko-pwa-iks	Small Brittle Fat.
Kah'-mi-taiks	Buffalo Dung.
Kut-ai-sot'-si-man	No Parfleche.

Ni-tot'-si-ksis-stan-iks	Kill Close By.
Mo-twai'-naiks	All Chiefs.
Mo-kŭm'-iks	Red Round Robes.
Mo-tah'-tos-iks	Many Medicines.

It will be readily seen from the translations of the above that each gens takes its name from some peculiarity or habit it is supposed to possess. It will also be noticed that each tribe has a few gentes common to one or both of the other tribes. This is caused by persons leaving their own tribe to live with another one, but, instead of uniting with some gens of the adopted tribe, they have preserved the name of their ancestral gens for themselves and their descendants.

The Blackfoot terms of relationship will be found interesting. The principal family names are as follows : —

My father	*Ni'-nah.*
My mother	*Ni-kis'-ta.*
My elder brother	*Nis'-ah*
My younger brother	*Nis-kun'.*
My older sister	*Nin'-sta.*
My younger sister	*Ni-sis'-ah.*
My uncle	*Nis'-ah.*
My aunt	*Ni-kis'-ta.*
My cousin, male	Same as brother.
My cousin, female	Same as sister.
My grandfather	*Na-ahks'.*
My grandmother	*Na-ahks'.*
My father-in-law	*Na-ahks'.*
My mother-in-law	*Na-ahks'.*
My son	*No-ko'-i.*
My daughter	*Ni-tun'.*
My son-in-law	*Nis'-ah.*
My daughter-in-law	*Ni-tot'-o-kē-man.*
My brother-in-law older than self	*Nis-tum-o'.*
My brother-in-law younger than self	*Nis-tum-o'-kun.*
My sister-in-law	*Ni-tot'-o-ke-man.*
My second cousin	*Nimp'-sa.*
My wife	*Nit-o-kē'-man.*
My husband	*No'-ma.*

As the members of a gens were all considered as relatives, however remote, there was a law prohibiting a man from marrying within his gens.   Originally this law was strictly enforced, but like many of the ancient customs it is no longer observed.   Lately, within the last forty or fifty years, it has become not uncommon for a man and his family, or even two or three families, on account of some quarrel or some personal dislike of the chief of their own gens, to leave it and join another band.   Thus the gentes often received outsiders, who were not related by blood to the gens ; and such people or their descendants could marry within the gens.   Ancestry became no longer necessary to membership.

As a rule, before a young man could marry, he was required to have made some successful expeditions to war against the enemy, thereby proving himself a brave man, and at the same time acquiring a number of horses and other property, which would enable him to buy the woman of his choice, and afterwards to support her.

Marriages usually took place at the instance of the parents, though often those of the young man were prompted by him.   Sometimes the father of the girl, if he desired to have a particular man for a son-in-law, would propose to the father of the latter for the young man as a husband for his daughter.

The marriage in the old days was arranged after this wise : The chief of one of the bands may have a marriageable daughter, and he may know of a young man, the son of a chief of another band, who is a brave warrior, of good character, sober-minded, steadfast, and trustworthy, who he thinks will make a good husband for his daughter and a good son-in-law.   After he has made up his mind about this, he is very likely to call in a few of his close relations, the principal men among them, and state to them his conclusions, so as to get their opinions about it.   If nothing is said to change his mind, he sends to the father of the boy a messenger to state his own views, and ask how the father feels about the matter.

On receiving this word, the boy's father probably calls together his close relations, discusses the matter with them, and, if the match is satisfactory to him, sends back word to that effect. When this message is received, the relations of the girl proceed to fit her out with the very best that they can provide. If she is the daughter of well-to-do or wealthy people, she already has many of the things that are needed, but what she may lack is soon supplied. Her mother makes her a new cowskin lodge, complete, with new lodge poles, lining, and back rests. A chief's daughter would already have plenty of good clothing, but if the girl lacks anything, it is furnished. Her dress is made of antelope skin, white as snow, and perhaps ornamented with two or three hundred elk tushes. Her leggings are of deer skin, heavily beaded and nicely fringed, and often adorned with bells and brass buttons. Her summer blanket or sheet is an elk skin, well tanned, without the hair and with the dew-claws left on. Her moccasins are of deer skin, with parfleche soles and worked with porcupine quills. The marriage takes place as soon as these things can be provided.

During the days which intervene between the proposal and the marriage, the young woman each day selects the choicest parts of the meat brought to the lodge, — the tongue, " boss ribs," some choice berry pemmican or what not, — cooks these things in the best style, and, either alone, or in company with a young sister, or a young friend, goes over to the lodge where the young man lives, and places the food before him. He eats some of it, little or much, and if he leaves anything, the girl offers it to his mother, who may eat of it. Then the girl takes the dishes and returns to her father's lodge. In this way she provides him with three meals a day, morning, noon, and night, until the marriage takes place. Every one in camp who sees the girl carrying the food in a covered dish to the young man's lodge, knows that a marriage is to take place ; and the girl is watched by idle persons as she passes to and fro, so that the task is quite a trying one for people as shy and bashful as Indians are. When the time for the marriage has come, — in other words, when the girl's parents are ready, — the girl, her mother assisting her, packs the new lodge and her own things on the horses, and moves out into the middle of the circle — about which all the lodges of the tribe are arranged — and there the new lodge is unpacked and set up. In front of the lodge are tied, let us say, fifteen horses, the girl's dowry given by her father. Very likely, too, the father has sent over to the young man his own war clothing and arms, a lance, a fine shield, a bow and arrows in otter-skin case, his war bonnet, war shirt, and war leggings ornamented with scalps, — his complete equipment. This is set up on a tripod in front of the lodge. The gift of these things is an evidence of the great respect felt by the girl's father for his son-in-law. As soon as the young man has seen the preparations being made for setting up the girl's lodge in the centre of the circle, he sends over to his father-in-law's lodge just twice the number of horses that the girl brought with her, — in this supposed case, thirty.

As soon as this lodge is set up, and the girl's mother has taken her departure and gone back to her own lodge, the young man, who, until he saw these preparations, had no knowledge of when the marriage was to take place, leaves his father's lodge, and, going over to the newly erected one, enters and takes his place at the back of it. Probably during the day he will order his wife to take down the lodge, and either move away from the camp, or at least move into the circle of lodges ; for he will not want to remain with his young wife in the most conspicuous place in the camp. Often, on the same day, he will send for six or eight of his friends, and, after feasting them, will announce his intention of going to war, and will start off the same night.   If he does so, and is successful, returning with horses or scalps, or both, he at once, on arrival at the camp, proceeds to his father-in-law's lodge and leaves there everything he has brought back, returning to his own lodge on foot, as poor as he left it.

We have supposed the proposal in this case to come from the father of the girl, but if a boy desires a particular girl for his wife, the proposal will come from his father ; otherwise matters are managed in the same way.

This ceremony of moving into the middle of the circle was only performed in the case of important people.   The custom was observed in what might be called a fashionable wedding among the Blackfeet.   Poorer, less important people married more quietly.   If the girl had reached marriageable age without having been asked for as a wife, she might tell her mother that she would like to marry a certain young man, that he was a man she could love and respect. The mother communicates this to the father of the girl, who invites the young man to the lodge to a feast, and proposes the match.   The young man returns no answer at the time, but, going back to his father's lodge, tells him of the offer, and expresses his feelings about it.   If he is inclined to accept, the relations are summoned, and the matter talked over.   A favorable answer being returned, a certain number of horses — what the young man or his father, or both together, can spare — are sent over to the girl's father. They send as many as they can, for the more they send, the more they are thought of and looked up to.   The girl, unless her parents are very poor, has her outfit, a saddle horse and pack horse with saddle and pack saddle, parfleches, etc. If the people are very poor, she may have only a riding horse.   Her relations get together, and do all in their power to give her a good fitting out, and the father, if he can possibly do so, is sure to pay them back what they have given.

If he cannot do so, the things are still presented ; for, in the case of a marriage, the relations on both sides are anxious to do all that they can to give the young people a good start in life.   When all is ready, the girl goes to the lodge where her husband lives, and goes in.   If this lodge is too crowded to receive the couple, the young man will make arrangements for space in the lodge of a brother, cousin, or uncle, where there is more room.   These are all his close relations, and he is welcome in any of their lodges, and has rights there.

Sometimes, if two young people are fond of each other, and there is no prospect of their being married, they may take riding horses and a pack horse, and elope at night, going to some other camp for a while.   This makes the girl's father angry, for he feels that he has been defrauded of his payments.   The young man knows that his father-in-law bears him a grudge, and if he afterwards goes to war and is successful, returning with six or seven horses, he will send them all to the camp where his father-in-law lives, to be tied in front of his lodge.   This at once heals the breach, and the couple may return.   Even if he has not been successful in war and brought horses, which of course he does not always accomplish, he from time to time sends the old man a present, the best he can.   Notwithstanding these efforts at conciliation, the parents feel very bitterly against him.   The girl has been stolen.   The union is no marriage at all.   The old people are ashamed and disgraced for their daughter.   Until the father has been pacified by satisfactory payments, there is no marriage.   Moreover, unless the young man had made a payment, or at least had endeavored to do so, he would be little thought of among his fellows, and looked down on as a poor creature without any sense of honor.

The Blackfeet take as many wives as they wish ; but these ceremonies are only carried out in the case of the first wife, the " sits-beside-him " woman.   In the case of subsequent marriages, if the man had proved a good, kind husband to his first wife, other men, who thought a good deal of their daughters, might propose to give them to him, so that they would be well treated. The man sent over the horses to the new father-in-law's lodge, and the girl returned to his, bringing her things with her. Or if the man saw a girl he liked, he would propose for her to her father.

Among the Blackfeet, there was apparently no form of courtship, such as prevails among our southern Indians. Young men seldom spoke to young girls who were not relations, and the girls were carefully guarded. They never went out of the lodge after dark, and never went out during the day, except with the mother or some other old woman. The girl, therefore, had very little choice in the selection of a husband. If a girl was told she must marry a certain man, she had to obey. She might cry, but her father's will was law, and she might be beaten or even killed by him, if she did not do as she was ordered. As a consequence of this severity, suicide was quite common among the Blackfoot girls. A girl ordered to marry a man whom she did not like would often watch her chance, and go out in the brush and hang herself. The girl who could not marry the man she wanted to was likely to do the same thing.

The man had absolute power over his wife. Her life was in his hands, and if he had made a payment for her, he could do with her about as he pleased. On the whole, however, women who behaved themselves were well treated and received a good deal of consideration. Those who were light-headed, or foolish, or obstinate and stubborn were sometimes badly beaten. Those who were unfaithful to their husbands usually had their noses or ears, or both, cut off for the first offence, and were killed either by the husband or some relation, or by the *I-kun-uh'-kah-tsi* for the second. Many of the doctors of the highest reputation in the tribe were women.

It is a common belief among some of those who have investigated the subject that the wife in Indian marriage was actually purchased, and became the absolute property of her husband. Though I have a great respect for some of the opinions which have been expressed on this subject, I am obliged to take an entirely different view of the matter. I have talked this subject over many times with young men and old men of a number of tribes, and I cannot learn from them, or in any other way, that in primitive times the woman was purchased from her father. The husband did not have property rights in his wife. She was not a chattel that he could trade away. He had all personal rights, could beat his wife, or, for cause, kill her, but he could not sell her to another man.

All the younger sisters of a man's wife were regarded as his potential wives. If he was not disposed to marry them, they could not be disposed of to any other man without his consent.

Not infrequently, a man having a marriageable daughter formally gave her to some young man who had proved himself brave in war, successful in taking horses, and, above all, of a generous disposition. This was most often done by men who had no sons to support them in their old age.

It is said that in the old days, before they had horses, young men did not expect to marry until they had almost reached middle life, — from thirty-five to forty years of age. This statement is made by Wolf Calf, who is now very old, almost one hundred years, he believes, and can remember back nearly or quite to the time when the Blackfeet obtained their first horses. In those days, young women did not marry until they were grown up, while of late years fathers not infrequently sell their daughters as wives when they are only children.

The first woman a man marries is called his sits-beside-him wife. She is invested with authority over all the other wives, and does little except to direct the others in their work, and look after the comfort of her husband. Her place in the lodge is on his right-hand side, while the others have their places or seats near the door-way. This wife is even allowed at informal gatherings to take a whiff at the pipe, as it is passed around the circle, and to participate in the conversation.

In the old days, it was a very poor man who did not have three wives. Many had six, eight, and some more than a dozen. I have heard of one who had sixteen. In those times, provided a man had a good-sized band of horses, the more wives he had, the richer he was. He could always find young men to hunt for him, if he furnished the mounts, and, of course, the more wives he had, the more robes and furs they would tan for him.

If, for any cause, a man wished to divorce himself from a woman, he had but to send her back to her parents and demand the price paid for her, and the matter was accomplished. The woman was then free to marry again, provided her parents were willing.

When a man dies, his wives become the potential wives of his oldest brother. Unless, during his life, he has given them outright horses and other property, at his death they are entitled to none of his possessions. If he has sons, the property is divided among them, except a few horses, which are given to his brothers. If he has no sons, all the property goes to his brothers, and if there are no brothers, it goes to the nearest male relatives on the father's side.

The Blackfeet cannot be said to have been slave-holders. It is true that the Crees call the Blackfeet women " Little Slaves." But this, as elsewhere suggested, may refer to the region whence they originally came, though it is often explained that it is on account of the manner in which the Blackfeet treat their women, killing them or mutilating their features for adultery and other serious offences.

Although a woman, all her life, was subject to some one's orders, either parent, relative, or husband, a man from his earliest childhood was free and independent. His father would not punish him for any misconduct, his mother dared not. At an early age he was taught to ride and shoot, and horses were given to him. By the time he was twelve, he had probably been on a war expedition or two. As a rule in later times, young men married when they were seventeen or eighteen years of age; and often they resided for several years with their fathers, until the family became so large that there was not room for them all in the lodge.

There were always in the camp a number of boys, orphans, who became the servants of wealthy men for a consideration; that is, they looked after their patron's horses and hunted, and in return they were provided with suitable food and clothing.

Among the Blackfeet, all men were free and equal, and office was not hereditary. Formerly each gens was governed by a chief, who was entitled to his office by virtue of his bravery and generosity. The head chief was chosen by the chiefs of the gentes from their own number, and was usually the one who could show the best record in war, as proved at the Medicine Lodge,[1] at which time he was elected; and for the ensuing year he was invested with the supreme power. But no matter how brave a man might have been, or how successful in war, he could not hope to be the chief either of a gens or of the tribe, unless he was kind-hearted, and willing to share his prosperity with the poor. For this reason, a chief was never a wealthy man, for what he acquired with one hand he gave away with the other. It was he who decided when the people should move camp, and where they should go. But in this, as in all other important affairs, he generally asked the advice of the minor chiefs.

The *I-kun-uh'-kah-tsi* (All Comrades) were directly under

---

[1] See chapter on Religion.

the authority of the head chief, and when any one was to be punished, or anything else was to be done which came within their province as the tribal police, it was he who issued the orders. The following were the crimes which the Blackfeet considered sufficiently serious to merit punishment, and the penalties which attached to them.

Murder: A life for a life, or a heavy payment by the murderer or his relatives at the option of the murdered man's relatives. This payment was often so heavy as absolutely to strip the murderer of all property.

Theft: Simply the restoration of the property.

Adultery: For the first offence the husband generally cut off the offending wife's nose or ears; for the second offence she was killed by the All Comrades. Often the woman, if her husband complained of her, would be killed by her brothers or first cousins, and this was more usual than death at the hands of the All Comrades. However, the husband could have her put to death for the first offence, if he chose.

Treachery (that is, when a member of the tribe went over to the enemy or gave them any aid whatever) : Death at sight.

Cowardice: A man who would not fight was obliged to wear woman's dress, and was not allowed to marry.

If a man left camp to hunt buffalo by himself, thereby driving away the game, the All Comrades were sent after him, and not only brought him back by main force, but often whipped him, tore his lodge to shreds, broke his travois, and often took away his store of dried meat, pemmican, and other food.

The tradition of the origin of the *I-kun-uh'-kah-tsi* has elsewhere been given. This association of the All Comrades consisted of a dozen or more secret societies, graded according to age, the whole constituting an association which was in part benevolent and helpful, and in part military, but whose main function was to punish offences against society at large. All these societies were really law and order associations. The Mŭt'-sĭks, or Braves, was the chief society, but the others helped the Braves.

A number of the societies which made up the *I-kun-uh'-kah-tsi* have been abandoned in recent years, but several of them still exist. Among the Pi-kun'-i, the list — so far as I have it — is as follows, the societies being named in order from those of boyhood to old age : —

SOCIETIES OF THE ALL COMRADES

Tsĭ-stĭks',	Little Birds,	includes boys from 15 to 20 years old.
K'ŭk-kŭīks',	Pigeons,	men who have been to war several times.
Tŭis-kĭs'-tĭks,	Mosquitoes,	men who are constantly going to war.
Mŭt'-sĭks,	Braves,	tried warriors.
Knăts-o-mi'-ta,	All Crazy Dogs,	about forty years old.
Ma-stoh'-pa-ta-kĭks	Raven Bearers.	.
E'-mi-taks,	Dogs,	⎤ old men. Dogs and Tails
		⎥ are different societies, but
Is'-sui,	Tails,	⎥ they dress alike and dance
		⎦ together and alike.
Ēts-kaī'-nah,	Horns, Bloods,	⎫ obsolete among the Piegans,
Sĭn'-o-pah,	Kit-foxes, Piegans,	⎭ but still exists with Bloods.
Ē-in'-a-ke,	Catchers or Soldiers,	obsolete for 25 or 30 years, perhaps longer.
Stŭ'mĭks,	Bulls,	obsolete for 50 years.

There may be other societies of the All Comrades, but these are the only ones that I know of at present. The Mŭt'-sĭks, Braves, and the Knats-o-mi'-ta, All Crazy Dogs, still exist, but many of the others are being forgotten. Since the necessity for their existence has passed, they are no longer kept up. They were a part of the old wild life, and when the buffalo disappeared, and the Blackfeet came to live about an agency, and to try to work for a subsistence, the societies soon lost their importance.

The societies known as Little Birds, Mosquitoes, and Doves are not really bands of the All Comrades, but are societies among the boys and young men in imitation of the *I-kun-uh'-kah-tsi*, but of comparatively recent origin. Men not more than fifty years old can remember when these societies came into existence. Of all the societies of the *I-kun-uh'-kah-tsi*, the Sin'-o-pah, or Kit-fox band, has the strongest medicine. This corresponds to the Horns society among the Bloods. They are the same band with different names. They have certain peculiar secret and sacred ceremonies, not to be described here.

The society of the Stum'-īks, or Bulls, became obsolete more than fifty years ago. Their dress was very fine, — bulls' heads and robes.

The members of the younger society purchased individually, from the next older one, its rights and privileges, paying horses for them. For example, each member of the Mosquitoes would purchase from some member of the Braves his right of membership in the latter society. The man who has sold his rights is then a member of no society, and if he wishes to belong to one, must buy into the one next higher. Each of these societies kept some old men as members, and these old men acted as messengers, orators, and so on.

The change of membership from one society to another was made in the spring, after the grass had started. Two, three, or more lodge coverings were stretched over poles, making one very large lodge, and in this the ceremonies accompanying the changes took place.

In later times, the Braves were the most important and best known of any of the All Comrades societies. The members of this band were soldiers or police. They were the constables of the camp, and it was their duty to preserve order, and to punish offenders. Sometimes young men would skylark in camp at night, making a great noise when people wanted to sleep, and would play rough practical jokes, that were not at all relished by those who suffered from them. One of the forms which their high spirits took was to lead and p sh a young colt up to the door of a lodge, after people were asleep, and then, lifting the door, to shove the animal inside and close the door again. Of course the colt, in its efforts to get out to its mother, would run round and round the lodge, trampling over the sleepers and roughly awakening them, knocking things down and creating the utmost confusion, while the mare would be whinnying outside the lodge, and the people within, bewildered and confused, did not know what the disturbance was all about.

The Braves would punish the young men who did such things, — if they could catch them, — tearing up their blankets, taking away their property, and sometimes whipping them severely. They were the peace officers of the camp, like the *lari pūk'ūs* among the Pawnees.

Among the property of the Brave society were two stone-pointed arrows, one " shield you don't sit down with," and one rattle. The man who carried this rattle was known as Brave Dog, and if it passed from one member of the society to another, the new owner became known as Brave Dog. The man who received the shield could not sit down for the next four days and four nights, but for all that time was obliged to run about the camp, or over the prairie, whistling like a rabbit.

The societies known as Soldiers and Bulls had passed out of existence before the time of men now of middle age. The pipe of the Soldier society is still in existence, in the hands of Double Runner. The bull's head war bonnet, which was the insignia of the Bulls society, was formerly in the possession of Young Bear Chief, at present chief of the Don't Laugh band of the Piegans. He gave it to White Calf, who presented it to a recent agent.

In the old days, and, indeed, down to the time of the

disappearance of the buffalo, the camp was always arranged
in the form of a circle, the lodges standing at intervals
around the circumference, and in the wide inner space there
was another circle of lodges occupied by the chief of certain
bands of the *I-kun-uh'-kah-tsi*. When all the gentes of the
tribe were present, each had its special position in the
circle, and always occupied it. The lodge of the chief of
the gens stood just within the circle, and about it his people
camped. The order indicated in the accompanying diagram
represents the Piegan camp as it used to stand thirty-five
or forty years ago. A number of the gentes are now extinct,
and it is not altogether certain just what the position of
those should be ; for while all the older men agree on the
position to be assigned to certain of the gentes, there are
others about which there are differences of opinion or much
uncertainty. It is stated that the gentes known as Seldom
Lonesome, Dried Meat, and No Parfleche belong to that
section of the tribe known as North Piegans, which, at the
time of the first treaty, separated from the Pi-kŭn'-i, and
elected to live under British rule.

The lodges of the chiefs of the *I-kun-uh'-kah-tsi* which
were within the circle served as lounging and eating places
for such members of the bands as were on duty, and were
council lodges or places for idling, as the occasion demanded.

When the camp moved, the Blood gens moved first and
was followed by the White Breast gens, and so on around
the circle to number 24. On camping, the Bloods camped
first, and the others after them in the order indicated, number 24 camping last and closing up the circle.

Diagram of Old-time Piegan Camp, say 1850 to 1855. Twenty-
four Lodges of Chiefs of the Gentes about the Outer Circle.
The inner circle shows lodges of chiefs of certain bands of the *I-kun-uh'-kah-tsi*.

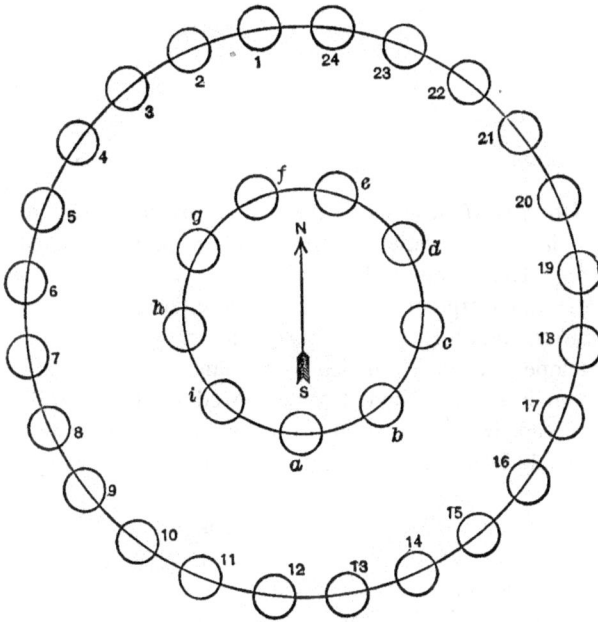

GENTES OF THE PI-KUN'-I

1. Blood People.
2. White Breasts.
3. Dried Meat.
4. Black Patched Moc-
   casins.
5. Black Fat Roasters.
6. Early Finished Eat-
   ing.
7. Don't Laugh.
8. Fat Roasters.
9. Black Doors.
10. Lone Eaters.
11. Skunks.
12. Seldom Lonesome.
13. Obstinate.
14. Lone Fighters.
15. Small Robes.
16. Big Topknots.
17. Worm People.
18. Small Brittle Fat.
19. Buffalo Dung.
20. No Parfleche.
21. Kill Close By.
22. All Chiefs.
23. Red Round Robes,
24. Many Medicines.

BANDS OF THE I-KUN-UH'-KAH-TSI

a. All Crazy Dogs.
b. Dogs.
c. Tails.
d. Kit-foxes.
e. Raven Bearers.
f. Braves.
g. Mosquitoes.
h. Soldiers.
i. Doves.

225

HUNTING

THE Blackfoot country probably contained more game and in greater variety than any other part of the continent. Theirs was a land whose physical characteristics presented sharp contrasts. There were far-stretching grassy prairies, affording rich pasturage for the buffalo and the antelope; rough breaks and bad lands for the climbing mountain sheep; wooded buttes, loved by the mule deer; timbered river bottoms, where the white-tailed deer and the elk could browse and hide; narrow, swampy valleys for the moose; and snow-patched, glittering pinnacles of rock, over which the sure-footed white goat took his deliberate way. The climate varied from arid to humid; the game of the prairie, the timber, and the rocks, found places suited to their habits. Fur-bearing animals abounded. Noisy hordes of wild fowl passed north and south in their migrations, and many stopped here to breed.

The Blackfoot country is especially favored by the warm chinook winds, which insure mild winters with but little snow; and although on the plains there is usually little rain in summer, the short prairie grasses are sweet and rich. All over this vast domain, the buffalo were found in countless herds. Elk, deer, antelope, mountain sheep, and bear without number were there. In those days, sheep were to be found on every ridge, and along the rough bad lands far from the mountains. Now, except a few in the " breaks " of the Missouri, they occur only on the highest and most inaccessible mountains, along with the white goats, which,

226

although pre-eminently mountain animals, were in early days sometimes found far out on the prairie.

Buffalo

The Blackfeet were a race of meat-eaters, and, while they killed large quantities of other game, they still depended for subsistence on the buffalo. This animal provided them with almost all that they needed in the way of food, clothing, and shelter, and when they had an abundance of the buffalo they lived in comfort.

Almost every part of the beast was utilized. The skin, dressed with the hair on, protected them from the winter's cold ; freed from the hair, it was used for a summer sheet or blanket, for moccasins, leggings, shirts, and women's dresses. The tanned cowskins made their lodges, the warmest and most comfortable portable shelters ever devised. From the rawhide, the hair having been shaved off, were made parfleches, or trunks, in which to pack small articles. The tough, thick hide of the bull's neck, spread out and allowed to shrink smooth, made a shield for war which would stop an arrow, and turn a lance thrust or the ball from an old-fashioned, smooth-bore gun. The green hide served as a kettle, in which to boil meat. The skin of the hind leg, cut off above the pastern and again some distance above the hock, was sometimes used as a moccasin or boot, the lower opening being sewed up for the toe. A variety of small articles, such as cradles, gun covers, whips, mittens, quivers, bow cases, knife-sheaths, etc., were made from the hide. Braided strands of hide furnished them with ropes and lines. The hair was used to stuff cushions and, later, saddles, and parts of the long black flowing beard to ornament wearing apparel and implements of war, such as shields and quivers. The horns gave them spoons and ladles — sometimes used as small dishes — and ornamented their war bonnets. From the hoofs they made a glue, which they used in fastening the

heads and feathers on their arrows, and the sinew backs
on their bows. The sinews which lie along the back
and on the belly were used as thread and string, and as
backing for bows to give them elasticity and strength.
From the ribs were made scrapers used in dressing hides,
and runners for small sledges drawn by dogs; and they
were employed by the children in coasting down hill
on snow or ice. The shoulder-blades, lashed to a wooden
handle, formed axes, hoes, and fleshers. From the cannon
bones (metatarsals and metacarpals) were made scrapers
for dressing hides. The skin of the tail, fitted on a stick,
was used as a fly brush. These are but a few of the uses to
which the product of the buffalo was put. As has been
said, almost every part of the flesh was eaten.

Now it must be remembered that in early days the hunting weapons of this people consisted only of stone-pointed
arrows, and with such armament the capture of game of the
larger sorts must have been a matter of some uncertainty.
To drive a rude stone-headed arrow through the tough hide
and into the vitals of the buffalo, could not have been —
even under the most favorable circumstances — other than
a difficult matter; and although we may assume that, in those
days, it was easy to steal up to within a few yards of the un-
suspicious animals, we can readily conceive that many arrows must have been shot without effect, for one that brought
down the game.

Certain ingenious methods were therefore devised to insure the taking of game in large numbers at one time. This
was especially the case with the buffalo, which were the food
and raiment of the people. One of these contrivances was
called pis'kun, deep-kettle; or, since the termination of the
word seems to indicate the last syllable of the word *ah'-pun*,
blood, it is more likely deep-blood-kettle. This was a large
corral, or enclosure, built out from the foot of a perpendicular cliff or bluff, and formed of natural banks, rocks, and

logs or brush, — anything in fact to make a close, high barrier. In some places the enclosure might be only a fence of brush, but even here the buffalo did not break it down, for they did not push against it, but ran round and round within, looking for a clear space through which they might pass. From the top of the bluff, directly over the pis'kun, two long lines of rock piles and brush extended far out on the prairie, ever diverging from each other like the arms of the letter V, the opening over the pis'kun being at the angle.

In the evening of the day preceding a drive of buffalo into the pis'kun a medicine man, usually one who was the possessor of a buffalo rock, In-is'-kim, unrolled his pipe, and prayed to the Sun for success. Next morning the man who was to call the buffalo arose very early, and told his wives that they must not leave the lodge, nor even look out, until he returned ; that they should keep burning sweet grass, and should pray to the Sun for his success and safety. Without eating or drinking, he then went up on the prairie, and the people followed him, and concealed themselves behind the rocks and bushes which formed the V, or chute. The medicine man put on a head-dress made of the head of a buffalo, and a robe, and then started out to approach the animals. When he had come near to the herd, he moved about until he had attracted the attention of some of the buffalo, and when they began to look at him, he walked slowly away toward the entrance of the chute. Usually the buffalo followed, and, as they did so, he gradually increased his pace. The buffalo followed more rapidly, and the man continually went a little faster. Finally, when the buffalo were fairly within the chute, the people began to rise up from behind the rock piles which the herd had passed, and to shout and wave their robes. This frightened the hindermost buffalo, which pushed forward on the others, and before long the whole herd was running at headlong speed toward the precipice, the rock piles directing them to the point over the enclosure. When they reached it, most of the animals were pushed over, and usually even the last of the band plunged blindly down into the pis'kun. Many were killed outright by the fall; others had broken legs or broken backs, while some perhaps were uninjured. The barricade, however, prevented them from escaping, and all were soon killed by the arrows of the Indians.

It is said that there was another way to get the buffalo into this chute. A man who was very skilful in arousing the buffalo's curiosity, might go out without disguise, and by wheeling round and round in front of the herd, appearing and disappearing, would induce them to move toward him, when it was easy to entice them into the chute. Once there, the people began to rise up behind them, shouting and waving their robes, and the now terror-stricken animals rushed ahead, and were driven over the cliff into the pis'kun, where all were quickly killed and divided among the people, the chiefs and the leading warrior getting the best and fattest animals.

The pis'kun was in use up to within thirty-five or forty years, and many men are still living who have seen the buffalo driven over the cliff. Such men even now speak with enthusiasm of the plenty that successful drives brought to the camp.

The pis'kuns of the Sik'-si-kau, or Blackfoot tribe, differed in some particulars from those constructed by the Bloods and the Piegans, who live further to the south, nearer to the mountains, and so in a country which is rougher and more broken. The Sik'-si-kau built their pis'kuns like the Crees, on level ground and usually near timber. A large pen or corral was made of heavy logs about eight feet high. On the side where the wings of the chute come together, a bridge, or causeway, was built, sloping gently up from the prairie to the walls of the corral, which at this point were cut away to the height of the bridge above the ground, — here about four feet, — so that the animals running up the causeway could jump down into the corral. The causeway was fenced in on either side by logs, so that the buffalo could not run off it. After they had been lured within the wings of the chute, they were driven toward the corral as already described. When they reached the end of the >, they ran up the bridge, and jumped down into the pen. When it was full, or all had entered, Indians, who had lain hidden near by, ran upon the bridge, and placed poles, prepared beforehand, across the opening through which the animals had entered, and over these poles hung robes, so as entirely to close the opening. The buffalo will not dash themselves against a barrier which is entirely closed, even though it be very frail; but if they can see through it to the outside, they will rush against it, and their great weight and strength make it easy for them to break down any but a heavy wall. Mr. Hugh Monroe tells me that he has seen a pis'kun built of willow brush; and the Cheyennes have stated to me that their buffalo corrals were often built of brush. Sometimes, if the walls of the pis'kun were not high, the buffalo tried to jump or climb over them, and, in doing this, might break them down, and some or all escape. As soon, however, as the animals were in the corral, the people — women and children included — ran up and showed themselves all about the walls, and by their cries kept the buffalo from pressing against the walls. The animals ran round and round within, and the men standing on the walls shot them down as they passed. The butchering was done in the pis'kun, and after this was over, the place was cleaned out, the heads, feet, and least perishable offal being removed. Wolves, foxes, badgers, and other small carnivorous animals visited the pis'kun, and soon made away with the entrails.

In winter, when the snow was on the ground, and the buffalo were to be led to the pis'kun, the following method was adopted to keep the herd travelling in the desired

direction after they had got between the wings of the chute.
A line of buffalo chips, each one supported on three small
sticks, so that it stood a few inches above the snow, was
carried from the mouth of the pis'kun straight out toward
the prairie. The chips were about thirty feet apart, and
ran midway between the wings of the chute. This line was,
of course, conspicuous against the white snow, and when the
buffalo were running down the chute, they always followed
it, never turning to the right nor to the left. In the latter
days of the pis'kun, the man who led the buffalo was often
mounted on a white horse.

Often, when they drove the buffalo over a high vertical
cliff, no corral was built beneath. Most of those driven
over were killed or disabled by the fall, and only a few got
away. The pis'kuns, as a rule, were built under low-cut
bluffs, and sometimes the buffalo were driven in by moon-
light.

In connection with the subject of leading or decoying the
buffalo, another matter not generally known may be mentioned. Sometimes, as a matter of convenience, a herd was
brought from a long distance close up to the camp. This
was usually done in the spring of the year, when the horses
were thin in flesh and not in condition to stand a long chase.
I myself have never seen this; but my friend, William
Jackson, was once present at such a drive by the Red River
half-breeds, and has described to me the way in which it
was done.

The camp was on Box Elder Creek near the Musselshell
River. It was in the spring of 1881, and the horses were
all pretty well run down and thin, so that their owners
wished to spare them as much as possible. The buffalo
were seven or eight miles distant, and two men were sent
out to bring them to the camp. Other men, leading fresh
horses, went with them, and hid themselves among the hills
at different points along the course that the buffalo were

expected to take, at intervals of a mile and a half. They watched the herd, and were on hand to supply the fresh horses to the men who were bringing it.

The buffalo were on a wide flat, and the men rode over the hill and advanced toward the herd at a walk. At length the buffalo noticed them, and began to huddle up together and to walk about, and at length to walk away. Then the men turned, and rode along parallel to the buffalo's course, and at the same gait that these were taking. When the buffalo began to trot, the men trotted, and when the herd began to lope, the men loped, and at length they were all running pretty fast. The men kept about half a mile from the herd, and up even with the leaders. As they ran, the herd kept constantly edging a little toward the riders, as if trying to cross in front of them. This inclination toward the men was least when they were far off, and greatest when they drew nearer to them. At no time were the men nearer to the herd than four hundred yards. If the buffalo edged too much toward the riders, so that the course they were taking would lead them away from camp, the men would drop back and cross over behind the herd to the other side, and then, pushing their horses hard, would come up with the leaders, — but still at a distance from them, — and then the buffalo would begin to edge toward them, and the herd would be brought back again to the desired course. If necessary, this was repeated, and so the buffalo were kept travelling in a course approximately straight.

By the time the buffalo had got pretty near to the camp, they were pretty well winded, and the tongues of many of them were hanging out. This herd was led up among the rolling hills about a mile from the camp, and there the people were waiting for them, and charged them, when the herd broke up, the animals running in every direction.

Occasionally it would happen that for a long time the

buffalo would not be found in a place favorable for driving
over the cliff or into a pen. In such cases, the Indians
would steal out on foot, and, on a day when there was no
wind, would stealthily surround the herd. Then they would
startle the buffalo, and yet would keep them from breaking
through the circle. The buffalo would "mill" around until
exhausted, and at length, when worn out, would be shot
down by the Indians. This corresponds almost exactly
with one of the methods employed in killing buffalo by the
Pawnees in early days before they had horses.[1] In those
days the Pi-kŭn'-i were very numerous, and sometimes when
a lot of buffalo were found in a favorable position, and there
was no wind, the people would surround them, and set up
their lodges about them, thus practically building a corral of
lodges. After all preparations had been made, they would
frighten the buffalo, which, being afraid to pass through
between the lodges, would run round and round in a great
circle, and when they were exhausted the people would kill
them.

Then they always had plenty of buffalo — if not fresh
meat, that which they had dried. For in winter they
would kill large numbers of buffalo, and would prepare
great stores of dried meat. As spring opened, the buffalo
would move down to the more flat prairie country away
from the pis'kuns. Then the Blackfeet would also move
away. As winter drew near, the buffalo would again move
up close to the mountains, and the Indians, as food began
to become scarce, would follow them toward the pis'kuns.
In the last of the summer and early autumn, they always had
runners out, looking for the buffalo, to find where they were,
and which way they were moving. In the early autumn, all
the pis'kuns were repaired and strengthened, so as to be in
good order for winter.

In the days before they had horses, and even in later

[1] Pawnee Hero Stories and Folk-Tales, p. 250.

times when the ground was of such a character as to prevent running the buffalo, an ingenious method of still-hunt-
ing them was practised. A story told by Hugh Monroe
illustrates it. He said: "I was often detailed by the
Hudson's Bay Company to go out in charge of a number of
men, to kill meat for the fort. When the ground was full
of holes and wash-outs, so that running was dangerous, I
used to put on a big timber wolf's skin, which I carried for
the purpose, tying it at my neck and waist, and then to sneak
up to the buffalo. I used a bow and arrows, and generally
shot a number without alarming them. If one looked sus-
piciously at me, I would howl like a wolf. Sometimes the
smell of the blood from the wounded and dying would set
the bulls crazy. They would run up and lick the blood,
and sometimes toss the dead ones clear from the ground.
Then they would bellow and fight each other, sometimes
goring one another so badly that they died. The great
bulls, their tongues covered with blood, their eyes flashing,
and tails sticking out straight, roaring and fighting, were terrible to see; and it was a little dangerous for me, because
the commotion would attract buffalo from all directions to
see what was going on. At such times, I would signal to
my men, and they would ride up and scare the buffalo
away."

In more modern times, the height of pleasure to a Blackfoot was to ride a good horse and run buffalo. When bows
and arrows, and, later, muzzle-loading "fukes" were the
only weapons, no more buffalo were killed than could actually be utilized. But after the Winchester repeater came
in use, it seemed as if the different tribes vied with each
other in wanton slaughter. Provided with one of these
weapons and a couple of belts of cartridges, the hunters
would run as long as their horses could keep up with the
band, and literally cover the prairie with carcasses, many of
which were never even skinned.

Antelope

It is said that once in early times the men determined that they would use antelope skins for their women's dresses, instead of cowskins. So they found a place where antelope were plenty, and set up on the prairie long lines of rock piles, or of bushes, so as to form a chute like a >. Near the point where the lines joined, they dug deep pits, which they roofed with slender poles, and covered these with grass and a little dirt. Then the people scattered out, and while most of them hid behind the rock piles and bushes, a few started the antelope toward the mouth of the chute. As they ran by them, the people showed themselves and yelled, and the antelope ran down the chute and finally reached the pits, and falling into them were taken, when they were killed and divided among the hunters. Afterward, this was the common method of securing antelopes up to the coming of the whites.

Eagles

Before the whites came to the Blackfoot country, the Indian standard of value was eagle tail-feathers. They were used to make war head-dresses, to tie on the head, and to ornament shields, lances, and other weapons. Besides this, the wings were used for fans, and the body feathers for arrow-making. Always a wary bird, the eagle could seldom be approached near enough for killing with the bow and arrow ; and, in fact, it seems as if it was considered improper to kill it in that way. The capture of these birds appears to have had about it something of a sacred nature, and, as was always the case among wild Indians when anything important was to be undertaken, it was invariably preceded by earnest prayers to the Deity for help and for success.

There are still living many men who have caught eagles in the ancient method, and, from several of these, accounts have been received, which, while essentially similar, yet differ in certain particulars, especially in the explanations of certain features of the ceremony.

Wolf Calf's account of this ceremony is as follows : —

"A man who started out to catch eagles moved his lodge and his family away from the main camp, to some place where the birds were abundant. A spot was chosen on top of a mound or butte within a few miles of his lodge, and here he dug a pit in the ground as long as his body and somewhat deeper. The earth removed was carried away to a distance, and scattered about so as to make no show. When the pit had been made large enough, it was roofed over with small willow sticks, on which grass was scattered, and over the grass a little earth and stones were laid, so as to give the place a natural look, like the prairie all about it.

"The bait was a piece of bloody neck of a buffalo. This, of course, could be seen a long way off, and by the meat a stuffed wolf skin was often placed, standing up, as if the animal were eating. To the piece of neck was tied a rope, which passed down through the roof of the pit and was held in the watcher's hand.

"After all had been made ready, the next day the man rose very early, before it was light, and, after smoking and praying, left his camp, telling his wives and children not to use an awl while he was gone. He endeavored to reach the pit early in the morning, before it became light, and lay down in it, taking with him a slender stick about six feet long, a human skull, and a little pemmican. Then he waited.

"When the morning came, and the eagles were flying, one of them would see the meat and descend to take it away from the wolf. Finding it held fast by the rope, the bird began to feed on it ; and while it was pecking at the bait, the watcher seized it by the legs, and drew it into the pit, where he killed it, either by twisting its neck, or by crushing it with his knees. Then he laid it to one side, first opening the bill and putting a little piece of pemmican in its mouth. This was done to make the other eagles hungry. While he was in the pit, the man neither ate, drank, nor slept. He had a sleeping-place not far off, to which he repaired each night after dark, and there he ate and drank.

"The reason for taking the skull into the hole with the catcher was, in part, for his protection. It was believed that the ghost of the person to whom the skull had belonged would protect the watcher against harm from the eagle, and besides that, the skull, or ghost, would make the watcher invisible, like a ghost. The eagle would not see him.

"The stick was used to poke or drive away smaller birds, such as magpies, crows, and ravens, which might alight on the roof of the pit, and try to feed on the bait. It was used, also, to drive away the white-headed eagle, which they did not care to catch. These are powerful birds; they could almost kill a person.

"There are two sacred things connected with the catching of eagles, — two things which must be observed if the eagle-catcher is to have good luck. The man who is watching must not eat rosebuds. If he does, the eagle, when he comes down and alights by the bait, will begin to scratch himself and will not attack the bait. The rosebuds will make him itch. Neither the man nor his wife must use an awl while he is absent from his lodge, and is trying to catch the birds. If this is done, the eagles will scratch the catcher. Sometimes one man would catch a great many eagles."

In his day, John Monroe was a famous eagle-catcher, and he has given me the following account of the method as he has practised it. The pit is dug, six feet long, three wide, and four deep, on top of the highest knoll that can be found near a stream. The earth taken out is carried a long way off. Over the pit they put two long poles, one on each side, running lengthwise of the pit, and other smaller sticks are laid across, resting on the poles. The smaller sticks are covered with juniper twigs and long grass. The skin of a wolf, coyote, or fox, is stuffed with grass, and made to look as natural as possible. A hole is cut in the wolf skin and a rope is passed through it, one end being tied to a large piece of meat which lies by the skin, and the other passing through the roof down into the pit. The bait is now covered with grass, and the man returns to his lodge for the night.

During the night, he sings his eagle songs and burns sweet grass for the eagles, rubbing the smoke over his own body to purify himself, so that on the morrow he will give out no scent. Before day he leaves his lodge without eating or drinking, goes to the pit and lies down in it. He uncovers the bait, arranges the roof, and sits there all day holding the rope. Crows and other birds alight by the bait and peck at it, but he pays no attention to them.

The eagle, sailing about high in air, sees the bait, and settles down slowly. It takes it a long time to make up its mind to come to the bait. In the pit, the man can hear the sound of the eagle coming. When the bird settles on the ground, it does not alight on the bait, but at one side of it, striking the ground with a thud—heavily. The man never mistakes anything else for that sound. The eagle walks toward the bait, and all the other birds fly away. It walks on to the roof; and, through the crevices that have been left between the sticks, the man can see in which direction the bird's head is. He carefully pushes the stick aside and, reaching out, grasps the eagle by the two feet. The bird does not struggle much. It is drawn down into the pit, and the man wrings its neck. Then the opening is closed, and the roof arranged as before. So the man waits and catches the eagles that come through the day. Sometimes he sits all day and gets nothing; again he may get eight or ten in a day.

When darkness comes, the man leaves his hiding-place,

takes his eagles, and goes home. He carries the birds to a special lodge, prepared outside of the camp, which is called the eagles' lodge. He places them on the ground in a row, and raises their heads, resting them on a stick laid in front of the row. In the mouth of each one is put a piece of pemmican, so that they may not be afraid of the people. The object of feeding the eagles is that their spirits may tell other eagles how they are being treated — that they are being fed by the people. In the lodge is a human skull, and they pray to it, asking the ghost to help them get the eagles.

It is said that in one pit, once, forty eagles were killed in a day. The larger hawks were caught, as well as eagles, though the latter were the most highly valued. Five eagles used to be worth a good horse, a valuation which shows that, in the Blackfoot country, eagles were more plenty, or horses more valuable, than farther south, where, in old times, two eagles would purchase a horse.

Other Game

They had no special means of capturing deer in any numbers. These were usually killed singly. The hunters used to creep up on elk and deer in the brush, and when they had come close to them, they could drive even their stone-pointed arrows deep in the flesh. Often their game was killed dead on the spot, but if not, they left it alone until the next day, when, on going back to the place, it was usually found near by, either dead or so desperately wounded that they could secure it.

Deadfalls were used to catch wolves, foxes, and other fur animals, and small apertures in the pis'kun walls were provided with nooses and snares for the same purpose.

Another way to catch wolves and coyotes was to set heavy stakes in the ground in a circle, about the carcasses of one or two dead buffalo. The stakes were placed at an angle of about forty-five degrees, a few inches apart, and all pointing toward the centre of the circle. At one place, dirt was piled up against the stakes from the outside, and the wolves, climbing up on this, jumped down into the enclosure, but were unable to jump out. Hugh Monroe tells me that, about thirty years ago, he and his sons made a trap like this, and in one night caught eighty-three wolves and coyotes.

In early times, beaver were very abundant and very tame, and were shot with bows and arrows.

The Blackfeet were splendid prairie hunters. They had no superiors in the art of stalking and killing such wary animals as the antelope. Sometimes they wore hats made of the skin and horns of an antelope head, which were very useful when approaching the game. Although the prairie was pre-eminently their hunting-ground, they were also skilful in climbing mountains and killing sheep and goats. On the other hand, the northern Crees, who also are a prairie people, are poor mountain hunters.

THE BLACKFOOT IN WAR

THE Blackfeet were a warlike people. How it may have been in the old days, before the coming of the white men, we do not know. Very likely, in early times, they were usually at peace with neighboring tribes, or, if quarrels took place, battles were fought, and men killed, this was only in angry dispute over what each party considered its rights. Their wars were probably not general, nor could they have been very bloody. When, however, horses came into the possession of the Indians, all this must have soon become changed. Hitherto there had really been no incentive to war. From time to time expeditions may have gone out to kill enemies, — for glory, or to take revenge for some injury, — but war had not yet been made desirable by the hope of plunder, for none of their neighbors — any more than themselves — had property which was worth capturing and taking away. Primitive arms, dogs, clothing, and dried meat were common to all the tribes, and were their only possessions, and usually each tribe had an abundance of all these. It was not worth any man's while to make long journeys and to run into danger merely to increase his store of such property, when his present possessions were more than sufficient to meet all his wants. Even if such things had seemed desirable plunder, the amount of it which could be carried away was limited, since — for a war party — the only means of transporting captured articles from place to place was on men's backs, nor could men burdened with loads either run or fight. But when horses became known,

and the Indians began to realize what a change the possession of these animals was working in their mode of life, when
they saw that, by enormously increasing the transporting
power of each family, horses made far greater possessions
practicable, that they insured the food supply, rendered the
moving of the camp easier and more rapid, made possible
long journeys with a minimum of effort, and that they had a
value for trading, the Blackfoot mind received a new idea,
the idea that it was desirable to accumulate property. The
Blackfoot saw that, since horses could be exchanged for
everything that was worth having, no one had as many horses
as he needed. A pretty wife, a handsome war bonnet, a
strong bow, a finely ornamented woman's dress, — any or all
of these things a man might obtain, if he had horses to
trade for them. The gambler at "hands," or at the ring
game, could bet horses. The man who was devoted to his
last married wife could give her a horse as an evidence of
his affection.

We can readily understand what a change the advent of
the horse must have worked in the minds of a people like
the Blackfeet, and how this changed mental attitude would
react on the Blackfoot way of living. At first, there were
but few horses among them, but they knew that their neighbors to the west and south — across the mountains and on
the great plains beyond the Missouri and the Yellowstone —
had plenty of them; that the Kūtenais, the Kalispels, the
Snakes, the Crows, and the Sioux were well provided. They
soon learned that horses were easily driven off, and that,
even if followed by those whose property they had taken,
the pursued had a great advantage over the pursuers; and
we may feel sure that it was not long before the idea of
capturing horses from the enemy entered some Blackfoot
head and was put into practice.

Now began a systematic sending forth of war parties against
neighboring tribes for the purpose of capturing horses, which

continued for about seventy-five or eighty years, and has only been abandoned within the last six or seven, and since the settlement of the country by the whites made it impossible for the Blackfeet longer to pass backward and forward through it on their raiding expeditions. Horse-taking at once became what might be called an established industry among the Blackfeet. Success brought wealth and fame, and there was a pleasing excitement about the war journey. Except during the bitterest weather of the winter, war parties of Blackfeet were constantly out, searching for camps of their enemies, from whom they might capture horses. Usually the only object of such an expedition was to secure plunder, but often enemies were killed, and sometimes the party set out with the distinct intention of taking both scalps and horses.

Until some time after they had obtained guns, the Blackfeet were on excellent terms with the northern Crees, but later the Chippeways from the east made war on the Blackfeet, and this brought about general hostilities against all Crees, which have continued up to within a few years. If I recollect aright, the last fight which occurred between the Pikun'-i and the Crees took place in 1886. In this skirmish, which followed an attempt by the Crees to capture some Piegan horses, my friend, Tail-feathers-coming-in-sight-over-the-Hill, killed and counted *coup* on a Cree whose scalp he afterward sent me, as an evidence of his prowess.

The Gros Ventres of the prairie, of Arapaho stock, known to the Blackfeet as *At-séna*, or Gut People, had been friends and allies of the Blackfeet from the time they first came into the country, early in this century, up to about the year 1862, when, according to Clark, peace was broken through a mistake.[1] A war party of Snakes had gone to a Gros Ventres camp near the Bear Paw Mountains and there killed two Gros Ventres and taken a white pony, which they subse-

[1] Indian Sign Language, p. 70.

quently gave to a party of Piegans whom they met, and with whom they made peace. The Gros Ventres afterward saw this horse in the Piegan camp and supposed that the latter had killed their tribesman, and this led to a long war. In the year 1867, the Piegans defeated the allied Crows and Gros Ventres in a great battle near the Cypress Mountains, in which about 450 of the enemy are said to have been killed.

An expression often used in these pages, and which is so familiar to one who has lived much with Indians as to need no explanation, is the phrase to count *coup*. Like many of the terms common in the Northwest, this one comes down to us from the old French trappers and traders, and a *coup* is, of course, a blow. As commonly used, the expression is almost a direct translation of the Indian phrase to strike the enemy, which is in ordinary use among all tribes. This striking is the literal inflicting a blow on an individual, and does not mean merely the attack on a body of enemies.

The most creditable act that an Indian can perform is to show that he is brave, to prove, by some daring deed, his physical courage, his lack of fear. In practice, this courage is shown by approaching near enough to an enemy to strike or touch him with something that is held in the hand — to come up within arm's length of him. To kill an enemy is praiseworthy, and the act of scalping him may be so under certain circumstances, but neither of these approaches in bravery the hitting or touching him with something held in the hand. This is counting *coup*.

The man who does this shows himself without fear and ·is respected accordingly. With certain tribes, as the Pawnees, Cheyennes, and others, it was not very uncommon for a warrior to dash up to an enemy and strike him before making any attempt to injure him, the effort to kill being secondary to the *coup*. The blow might be struck with anything held in the hand, — a whip, coupstick, club, lance,

the muzzle of a gun, a bow, or what not. It did not necessarily follow that the person on whom the *coup* had been
counted would be injured. The act was performed in the
case of a woman, who might be captured, or even on a
child, who was being made prisoner.

Often the dealing the *coup* showed a very high degree
of courage. As already implied, it might be counted on a
man who was defending himself most desperately, and was
trying his best to kill the approaching enemy, or, even if
the attempt was being made on a foe who had fallen, it was
never certain that he was beyond the power of inflicting injury.
He might be only wounded, and, just when the enemy had
come close to him, and was about to strike, he might have
strength enough left to raise himself up and shoot him dead.
In their old wars, the Indians rarely took men captive. The
warrior never expected quarter nor gave it, and usually men
fought to the death, and died mute, defending themselves to
the last — to the last, striving to inflict some injury on the
enemy.

The striking the blow was an important event in a man's
life, and he who performed this feat remembered it. He
counted it. It was a proud day for the young warrior when
he counted his first *coup*, and each subsequent one was
remembered and numbered in the warrior's mind, just as
an American of to-day remembers the number of times he
has been elected to Congress. At certain dances and religious ceremonies, like that of the Medicine Lodge, the warriors counted — or rather re-counted — their *coups*.

While the *coup* was primarily, and usually, a blow with
something held in the hand, other acts in warfare which involved great danger to him who performed them were also
reckoned *coups* by some tribes. Thus, for a horseman to
ride over and knock down an enemy, who was on foot, was
regarded among the Blackfeet as a *coup*, for the horseman
might be shot at close quarters, or might receive a lance

thrust. It was the same to ride one's horse violently against a mounted foe. An old Pawnee told me of a *coup* that he had counted by running up to a fallen enemy and jumping on him with both feet. Sometimes the taking of horses counted a *coup*, but this was not always the case.

As suggested by what has been already stated, each tribe of the Plains Indians held its own view as to what constituted a *coup*. The Pawnees were very strict in their interpretation of the term, and with them an act of daring was not in itself deemed a *coup*. This was counted only when the person of an enemy was actually touched. One or two incidents which have occurred among the Pawnees will serve to illustrate their notions on this point.

In the year 1867, the Pawnee scouts had been sent up to Ogallalla, Nebraska, to guard the graders who were working on the Union Pacific railroad. While they were there, some Sioux came down from the hills and ran off a few mules, taking them across the North Platte. Major North took twenty men and started after them. Crossing the river, and following it up on the north bank, he headed them off, and before long came in sight of them.

The six Sioux, when they found that they were pursued, left the mules that they had taken, and ran ; and the Pawnees, after chasing them eight or ten miles, caught up with one of them, a brother of the well-known chief Spotted Tail. Baptiste Bahele, a half-breed Skidi, had a very fast horse, and was riding ahead of the other Pawnees, and shooting arrows at the Sioux, who was shooting back at him. At length Baptiste shot the enemy's horse in the hip, and the Indian dismounted and ran on foot toward a ravine. Baptiste shot at him again, and this time sent an arrow nearly through his body, so that the point projected in front. The Sioux caught the arrow by the point, pulled it through his body, and shot it back at his pursuer, and came very near hitting him. About that time, a ball from a carbine hit the Sioux and knocked him down.

Then there was a race between Baptiste and the Pawnee next behind him, to see which should count *coup* on the fallen man. Baptiste was nearest to him and reached him first, but just as he got to him, and was leaning over from his horse, to strike the dead man, the animal shied at the body, swerving to one side, and he failed to touch it. The horse ridden by the other Pawnee ran right over the Sioux, and his rider leaned down and touched him.

Baptiste claimed the *coup* — although acknowledging that he had not actually touched the man — on the ground that he had exposed himself to all the danger, and would have hit the man if his horse had not swerved as it did from the body ; but the Pawnees would not allow it, and all gave the credit of the *coup* to the other boy, because he had actually touched the enemy.

On another occasion three or four young men started on the warpath from the Pawnee village. When they came near to Spotted Tail's camp on the Platte River, they crossed the stream, took some horses, and got them safely across the river. Then one of the boys recrossed, went back to the camp, and cut loose another horse. He had almost got this one out of the camp, when an Indian came out of a lodge near by, and sat down. The Pawnee shot the Sioux, counted *coup* on him, scalped him, and then hurried across the river with the whole Sioux camp in pursuit. When the party returned to the Pawnee village, this boy was the only one who received credit for a *coup*.

Among the Blackfeet the capture of a shield, bow, gun, war bonnet, war shirt, or medicine pipe was deemed a *coup*.

Nothing gave a man a higher place in the estimation of the people than the counting of *coups*, for, I repeat, personal bravery is of all qualities the most highly respected by

Indians. On special occasions, as has been said, men counted over again in public their *coups*. This served to gratify personal vanity, and also to incite the young men to the performance of similar brave deeds. Besides this, they often made a more enduring record of these acts, by reproducing them pictographically on robes, cowskins, and other hides. There is now in my possession an illuminated cowskin, presented to me by Mr. J. Kipp, which contains the record of the *coups* and the most striking events in the life of Red Crane, a Blackfoot warrior, painted by himself. These pictographs are very rude and are drawn after the style common among Plains Indians, but no doubt they were sufficiently lifelike to call up to the mind of the artist each detail of the stirring events which they record.

The Indian warrior who stood up to relate some brave deed which he had performed was almost always in a position to prove the truth of his statements. Either he had the enemy's scalp, or some trophy captured from him, to produce as evidence, or else he had a witness of his feat in some companion. A man seldom boasted of any deed unless he was able to prove his story, and false statements about exploits against the enemy were most unusual. Temporary peace was often made between tribes usually at war, and, at the friendly meetings which took place during such times of peace, former battles were talked over, the performances of various individuals discussed, and the acts of particular men in the different fights commented on. In this way, if any man had falsely claimed to have done brave deeds, he would be detected.

An example of this occurred many years ago among the Cheyennes. At that time, there was a celebrated chief of the Skidi tribe of the Pawnee Nation whose name was Big Eagle. He was very brave, and the Cheyennes greatly feared him, and it was agreed among them that the man who could count *coup* on Big Eagle should be made war chief of the Cheyennes. After a fight on the Loup River, a Cheyenne warrior claimed to have counted *coup* on Big Eagle by thrusting a lance through his buttocks. On the strength of the claim, this man was made war chief of the Cheyennes. Some years later, during a friendly visit made by the Pawnees to the Cheyennes, this incident was mentioned. Big Eagle was present at the time, and, after inquiring into the matter, he rose in council, denied that he had ever been struck as claimed, and, throwing aside his robe, called on the Cheyennes present to examine his body and to point out the scars left by the lance. None were found. It was seen that Big Eagle spoke the truth; and the lying Cheyenne, from the proud position of war chief, sank to a point where he was an object of contempt to the meanest Indian in his tribe.

Among the Blackfeet a war party usually, or often, had its origin in a dream. Some man who has a dream, after he awakes tells of it. Perhaps he may say: "I dreamed that on a certain stream is a herd of horses that have been given to me, and that I am going away to get. I am going to war. I shall go to that place and get my band of horses." Then the men who know him, who believe that his medicine is strong and that he will have good luck, make up their minds to follow him. As soon as he has stated what he intends to do, his women and his female relations begin to make moccasins for him, and the old men among his relations begin to give him arrows and powder and ball to fit him out for war. The relations of those who are going with him do the same for them.

The leader notifies the young men who are going with him on what day and at what hour he intends to start. He determines the time for himself, but does not let the whole camp know it in advance. Of late years, large war parties have not been desirable. They have preferred to go out in small bodies.

Just before a war party sets out, its members get together and sing the " peeling a stick song," which is a wolf song. Then they build a sweat lodge and go into it, and with them goes in an old man, a medicine-pipe man, who has been a good warrior. They fill the pipe and ask him to pray for them, that they may have good luck, and may accomplish what they desire. The medicine-pipe man prays and sings and pours water on the hot stones, and the warriors with their knives slice bits of skin and flesh from their bodies, — their arms and breasts and sometimes from the tip of the tongue, — which they offer to the Sun. Then, after the ceremony is over, all dripping with perspiration from their vapor bath, the men go down to the river and plunge in.

In starting out, a war party often marches in the daytime, but sometimes they travel at night from the beginning. Often they may make an all night march across a wide prairie, in passing over which they might be seen if they travelled in the day. They journey on foot, always. The older men carry their arms, while the boys bear the moccasins, the ropes, and the food, which usually consists of dried meat or pemmican. They carry also coats and blankets and their war bonnets and otter skin medicine. The leader has but little physical labor to perform. His mind is occupied in planning the movements of his party. He is treated with the greatest respect. The others mend his moccasins, and give him the best of the food which they carry.

After they get away from the main camp, the leader selects the strongest of the young men, and sends him ahead to some designated butte, saying, " Go to that place, and look carefully over the country, and if you see nothing, make signals to us to come on." This scout goes on ahead, travelling in the ravines and coulées, and keeps himself well hidden. After he has reconnoitred and made signs that he sees nothing, the party proceeds straight toward him.

The party usually starts early in the morning and travels

all day, making camp at sundown.   During the day, if they
happen to come upon an antelope or a buffalo, they kill it,
if possible, and take some of the meat with them.   They try
in every way to economize their pemmican.   They always
endeavor to make camp in the thick timber, where they cannot be seen ; and here, when it is necessary, on account of
bad weather or for other reasons, they build a war lodge.
Taking four young cotton-woods or aspens, on which the
leaves are left, and lashing them together like lodge poles,
but with the butts up, about these they place other similar
trees, also butts up and untrimmed.   The leaves keep the
rain off, and prevent the light of the fire which is built
in the lodge from showing through.   Sometimes, when on
the prairie, where there is no wood, in stormy weather they
will build a shelter of rocks.   When the party has come
close to the enemy, or into a country where the enemy are
likely to be found, they build no more fires, but eat their
food uncooked.

When they see fresh tracks of people, or signs that enemies
are in the country, they stop travelling in the daytime and
move altogether by night, until they come to some good
place for hiding, and here they stop and sleep.   When day
comes, the leader sends out young men to the different
buttes, to look over the country and see if they can discover
the enemy.   If some one of the scouts reports that he has
seen a camp, and that the enemy have been found, the
leader directs his men to paint themselves and put on their
war bonnets.   This last is a figure of speech, since the war
bonnets, having of late years been usually ornamented with
brass bells, could not be worn in a secret attack, on account
of the noise they would make.   Before painting themselves, therefore, they untie their war bonnets, and spread
them out on the ground, as if they were about to be worn,
and then when they have finished painting themselves, tie
them up again.   When it begins to get dark, they start on

the run for the enemy's camp. They leave their food in camp, but carry their ropes slung over the shoulder and under the arm, whips stuck in belts, guns and blankets.

After they have crept up close to the lodges, the leader chooses certain men that have strong hearts, and takes them with him into the camp to cut loose the horses. The rest of the party remain outside the camp, and look about its outskirts, driving in any horses that may be feeding about, not tied up. Of those who have gone into the camp, some cut loose one horse, while others cut all that may be tied about a lodge. Some go only once into the camp, and some go twice to get the horses. When they have secured the horses, they drive them off a little way from the camp, at first going slowly, and then mount and ride off fast. Generally, they travel two nights and one day before sleeping.

This is the usual method of procedure of an ordinary expedition to capture horses, and I have given it very nearly in the language of the men who explained it to me.

In their hostile encounters, the Blackfeet have much that is common to many Plains tribes, and also some customs that are peculiar to themselves. Like most Indians, they are subject to sudden, apparently causeless, panics, while at other times they display a courage that is heroic. They are firm believers in luck, and will follow a leader who is fortunate in his expeditions into almost any danger. On the other hand, if the leader of a war party loses his young men, or any of them, the people in the camp think that he is unlucky, and does not know how to lead a war party. Young men will not follow him as a leader, and he is obliged to go as a servant or scout under another leader. He is likely never again to lead a war party, having learned to distrust his luck.

If a war party meets the enemy, and kills several of them, losing in the battle one of its own number, it is likely, as the phrase is, to "cover" the slain Blackfoot with all the

dead enemies save one, and to have a scalp dance over that
remaining one.   If a party had killed six of the enemy and
lost a man, it might "cover" the slain Blackfoot with five
of the enemy.   In other words, the five dead enemies would
pay for the one which the war party had lost.   So far,
matters would be even, and they would feel at liberty to
rejoice over the victory gained over the one that is left.

The Blackfeet sometimes cut to pieces an enemy killed
in battle.   If a Blackfoot had a relation killed by a member
of another tribe, and afterward killed one of this tribe, he
was likely to cut him all to pieces "to get even," that is,
to gratify his spite — to obtain revenge.   Sometimes, after
they had killed an enemy, they dragged his body into camp,
so as to give the children an opportunity to count *coup* on it.
Often they cut the feet and hands off the dead, and took
them away and danced over them for a long time.   Sometimes they cut off an arm or a leg, and often the head, and
danced and rejoiced over this trophy.

Women and children of hostile tribes were often captured,
and adopted into the Blackfoot tribes with all the rights and
privileges of indigenous members.   Men were rarely captured.   When they were taken, they were sometimes killed
in cold blood, especially if they had made a desperate
resistance before being captured.   At other times, the captive would be kept for a time, and then the chief would take
him off away from the camp, and give him provisions,
clothing, arms, and a horse, and let him go.   The captive
man always had a hard time at first.   When he was
brought into the camp, the women and children threw dirt
on him and counted *coups* on him, pounding him with sticks
and clubs.   He was rarely tied, but was always watched.
Often the man who had taken him prisoner had great
trouble to keep his tribesmen from killing him.

In the very early days of this century, war parties used
commonly to start out in the spring, going south to the land

where horses were abundant, being absent all summer and the next winter, and returning the following summer or autumn, with great bands of horses. Sometimes they were gone two years. They say that on such journeys they used to go to *Spai'yu ksah'ku*, which means the Spanish lands — *Spai'yu* being a recently made word, no doubt from the French *espagnol*. That they did get as far as Mexico, or at least New Mexico, is indicated by the fact that they brought back branded horses and a few branded mules; for in these early days there was no stock upon the Plains, and animals bearing brands were found only in the Spanish American settlements. The Blackfeet did not know what these marks meant. From their raids into these distant lands, they sometimes brought back arms of strange make, lances, axes, and swords, of a form unlike any that they had seen. The lances had broad heads; some of the axes, as described, were evidently the old "T. Gray" trade axes of the southwest. A sword, described as having a long, slender, straight blade, inlaid with a flower pattern of yellow metal along the back, was probably an old Spanish rapier.

In telling of these journeys to Spanish lands, they say of the very long reeds which grow there, that they are very large at the butt, are jointed, very hard, and very tall; they grow in marshy places; and the water there has a strange, mouldy smell.

It is said, too, that there have been war parties who have crossed the mountains and gone so far to the west that they have seen the big salt water which lies beyond, or west of, the Great Salt Lake. Journeys as far south as Salt Lake were not uncommon, and Hugh Monroe has told me of a war party he accompanied which went as far as this.

RELIGION

In ancient times the chief god of the Blackfeet—their
Creator—was *Na'pi* (Old Man). This is the word used to
indicate any old man, though its meaning is often loosely
given as white. An analysis of the word *Na'pi*, however,
shows it to be compounded of the word *Ni'nah*, man, and
the particle *a'pi*, which expresses a color, and which is never
used by itself, but always in combination with some other
word. The Blackfoot word for white is *Ksik-si-num'*, while
a'pi, though also conveying the idea of whiteness, really describes the tint seen in the early morning light when it first
appears in the east—the dawn—not a pure white, but
that color combined with a faint cast of yellow. *Na'pi*,
therefore, would seem to mean dawn-light-color-man, or
man-yellowish-white. It is easy to see why old men should
be called by this latter name, for it describes precisely the
color of their hair.

Dr. Brinton, in his valuable work, American Hero Myths,
has suggested a more profound reason why such a name
should be given to the Creator. He says: "The most important of all things to life is light. This the primitive
savage felt, and personifying it, he made light his chief god.
The beginning of day served, by analogy, for the beginning
of the world. Light comes before the Sun, brings it forth,
creates it, as it were. Hence the Light god is not the Sun
god but his antecedent and Creator."

It would be absurd to attribute to the Blackfoot of to-day
any such abstract conception of the name of the Creator as

256

that expressed in the foregoing quotation. The statement that Old Man was merely light personified would be beyond his comprehension, and if he did understand what was meant, he would laugh at it, and aver that *Na'pi* was a real man, a flesh and blood person like himself.

The character of Old Man, as depicted in the stories told of him by the Blackfeet, is a curious mixture of opposite attributes. In the serious tales, such as those of the creation, he is spoken of respectfully, and there is no hint of the impish qualities which characterize him in other stories, in which he is powerful, but also at times impotent ; full of all wisdom, yet at times so helpless that he has to ask aid from the animals. Sometimes he sympathizes with the people, and at others, out of pure spitefulness, he plays them malicious tricks that are worthy of a demon. He is a combination of strength, weakness, wisdom, folly, childishness, and malice.

Under various names Old Man is known to the Crees, Chippeways, and other Algonquins, and many of the stories that are current among the Blackfeet are told of him among those tribes. The more southern of these tribes do not venerate him as of old, but the Plains and Timber Crees of the north, and the north Chippeways, are said still to be firm believers in Old Man. He was their Creator, and is still their chief god. He is believed in less by the younger generation than the older. The Crees are regarded by the Indians of the Northwest as having very powerful medicine, and this all comes from Old Man.

Old Man can never die. Long ago he left the Blackfeet and went away to the West, disappearing in the mountains. Before his departure he told them that he would always take care of them, and some day would return. Even now, many of the old people believe that he spoke the truth, and that some day he will come back, and will bring with him the buffalo, which they believe the white men have hidden. It is sometimes said, however, that when he left them he told them also that, when he returned, he would find them changed — a different people and living in a different way from that which they practised when he went away. Sometimes, also, it is said that when he disappeared he went to the East.

It is generally believed that Old Man is no longer the principal god of the Blackfeet, that the Sun has taken his place. There is some reason to suspect, however, that the Sun and Old Man are one, that *Nātōs'* is only another name for *Na'pi*, for I have been told by two or three old men that "the Sun is the person whom we call Old Man." However this may be, it is certain that *Na'pi* — even if he no longer occupies the chief place in the Blackfoot religious system — is still reverenced, and is still addressed in prayer. Now, however, every good thing, success in war, in the chase, health, long life, all happiness, come by the special favor of the Sun.

The Sun is a man, the supreme chief of the world. The flat, circular earth in fact is his home, the floor of his lodge, and the over-arching sky is its covering. The moon, *Kŏ-kŏ-mik'-ē-ĭs*, night light, is the Sun's wife. The pair have had a number of children, all but one of whom were killed by pelicans. The survivor is the morning star, *A-pi-su'-ahts* — early riser.

In attributes the Sun is very unlike Old Man. He is a beneficent person, of great wisdom and kindness, good to those who do right. As a special means of obtaining his favor, sacrifices must be made. These are often presents of clothing, fine robes, or furs, and in extreme cases, when the prayer is for life itself, the offering of a finger, or — still dearer — a lock of hair. If a white buffalo was killed, the robe was always given to the Sun. It belonged to him. Of the buffalo, the tongue — regarded as the greatest delicacy of the whole animal — was especially sacred to the Sun.

The sufferings undergone by men in the Medicine Lodge each year were sacrifices to the Sun. This torture was an actual penance, like the sitting for years on top of a pillar, the wearing of a hair shirt, or fasting in Lent. It was undergone for no other purpose than that of pleasing God — as a propitiation or in fulfilment of vows made to him. Just as the priests of Baal slashed themselves with knives to induce their god to help them, so, and for the same reason, the Blackfoot men surged on and tore out the ropes tied to their skins. It is merely the carrying out of a religious idea that is as old as history and as widespread as the globe, and is closely akin to the motive which to-day, in our own centres of enlightened civilization, prompts acts of self-denial and penance by many thousands of intelligent cultivated people. And yet we are horrified at hearing described the tortures of the Medicine Lodge.

Besides the Sun and Old Man, the Blackfoot religious system includes a number of minor deities or rather natural qualities and forces, which are personified and given shape. These are included in the general terms Above Persons, Ground Persons, and Under Water Persons. Of the former class, Thunder is one of the most important, and is worshipped as is elsewhere shown. He brings the rain. He is represented sometimes as a bird, or, more vaguely, as in one of the stories, merely as a fearful person. Wind Maker is an example of an Under Water Person, and it is related that he has been seen, and his form is described. It is believed by some that he lives under the water at the head of the Upper St. Mary's Lake. Those who believe this say that when he wants the wind to blow, he makes the waves roll, and that these cause the wind to blow, — another example of mistaking effect for cause, so common among the Indians. The Ground Man is another below person. He lives under the ground, and perhaps typifies the power of the earth, which is highly respected by all Indians of the west. The

Cheyennes also have a Ground Man whom they call The Lower One, or Below Person (*Pun'-ŏ-tsĭ-hyo*). The cold and snow are brought by Cold Maker (*Ai'-so-yim-stan*). He is a man, white in color, with white hair, and clad in white apparel, who rides on a white horse. He brings the storm with him. They pray to him to bring, or not to bring, the storm.

Many of the animals are regarded as typifying some form of wisdom or craft. They are not gods, yet they have power, which, perhaps, is given them by the Sun or by Old Man. Examples of this are shown in some of the stories.

Among the animals especially respected and supposed to have great power, are the buffalo, the bear, the raven, the wolf, the beaver, and the kit-fox. Geese too, are credited with great wisdom and with foreknowledge of the weather. They are led by chiefs. As is quite natural among a people like the Blackfeet, the buffalo stood very high among the animals which they reverenced. It symbolized food and shelter, and was *Nato'yĕ* (of the Sun), sacred. Not a few considered it a medicine animal, and had it for their dream, or secret helper. It was the most powerful of all the animal helpers. Its importance is indicated by the fact that buffalo skulls were placed on the sweat houses built in connection with the Medicine Lodge. A similar respect for the buffalo exists among many Plains tribes, which were formerly dependent on it for food and raiment. A reverence for the bear appears to be common to all North American tribes, and is based not upon anything that the animal's body yields, but perhaps on the fact that it is the largest carnivorous mammal of the continent, the most difficult to kill and extremely keen in all its senses. The Blackfeet believe it to be part brute and part human, portions of its body, particularly the ribs and feet, being like those of a man. The raven is cunning. The wolf has great endurance and much craft. He can steal close to one without being seen. In the stories given in the earlier pages of this book, many of the attributes of the different animals are clearly set forth.

There were various powers and signs connected with these animals so held in high esteem by the Blackfeet, to which the people gave strict heed. Thus the raven has the power of giving people far sight. It was also useful in another way. Often, in going to war, a man would get a raven's skin and stuff the head and neck, and tie it to the hair of the head behind. If a man wearing such a skin got near the enemy without knowing it, the skin would give him warning by tapping him on the back of the head with its bill. Then he would know that the enemy was near, and would hide. If a raven flew over a lodge, or a number of lodges, and cried, and then was joined by other ravens, all flying over the camp and crying, it was a sure sign that during the day some one would come and tell the news from far off. The ravens often told the people that game was near, calling to the hunter and then flying a little way, and then coming back, and again calling and flying toward the game.

The wolves are the people's great friends; they travel with the wolves. If, as they are travelling along, they pass close to some wolves, these will bark at the people, talking to them. Some man will call to them, " No, I will not give you my body to eat, but I will give you the body of some one else, if you will go along with us." This applies both to wolves and coyotes. If a man goes away from the camp at night, and meets a coyote, and it barks at him, he goes back to the camp, and says to the people : " Look out now; be smart. A coyote barked at me to-night." Then the people look out, and are careful, for it is a sure sign that something bad is going to happen. Perhaps some one will be shot ; perhaps the enemy will charge the camp.

If a person is hungry and sings a wolf song, he is likely to find food. Men going on a hunting trip sing these songs, which bring them good luck.

The bear has very powerful medicine. Sometimes he takes pity on people and helps them, as in the story of Mik'-api.

Some Piegans, if they wish to travel on a certain day, have the power of insuring good weather on that day. It is supposed that they do this by singing a powerful song. Some of the enemy can cause bad weather, when they want to steal into the camp.

People who belonged to the *Sin'-o-pah* band of the *I-kun-uh'-kah-tsi*, if they were at war in summer and wanted a storm to come up, would take some dirt and water and rub it on the kit-fox skin, and this would cause a rain-storm to come up. In winter, snow and dirt would be rubbed on the skin and this would bring up a snow-storm.

Certain places and inanimate objects are also greatly reverenced by the Blackfeet, and presents are made to them.

The smallest of the three buttes of the Sweet Grass Hills is regarded as sacred. "All the Indians are afraid to go there," Four Bears once told me. Presents are sometimes thrown into the Missouri River, though these are not offerings made directly to the stream, but are given to the Under Water People, who live in it.

Mention has already been made of the buffalo rock, which gives its owner the power to call the buffalo.

Another sacred object is the medicine rock of the Marias. It is a huge boulder of reddish sandstone, two-thirds the way up a steep hill on the north bank of the Marias River, about five miles from Fort Conrad. Formerly, this rock rested on the top of the bluff, but, as the soil about it is worn away by the wind and the rain, it is slowly moving down the hill. The Indians believe it to be alive, and make presents to it. When I first visited it, the ground about it was strewn with decaying remnants of offerings that had been made to it in the past. Among these I noticed, besides fragments of clothing, eagle feathers, a steel finger ring, brass ear-rings, and a little bottle made of two copper cartridge cases.

Down on Milk River, east of the Sweet Grass Hills, is another medicine rock. It is shaped something like a man's body, and looks like a person sitting on top of the bluff. Whenever the Blackfeet pass this rock, they make presents to it. Sometimes, when they give it an article of clothing, they put it on the rock, "and then," as one of them once said to me, "when you look at it, it seems more than ever like a person." Down in the big bend of the Milk River, opposite the eastern end of the Little Rocky Mountains, lying on the prairie, is a great gray boulder, which is shaped like a buffalo bull lying down. This is greatly reverenced by all Plains Indians, Blackfeet included, and they make presents to it. Many other examples of similar character might be given.

The Blackfeet make daily prayers to the Sun and to Old Man, and nothing of importance is undertaken without asking for divine assistance. They are firm believers in dreams. These, they say, are sent by the Sun to enable us to look ahead, to tell what is going to happen. A dream, especially if it is a strong one, — that is, if the dream is very clear and vivid, — is almost always obeyed. As dreams start them on the war path, so, if a dream threatening bad luck comes to a member of a war party, even if in the enemy's country and just about to make an attack on a camp, the party is likely to turn about and go home without making any hostile demonstrations. The animal or object which appears to the boy, or man, who is trying to dream for power, is, as has been said, regarded thereafter as his secret helper, his medicine, and is usually called his dream (*Nits-o'-kan*).

The most important religious occasion of the year is the ceremony of the Medicine Lodge. This is a sacrifice, which, among the Blackfeet, is offered invariably by women. If a woman has a son or husband away at war, and is anxious about him, or if she has a dangerously sick child, she may make to the Sun a vow in the following words : —

"Listen, Sun. Pity me. You have seen my life. You know that I am pure. I have never committed adultery with any man. Now, therefore, I ask you to pity me. I will build you a lodge. Let my son survive. Bring him back to health, so that I may build this lodge for you."

The vow to build the Medicine Lodge is repeated in a loud voice, outside her lodge, so that all the people may hear it, and if any man can impeach the woman, he is obliged to speak out, in which case she could be punished according to the law. The Medicine Lodge is always built in summer, at the season of the ripening of the sarvis berries, and if, before this time, the person for whom the vow is made dies, the woman is not obliged to fulfil her vow. She is regarded with suspicion, and it is generally believed that she has been guilty of the crime she disavowed. As this cannot be proved, however, she is not punished.

When the time approaches for the building of the lodge, a suitable locality is selected, and all the people move to it, putting up their lodges in a circle about it. In the meantime, at least a hundred buffalo tongues have been collected, cut, and dried by the woman who may be called the Medicine Lodge woman. No one but she is allowed to take part in this work.

Before the tongues are cut and dried, they are laid in a pile in the medicine woman's lodge. She then gives a feast to the old men, and one of them, noted for his honesty, and well liked by all, repeats a very long prayer, asking in substance that the coming Medicine Lodge may be acceptable to the Sun, and that he will look with favor on the people, and will give them good health, plenty of food, and success in war. A hundred songs are then sung, each one different from the others. The feast and singing of these songs lasts a day and a half.

Before the Medicine Lodge is erected, four large sweat lodges are built, all in a line, fronting to the east or toward the rising sun. Two stand in front of the Medicine Lodge, and two behind it. The two nearest the Medicine Lodge are built one day, and the others on the day following. The sticks for the framework of these lodges are cut only by renowned warriors, each warrior cutting one, and, as he brings it in and lays it down, he counts a *coup*, which must be of some especially brave deed. The old men then take the sticks and erect the lodges, placing on top of each a buffalo skull, one half of which is painted red, the other black, to represent day and night, or rather the sun and the moon. When the lodges are finished and the stones heated, the warriors go in to sweat, and with them the medicine pipe men, who offer up prayers.

While this is going on, the young men cut the centre post for the Medicine Lodge, and all the other material for its construction. The women then pack out the post and the poles on horses, followed by the men shouting, singing, and shooting.

In the morning of this day the medicine woman begins a fast, which must last four days and four nights, with only one intermission, as will shortly appear. During that time she may not go out of doors, except between sunset and sunrise. During the whole ceremony her face, hands, and clothing are covered with the sacred red paint.

When all the material has been brought to the spot where the lodge is to be erected, that warrior who, during the previous year, has done the most cutting and stabbing in battle is selected to cut the rawhide to bind it, and while he cuts the strings he counts three *coups*.

The centre post is now placed on the ground, surrounded by the poles and other smaller posts ; and two bands of the

I-kun-uh'-kah-tsi, the Braves, and the All Crazy Dogs approach. Each band sings four songs, and then they raise the lodge amid the shouting of the people. It is said that, in old times, all the bands of the *I-kun-uh'-kah-tsi* took part in this ceremony. For raising the centre post, which is very heavy, lodge poles are tied in pairs, with rawhide, so as to form "shears," each pair being handled by two men. If one of the ropes binding the shears breaks, the men who hold the pair are said to be unlucky; it is thought that they are soon to die. As soon as the centre post is up, the wall posts are erected, and the roof of poles put on, the whole structure being covered with brush. The door-way faces east or southeast, and the lodge is circular in shape, about forty feet in diameter, with walls about seven feet high.

Inside the Medicine Lodge, at the back, or west side, in the principal place in the lodge, is now built a little box-shaped house, about seven feet high, six feet long, and four wide. It is made of brush, so tightly woven that one cannot see inside of it. This is built by a medicine man, the high priest of this ceremony, who, for four days, the duration of the ceremony, neither eats nor goes out of it in the daytime. The people come to him, two at a time, and he paints them with black, and makes for them an earnest prayer to the Sun, that they may have good health, long lives, and good food and shelter. This man is supposed to have power over the rain. As rain would interfere with the ceremonies, he must stop it, if it threatens.

In the meantime, the sacred dried tongues have been placed in the Medicine Lodge. The next morning, the Medicine Lodge woman leaves her own lodge, and, walking very slowly with bowed head, and praying at every step, she enters the Medicine Lodge, and, standing by the pile of tongues, she cuts up one of them and holds it toward heaven, offering it to the Sun; then she eats a part of it and buries the rest in the dirt, praying to the Ground Man, and calling him to bear witness that she has not defiled his body by committing adultery. She then proceeds to cut up the tongues, giving a very small piece to every person, man, woman, or child. Each one first holds it up to the Sun, and then prays to the Sun, Na'-pi, and the Ground Man for long life, concluding by depositing a part of the morsel of tongue on the ground, saying, " I give you this sacred tongue to eat." And now, during the four days, outside the lodge, goes on the counting of the *coups*. Each warrior in turn recounts his success in war, — his battles or his horse-takings. With a number of friends to help him, he goes through a pantomime of all these encounters, showing how he killed this enemy, took a gun from that one, or cut horses loose from the lodge of another. When he has concluded, an old man offers a prayer, and ends by giving him a new name, saying that he hopes he will live well and long under it.

Inside the lodge, rawhide ropes are suspended from the centre post, and here the men fulfil the vows that they have made during the previous year. Some have been sick, or in great danger at war, and they then vowed that if they were permitted to live, or escape, they would swing at the Medicine Lodge. Slits are cut in the skin of their breast, ropes passed through and secured by wooden skewers, and then the men swing and surge until the skin gives way and tears out. This is very painful, and some fairly shriek with agony as they do it, but they never give up, for they believe that if they should fail to fulfil their vow, they would soon die.

On the fourth day every one has been prayed for, every one has made to the Sun his or her present, which is tied to the centre post, the sacred tongues have all been consumed, and the ceremony ends, every one feeling better, assured of long life and plenty.

Most persons have an entirely erroneous idea of the

purpose of this annual ceremony. It has been supposed
that it was for the purpose of making warriors. This is not
true. It was essentially a religious festival, undertaken for
the bodily and spiritual welfare of the people according to
their beliefs. Incidentally, it furnished an opportunity for
the rehearsal of daring deeds. But among no tribes who
practised it were warriors made by it. The swinging by the
breast and other self-torturings were but the fulfilment of
vows, sacred promises made in time of danger, penances performed, and not, as many believe, an occasion for young men
to test their courage.

From the Indians of the tribe, the Medicine Lodge woman
receives a very high measure of respect and consideration.
Blackfoot men have said to me, " We look on the Medicine
Lodge woman as you white people do on the Roman Catholic
sisters." Not only is she virtuous in deed, but she must be
serious and clean-minded. Her conversation must be sober.

Before the coming of the whites, the Blackfeet used to
smoke the leaves of a plant which they call *na-wuh'-to-ski*,
and which is said to have been received long, long ago from
a medicine beaver. It was used unmixed with any other
plant. The story of how this came to the tribe is told elsewhere.[1] This tobacco is no longer planted by the Piegans,
nor by the Bloods, though it is said that an old Blackfoot
each year still goes through the ceremony, and raises a little.
The plant grows about ten inches high and has a long seed
stalk growing from the centre. White Calf, the chief of the
Piegans, has the secrets of the tobacco and is perhaps the
only person in the tribe who knows them. From him I have
received the following account of the ceremonies connected
with it : —

Early in the spring, after the last snow-storm, when the
flowers begin to bud (early in the month of May), the
women and children go into the timber and prepare a large

[1] The Beaver Medicine, p. 117.

bed, clearing away the underbrush, weeds and grass and leaves and sticks, raking the ground till the earth is thoroughly pulverized. Elk, deer, and mountain sheep droppings are collected, pounded fine, and mixed with the seed which is to be sown.

On the appointed day all the men gather at the bed. Each one holds in his hand a short, sharp-pointed stick, with which to make a hole in the ground. The men stand in a row extending across the bed. At a signal they make the holes in the ground, and drop in some seed, with some sacred sarvis berries. The tobacco song is sung by the medicine men, all take a short step forward, make another hole, a foot in front of the last, and then drop in it some more seed. Another song is sung, another step taken, and seed is again planted ; and this continues until the line of men has moved all the way across the bed, and the planting is completed. The tobacco dance follows the planting.

After the seed has been planted, they leave it and go off after the buffalo. While away during the summer, some important man — one of the medicine men who had taken part in the planting — announces to the people his purpose to go back to look after the crop. He starts, and after he has reached the place, he builds a little fire in the bed, and offers a prayer for the crop, asking that it may survive and do well. Then he pulls up one of the plants, which he takes back with him and shows to the people, so that all may see how the crop is growing. He may thus visit the place three or four times in the course of the summer.

From time to time, while they are absent from the tobacco patch in summer, moving about after the buffalo, the men gather in some lodge to perform a special ceremony for the protection of the crop. Each man holds in his hand a little stick. They sing and pray to the Sun and Old Man, asking that the grasshoppers and other insects may not eat their plants. At the end of each song they strike the ground with their sticks, as if killing grasshoppers and worms. It has sometimes happened that a young man has said that he does not believe that these prayers and songs protect the plants, that the Sun does not send messengers to destroy the worms. To such a one a medicine man will say, " Well, you can go to the place and see for yourself." The young man gets on his horse and travels to the place. When he comes to the edge of the patch and looks out on it, he sees many small children at work there, killing worms. He has not believed in this before, but now he goes back convinced. Such a young man does not live very long.

At length the season comes for gathering the crop, and, at a time appointed, all the camps begin to move back toward the tobacco patch, timing their marches so that all may reach it on the same day. When they get there, they camp near it, but no one visits it except the head man of the medicine men who took charge of the planting. This man goes to the bed, gathers a little of the plant, and returns to the camp.

A small boy, six or eight years old, is selected to carry this plant to the centre of the circle. The man who gathered the tobacco ties it to a little stick, and, under the tobacco, to the stick he ties a baby's moccasin. The little boy carries this stick to the centre of the camp, and stands it in the ground in the middle of the circle, the old man accompanying him and showing him where to put it. It is left there all night. The next day there is a great feast, and the kettles of food are all brought to the centre of the camp. The people all gather there, and a prayer is made. Then they sing the four songs which belong especially to this festival. The first and fourth are merely airs without words ; the second has words, the purport of which is, " The sun goes with us." The third song says, " Hear your children's prayer." After the ceremony is over, every one is at liberty to go and gather the tobacco. It is dried and put in sacks for use during the year. The seed is collected for the next planting.

When they reach the patch, if the crop is good, every one is glad. After the gathering, they all move away again after the buffalo.

Sometimes a man who was lazy, and had planted no tobacco, would go secretly to the patch, and pull a number of plants belonging to some one else, and hide them for his own use. Now, in these prayers that they offer, they do not ask for mercy for thieves. A man who had thus taken what did not belong to him would have a lizard appear to him in a dream, and then he would fall sick and die. The medicine men would know of all this, but they would not do anything. They would just let him die.

This tobacco was given us by the one who made us.

The Blackfoot cosmology is imperfect and vague, and I have been able to obtain nothing like a complete account of it, for I have found no one who appeared to know the story of the beginning of all things.

Some of the Blackfeet now say that originally there was a great womb, in which were conceived the progenitors of all animals now on earth. Among these was Old Man. As the time for their birth drew near, the animals used to quarrel as to which should be the first to be born, and one day, in a fierce struggle about this, the womb burst, and Old Man jumped first to the ground. For this reason, he named all the animals Nis-kum'-iks, Young Brothers ; and they, because he was the first-born, called him Old Man.

There are several different accounts of the creation of the people by Old Man. One is that he married a female dog, and that their progeny were the first people. Others, and the ones most often told, have been given in the Old Man stories already related.

There is an account of the creation which is essentially an Algonquin myth, and is told by most of the tribes of this stock from the Atlantic to the Rocky Mountains, though the

hero is variously named.   Here is the Blackfoot version of
it : —

In the beginning, all the land was covered with water,
and Old Man and all the animals were floating around on a
large raft.   One day Old Man told the beaver to dive and
try to bring up a little mud.   The beaver went down, and
was gone a long time, but could not reach the bottom.
Then the loon tried, and the otter, but the water was too
deep for them.   At last the muskrat dived, and he was gone
so long that they thought he had drowned, but he finally
came up, almost dead, and when they pulled him on to the
raft, they found, in one of his paws, a little mud.   With this,
Old Man formed the world, and afterwards he made the
people.

This myth, while often related by the Blackfoot tribe,
is seldom heard among the Bloods or Piegans.   It is
uncertain whether all three tribes used to know it, but have
forgotten it, or whether it has been learned in comparatively
modern times by the Blackfeet from the Crees, with whom
they have always had more frequent intercourse and a closer
connection than the other two tribes.

There is also another version of the origin of death.   When
Old Man made the first people, he gave them very strong
bodies, and for a long time no one was sick.   At last, a little
child fell ill.   Each day it grew weaker and weaker, and at
last it fainted.   Then the mother went to Old Man, and
prayed him to do something for it.

"This," said Old Man, "will be the first time it has
happened to the people.   You have seen the buffalo fall to
the ground when struck with an arrow.   Their hearts stop
beating, they do not breathe, and soon their bodies become
cold.   They are then dead.   Now, woman, it shall be for
you to decide whether death shall come to the people as
well as to the other animals, or whether they shall live
forever.   Come now with me to the river."

When they reached the water's edge, Old Man picked up from the ground a dry buffalo chip and a stone. " Now, woman," he said, " you will tell me which one of these to throw into the water. If what I throw floats, your child shall live ; the people shall live forever. If it sinks, then your child shall die, and all the people shall die, each one when his time comes."

The woman stood still a long time, looking from the stone to the buffalo chip, and from the chip to the stone. At last she said, "Throw the stone." Then Old Man tossed it into the river, and it sank to the bottom. "Woman," he cried, "go home ; your child is dead." Thus, on account of a foolish woman, we all must die.

The shadow of a person, the Blackfeet say, is his soul. Northeast of the Sweet Grass Hills, near the international boundary line, is a bleak, sandy country called the Sand Hills, and there all the shadows of the deceased good Blackfeet are congregated. The shadows of those who in this world led wicked lives are not allowed to go there. After death, these wicked persons take the shape of ghosts (*Sta-au'* [1]), and are compelled ever after to remain near the place where they died. Unhappy themselves, they envy those who are happy, and continually prowl about the lodges of the living, seeking to do them some injury. Sometimes they tap on the lodge skins and whistle down the smoke hole, but if the fire is burning within they will not enter.

Outside in the dark they do much harm, especially the ghosts of enemies who have been killed in battle. These sometimes shoot invisible arrows into persons, causing sickness and death. They have hit people on the head, causing them to become crazy. They have paralyzed people's limbs, and drawn their faces out of shape, and done much other harm.

[1] The human skeleton is also called *Sta-au'*, *i.e.* ghost. Compare Cheyenne *Mis-tai'*, ghost.

Ghosts walk above the ground, not on it. An example of this peculiarity is seen in the case of the young man who visited the lodge of the starving family, in the story entitled Origin of the *I-kun-uh'-kah-tsi*.

Ghosts sometimes speak to people. An instance of this is the following, which occurred to my friend Young Bear Chief, and which he related to me. He said: " I once went to war, and took my wife with me. I went to Buffalo Lip Butte, east of the Cypress Mountains; a little creek runs by it. I took eighteen horses from an Assinaboine camp one night, when it was very foggy. I found sixteen horses feeding on the hills, and went into the camp and cut loose two more. Then we went off with the horses. When we started, it was so foggy that I could not see the stars, and I did not know which way to run. I kept travelling in what I supposed was the direction toward home, but I did not know where I was going. After we had gone a long way, I stopped and got off my horse to fix my belt. My wife did not dismount, but sat there waiting for me to mount and ride on.

" I spoke to my wife, and said to her, 'We don't know which way to go.' A voice spoke up right behind me and said: 'It is well; you go ahead. You are going right.' When I heard the voice, the top of my head seemed to lift up and felt as if a lot of needles were sticking into it. My wife, who was right in front of me, was so frightened that she fainted and fell off her horse, and it was a long time before she came to. When she got so she could ride, we went on, and when morning came I found that we were going straight, and were on the west side of the West Butte of the Sweet Grass Hills. We got home all right. This must have been a ghost."

Now and then among the Blackfeet, we find evidences of a belief that the soul of a dead person may take up its abode in the body of an animal. An example of this is seen in the story of E-kūs'-kini, p. 90. Owls are thought to be the ghosts of medicine men.

The Blackfeet do not consider the Sand Hills a happy hunting ground. There the dead, who are themselves shadows, live in shadow lodges, hunt shadow buffalo, go to war against shadow enemies, and in every way lead an existence which is but a mimicry of this life. In this respect the Blackfeet are almost alone. I know of scarcely any other American tribe, certainly none east of the Rocky Mountains, who are wholly without a belief in a happy future state. The Blackfeet do not especially say that this future life is an unhappy one, but, from the way in which they speak of it, it is clear that for them it promises nothing desirable. It is a monotonous, never ending, and altogether unsatisfying existence, — a life as barren and desolate as the country which the ghosts inhabit. These people are as much attached to life as we are. Notwithstanding the unhappy days which have befallen them of late years, — days of privation and hunger, — they cling to life. Yet they seem to have no fear of death. When their time comes, they accept their fate without a murmur, and tranquilly, quietly pass away.

MEDICINE PIPES AND HEALING

THE person whom the whites term " medicine man " is called by the Blackfeet *Ni-namp'-skan*. Mr. Schultz believes this word to be compounded of *nin'nah*, man, and *namp'-ski*, horned toad (*Phrynosoma*), and in this he is supported by Mr. Thomas Bird, a very intelligent half-breed, who has translated a part of the Bible into the Blackfoot language for the Rev. S. Trivett, a Church of England missionary. These gentlemen conclude that the word means " all-face man." The horned toad is called *namp'-ski*, all-face ; and as the medicine man, with his hair done up in a huge topknot, bore a certain resemblance to this creature, he was so named. No one among the Blackfeet appears to have any idea as to what the word means.

The medicine pipes are really only pipe stems, very long, and beautifully decorated with bright-colored feathers and the fur of the weasel and other animals. It is claimed that these stems were given to the people long, long ago, by the Sun, and that those who own them are regarded by him with special favor.

Formerly these stems were valued at from fifteen to thirty head of horses, and were bought and sold like any other property. When not in use, they were kept rolled up in many thicknesses of fine tanned fur, and with them were invariably a quantity of tobacco, a sacred whistle, two sacred rattles, and some dried sweet grass, and sweet pine needles.

In the daytime, in pleasant weather, these sacred bundles were hung out of doors behind the owners' lodges, on tripods.

276

At night they were suspended within, above the owners' seat. It was said that if at any time a person should walk completely around the lodge of a medicine man, some bad luck would befall him. Inside the lodge, no one was allowed to pass between the fireplace and the pipe stem. No one but a medicine man and his head wife could move or unroll the bundle. The man and his wife were obliged always to keep their faces, hands, and clothing painted with *nits'-i-san*, a dull red paint, made by burning a certain clay found in the bad lands.

The *Ni-namp'-skan* appears to be a priest of the Sun, and prayers offered through him are thought to be specially favored. So the sacred stem is frequently unrolled for the benefit of the sick, for those who are about to undertake a dangerous expedition, such as a party departing to war, for prayers for the general health and prosperity of the people, and for a bountiful supply of food. At the present time these ancient ceremonies have largely fallen into disuse. In fact, since the disappearance of the buffalo, most of the old customs are dying out.

The thunder is believed to bring the rain in spring, and the rain makes the berries grow. It is a rule that after the first thunder is heard in the spring, every medicine man must give a feast and offer prayers for a large berry crop. I have never seen this ceremony, but Mr. Schultz was once permitted to attend one, and has given me the following account of it. He said : " When I entered the lodge with the other guests, the pipe stem had already been unrolled. Before the fire were two huge kettles of cooked sarvis berries, a large bowlful of which was soon set before each guest. Each one, before eating, took a few of the berries and rubbed them into the ground, saying, ' Take pity on us, all Above People, and give us good.'

"When all had finished eating, a large black stone pipe bowl was filled and fitted to the medicine stem, and the medicine man held it aloft and said : ' Listen, Sun ! Listen, Thunder !   Listen, Old Man !   All Above Animals, all Above People, listen. Pity us ! You will smoke. We fill the sacred pipe. Let us not starve. Give us rain during this summer. Make the berries large and sweet. Cover the bushes with them. Look down on us all and pity us. Look at the women and the little children ; look at us all. Let us reach old age. Let our lives be complete. Let us destroy our enemies. Help the young men in battle. Man, woman, child, we all pray to you ; pity us and give us good. Let us survive.'

" He then danced the pipe dance, to be described further on. At this time, another storm had come up, and the thunder crashed directly over our heads.

"' Listen,' said the medicine man. ' It hears us. We are not doing this uselessly ' ; and he raised his face, animated with enthusiasm, toward the sky, his whole body trembling with excitement ; and, holding the pipe aloft, repeated his prayer.   All the rest of the people were excited, and repeatedly clasped their arms over their breasts, saying : ' Pity us ; good give us ; good give us. Let us survive.'

" After this, the pipe was handed to a man on the right of the semi-circle. Another warrior took a lighted brand from the fire, and counted four *coups*, at the end of each *coup* touching the pipe bowl with the brand. When he had counted the fourth *coup*, the pipe was lighted. It was then smoked in turn around the circle, each one, as he received it, repeating a short prayer before he put the stem to his lips. When it was smoked out, a hole was dug in the ground, the ashes were knocked into it and carefully covered over, and the thunder ceremony was ended."

In the year 1885, I was present at the unwrapping of the medicine pipe by Red Eagle, an aged *Ni-namp'-skan*, since dead. On this occasion prayers were made for the success of a party of Piegans who had started in pursuit of some

Crows who had taken a large band of horses from the Piegans the day before. The ceremony was a very impressive one, and prayers were offered not only for the success of this war party, but also for the general good, as well as for the welfare of special individuals, who were mentioned by name. The concluding words of the general prayer were as follows: "May all people have full life. Give to all heavy bodies. Let the young people grow; increase their flesh. Let all men, women, and children have full life. Harden the bodies of the old people so that they may reach great age."

In 1879, Mr. Schultz saw a sacred pipe unwrapped for the benefit of a sick woman, and on various occasions since he has been present at this ceremony. All accounts of what takes place agree so closely with what I saw that I give only one of them. Mr. Schultz wrote me of the first occasion: "When I entered the lodge, it was already well filled with men who had been invited to participate in the ceremony. The medicine man was aged and gray-headed, and his feeble limbs could scarcely support his body. Between him and his wife was the bundle which contained the medicine pipe, as yet unwrapped, lying on a carefully folded buffalo robe. Plates of food were placed before each guest, and after all had finished eating, and a common pipe had been lighted to be smoked around the circle, the ceremony began.

"With wooden tongs, the woman took a large coal from the fire, and laid it on the ground in front of the sacred stem. Then, while every one joined in singing a chant, a song of the buffalo (without words), she took a bunch of dried sweet grass, and, raising and lowering her hand in time to the music, finally placed the grass on the burning coals. As the thin column of perfumed smoke rose from the burning herb, both she and the medicine man grasped handfuls of it and rubbed it over their persons, to purify themselves before touching the sacred roll. They also took each a small piece of some

root from a little pouch, and ate it, signifying that they purified themselves without and within.

"The man and woman now faced each other and again
began the buffalo song, keeping time by touching with the
clenched hands — the right and left alternately — the wrappings of the pipe, occasionally making the sign for buffalo.
Now, too, one could occasionally hear the word *Nai-ai'* [1] in
the song. After singing this song for about ten minutes, it
was changed to the antelope song, and, instead of touching
the roll with the clenched hands, which represented the
heavy tread of buffalo, they closed the hands, leaving the
index finger extended and the thumbs partly open, and in
time to the music, as in the previous song, alternately touched
the wrappers with the tips of the left and right forefinger,
the motions being quick and firm, and occasionally brought
the hands to the side of the head, making the sign for
antelope, and at the same time uttering a loud '*Kuh*,' to
represent the whistling or snorting of that animal.

"At the conclusion of this song, the woman put another
bunch of sweet grass on a coal, and carefully undid the wrappings of the pipe, holding each one over the smoke to keep
it pure. When the last wrapping was removed, the man
gently grasped the stem and, every one beginning the pipe
song, he raised and lowered it several times, shaking it as he
did so, until every feather and bit of fur and scalp hung loose
and could be plainly seen.

"At this moment the sick woman entered the lodge, and
with great difficulty, for she was very weak, walked over to
the medicine woman and knelt down before her. The
medicine woman then produced a small bag of red paint, and
painted a broad band across the sick woman's forehead, a
stripe down the nose, and a number of round dots on each
cheek. Then picking up the pipe stem, which the man had
laid down, she held it up toward the sky and prayed, saying,

[1] My shelter; my covering; my robe.

'Listen, Sun, pity us! Listen, Old Man, pity us! Above
People, pity us! Under Water People, pity us! Listen,
Sun! Listen, Sun! Let us survive, pity us! Let us survive. Look down on our sick daughter this day. Pity her
and give her a complete life.' At the conclusion of this
short prayer, all the people uttered a loud *m-m-m-h*, signifying that they took the words to their hearts. Every one now
commenced the pipe song, and the medicine woman passed
the stem over different parts of the sick woman's body, after
which she rose and left the lodge.

"The medicine man now took a common pipe which had
been lighted, and blew four whiffs of smoke toward the sky,
four toward the ground, and four on the medicine pipe
stem, and prayed to the Sun, Old Man, and all medicine
animals, to pity the people and give them long life. The
drums were then produced, the war song commenced, and
the old man, with a rattle in each hand, danced four times
to the door-way and back. He stooped slightly, kept all his
limbs very rigid, extending his arms like one giving a
benediction, and danced in time to the drumming and
singing with quick, sudden steps. This is the medicine pipe
dance, which no one but a pipe-owner is allowed to perform.
Afterward, he picked up the pipe stem, and, holding it
aloft in front of him, went through the same performance.
At the conclusion of the dance, the pipe stem was passed
from one to another of the guests, and each one in turn held
it aloft and repeated a short prayer. The man on my right
prayed for the health of his children, the one on my left for
success in a proposed war expedition. This concluded the
ceremony."

Disease among the Blackfeet is supposed to be caused by
evil spirits, usually the spirits or ghosts of enemies slain in
battle. These spirits are said to wander about at night, and
whenever opportunity offers, they shoot invisible arrows into
persons. These cause various internal troubles, such as

consumption, hemorrhages, and diseases of the digestive organs. Mice, frogs, snakes, and tailed batrachians are said to cause much disease among women, and hence should be shunned, and on no account handled.

Less important external ailments and hurts, such as ulcers, boils, sprains, and so on, are treated by applying various lotions or poultices, compounded by boiling or macerating certain roots or herbs, known only to the person supplying them. Rheumatic pains are treated in several ways. Sometimes the sweat lodge is used, or hot rocks are applied over the place where the pain is most severe, or actual cautery is practised, by inserting prickly pear thorns in the flesh, and setting fire to them, when they burn to the very point.

The sweat lodge, so often referred to, is used as a curative agent, as well as in religious ceremonies, and is considered very beneficial in illness of all kinds. The sweat lodge is built in the shape of a rough hemisphere, three or four feet high and six or eight in diameter. The frame is usually of willow branches, and is covered with cowskins and robes. In the centre of the floor, a small hole is dug out, in which are to be placed red hot stones. Everything being ready, those who are to take the sweat remove their clothing and crowd into the lodge. The hot rocks are then handed in from the fire outside, and the cowskins pulled down to the ground to exclude any cold air. If a medicine pipe man is not at hand, the oldest person present begins to pray to the Sun, and at the same time sprinkles water on the hot rocks, and a dense steam rises, making the perspiration fairly drip from the body. Occasionally, if the heat becomes too intense, the covering is raised for a few minutes to admit a little air. The sweat bath lasts for a long time, often an hour or more, during which many prayers are offered, religious songs chanted, and several pipes smoked to the Sun. As has been said, the sweat lodge is built to represent the Sun's own lodge or home, that is, the world. The ground inside the lodge stands for its surface, which, according to Blackfoot philosophy, is flat and round. The framework represents the sky, which far off, on the horizon, reaches down to and touches the world.

As soon as the sweat is over, the men rush out, and plunge into the stream to cool off. This is invariably done, even in winter, when the ice has to be broken to make a hole large enough to bathe in. It is said that, when the small-pox was raging among these Indians, they used the sweat lodge daily, and that hundreds of them, sick with the disease, were unable to get out of the river, after taking the bath succeeding a sweat, and were carried down stream by the current and drowned.

It is said that wolves, which in former days were extremely numerous, sometimes went crazy, and bit every animal they met with, sometimes even coming into camps and biting dogs, horses, and people. Persons bitten by a mad wolf generally went mad, too. They trembled and their limbs jerked, they made their jaws work and foamed at the mouth, often trying to bite other people. When any one acted in this way, his relations tied him hand and foot with ropes, and, having killed a buffalo, they rolled him up in the green hide, and then built a fire on and around him, leaving him in the fire until the hide began to dry and burn. Then they pulled him out and removed the buffalo hide, and he was cured. While in the fire, the great heat caused him to sweat profusely, so much water coming out of his body that none was left in it, and with the water the disease went out, too. All the old people tell me that they have seen individuals cured in this manner of a mad wolf's bite.

Whenever a person is really sick, a doctor is sent for. Custom requires that he shall be paid for his services before rendering them. So when he is called, the messenger says to him, " A—— presents to you a horse, and asks you to come and doctor him." Sometimes the fee may be several horses, and sometimes a gun, saddle, or some article of wearing-apparel. This fee pays only for one visit, but the duration of the visit is seldom less than twelve hours, and sometimes exceeds forty-eight. If, after the expiration of the visit, the patient feels that he has been benefited, he will probably send for the doctor again, but if, on the other hand, he continues to grow worse, he is likely to send for another.   Not infrequently two or more doctors may be present at the same time, taking turns with the patient.   In early days, if a man fell sick, and remained so for three weeks or a month, he had to start anew in life when he recovered ; for, unless very wealthy, all his possessions had gone to pay doctor's fees.   Often the last horse, and even the lodge, weapons, and extra clothing were so parted with. Of late years, however, since the disappearance of the buffalo, the doctors' fees are much more moderate.

The doctor is named *I-so-kin'-ŭh-kin*, a word difficult to translate.   The nearest English meaning of the word seems to be " heavy singer for the sick."   As a rule all doctors sing while endeavoring to work their cures, and, as helpers, a number of women are always present.   Disease being caused by evil spirits, prayers, exhortations, and certain mysterious methods must be observed to rid the patient of their influence.   No two doctors have the same methods or songs. Herbs are sometimes used, but not always.   One of their medicines is a great yellow fungus which grows on the pine trees.   This is dried and powdered, and administered either dry or in an infusion.   It is a purgative.   As a rule, these doctors, while practising their rites, will not allow any one in the lodge, except the immediate members of the sick man's family.   Mr. Schultz, who on more than one occasion has been present at a doctoring, gives the following account of one of the performances.

" The patient was a man in the last stages of consumption.

When the doctor entered the lodge, he handed the sick man
a strip of buckskin, and told him to tie it around his chest.
The patient then reclined on a couch, stripped to the waist,
and the doctor kneeled on the floor beside him. Having
cleared a little space of the loose dirt and dust, the doctor
took two coals from the fire, laid them in this place, and put
a pinch of dried sweet grass on each of them. As the smoke
arose from the burning grass, he held his drum over it, turning it from side to side, and round and round. This was
supposed to purify it. Laying aside the drum, he held his
hands in the smoke, and rubbed his arms and body with it.
Then, picking up the drum, he began to tap it rapidly, and
prayed, saying : ' Listen, my dream. This you told me
should be done. This you said should be the way. You
said it would cure the sick. Help me now. Do not lie to
me. Help me, Sun person. Help me to cure this sick man.'

" He then began to sing, and as soon as the women had
caught the air, he handed the drum to one of them to beat,
and, still singing himself, took an eagle's wing and dipped
the tip of it in a cup of ' medicine.' It was a clear liquid,
and looked as if it might be simply water. Placing the tip
of the wing in his mouth, he seemed to bite off the end of it,
and, chewing it a little, spat it out on the patient's breast.
Then, in time to the singing, he brushed it gently off, beginning at the throat and ending at the lower ribs. This was
repeated three times. Next he took the bandage from the
patient, dipped it in the cup of medicine, and, wringing it out,
placed it on the sick man's chest, and rubbed it up and
down, and back and forth, after which he again brushed the
breast with the eagle wing. Finally, he lighted a pipe, and,
placing the bowl in his mouth, blew the smoke through the
stem all over the patient's breast, shoulders, neck, and arms,
and finished the ceremony by again brushing with the wing.
At intervals of two or three hours, the whole ceremony was
repeated. The doctor arrived at the lodge of the sick man

about noon, and left the next morning, having received for his services a saddle and two blankets."

" Listen, my dream — " This is the key to most of the Blackfoot medicine practices. These doctors for the most part effect their cures by prayer. Each one has his dream, or secret helper, to whom he prays for aid, and it is by this help that he expects to restore his patient to health. No doubt the doctors have the fullest confidence that their practices are beneficial, and in some cases they undoubtedly do good because of the implicit confidence felt in them by the patient.

Often, when a person is sick, he will ask some medicine man to unroll his pipe. If able to dance, he will take part in the ceremony, but if not, the medicine man paints him with the sacred symbols. In any case a fervent prayer is offered by the medicine man for the sick person's recovery. The medicine man administers no remedies ; the ceremony is purely religious. Being a priest of the Sun, it is thought that god will be more likely to listen to him than he would to an ordinary man.

Although the majority of Blackfoot doctors are men, there are also many women in the guild, and some of them are quite noted for their success. Such a woman, named Wood Chief Woman, is now alive on the Blackfoot reservation. She has effected many wonderful cures. Two Bear Woman is a good doctor, and there are many others.

In the case of gunshot wounds a man's " dream," or " medicine," often acts directly and speedily. Many cases are cited in which this charm, often the stuffed skin of some bird or animal, belonging to the wounded man, becomes alive, and by its power effects a cure. Many examples of this might be given but for lack of space. Entirely honest Indians and white men have seen such cures and believe in them.

THE BLACKFOOT OF TO-DAY

In the olden times the Blackfeet were very numerous, and it is said that then they were a strong and hardy people, and few of them were ever sick. Most of the men who died were killed in battle, or died of old age. We may well enough believe that this was the case, because the conditions of their life in those primitive times were such that the weakly and those predisposed to any constitutional trouble would not survive early childhood. Only the strongest of the children would grow up to become the parents of the next generation. Thus a process of selection was constantly going on, the effect of which was no doubt seen in the general health of the people.

With the advent of the whites, came new conditions. Various special diseases were introduced and swept off large numbers of the people. An important agent in their destruction was alcohol.

In the year 1845, the Blackfeet were decimated by the small-pox. This disease appears to have travelled up the Missouri River; and in the early years, between 1840 and 1850, it swept away hosts of Mandans, Rees, Sioux, Crows, and other tribes camped along the great river. I have been told, by a man who was employed at Fort Union in 1842–43, that the Indians died there in such numbers that the men of the fort were kept constantly at work digging trenches in which to bury them, and when winter came, and the ground froze so hard that it was no longer practicable to bury the dead, their bodies were stacked up like cord wood in great piles to await the coming of spring. The disease spread from tribe to tribe, and finally reached the Blackfeet. It is said by whites who were in the country at the time, that this small-pox almost swept the Plains bare of Indians.

In the winter of 1857–58, small-pox again carried off great numbers, but the mortality was not to be compared with that of 1845. In 1864, measles ran through all the Blackfoot camps, and was very fatal, and again in 1869 they had the small-pox.

Between the years 1860 and 1875, a great deal of whiskey was traded to the Blackfeet. Having once experienced the delights of intoxication, the Indians were eager for liquor, and the traders found that robes and furs could be bought to better advantage for whiskey than for anything else. To be sure, the personal risk to the trader was considerably in-creased by the sale of whiskey, for when drunk the Indians fought like demons among themselves or with the traders. But, on the other hand, whiskey for trading to Indians cost but a trifle, and could be worked up, and then diluted, so that a little would go a long way.

As a measure of partial self-protection, the traders used to deal out the liquor from the keg or barrel in a tin scoop so constructed that it would not stand on a flat surface, so that an Indian, who was drinking, had to keep the vessel in his hand until the liquor was consumed, or else it would be spilled and lost. This lessened the danger of any shooting or stabbing while the Indian was drinking, and an effort was usually made to get him out of the store as soon as he had finished. Nevertheless, drunken fights in the trading-stores were of common occurrence, and the life of a whiskey-trader was one of constant peril. I have talked with many men who were engaged in this traffic, and some of the stories they tell are thrilling. It was a common thing in winter for the man who unbarred and opened the store in the morning to have a dead Indian fall into his arms as the door swung

open.   To prop up against the door a companion who had
been killed or frozen to death during the night seems to have
been regarded by the Indians as rather a delicate bit of
humor, in the nature of a joke on the trader.   Long histories
of the doings of these whiskey trading days have been related
to me, but the details are too repulsive to be set down.
The traffic was very fatal to the Indians.

The United States has laws which prohibit, under severe
penalties, the sale of intoxicants to Indians, but these laws
are seldom enforced.   To the north of the boundary line,
however, in the Northwest Territories, the Canadian Mounted
Police have of late years made whiskey-trading perilous
business.   Of Major Steell's good work in putting down the
whiskey traffic on the Blackfoot agency in Montana, I shall
speak further on, and to-day there is not very much whiskey
sold to the Blackfeet.   Constant vigilance is needed, however, to keep traders from the borders of the reservation.

In the winter of 1883–84 more than a quarter of the Piegan
tribe of the Blackfeet, which then numbered about twenty-
five or twenty-six hundred, died from starvation.   It had
been reported to the Indian Bureau that the Blackfeet were
practically self-supporting and needed few supplies.   As a
consequence of this report, appropriations for them were
small.   The statement was entirely and fatally misleading.
The Blackfeet had then never done anything toward self-
support, except to kill buffalo.   But just before this, in
the year 1883, the buffalo had been exterminated from the
Blackfoot country.   In a moment, and without warning, the
people had been deprived of the food supply on which they
had depended.   At once they had turned their attention to
the smaller game, and, hunting faithfully the river bottoms,
the brush along the small streams, and the sides of the mountains, had killed off all the deer, elk, and antelope; and at
the beginning of the winter found themselves without their
usual stores of dried meat, and with nothing to depend on,

except the scanty supplies in the government storehouse.
These were ridiculously inadequate to the wants of twenty-
five hundred people, and food could be issued to them only
in driblets quite insufficient to sustain life. The men devoted themselves with the utmost faithfulness to hunting,
killing birds, rabbits, prairie-dogs, rats, anything that had
life ; but do the best they might, the people began to starve.
The very old and the very young were the first to perish ;
after that, those who were weak and sickly, and at last some
even among the strong and hardy. News of this suffering
was sent East, and Congress ordered appropriations to relieve
the distress ; but the supplies had to be freighted in wagons
for one hundred and fifty or two hundred miles before they
were available. If the Blackfeet had been obliged to depend
on the supplies authorized by the Indian Bureau, the whole
tribe might have perished, for the red tape methods of the
Government are not adapted to prompt and efficient action
in times of emergency. Happily, help was nearer at hand.
The noble people of Montana, and the army officers stationed
at Fort Shaw, did all they could to get supplies to the suf-
ferers. One or two Montana contractors sent on flour and
bacon, on the personal assurance of the newly appointed
agent that he would try to have them paid. But it took a
long time to get even these supplies to the agency, over
roads sometimes hub deep in mud, or again rough with
great masses of frozen clay ; and all the time the people
were dying.

During the winter, Major Allen had been appointed agent
for the Blackfeet, and he reached the agency in the midst
of the worst suffering, and before any effort had been made
to relieve it. He has told me a heart-rending story of the
frightful suffering which he found among these helpless
people.

In his efforts to learn exactly what was their condition,
Major Allen one day went into twenty-three houses and

lodges to see for himself just what the Indians had to eat. In only two of these homes did he find anything in the shape of food. In one house a rabbit was boiling in a pot. The man had killed it that morning, and it was being cooked for a starving child. In another lodge, the hoof of a steer was cooking, — only the hoof, — to make soup for the family. Twenty-three lodges Major Allen visited that day, and the little rabbit and the steer's hoof were all the food he found. "And then," he told me, with tears in his eyes, "I broke down. I could go no further. To see so much misery, and feel myself utterly powerless to relieve it, was more than I could stand."

Major Allen had calculated with exactest care the supplies on hand, and at this time was issuing one-seventh rations. The Indians crowded around the agency buildings and begged for food. Mothers came to the windows and held up their starving babies that the sight of their dull, pallid faces, their shrunken limbs, and their little bones sticking through their skins might move some heart to pity. Women brought their young daughters to the white men in the neighborhood, and said, " Here, you may have her, if you will feed her ; I want nothing for myself; only let her have enough to eat, that she may not die." One day, a deputation of the chiefs came to Major Allen, and asked him to give them what he had in his storehouses. He explained to them that it must be some time before the supplies could get there, and that only by dealing out what he had with the greatest care could the people be kept alive until provisions came. But they said : "Our women and children are hungry, and we are hungry. Give us what you have, and let us eat once and be filled. Then we will die content; we will not beg any more." He took them into the storehouse, and showed them just what food he had, — how much flour, how much bacon, how much rice, coffee. sugar, and so on through the list — and then told them that if this was issued all at once, there was no hope for them, they would surely die, but that he expected supplies by a certain day. "And," said he, "if they do not come by that time, you shall come in here and help yourselves. That I promise you." They went away satisfied.

Meanwhile, the supplies were drawing near. The officer in command of Fort Shaw had supplied fast teams to hurry on a few loads to the agency, but the roads were so bad that the wagon trains moved with appalling slowness. At length, however, they had advanced so far that it was possible to send out light teams, to meet the heavily laden ones, and bring in a few sacks of flour and bacon; and every little helped. Gradually the suffering was relieved, but the memory of that awful season of famine will never pass from the minds of those who witnessed it.

There is a record of between four and five hundred Indians who died of hunger at this time, and this includes only those who were buried in the immediate neighborhood of the agency and for whom coffins were made. It is probable that nearly as many more died in the camps on other creeks, but this is mere conjecture. It is no exaggeration to say, however, that from one-quarter to one-third of the Piegan tribe starved to death during that winter and the following spring.

The change from living in portable and more or less open lodges to permanent dwellings has been followed by a great deal of illness, and at present the people appear to be sickly, though not so much so as some other tribes I have known, living under similar conditions further south.

Like other Indians, the Blackfeet have been several times a prey to bad agents, — men careless of their welfare, who thought only about drawing their own pay, or, worse, who used their positions simply for their own enrichment, and stole from the government and Indians alike everything upon which they could lay hands. It was with great satisfaction that I secured the discharge of one such man a few years ago, and I only regret that it was not in my power to have carried the matter so far that he might have spent a few years in prison.

The present agent of the Blackfeet, Major George Steell, is an old-timer in the country and understands Indians very thoroughly. In one respect, he has done more for this people than any other man who has ever had charge of them, for he has been an uncompromising enemy of the whiskey traffic, and has relentlessly pursued the white men who always gather about an agency to sell whiskey to the Indians, and thus not only rob them of their possessions, but degrade them as well. The prison doors of Deer Lodge have more than once opened to receive men sent there through the energy of Major Steell. For the good work he has done in this respect, this gentleman deserves the highest credit, and he is a shining example among Indian agents.

As recently as 1887 it was rather unusual to see a Blackfoot Indian clad in white men's clothing; the only men who wore coats and trousers were the police and a few of the chiefs; to-day it is quite as unusual to see an Indian wearing a blanket. Not less striking than this difference in their way of life, is the change which has taken place in the spirit of the tribe.

I was passing through their reservation in 1888, when the chiefs asked me to meet them in council and listen to what they had to say.

I learned that they wished to have a message taken to the Great Father in the East, and, after satisfying myself that their complaint was well grounded, I promised to do for them what I could. I accomplished what they desired, and since that time I have taken much active interest in this people, and my experience with them has shown me very clearly how much may be accomplished by the unaided efforts of a single individual who thoroughly understands the needs of a tribe of Indians.   During my annual visits to the Blackfeet reservation, which have extended over two, three, or four months each season, I see a great many of the men and have long conversations with them.   They bring their troubles to me, asking what they shall do, and how their condition may be improved.   They tell me what things they want, and why they think they ought to have them.   I listen, and talk to them just as if they were so many children.   If their requests are unreasonable, I try to explain to them, step by step, why it is not best that what they desire should be done, or tell them that other things which they ask for seem proper, and that I will do what I can to have them granted.   If one will only take the pains necessary to make things clear to him, the adult Indian is a reasonable being, but it requires patience to make him understand matters which to a white man would need no explanation.   As an example, let me give the substance of a conversation had last autumn with a leading man of the Piegans who lives on Cut Bank River, about twenty-five miles from the agency.   He said to me : —

"We ought to have a storehouse over here on Cut Bank, so that we will not be obliged each week to go over to the agency to get our food.   It takes us a day to go, and a day to come, and a day there ; nearly three days out of every week to get our food.   When we are at work cutting hay, we cannot afford to spend so much time travelling back and forth.   We want to get our crops in, and not to be travelling about all the time.   It would be a good thing, too, to have a blacksmith shop here, so that when our wagons break down, we will not have to go to the agency to get them mended."

This is merely the substance of a much longer speech, to which I replied by a series of questions, something like the following : —

"Do you remember talking to me last year, and telling me

on this same spot that you ought to have beef issued to you
here, and ought not to have to make the long journey to the
agency for your meat?"   "Yes."

"And that I told you I agreed with you, and believed that
some of the steers could just as well be killed here by the
agency herder and issued to those Indians living near here?"
"Yes."

"That change has been made, has it not?   You now get
your beef here, don't you?"   "Yes."

"You know that the Piegans have a certain amount of
money coming to them every year, don't you?"   "Yes."

"And that some of that money goes to pay the expenses
of the agency, some for food, some to pay clerks and black-
smiths, some to buy mowing-machines, wagons, harness, and
rakes, and some to buy the cattle which have been issued to
you?"   "Yes."

"Now, if a government storehouse were to be built over
here, clerks hired to manage it, a blacksmith shop built and
another blacksmith hired, that would all cost money, wouldn't
it?"   "Yes."

"And that money would be taken out of the money coming next year to the Piegans, wouldn't it?"   "Yes."

"And if that money were spent for those things, the people
would have just so many fewer wagons, mowing-machines,
rakes, and cattle issued to them next year, wouldn't they?"
"Yes."

"Well, which would be best for the tribe, which would
you rather have, a store and a blacksmith shop here on Cut
Bank, or the money which those things would cost in cows
and farming implements?"

"I would prefer that we should have the cattle and the
tools."

"I think you are right.   It would save trouble to each
man, if the government would build a storehouse for him
right next his house, but it would be a waste of money.

Many white men have to drive ten, twenty, or thirty miles to the store, and you ought not to complain if you have to do so."

After this conversation the man saw clearly that his request was an unreasonable one, but if I had merely told him that he was a fool to want a store on Cut Bank, he would never have been satisfied, for his experiences were so limited that he could not have reasoned the thing out for himself.

In my talks with these people, I praise those who have worked hard and lived well during the past year, while to those who have been idle or drunken or have committed crimes, I explain how foolish their course has been and try to show them how impossible it is for a man to be successful if he acts like a child, and shows that he is a person of no sense. A little quiet talk will usually demonstrate to them that they have been unwise, and they make fresh resolutions and promise amendment. Of course the only argument I use is to tell them that one course will be for their material advancement, and is the way a white man would act, while the other will tend to keep them always poor.

Some years ago, the Blackfeet made a new treaty, by which they sold to the government a large portion of their lands. By this treaty, which was ratified by Congress in May, 1887, they are to receive $150,000 annually for a period of ten years, when government support is to be withdrawn. This sum is a good deal more than is required for their subsistence, and, by the terms of the treaty, the surplus over what is required for their food and clothing is to be used in furnishing to the Indians farming implements, seed, live stock, and such other things as will help them to become self-supporting.

The country which the Blackfeet inhabit lies just south of the parallel of 49°, close to the foot of the Rocky Mountains, and is very cold and dry. Crops can be grown there successfully not more than once in four or five years, and the sole products to be depended on are oats and potatoes, which are raised only by means of irrigation. It is evident, therefore, that the Piegan tribe of the Blackfeet can never become an agricultural people. Their reservation, however, is well adapted to stock-raising, and in past years the cattle-men from far and from near have driven their herds on to the reservation to eat the Blackfoot grass ; and the remonstrances of the Indians have been entirely disregarded. Some years ago, I came to the conclusion that the proper occupation for these Indians was stock-raising. Horses they already had in some numbers, but horses are not so good for them as cattle, because horses are more readily sold than cattle, and an Indian is likely to trade his horse for whiskey and other useless things. Cattle they are much less likely to part with, and besides this, require more attention than horses, and so are likely to keep the Indians busy and to encourage them to work.

Within the past three or four years, I have succeeded in inducing the Indian Bureau to employ a part of the treaty money coming to the Blackfeet in purchasing for them cattle.

It was impressed upon them that they must care for the cattle, not kill and eat any of them, but keep them for breed-ing purposes. It was represented to them that, if properly cared for, the cattle would increase each year, until a time might come when each Indian would be the possessor of a herd, and would then be rich like the white cattle-men.

The severe lesson of starvation some years before had not failed to make an impression, and it was perhaps owing to this terrible experience that the Piegans did not eat the cows as soon as they got them, as other Indian tribes have so often done. Instead of this, each man took the utmost care of the two or three heifers he received. Little shelters and barns were built to protect them during the winter.

Indians who had never worked before, now tried to borrow a mowing-machine, so as to put up some hay for their animals. The tribe seemed at once to have imbibed the idea of property, and each man was as fearful lest some accident should happen to his cows as any white man might have been. Another issue of cattle was made, and the result is that now there is hardly an individual in the tribe who is not the possessor of one or more cows. Scarcely any of the issued cattle have been eaten; there has been almost no loss from lack of care; the original stock has increased and multiplied, and now the Piegans have a pretty fair start in cattle.

This material advancement is important and encouraging. But richer still is the promise for the future. A few years ago, the Blackfeet were all paupers, dependent on the bounty of the government and the caprice of the agent. Now, they feel themselves men, are learning self-help and self-reliance, and are looking forward to a time when they shall be self-supporting. If their improvement should be as rapid for the next five years as it has been for the five preceding 1892, a considerable portion of the tribe will be self-supporting at the date of expiration of the treaty.

It is commonly believed that the Indian is hopelessly lazy, and that he will do no work whatever. This misleading notion has been fostered by the writings of many ignorant people, extending over a long period of time. The error had its origin in the fact that the work which the savage Indian does is quite different from that performed by the white laborer. But it is certain that no men ever worked harder than Indians on a journey to war, during which they would march on foot hundreds of miles, carrying heavy loads on their backs, then have their fight, or take their horses, and perhaps ride for several days at a stretch, scarcely stopping to eat or rest. That they did not labor regularly is of course true, but when they did work, their toil was very much harder than that ever performed by the white man.

The Blackfeet now are willing to work in the same way that the white man works. They appreciate, as well as any one, the fact that old things have passed away, and that they must now adapt themselves to new surroundings. Therefore, they work in the hay fields, tend stock, chop logs in the mountains, haul firewood, drive freighting teams, build houses and fences, and, in short, do pretty much all the work that would be done by an ordinary ranchman. They do not perform it so well as white men would ; they are much more careless in their handling of tools, wagons, mowing-machines, or other implements, but they are learning all the time, even if their progress is slow.

The advance toward civilization within the past five years is very remarkable and shows, as well as anything could show, the adaptability of the Indian. At the same time, I believe that if it had not been for that fateful experience known as "the starvation winter," the progress made by the Blackfeet would have been very much less than it has been. The Indian requires a bitter lesson to make him remember.

But besides this lesson, which at so terrible a cost demonstrated to him the necessity of working, there has been another factor in the progress of the Blackfoot. If he has learned the lesson of privation and suffering, the record given in these pages has shown that he is not less ready to respond to encouragement, not less quickened and sustained by friendly sympathy. Without such encouragement he will not persevere. If his crops fail him this year, he has no heart to plant the next. A single failure brings despair. Yet if he is cheered and helped, he will make other efforts. The Blackfeet have been thus sustained ; they have felt that there was an inducement for them to do well, for some one whom they trusted was interested in their welfare, was watching their progress, and was trying to help them. They knew that this person had no private interest to serve, but wished to do the best that he could for his people. Having an exaggerated idea of his power to aid them, they have tried to follow his advice, so as to obtain his good-will and secure his aid with the government. Thus they have had always before them a definite object to strive for.

The Blackfoot of to-day is a working man. He has a little property which he is trying to care for and wishes to add to. With a little help, with instruction, and with encouragement to persevere, he will become in the next few years self-supporting, and a good citizen.

INDEX

BLACKFEET
INDIAN STORIES

BY

GEORGE BIRD GRINNELL

AUTHOR OF

"BLACKFEET LODGE TALES," "TRAILS OF THE PATHFINDERS," ETC.

NEW YORK

CHARLES SCRIBNER'S SONS

TO THE READER

Those who wish to know something about how the people lived who told these stories will find their ways of life described in the last chapter of this book

The Blackfeet were hunters, travelling from place to place on foot. They used implements of stone, wood, or bone, wore clothing made of skins, and lived in tents covered by hides. Dogs, their only tame animals, were used as beasts of burden to carry small packs and drag light loads.

The stories here told come down to us from very ancient times. Grandfathers have told them to their grandchildren, and these again to their grandchildren, and so from mouth to mouth, through many generations, they have reached our time.

CONTENTS

vii

CONTENTS

BLACKFEET INDIAN STORIES

Blackfeet Indian Stories

TWO FAST RUNNERS

ONCE, a long time ago, the antelope and
the deer happened to meet on the prairie. They spoke together, giving each other
the news, each telling what he had seen and
done. After they had talked for a time the
antelope told the deer how fast he could run,
and the deer said that he could run fast too,
and before long each began to say that he could
run faster than the other. So they agreed that
they would have a race to decide which could
run the faster, and on this race they bet their
galls. When they started, the antelope ran
ahead of the deer from the very start and won
the race and so took the deer's gall.

But the deer began to grumble and said,
"Well, it is true that out here on the prairie

1

you have beaten me, but this is not where I
live. I only come out here once in a while to
feed or to cross the prairie when I am going
somewhere. It would be fairer if we had a race
in the timber. That is my home, and there I
can run faster than you. I am sure of it."

The antelope felt so glad and proud that he
had beaten the deer in the race that he was
sure that wherever they might run he could
beat him, so he said, "All right, I will run you
a race in the timber. I have beaten you out
here on the flat and I can beat you there." On
this race they bet their dew-claws.

They started and ran this race through the
thick timber, among the bushes, and over fallen
logs, and this time the antelope ran slowly, for
he was afraid of hitting himself against the trees
or of falling over the logs. You see, he was not
used to this kind of travelling. So the deer
easily beat him and took his dew-claws.

Since that time the deer has had no gall and
the antelope no dew-claws.

2

THE WOLF MAN

A LONG time ago there was a man who
had two wives. They were not good
women; they did not look after their home
nor try to keep things comfortable there. If
the man brought in plenty of buffalo cow skins
they did not tan them well, and often when
he came home at night, hungry and tired after
his hunting, he had no food, for these women
would be away from the lodge, visiting their
relations and having a good time.

The man thought that if he moved away
from the big camp and lived alone where there
were no other people perhaps he might teach
these women to become good; so he moved his
lodge far off on the prairie and camped at the
foot of a high butte.

Every evening about sundown the man used
to climb up to the top of this butte and sit
there and look all over the country to see where

3

the buffalo were feeding and whether any enemies were moving about. On top of the hill there was a buffalo skull, on which he used to sit.

One day one of the women said to the other, "It is very lonely here; we have no one to talk with or to visit."

"Let us kill our husband," said the other; "then we can go back to our relations and have a good time."

Early next morning the man set out to hunt, and as soon as he was out of sight his wives went up on top of the butte where he used to sit. There they dug a deep hole and covered it over with light sticks and grass and earth, so that it looked like the other soil near by, and placed the buffalo skull on the sticks which covered the hole.

In the afternoon, as they watched for their returning husband, they saw him come over the hill loaded down with meat that he had killed. When he threw down his load outside the lodge, they hurried to cook something for him. After he had eaten he went up on the

4

butte and sat down on the skull. The slender
sticks broke and he fell into the hole. His
wives were watching him, and when they saw
him disappear, they took down the lodge and
packed their dogs and set out to go to the
main camp. As they drew near it, so that
people could hear them, they began to cry and
mourn.

Soon some people came to meet them and
said, "What is this? Why are you mourning?
Where is your husband?"

"Ah," they replied, "he is dead. Five days
ago he went out to hunt and he did not come
back. What shall we do? We have lost him
who cared for us"; and they cried and mourned
again.

Now, when the man fell into the pit he was
hurt, for the hole was deep. After a time he
tried to climb out, but he was so badly bruised
that he could not do so. He sat there and
waited, thinking that here he must surely die
of hunger.

But travelling over the prairie was a wolf
that climbed up on the butte and came to the

hole and, looking in, saw the man and pitied him.

"Ah-h-w-o-o-o! Ah-h-w-o-o-o-o!" he howled, and when the other wolves heard him they all came running to see what was the matter. Following the big wolves came also many coyotes, badgers, and kit-foxes. They did not know what had happened, but they thought perhaps there was food here.

To the others the wolf said, "Here in this hole is what I have found. Here is a man who has fallen in. Let us dig him out and we will have him for our brother."

All the wolves thought that this talk was good, and they began to dig, and before very long they had dug a hole down almost to the bottom of the pit.

Then the wolf who had found the man said, "Hold on; wait a little; I want to say a few words." All the animals stopped digging and began to listen, and the wolf said, "We will all have this man for our brother; but I found him, and so I think he ought to live with us big wolves." All the others thought that this was

6

good, and the wolf that had found the man went into the hole that had been dug, and tearing down the rest of the earth, dragged out the poor man, who was now almost dead, for he had neither eaten nor drunk anything since he fell in the hole. They gave the man a kidney to eat, and when he was able to walk the big wolves took him to their home. Here there was a very old blind wolf who had great power and could do wonderful things. He cured the man and made his head and his hands look like those of a wolf. The rest of his body was not changed.

In those days the people used to make holes in the walls of the fence about the enclosure into which they led the buffalo. They set snares over these holes, and when wolves and other animals crept through them so as to get into the pen and feed on the meat they were caught by the neck and killed, and the people used their skins for clothing.

One night all the wolves went down to the pen to get meat, and when they had come close to it, the man-wolf said to his brothers, "Stop here for a little while and I will go down and fix the places so that you will not be caught." He went down to the pen and sprung all the snares, and then went back and called the wolves and the others—the coyotes, badgers, and kit-foxes—and they all went into the pen and feasted and took meat to carry home to their families. In the morning the people found the meat gone and all their snares sprung, and they were surprised and wondered how this could have happened. For many nights the nooses were pulled tight and the meat taken; but once when the wolves went there to eat they found only the meat of a lean and sickly bull. Then the man-wolf was angry, and he cried out like a wolf, "Bad-food-you-give-us-o-o-o! Bad-food-you-give-us-o-o-o-o!"

When the people heard this they said to one another, "Ah, it is a man-wolf who has done all this. We must catch him." So they took down to the piskun[1] pemmican and nice back fat and placed it there, and many of them hid

[1] A pen or enclosure, usually—among the Blackfeet—at the foot of a cliff, over which the buffalo were induced to jump. Pronounced pĭ'skŭn.

close by. After dark the wolves came, as was their custom, and when the man-wolf saw the good food, he ran to it and began to eat. Then the people rushed upon him from every side and caught him with ropes, and tied him and took him to a lodge, and when they had brought him inside to the light of the fire, at once they knew who it was. They said, "Why, this is the man who was lost."

"No," said the man, "I was not lost. My wives tried to kill me. They dug a deep hole and I fell into it, and I was hurt so badly I could not get out; but the wolves took pity on me and helped me or I would have died there."

When the people heard this they were angry, and they told the man to do something to punish these women.

"You say well," he replied; "I give those women to the punishing society. They know what to do."

After that night the two women were never seen again.

KŬT-O-YĬS', THE BLOOD BOY

A S the children whose ancestors came from
Europe have stories about the heroes who
killed wicked and cruel monsters—like Jack the
Giant Killer, for example—so the Indian children hear stories about persons who had magic
power and who went about the world destroying those who treated cruelly or killed the Indians of the camps. Such a hero was Kŭt-o-
yĭs', and this is how he came to be alive and
to travel about from place to place, helping the
people and destroying their enemies.

It was long, long ago, down where Two Medicine and Badger Rivers come together, that an
old man lived with his wife and three daughters.
One day there came to his camp a young man,
good-looking, a good hunter, and brave. He
stayed in the camp for some time, and whenever he went hunting he killed game and
brought in great loads of meat.

All this time the old man was watching him, for he said in his heart, "This seems a good young man and a good hunter. Perhaps I will give him my daughters for wives, and then he will stay here and help me always."

After a time the old man decided to do this, and he gave the young man his daughters; and because these three were his only children he gave his son-in-law his dogs and all his property, and for himself and his wife he kept only a little lodge. The young man's wives tanned plenty of cow skins and made a big fine lodge, and in this the son-in-law lived with his wives.

For some time after this the son-in-law was very good and kind to the old people. When he killed any animal he gave them part of the meat, and gave them skins which his mother-in-law tanned for robes or for clothing.

As time went on the son-in-law began to grow stingy, and pretty soon he gave nothing to his father-in-law's lodge, but kept everything for his own.

Now, the son-in-law was a person of much mysterious power, and he kept the buffalo hid-

den under a big log-jam in the river. Whenever he needed food and wished to kill anything,
he would take his father-in-law with him to
help. He would send the old man out to stamp
on the log-jam and frighten the buffalo, and
when they ran out from under it the young
man would shoot one or two with his arrows,
never killing more than he needed. But often
he gave the old people nothing at all to eat.
They were hungry all the time, and at length
they began to grow thin and weak.

One morning early the young man asked his
father-in-law to come and hunt with him. They
went to the log-jam and the old man drove
out the buffalo and his son-in-law killed a fat
buffalo cow. Then he said to his father-in-law,
"Hurry back now to the camp and tell your
daughters to come and carry home the meat,
and then you can have something to eat." The
old man set out for the camp, thinking, as he
walked along, "Now, at last, my son-in-law has
taken pity on me; he will give me some of this
meat."

When he returned with his daughters they

skinned the cow and cut it up and, carrying it, went home. The young man had his wives leave the meat at his own lodge and told his father-in-law to go home. He did not give him even a little piece of the meat. The two older daughters gave their parents nothing to eat, but sometimes the youngest one had pity on them and took a piece of meat and, when she could, threw it into the lodge to the old people. The son-in-law had told his wives not to give the old people anything to eat. Except for the good heart of the youngest daughter they would have died of hunger.

Another day the son-in-law rose early in the morning and went over to the old man's lodge and kicked against the poles, calling to him, "Get up now and help me; I want you to go and stamp on the log-jam to drive out the buffalo." When the old man moved his feet on the jam and a buffalo ran out, the son-in-law was not ready for it, and it passed by him before he shot the arrow; so he only wounded it. It ran away, but at last it fell down and died.

The old man followed close after it, and as he ran along he came to a place where a great clot of blood had fallen from the buffalo's wound. When he came to where this clot of blood was lying on the ground, he stumbled and fell and spilled his arrows out of his quiver, and while he was picking them up he picked up also the clot of blood and hid it in his quiver.

"What are you picking up?" called the son-in-law.

"Nothing," replied the old man. "I fell down and spilled my arrows, and I am putting them back."

"Ah, old man," said the son-in-law, "you are lazy and useless. You no longer help me. Go back now to the camp and tell your daughters to come down here and help carry in this meat."

The old man went to the camp and told his daughters of the meat that their husband had killed, and they went down to the killing ground. Then he went to his own lodge and said to his wife, "Hurry, now, put the stone kettle on the fire. I have brought home something from the killing."

14

"Ah," said the old woman, "has our son-in-law been generous and given us something nice to eat?"

"No," replied the old man, "but hurry and put the kettle on the fire."

After a time the water began to boil and the old man turned his quiver upside down over the pot, and immediately there came from it a sound of a child crying, as if it were being hurt. The old people both looked in the kettle and there they saw a little boy, and they quickly took him out of the water. They were surprised and did not know where the child had come from. The old woman wrapped the child up and wound a line about its wrappings to keep them in place, making a lashing for the child. Then they talked about it, wondering what should be done with it. They thought that if their son-in-law knew it was a boy he would kill it; so they determined to tell their daughters that the baby was a girl, for then their son-in-law would think that he was going to have another wife. So he would be glad. They called the child Kŭt-o-yĭs'—Clot of Blood.

15

The son-in-law and his wives came home, bringing the meat, and after a little time they heard the child in the next lodge crying. The son-in-law said to his youngest wife, "Go over to your mother's and see whether that baby is a boy or a girl. If it is a boy, tell your parents to kill it."

Soon the young woman came back and said to her husband, "It is a girl baby. You are to have another wife."

The son-in-law did not know whether to believe this, and sent his oldest wife to ask the same question. When she came back and told him the same thing he believed that it was really a girl. Then he was glad, for he said to himself, "Now, when this child has grown up, I shall have another wife." He said to his youngest wife, "Take some back fat and pemmican over to your mother; she must be well fed now that she has to nurse this child."

On the fourth day after he had been born the child spoke and said to his mother, "Hold me in turn to each one of these lodge poles, and when I come to the last one I shall fall out of

16

my lashings and be grown up." The old woman did as he had said, and as she held him to one pole after another he could be seen to grow; and finally when he was held to the last pole he was a man.

After Kŭt-o-yĭs' had looked about the lodge he put his eye to a hole in the lodge-covering and looked out. Then he turned around and said to the old people, "How is it that in this lodge there is nothing to eat? Over by the other lodge I see plenty of food hanging up."

"Hush," said the old woman, raising her hand, "you will be heard. Our son-in-law lives over there. He does not give us anything at all to eat."

"Well," said the young man, "where is your piskun—where do you kill buffalo?"

"It is down by the river," the old woman answered. "We pound on it and the buffalo run out."

For some time they talked together and the old man told Kŭt-o-yĭs' how his son-in-law had abused him. He said to the young man, "He has taken from me my bow and my arrows and

17

has taken even my dogs; and now for many
days we have had nothing to eat, except sometimes a small piece of meat that our daughter
throws to us."

"Father," said Kŭt-o-yĭs', "have you no arrows?"

"No, my son," replied the old man, "but I
still have four stone arrow points."

"Go out then," said Kŭt-o-yĭs', "and get
some wood. We will make a bow and some
arrows, and in the morning we will go down to
where the buffalo are and kill something to
eat."

Early in the morning Kŭt-o-yĭs' pushed the
old man and said, "Come, get up now, and we
will go down and kill, when the buffalo come
out." It was still very early in the morning.

When they reached the river the old man
said, "This is the place to stand and shoot. I
will go down and drive them out."

He went down and stamped on the log-jam,
and presently a fat cow ran out and Kŭt-o-yĭs'
killed it.

Now, after these two had gone to the river

18

the son-in-law arose and went over to the old man's lodge, and knocked on the poles and called to the old man to get up and help him kill. The old woman called out to the son-in-law, saying, "Your father-in-law has already gone down to the piskun." This made the son-in-law angry, and he began to talk badly to the old woman and to threaten to harm her.

Presently he went on down to the log-jam, and as he got near the place he saw the old man at work there, bending over, skinning a buffalo; for Kŭt-o-yĭs′, when he had seen the son-in-law coming, had lain down on the ground and hidden himself behind the carcass.

When the son-in-law had come pretty close to where the buffalo lay he said to his father-in-law, "Old man, stand up and look all about you. Look carefully and well, for it will be the last time that you will ever see anything"; and while the son-in-law said this he took an arrow from his quiver.

Kŭt-o-yĭs′ spoke to the old man from his hiding-place and said, "Tell your son-in-law that he must take his last look, for that you are going

19

to kill him now." The old man said this as he had been told.

"Ah," said the son-in-law, "you talk back to me. That makes me still angrier at you." He put an arrow on the string and shot at the old man, but did not hit him. Kŭt-o-yĭs' said to the old man, "Pick up that arrow and shoot it back at him"; and the old man did so. Now, they shot at each other four times, and then the old man said to Kŭt-o-yĭs', "I am afraid now; get up and help me. If you do not, I think he will kill me." Then Kŭt-o-yĭs' rose to his feet and said to the son-in-law, "Here, what are you doing? I think you have been treating this old man badly for a long time. Why do you do it?"

"Oh no," said the son-in-law, and he smiled at Kŭt-o-yĭs' in a friendly way, for he was afraid of him. "Oh no; no one thinks more of this old man than I do. I have always been very good to him."

"No," said Kŭt-o-yĭs'. "You are saying what is not true, and I am going to kill you now."

Kŭt-o-yĭs' shot the son-in-law four times and

20

he fell down and died. Then the young man told his father to go and bring down to him the daughters who had acted badly toward him. The old man did so and Kŭt-o-yĭs' punished them. Then he went up to the lodges and said to the youngest woman, "Did you love your husband?" "Yes," said the girl, "I loved him." So Kŭt-o-yĭs' punished her too, but not so badly as he had the other daughters, because she had been kind to her parents.

To the old people he said, "Go over now to that lodge and live there. There is plenty of food, and when that is gone I will kill more. As for me, I shall make a journey. Tell me where there are any people. In what direction shall I go to find a camp?"

"Well," said the old man, "up here on Two Medicine Lodge Creek there are some people —up where the piskun is, you know."

Kŭt-o-yĭs' followed up the stream to where the piskun was and there found many lodges of people. In the centre of the camp was a big lodge, and painted on it the figure of a bear. He did not go to this lodge, but went into a

21

small lodge where two old women lived. When he had sat down they put food before him— lean dried meat and some belly fat.

"How is this, grandmothers?" he said. "Here is a camp with plenty of fat meat and back fat hanging up to dry; why do you not give me some of that?"

"Hush; be careful," said the old women. "In that big lodge over there lives a big bear and his wives and children. He takes all the best food and leaves us nothing. He is the chief of this place."

Early in the morning Kŭt-o-yĭs′ said to the old women, "Harness up your dogs to the travois now and go over to the piskun, and I will kill some fat meat for you."

When they got there, he killed a fat cow and helped the old women to cut it up, and they took it to the lodge. One of those old women said, "Ah me, the bears will be sure to come."

"Why do you say that?" he asked.

They said to him, "We shall be sorry to lose this back fat."

"Do not fear," he said. "No one shall take

22

this back fat from you. Now, take all those best pieces and hang them up, so that those who live in the bear lodge may see them."

They did so. Pretty soon the old bear chief said to one of his children, "By this time I think the people have finished killing. Go out now and look about; see where the nicest pieces are, and bring in some nice back fat."

One of the young bears went out of the lodge and stood up and looked about, and when it saw this meat hanging by the old women's lodge close by, it went over toward it.

"Ah," said the old women, "there are those bears."

"Do not be afraid," said Kŭt-o-yĭs'.

The young bear went over to where the meat was hanging and stood up and began to pull it down. Kŭt-o-yĭs' went out of the lodge and said, "Wait; wait! What are you doing, taking the old women's meat?"

The young bear answered, "My father told me that I should go out and get this meat and bring it home to him."

Kŭt-o-yĭs' hit the young bear over the head with a stick and it ran home crying.

When it had reached the lodge it told what had happened and the father bear said, "I will go over there myself; perhaps this person will hit me over the head."

When the old women saw the father and mother bear and all their relations coming they were afraid, but Kŭt-o-yĭs' jumped out of the lodge and killed the bears one after another; all except one little she-bear, a very small one, which got away.

"Well," said Kŭt-o-yĭs', "you may go and breed more bears."

He told the old women to move over to the bear-painted lodge and after this to live in it. It was theirs.

To the old women Kŭt-o-yĭs' then said, "Now, grandmothers, where are there any more people? I want to travel about and see them."

The old women said, "At the Point of Rocks —on Sun River—there is a camp. There is a piskun there."

So Kŭt-o-yĭs' set off for that place, and when

he came to the camp he went into an old woman's lodge.

The old woman gave him something to eat —a dish of bad food.

"Why is this, grandmother?" asked Kŭt-o-yĭs'. "Have you no food better than this to give to a visitor? Down there I see a piskun; you must kill plenty of buffalo and must have good food."

"Speak lower," said the old woman, "or you may be heard. We have no good food because there is a great snake here who is the chief of the camp. He takes all the best pieces. He lives over there in that snake-painted lodge."

The next morning when the buffalo were led in, Kŭt-o-yĭs' killed one, and they took the back fat and carried it to their lodge. Then Kŭt-o-yĭs' said, "I think I will visit that snake person." He went over and went into the lodge, and there he saw many women that the snake person had taken to be his wives. The women were cooking some service berries. Kŭt-o-yĭs' picked up the dish and ate the berries and threw the dish away. Then he went up to the big

25

snake, who was lying there asleep, and pricked him with his knife, saying, "Here, get up; I have come to visit you. Let us smoke together."

Then the snake was angry and he raised up his head and began to rattle, and Kŭt-o-yĭs' cut off his head and cut him in pieces. He cut off the heads of all the snake's wives and children; all except one little female snake which got away by crawling into a crack in the rocks.

"Oh, well," said Kŭt-o-yĭs', "you can go and breed snakes so there will be more. The people will not be afraid of little snakes."

Kŭt-o-yĭs' said to the old woman, "Now, grandmother, go into this snake lodge and take it for your own and everything that is in it."

Then he said to them, "Where are there some more people?" They told him there were some camps down the river and some up in the mountains, but they said, "Do not go up there. It is bad because there lives Āi-sĭn'-o-kō-kĭ— Wind Sucker. He will kill you."

Kŭt-o-yĭs' was glad to know that there was such a person, and he went to the mountains.

When he reached the place where Wind Sucker

26

lived, he looked into his mouth and saw there many dead people. Some were skeletons and some had only just died. He went in, and there he saw a fearful sight. The ground was white as snow with the bones of those who had died. There were bodies with flesh on them; some who had died not long before and some who were still living.

As he looked about, he saw hanging down above him a great thing that seemed to move— to grow a little larger and then to grow a little smaller.

Kŭt-o-yĭs' spoke to one of the people who was alive and asked, "What is that hanging down above us?"

The person answered him, "That is Wind Sucker's heart."

Then Kŭt-o-yĭs' spoke to all the living and said to them, "You who still draw a little breath try to move your heads in time to the song that I shall sing; and you who are still able to move stand up on your feet and dance. Take courage now; we are going to dance to the ghosts."

Then Kŭt-o-yĭs' tied his knife, point upward,

to the top of his head and began to dance, singing the ghost song, and all the others danced with him; and as he danced up and down he kept springing higher and higher into the air, and the point of his knife cut Wind Sucker's heart and killed him.

Then Kŭt-o-yĭs', with his knife, cut a hole between Wind Sucker's ribs, and he and all those who were able to move crawled out through the hole. He said to those who could still walk that they should go and tell their people to come here, to get the ones still alive but unable to travel.

To some of these people that he had freed he said, "Where are there any other people? I want to visit all the people."

"There is a camp to the westward, up the river," they replied; "but you must not take the left-hand trail going up because on that trail lives a woman who invites men to wrestle with her and then kills them. Avoid her."

Now, really, this was what Kŭt-o-yĭs' was looking for. This was what he was doing in the world, trying to kill off all the bad things.

28

He asked these people just where this woman lived and how it was best for him to go so that he should not meet her. He did this because he did not wish the people to know that he was going where she was.

He started, and after he had travelled some time he saw a woman standing not far from the trail. She called to him, saying, "Come here, young man, come here; I want to wrestle with you."

"No," he replied, "I am in a hurry; I cannot stop."

The woman called again, "No, no; do not go on; come now and wrestle once with me."

After she had called him the fourth time, Kŭt-o-yĭs' went to her.

Now on the ground where this woman wrestled with people she had placed many sharp, broken flint-stones, partly hiding them by the grass. The two seized each other and began to wrestle over these sharp stones, but Kŭt-o-yĭs' looked at the ground and did not step on them. He watched his chance and gave the woman a quick wrench, and threw her down on

29

a, large sharp flint which cut her in two; and the parts of her body fell asunder.

Kŭt-o-yĭs' then went on, and after a time came to where a woman had made a place for sliding downhill. At the far end of it she had fixed a rope which, when she raised it, would trip people up, and when they were tripped they fell over a high cliff into a deep water, where a great fish ate them.

When this woman saw Kŭt-o-yĭs' coming she cried out to him, "Come over here, young man, and slide with me."

"No," he replied, "I am in a hurry; I cannot wait." She kept calling to him, and when she had called him the fourth time he went over where he was to slide with her.

"This sliding," said the woman, "is very good fun."

"Ah, yes," said Kŭt-o-yĭs', "I will look at it."

As he went near the place he looked carefully and saw the hidden rope. He began to slide, and holding his knife in his hand, when he reached the rope he cut it just as the woman raised it and pulled on it, and the woman fell

30

over backward into the water and was eaten up by the big fish.

From here he went on again, and after a time he came to a big camp. A man-eater was the chief of this place.

Before Kŭt-o-yĭs' went to the chief's lodge he looked about and saw a little girl and called her to him and said, "Child, I am going into that lodge, to let that man-eater kill and eat me. Therefore, be on the watch, and if you can get hold of one of my bones take it out and call all the dogs to you, and when they have come to you throw down the bone and say, 'Kŭt-o-yis', the dogs are eating your bones.'"

Then Kŭt-o-yĭs' entered the lodge, and when the man-eater saw him he called out, "Oki, oki!" (welcome, welcome!) and seemed glad to see him, for he was a fat young man. The man-eater took a knife and walked up to Kŭt-o-yĭs' and cut his throat and put him into a great stone pot to cook. When the meat was cooked he pulled the kettle from the fire and ate the body, limb by limb, until it was all eaten.

After that the little girl who was watching

31

came into the lodge and said, "Pity me, man-eater, my mother is hungry and asks you for those bones." The old man gathered them together and handed them to her, and she took them out of the lodge. When she had gone a little way, she called all the dogs to her and threw down the bones to the dogs, crying out, "Look out, Kŭt-o-yĭs', the dogs are eating you," and when she said that, Kŭt-o-yĭs' arose from the pile of bones.

Again he went into the lodge, and when the man-eater saw him he cried out, "How, how, how! the fat young man has survived!" and he seemed surprised. Again he took his knife and cut the throat of Kŭt-o-yĭs' and threw him into the kettle. Again when the meat was cooked he ate it, and when the little girl asked for the bones again he gave them to her. She took them out and threw them to the dogs, crying, "Kŭt-o-yĭs', the dogs are eating you," and again Kŭt-o-yĭs' arose from the bones.

When the man-eater had cooked him four times Kŭt-o-yĭs' again went into the lodge, and seizing the man-eater, he threw him into the boiling kettle, and his wives and all his children, and boiled them to death.

The man-eater was the seventh and last of the bad things to be destroyed by Kŭt-o-yĭs'.

THE DOG AND THE ROOT DIGGER

THIS happened long ago.

In those days the people were hungry. No buffalo could be found, no antelope were seen on the prairie. Grass grew in the trails where the elk and the deer used to travel. There was not even a rabbit in the brush. Then the people prayed, "Oh, Napi, help us now or we must die. The buffalo and the deer are gone. It is useless to kindle the morning fires; our arrows are useless to us; our knives remain in their sheaths."

Then Napi set out to find where the game was, and with him went a young man, the son of a chief. For many days they travelled over the prairies. They could see no game; roots and berries were their only food. One day they climbed to the crest of a high ridge, and as they looked off over the country they saw far away by a stream a lonely lodge.

"Who can it be?" asked the young man.
"Who camps there alone, far from friends?"

"That," said Napi, "is he who has hidden
all the animals from the people. He has a wife
and a little son." Then they went down near
to the lodge and Napi told the young man what
to do. Napi changed himself into a little dog,
and he said, "This is I." The young man
changed himself into a root digger and he said,
"This is I." Pretty soon the little boy, who
was playing about near the lodge, found the
dog and carried it to his father, saying, "See
what a pretty little dog I have found."

The father said, "That is not a dog; throw it
away!" The little boy cried, but his father
made him take the dog out of the lodge. Then
the boy found the root digger, and again picking up the dog, he carried both into the lodge,
saying, "Look, mother; see what a pretty root
digger I have found."

"Throw them away," said his father; "throw
them both away. That is not a root digger; that
is not a dog."

"I want that root digger," said the woman.
"Let our son have the little dog."

"Let it be so, then," replied the husband; "but remember that if trouble comes, it is you who have brought it on yourself and on our son."

Soon after this the woman and her son went off to pick berries, and when they were out of sight the man went out and killed a buffalo cow and brought the meat into the lodge and covered it up. He took the bones and the skin and threw them in the water. When his wife came back he gave her some of the meat to roast, and while they were eating, the little boy fed the dog three times, and when he offered it more the father took the meat away.

In the night, when all were sleeping, Napi and the young man arose in their right shapes and ate some of the meat.

"You were right," said the young man. "This is surely the person who has hidden the buffalo."

"Wait," said Napi; and when they had finished eating they changed themselves again into the root digger and the dog.

Next morning the wife and the little boy went out to dig roots, and the woman took the root digger with her, while the dog followed the little boy.

As they travelled along looking for roots, they passed near a cave, and at its mouth stood a buffalo cow. The dog ran into the cave, and the root digger, slipping from the woman's hand, followed, gliding along over the ground like a snake. In this cave were found all the buffalo and the other game. They began to drive them out, and soon the prairie was covered with buffalo, antelope, and deer. Never before were so many seen.

Soon the man came running up, and he said to his wife, "Who is driving out my animals?" The woman replied, "The dog and the root digger are in there now."

"Did I not tell you," said her husband, "that those were not what they looked like. See now the trouble that you have brought upon us!" He put an arrow on his string and waited for them to come out, but they were cunning, and when the last animal, a big bull, was starting out the stick grasped him by the long hair under the neck and coiled up in it, and the dog held on by the hair underneath until they were far out on the prairie, when they changed into their true shapes and drove the buffalo toward the camp.

When the people saw the buffalo coming they led a big band of them to the piskun, but just as the leaders were about to jump over the cliff a raven came and flapped its wings in front of them and croaked, and they turned off and ran down another way. Every time a herd of buffalo was brought near to the piskun this raven frightened them away. Then Napi knew that the raven was the person who had kept the buffalo hidden.

Napi went down to the river and changed himself into a beaver and lay stretched out on a sandbar, as if dead. The raven was very hungry and flew down and began to pick at the beaver. Then Napi caught it by the legs and ran with it to the camp, and all the chiefs were called together to decide what should be done with the bird. Some said, "Let us kill it," but Napi said, "No, I will punish it," and he tied it up over the lodge, right in the smoke hole.

THE DOG AND THE ROOT DIGGER

As the days went by the raven grew thin and weak and its eyes were blinded by the thick smoke, and it cried continually to Napi asking him to pity it. One day Napi untied the bird and told it to take its right shape, and then said, "Why have you tried to fool Napi? Look at me. I cannot die. Look at me. Of all peoples and tribes I am the chief. I cannot die. I made the mountains; they are standing yet. I made the prairies and the rocks; you see them yet.

"Go home now to your wife and your child, and when you are hungry hunt like any one else. If you do not, you shall die."

THE CAMP OF THE GHOSTS

THERE was once a man who loved his wife dearly. After they had been married for a time they had a little boy. Some time after that the woman grew sick and did not get well. She was sick for a long time. The young man loved his wife so much that he did not wish to take a second woman. The woman grew worse and worse. Doctoring did not seem to do her any good. At last she died.

For a few days after this, the man used to take his baby on his back and travel out away from the camp, walking over the hills, crying and mourning. He felt badly, and he did not know what to do.

After a time he said to the little child, "My little boy, you will have to go and live with your grandmother. I shall go away and try to find your mother and bring her back."

He took the baby to his mother's lodge and asked her to take care of it and left it with her. Then he started away, not knowing where he was going nor what he should do.

When he left the camp, he travelled toward the Sand Hills. On the fourth night of his journeying he had a dream. He dreamed that he went into a little lodge in which was an old woman. This old woman said to him, "Why are you here, my son?"

The young man replied, "I am mourning day and night, crying all the while. My little son, who is the only one left me, also mourns."

"Well," asked the old woman, "for whom are you mourning?"

The young man answered, "I am mourning for my wife. She died some time ago. I am looking for her."

"Oh, I saw her," said the old woman; "she passed this way. I myself have no great power to help you, but over by that far butte beyond, lives another old woman. Go to her and she will give you power to continue your journey. You could not reach the place you are seeking

41

without help. Beyond the next butte from her lodge you will find the camp of the ghosts."

The next morning the young man awoke and went on toward the next butte. It took him a long summer's day to get there, but he found there no lodge, so he lay down and slept. Again he dreamed. In his dream he saw a little lodge, and saw an old woman come to the door and heard her call to him. He went into the lodge, and she spoke to him.

"My son, you are very unhappy. I know why you have come this way. You are looking for your wife who is now in the ghost country. It is a very hard thing for you to get there. You may not be able to get your wife back, but I have great power and I will do for you all that I can. If you act as I advise, you may succeed."

Other wise words she spoke to him, telling him what he should do; also she gave him a bundle of mysterious things which would help him on his journey.

She went on to say, "You stay here for a time and I will go over there to the ghosts' camp and try to bring back some of your relations who are there. If it is possible for me to bring them back, you may return there with them, but on the way you must shut your eyes. If you should open them and look about you, you would die. Then you would never come back. When you come to the camp you will pass by a big lodge and they will ask you, 'Where are you going and who told you to come here?' You must answer, 'My grandmother, who is standing out here with me, told me to come.' They will try to scare you; they will make fearful noises and you will see strange and terrible things, but do not be afraid."

The old woman went away, and after a time came back with one of the man's relations. He went with this relation to the ghosts' camp. When they came to the large lodge some one called out and asked the man what he was doing there, and he answered as the old woman had told him. As he passed on through the camp the ghosts tried to frighten him with many fearful sights and sounds, but he kept up a strong heart.

43

Presently he came to another lodge, and the man who owned it came out and spoke to him, asking where he was going. The young man said, "I am looking for my dead wife. I mourn for her so much that I cannot rest. My little boy too keeps crying for his mother. They have offered to give me other wives, but I do not want them. I want the one for whom I am searching."

The ghost said, "It is a fearful thing that you have come here; it is very likely that you will never go away. Never before has there been a person here."

The ghost asked him to come into his lodge, and he entered.

This chief ghost said to him, "You shall stay here for four nights and you shall see your wife, but you must be very careful or you will never go back. You will die here in this very place."

Then the chief ghost walked out of the lodge and shouted out for a feast, inviting the man's father-in-law and other relations who were in the camp to come and eat, saying, "Your son-

44

in-law invites you to a feast," as if he meant
that the son-in-law had died and become a
ghost and arrived at the camp of the ghosts.

Now when these invited ghosts had reached
the lodge they did not like to go in. They said
to each other, "There is a person here"; it
seemed as if they did not like the smell of a human being. The chief ghost burned sweet pine
on the fire, which took away this smell, and then
the ghosts came in and sat down.

The chief ghost said to them, "Now pity
this son-in-law of yours. He is looking for his
wife. Neither the great distance that he has
come nor the fearful sights that he has seen
here have weakened his heart. You can see
how tender-hearted he is. He not only mourns
because he has lost his wife, but he mourns
because his little boy is now alone, with no
mother; so pity him and give him back his
wife."

The ghosts talked among themselves, and
one of them said to the man, "Yes; you shall
stay here for four nights, and then we will give
you a medicine pipe—the Worm Pipe—and we

will give you back your wife and you may return to your home."

Now, after the third night the chief ghost
called together all the people, and they came, and
with them came the man's wife. One of the
ghosts was beating a drum, and following him
was another who carried the Worm Pipe, which
they gave to him.

Then the chief ghost said, "Now be very
careful; to-morrow you and your wife will start
on your journey homeward. Your wife will
carry the medicine pipe and for four days some
of your relations will go along with you. During this time you must keep your eyes shut;
do not open them, or you will return here and be
a ghost forever. Your wife is not now a person. But in the middle of the fourth day you
will be told to look, and when you have opened
your eyes you will see that your wife has become
a person, and that your ghost relations have
disappeared."

Before the man went away his father-in-law
spoke to him and said, "When you get near
home you must not go at once into the camp.

Let some of your relations know that you have come, and ask them to build a sweat-house for you. Go into that sweat-house and wash your body thoroughly, leaving no part of it, however small, uncleansed. If you fail in this, you will die. There is something about the ghosts that it is difficult to remove. It can only be removed by a thorough sweat. Take care now that you do what I tell you. Do not whip your wife, nor strike her with a knife, nor hit her with fire. If you do, she will vanish before your eyes and return here."

They left the ghost country to go home, and on the fourth day the wife said to her husband, "Open your eyes." He looked about him and saw that those who had been with them had disappeared, and he found that they were standing in front of the old woman's lodge by the butte. She came out of her lodge and said to them, "Stop; give me back those mysterious medicines of mine, whose power helped you to do what you wished." The man returned them to her, and then once more became really a living person.

47

When they drew near to the camp the woman went on ahead and sat down on a butte. Then some curious persons came out to see who this might be. As they approached the woman called out to them, "Do not come any nearer. Go and tell my mother and my relations to put up a lodge for us a little way from the camp, and near by it build a sweat-house." When this had been done the man and his wife went in and took a thorough sweat, and then they went into the lodge and burned sweet grass and purified their clothing and the Worm Pipe. Then their relations and friends came in to see them. The man told them where he had been and how he had managed to get his wife back, and that the pipe hanging over the doorway was a medicine pipe—the Worm Pipe—presented to him by his ghost father-in-law.

That is how the people came to possess the Worm Pipe. That pipe belongs to the band of Piegans known as the Worm People.

Not long after this, once in the night, this man told his wife to do something, and when she did not begin at once he picked up a brand from the fire and raised it—not that he intended to strike her with it, but he made as if he would —when all at once she vanished and was never seen again.

THE BUFFALO STONE

A SMALL stone, which is often a fossil shell, or sometimes only a queer shaped piece of flint, is called by the Blackfeet I-nĭs′kĭm, the buffalo stone. This stone has great power, and gives its owner good luck in bringing the buffalo close, so that they may be killed. The stone is found on the prairie, and any one who finds one is thought to be very lucky. Sometimes a man who is going along on the prairie will hear a queer faint chirp, such as a little bird might make. He knows this sound is made by a buffalo stone. He stops and searches for it on the ground, and if he cannot find it, marks the place and comes back next day to look for it again. If it is found, he and all his family are glad. The Blackfeet tell a story about how the first buffalo stone was found.

Long ago, one winter, the buffalo disappeared. The snow was deep, so deep that the people could not move in search of the buffalo; so the hunters went as far as they could up and down the river-bottoms and in the ravines, and killed deer and elk and other small game, and when these were all killed or driven away the people began to starve.

One day a young married man killed a prairie rabbit. He ran home as fast as he could, and told one of his wives to hurry and get a skin of water to cook it. She started down to the river for water, and as she was going along she heard a beautiful song. She looked all about, but could see no one who was singing.

The song seemed to come from a big cottonwood tree near the trail leading down to the water. As she looked closely at this tree she saw a queer stone jammed in a fork where the tree was split, and with it a few hairs from a buffalo which had rubbed against the tree. The woman was frightened and dared not pass the tree. Soon the singing stopped and the I-nĭs'kĭm said to the woman, "Take me to your lodge, and when it is dark call in the people and teach them the song you have just heard. Pray, too, that you may not starve, and that the buffalo may come back. Do this, and when day comes your hearts will be glad."

The woman went on and got the water, and when she came back she took the stone and gave it to her husband, telling him about the song and what the stone had said.

As soon as it was dark, the man called the chiefs and old men to his lodge, and his wife taught them the song that she had heard. They prayed too, as the stone had said should be done. Before long they heard far off a noise coming. It was the tramp of a great herd of buffalo. Then they knew that the stone was powerful, and since that time the people have taken care of it and have prayed to it.

HOW THE THUNDER PIPE CAME

YOU have heard the Thunder, for he is everywhere. He roars in the mountains, and far out on the prairie is heard his crashing. He strikes the high rocks, and they fall to pieces; a tree, and it is broken in slivers; the people, and they die. He is bad. He does not like the high cliff, the standing tree, or living man. He likes to strike and crush them to the ground. Of all things he is the most powerful. He cannot be resisted. But I have not told you the worst thing about him. Sometimes he takes away women.

Long ago, almost in the beginning, a man and his wife were sitting in their lodge when Thunder came and struck them. The man was not killed. At first he lay as if dead, but after a time he lived again, and, standing up, looked about him. He did not see his wife.

"Oh," he thought, "she has gone to get wood or water," and he sat down again. But when night came he went out of the lodge and asked the people about her. No one had seen her. He looked all through the camp, but could not find her. Then he knew that the Thunder had taken her away, and he went out on the hills and mourned. All night he sat there, trying to think what he might do to get back his wife.

When morning came he rose and wandered away, and whenever he met any of the animals he asked if they could tell him where the Thunder lived. The animals laughed, and most of them would not answer.

The Wolf said to him, "Do you think that we would look for the home of the only one we fear? He is our only danger. From all other enemies we can run away, but from him no one can run. He strikes and there we lie. Turn back; go home. Do not look for the place of that dreadful one."

The man kept on and travelled a long distance. At last, after many days, he came to a lodge—a strange lodge, for it was made of stone. Just like any other lodge it looked, only it was made of stone. This was the home of the Raven chief. The man entered.

"Welcome, friend," said the chief of the Ravens; "sit down there," and he pointed to a place. Soon food was placed before the poor man.

When he had finished eating, the Raven chief asked, "Why have you come here?"

"Thunder has stolen my wife," the man answered. "I am looking for his dwelling-place that I may find her."

"Are you brave enough to enter the lodge of that dreadful person?" asked the Raven. "He lives near here. His lodge is of stone like this one, and hanging in it are eyes—the eyes of those he has killed or taken away. He has taken out their eyes and hung them in his lodge. Now, then! Dare you enter there?"

"No," answered the man, "I am afraid. Who could look at such dreadful things and live?"

"No man can," said the Raven; "there is

only one old Thunder fears; there is but one he cannot kill. It is we. It is the Ravens. Now I will give you some medicine, and he shall not harm you. You shall enter there and try to find among those eyes your wife's, and if you find them tell the Thunder why you came and make him give them to you. Here, now, is a raven's wing. Point this at him and he will be afraid and start back; but if that should fail, take this arrow. Its shaft is made of elk horn. Take this, I say, and shoot it through the lodge."

"Why make a fool of me?" the poor man asked. "My heart is sad. I am crying." He covered his head with his robe and wept.

"Oh," said the Raven, "you do not believe me. Come outside, come outside, and I will make you believe."

When they stood outside the Raven asked, "Is the home of your people far?"

"A great distance," said the man.

"Can you tell how many days you have travelled?"

"No," he replied, "my heart was sad; I did

56

not count the days. Since I left, the berries have grown and ripened."

"Can you see your camp from here?" asked the Raven.

The man did not answer. Then the Raven rubbed some medicine on his eyes and said, "Look!" The man looked and saw the camp. It was near. He saw the people; he saw the smoke rising from the lodges; he saw the painting on some of the lodges.

"Now you will believe," said the Raven. "Take, then, the arrow and the wing, and go and get your wife." The man took these things and went to the Thunder's lodge. He entered and sat down by the doorway.

The Thunder sat at the back of the lodge and looked at him with awful eyes. The man looked above and saw hanging there many pairs of eyes. Among them were those of his wife.

"Why have you come?" said the Thunder in a dreadful voice.

"I seek my wife," said the man, "whom you have stolen. There hang her eyes."

57

"No man may enter my lodge and live," said the Thunder, and he rose to strike him. Then the man pointed the raven wing at the Thunder, and he fell back on his bed and shivered; but soon he recovered and rose again, and then the man fitted the elk-horn arrow to his bow and shot it through the lodge of stone. Right through that stone it pierced a hole and let the sunlight in.

"Wait," said the Thunder; "stop. You are the stronger, you have the greater medicine. You shall have your wife. Take down her eyes."

The man cut the string that held the eyes, and his wife stood beside him.

"Now," said the Thunder, "you know me. I have great power. In summer I live here; but when winter comes I go far south. I go south with the birds. Here is my pipe. It has strong power. Take it and keep it. After this, when first I come in the spring you shall fill this pipe and light it, and you shall smoke it and pray to me; you and the people. I bring the rain which makes the berries large and ripe.

HOW THE THUNDER PIPE CAME

I bring the rain which makes all things grow, and for this you shall pray to me; you and all the people."

Thus the people got their first medicine pipe. It was long ago.

COLD MAKER'S MEDICINE

THE last lodge had been set up in the Blackfeet winter camp. Evening was closing
over the travel-tired people. The sun had
dropped beyond the hills not far away. Women
were bringing water from the river at the edge
of the great circle. Men gathered in quiet
groups, weary after the long march of the day.
Children called sleepily to each other, and the
dogs sniffed about in well-fed content.

Lone Feather wrapped his robe more closely
around him and walked slowly from his lodge
door and from the camp, off toward the north.
He was thinking of many things, and hardly
noticed where he was going. Presently as he
walked, he heard the sound of persons talking.
He stopped to listen. The sound came from a
lodge made of stone, close by the river. Quietly
he went toward the lodge and saw a thin blue
line of smoke coming from the top.

As he approached, an old woman, bent with age and crippled, came from the lodge door and looked at him.

"Will you come into my lodge?" she said, greeting him.

Lone Feather looked at her for a moment in silence. She spoke again. He could not understand her speech, for she belonged to another tribe. By signs she made him know that she wished him to come into her lodge and rest. Lone Feather entered.

Far back from the door crouched two big grizzly bears. She made signs to show that the bears were friendly, and Lone Feather sat down near the door. She stirred the fire, and as she put on fresh wood the sparks flew up toward the smoke hole, which was opened only a little way.

By signs she told him she would go out and open the smoke hole wider, so that the fire might burn more brightly. She was gone for some time, and Lone Feather sat looking into the fire, still thinking of many things, when the air became thick with smoke. He looked up and saw that the smoke hole was closed. He

61

sprang up and went to the door, but the door covering was down. He raised it, and as he put his head out the old woman hit him with a large stone club and he was dead.

Before his spirit started for the Sand Hills he saw that with a large knife she cut up his body and put the pieces into a pot. Soon they were well cooked and the old woman and the two bears feasted on his flesh.

They threw his bones out of the door, where they fell among many others like them. The ground was strewn with the bones of the persons she had trapped and killed.

Day by day other persons disappeared from the winter camp, and more and more bones whitened on the ground outside the stone lodge on the river bank.

As Cold Maker was bringing the snow to the Blackfeet winter camp, he passed the Sand Hills. Lone Feather and other ghosts from the Blackfeet tribe were telling each other how the old woman had sent them there. Cold Maker heard their stories and he was angry.

When he reached the camp he went to the

lodge of Broken Bow—a brave young man, but very poor.

He shivered when Cold Maker entered his lodge and drew his ragged robe about him. They were close friends.

"Would you like to have a new robe?" asked Cold Maker.

"Yes," said Broken Bow.

"Come with me. You may kill two grizzly bears," said Cold Maker.

"My bow is broken. I cannot," said Broken Bow sadly.

"I will help you. Bring only a knife."

Together they went from the lodges toward the north. The sun was already hidden behind the nearby hills.

After they had travelled some distance they heard the sound of voices. They listened. Two bears were complaining that they wanted meat. A woman told them they must wait. The men saw the line of thin blue smoke rising from the top of the lodge of stone. All about whitening bones covered the ground. They went nearer.

Soon an old woman, bent with age and crip-

63

pled, came from the door and smiled as she saw the two persons coming.

"Come in and rest," she said. Broken Bow did not understand her language, but Cold Maker, who understands all tribes, said, "We are cold. Will you let us sit by your fire?"

The old woman smiled again.

"You are welcome," she said; "come in. Do not fear my bears. They are friendly. They will not harm you." The two friends entered the lodge, where a smouldering fire sent a feeble smoke up to the smoke hole, that was partly open. She put fresh wood on the fire and said, "I will open the smoke hole wider," and went out, dropping the door covering as she went.

Then she closed the smoke hole. The smoke began to fill the top of the lodge. It settled lower and lower. Broken Bow was afraid.

"Give me your pipe," said Cold Maker.

Broken Bow filled his pipe and handed it to him. He lighted it by a brand from the fire, and sent great puffs of smoke curling upward. This smoke met the other smoke and stopped it. It could not descend any lower.

Broken Bow saw the wonderful medicine of his friend. He was no longer afraid, but wondered what Cold Maker would do next. The grizzly bears growled low.

The old woman outside called to them, "Friends, is it smoking in there now?"

"Not a bit," replied Cold Maker. "We are very comfortable."

She waited. They did not come out. She stood near the door. Her stone club was ready. She grew impatient. She wondered what had gone wrong with her plans. The two friends were silent. She looked at the smoke hole, but it was closed securely. She lifted the door covering to see if the friends within had died. They sat perfectly still. She entered to look more closely, and as soon as she was fairly inside Cold Maker and Broken Bow rushed out and dropped the door covering. Before she could move they piled great heaps of stone in the door-way. The bears growled. She called for help. Cold Maker and Broken Bow went on down the river.

Then Cold Maker took from a little sack a

few white eagle-down feathers. He blew them from him. At once a fierce storm blew across the valley. The bitter cold froze the water, but only in this one place. It dammed the stream with fast forming ice. The water rose higher and higher. It spread out over the banks. Cold Maker and Broken Bow went far off on the hills and watched it. Little by little it rose. It reached the stone lodge. The bears roared. The woman screamed. The water reached the top and covered the lodge from sight. All sound ceased. A moment more, and the water was quiet. Once more Cold Maker blew from him a few white eagle-down feathers. The storm subsided. It became warm again. The ice melted. The water retreated to its channel.

Cold Maker and Broken Bow went to the stone lodge. The woman was lying beside the pot. The grizzly bears were close to the stones which blocked the door-way.

Cold Maker said, "Here is your new robe," and Broken Bow took from the bears their thick, warm skins.

COLD MAKER'S MEDICINE

On his way home Cold Maker again passed the Sand Hills. Entering the country was an old woman bent with age and crippled.

He hurried on.

THE ALL COMRADES SOCIETIES

IN the Blackfeet tribe was an association known as the All Comrades. This was made up of a dozen secret societies graded according to age, the members of the younger societies passing, after a few years, into the older ones. This association was in part benevolent and helpful and in part to encourage bravery in war, but its main purpose was to see that the orders of the chiefs were carried out, and to punish offences against the tribe at large. There are stories which explain how these societies came to be instituted, and this one tells how the Society of Bulls began.

THE BULLS SOCIETY

IT was long, long ago, very far back, that this happened. In those days the people used to kill the buffalo by driving them over a steep place near the river, down which they fell into a great pen built at the foot of the cliff, where the buffalo that had not been killed by the fall were shot with arrows by the men. Then the people went into the pen and skinned the buffalo and cut them up and carried the meat away to their camp. This pen they called piskun.

In those days the people had built a great piskun with high, strong walls. No buffalo could jump over it; not even if a great crowd of them ran against it, could they push it down.

The young men kept going out, as they always did, to try to bring the buffalo to the edge of the cliff, but somehow they would not jump over into the piskun. When they had come almost to the edge, they would turn off to one side or the other and run down the sloping hills and away over the prairie. So the people could get no food, and they began to be hungry, and at last to starve.

Early one morning a young woman, the daughter of a brave man, was going from her lodge down to the stream to get water, and as she went along she saw a herd of buffalo feeding on the prairie, close to the edge of the cliff above the great piskun.

"Oh," she called out, "if you will only jump off into the piskun I will marry one of you." She did not mean this, but said it just in fun, and as soon as she had said it, she wondered greatly when she saw the buffalo come jumping over the edge, falling down the cliff.

A moment later a big bull jumped high over the wall of the piskun and came toward her, and now truly she was frightened.

"Come," he said, taking hold of her arm.

"No, no," she answered, trying to pull herself away.

"But you said if the buffalo would only jump over, you would marry one of them. Look, the piskun is full."

She did not answer, and without saying anything more he led her up over the bluff and out on the prairie.

After the people had finished killing the buffalo and cutting up the meat, they missed this young woman. No one knew where she had gone, and her relations were frightened and very sad because they could not find her. So her father took his bow and quiver and put them on his back and said, "I will go and find her"; and he climbed the bluff and set out over the prairie.

He travelled some distance, but saw nothing of his daughter. The sun was hot, and at length he came to a buffalo wallow in which some water was standing, and drank and sat down to rest. A little way off on the prairie he saw a herd of buffalo. As the man sat there by the wallow, trying to think what he might do to find his daughter, a magpie came up and alighted on the ground near him. The man spoke to it, saying, "Măm-ĭ-ăt′sĭ-kĭmĭ—Magpie —you are a beautiful bird; help me, for I am very unhappy. As you travel about over the prairie, look everywhere, and if you see my daughter say to her, 'Your father is waiting by the wallow.'"

Soon the magpie flew away, and as he passed near the herd of buffalo he saw the young woman there, and alighting on the ground near her, he began to pick at things, turning his head this way and that, and seeming to look for food.

71

When he was close to the girl he said to her, "Your father is waiting by the wallow."

"Sh-h-h! Sh-h-h!" replied the girl in a whisper, looking about her very much frightened, for her bull husband was sleeping close by. "Do not speak so loud. Go back and tell him to wait."

"Your daughter is over there with the buffalo. She says 'Wait,'" said the magpie when he had flown back to the poor father.

After a little time the bull awoke and said to his wife, "Go and bring me some water." Then the woman was glad, and she took a horn from her husband's head and went to the wallow for water.

"Oh, why did you come?" she said to her father. "They will surely kill you."

"I came to take my daughter back to my lodge. Come, let us go."

"No," said the girl, "not now. They will surely chase us and kill us. Wait until he sleeps again and I will try to get away." Then she filled the horn with water and went back to the buffalo.

Her husband drank a swallow of the water, and when he took the horn it made a noise. "Ah," he said, as he looked about, "a person is somewhere close by."

"No one," replied the girl, but her heart stood still. The bull drank again. Then he stood up on his feet and moaned and grunted, "M-m-ah-oo! Bu-u-u!" Fearful was the sound. Up rose the other bulls, raised their tails in the air, tossed their heads and bellowed back to him. Then they pawed the earth, thrust their horns into it, rushed here and there, and presently, coming to the wallow, found there the poor man. They rushed over him, trampling him with their great hoofs, thrust their horns into his body and tore him to pieces, and trampled him again. Soon not even a piece of his body could be seen—only the wet earth cut up by their hoofs.

Then his daughter mourned in sorrow. "*Oh! Ah! Ni-nah-ah! Oh! Ah! Ni-nah-ah!*"—Ah, my father, my father.

"Ah," said her bull husband; "now you understand how it is that we feel. You mourn for your father; but we have seen our fathers, mothers, and many of our relations fall over the high cliffs, to be killed for food by your people. But now I will pity you, I will give you one chance. If you can bring your father to life, you and he may go back to your camp."

Then said the woman, "Ah, magpie, pity me, help me; for now I need help. Look in the trampled mud of the wallow and see if you can find even a little piece of my father's body and bring it to me."

Swiftly the magpie flew to the wallow, and alighting there, walked all about, looking in every hole and even tearing up the mud with his sharp beak. Presently he uncovered something white, and as he picked the mud from about it, he saw it was a bone, and pulling hard, he dragged it from the mud—the joint of a man's backbone. Then gladly he flew back with it to the woman.

The girl put the bone on the ground and covered it with her robe and began to sing. After she had sung she took the robe away, and there under it lay her father's body, as if he had just

74

died. Once again she covered the body with the robe and sang, and this time when she took the robe away the body was breathing. A third time she covered the body with the robe and sang, and when she again took away the robe, the body moved its arms and legs a little. A fourth time she covered it and sang, and when she took away the robe her father stood up.

The buffalo were surprised and the magpie was glad, and flew about making a great noise.

"Now this day we have seen a strange thing," said her bull husband. "The people's medicine is strong. He whom we trampled to death, whom our hoofs cut to pieces and mixed all up with the soil, is alive again. Now you shall go to your home, but before you go we will teach you our dance and our song. Do not forget them."

The buffalo showed the man and his daughter their dance and taught them the songs, and then the bull said to them, "Now you are to go back to your home, but do not forget what you have seen. Teach the people this dance and these songs, and while they are dancing it let them wear a bull's head and a robe. Those who are to be of the Bulls Society shall wear them."

When the poor man returned with his daughter, all the people were glad. Then after a time he called a council of the chiefs and told them the things that had happened. The chiefs chose certain young men to be Bulls, and the man taught them the dance and the song, and told them everything that they should do.

So began the Bull Society.

THE OTHER SOCIETIES

For a long time the buffalo had not been seen. Every one was hungry, for the hunters could find no food for the people.

A certain man, who had two wives, a daughter, and two sons, as he saw what a hard time they were having, said, "I shall not stop here to die. To-morrow we will move toward the mountains, where we may kill elk and deer and sheep and antelope, or, if not these, at least we shall find beaver and birds, and can get them. In this way we shall have food to eat and shall live."

Next morning they caught their dogs and harnessed them to the travois and took their loads on their backs and set out. It was still winter, and they travelled slowly. Besides, they were weak from hunger and could go only a short distance in a day. The fourth night came, and they sat in their lodge, tired and hungry. No one spoke, for people who are hungry do not care to talk. Suddenly, outside, the dogs began to bark, and soon the door was pushed aside and a young man entered.

"Welcome," said the man, and he motioned to a place where the stranger should sit.

Now during this day there had been blowing a warm wind which had melted the snow, so that the prairie was covered with water, yet this young man's moccasins and leggings were dry. They saw this, and were frightened. They sat there for a long time, saying nothing.

Then the young man spoke and asked, "Why is this? Why do you not give me food?"

"Ah," replied the father, "you see here people who are truly poor. We have no food. For many days the buffalo did not come in

77

sight, and we looked for deer and other animals which people eat, and when these had all been killed we began to starve. Then I said, 'We will not stay here to die from hunger,' and we set out for the mountains. This is the fourth night of our travels."

"Ah," said the young man, "then your travels are ended. You need go no farther. Close by here is our piskun. Many buffalo have been run in, and our parfleches are filled with dried meat. Wait a little; I will go and bring you some," and he went out.

As soon as he had gone they began to talk about this strange person. They were afraid of him and did not know what to do. The children began to cry, and the women tried to quiet them. Presently the young man came back, bringing some meat.

"There is food," said he, as he put it down by the woman. "Now to-morrow move your camp over to our lodges. Do not fear anything. No matter what strange things you may see, do not fear. All will be your friends. Yet about one thing I must warn you. In this you should

78

be careful. If you should find an arrow lying about anywhere, in the piskun or outside, do not touch it, neither you nor your wives nor your children." When he had said this he went out.

The father took his pipe and filled it, and smoked and prayed to all the powers, saying, "Hear now, Sun; listen, Above People; listen, Underwater People; now you have taken pity; now you have given us food. We are going to those mysterious ones who walk through water with dry moccasins. Protect us among these to-be-feared people. Let us live. Man, woman, and child, give us long life."

Now from the fire again arose the smell of roasting meat. The children ate and played. Those who so long had been silent now talked and laughed.

Early in the morning, as soon as the sun had risen, they took down their lodge and packed their dogs and started for the camp of the stranger. When they had come to where they could see it, they found it a wonderful place. There around the piskun, and stretching far up and down the valley, were pitched the lodges of the meat eaters. They could not see them all, but near by they saw the lodges of the Bear band, the Fox band, and the Raven band. The father of the young man who had visited them and given them meat was the chief of the Wolf band, and by that band they pitched their lodge. Truly that was a happy place. Food was plenty. All day long people were shouting out for feasts, and everywhere was heard the sound of drumming and singing and dancing.

The newly come people went to the piskun for meat, and there one of the children saw an arrow lying on the ground. It was a beautiful arrow, the stone point long, slender, and sharp, the shaft round and straight. The boy remembered what had been said and he looked around fearfully, but everywhere the people were busy. No one was looking. He picked up the arrow and put it under his robe.

Then there rose a terrible sound. All the animals howled and growled and rushed toward him, but the chief Wolf got to him first, and holding up his hand said, "Wait. He is young and not yet of good sense. We will let him go this time." They did nothing to him.

When night came some one shouted out, calling people to a feast and saying, "Listen, listen, Wolf, you are to eat; enter with your friend."

"We are invited," said the chief Wolf to his new friend, and together they went to the lodge from which the call came.

Within the lodge the fire burned brightly, and seated around it were many men, the old and wise of the Raven band. On the lodge lining, hanging behind the seats, were the paintings of many great deeds. Food was placed before the guests—pemican and berries and dried back fat—and after they had eaten the pipe was lighted and passed around the circle. Then the Raven chief spoke and said, "Now, Wolf, I am going to give our new friend a present. What do you think of that?"

"It shall be as you say," replied the Wolf; "our new friend will be glad."

From a long parfleche sack the Raven chief took a slender stick, beautifully ornamented with many-colored feathers. To the end of the stick was tied the skin of a raven—head, wings, feet, and tail.

"We," said the Raven chief, "are those who carry the raven (Măs-to-pāh'-tă-kĭks). Of all the fliers, of all the birds, what one is so smart as the raven? None. The raven's eyes are sharp, his wings are strong. He is a great hunter and never hungry. Far off on the prairie he sees his food, or if it is deep hidden in the forest it does not escape him. This is our song and our dance."

When he had finished singing and dancing he placed the stick in the sack and gave it to the man and said, "Take it with you, and when you have returned to your people you shall say, 'Now there are already the Bulls, and he who is the Raven chief said, "There shall be more. There shall be the All Friends (Ĭkŭn-ŭh'-kăh-tsĭ), so that the people may live, and of the All Friends shall be the Raven Bearers."' You shall call a council of the chiefs and wise old men, and they shall choose the persons who are to belong to the society. Teach them the song and the dance, and give them the medicine. It shall be theirs forever."

Soon they heard another person shouting out the feast call, and, going, they entered the lodge of the chief of the Kit-Foxes (Sĭn'-o-pah). Here, too, old men had gathered. After they had eaten of the food set before them, the chief said, "Those among whom you have just come are generous. They do not look carefully at the things they have, but give to the stranger and pity the poor. The kit-fox is a little animal, but what one is smarter? None. His hair is like the dead grass of the prairie; his eyes are keen; his feet make no noise when he walks; his brain is cunning. His ears receive the far-off sound. Here is our medicine. Take it." He gave the man the stick. It was long, crooked at one end, wound with fur, and tied here and there with eagle feathers. At the end was a kit-fox skin. Again the chief spoke and said, "Listen to our song. Do not forget it, and the dance, too, you must remember. When you reach home teach them to the people." He sang and danced. Then presently his guests departed.

83

Again they heard the feast shout, and he who called was the chief of the Bear society. After they had eaten and smoked the chief said,

"What is your opinion, friend Wolf? Shall we give our new friend a present?"

"It shall be as you say," replied the Wolf. "It is yours to give."

Then spoke the Bear, saying, "There are many animals and some of them are powerful; but the bear is the strongest and greatest of all. He fears nothing and is always ready to fight."

Then he put on a necklace of bear claws, a band of bear fur about his head, and a belt of bear fur, and sang and danced. When he had finished he gave the things he had worn to the man and said, "Teach the people our song and our dance, and give them this medicine. It is powerful."

It was very late. The Seven Stars had come to the middle of the night, yet again they heard the feast shout from the far end of the camp. In this lodge the men were painted with streaks of red, and their hair was all pushed to one side.

84

After the feast the chief said, "We are different from all others here. We are called the Braves (Mŭt'-sĭks). We know not fear; we are death. Even if our enemies are as many as the grass we do not turn away, but fight and conquer. Bows are good weapons, lances are better; but our weapon is the knife."

Then the chief sang and danced, and afterward he gave the Wolf chief's friend the medicine. It was a long knife and many scalps were tied on the handle. "This," said he, "is for the All Friends."

To one more lodge they were called that night and the lodge owner taught the man his song and dance, and gave him his medicine. Then the Wolf chief and his friend went home and slept.

Early next day the Blackfeet women began to take down the lodge and to get ready to move their camp. Many women came and made them presents of food, dried meat, pemican, and berries. They were given so much that they could not take it all with them. It was long before they joined the main camp, for it had moved south, looking for buffalo.

When they reached the camp, as soon as the lodge was pitched, the man called all the chiefs to come and feast with him, and told them what he had seen, and showed them the different medicines. Then the chiefs chose certain young men to belong to the different societies, and this man taught them the songs and dances, and gave its medicine to each society.

THE FIRST MEDICINE LODGE

THE chief god of the Blackfeet is the Sun. He made the world and rules it, and to him the people pray. One of his names is Napi —old man; but there is another Napi who is very different from the Sun, and instead of being great, wise, and wonderful, is foolish, mean, and contemptible. We shall hear about him further on.

Every year in summer, about the time the berries ripen, the Blackfeet used to hold the great festival and sacrifice which we call the ceremony of the Medicine Lodge. This was a time of happy meetings, of feasting, of giving presents; but besides this rejoicing, those men who wished to have good-luck in whatever they might undertake tried to prove their prayers sincere by sacrificing their bodies, torturing themselves in ways that caused great suffering.

In ancient times, as we are told in books of history, things like that used to happen among many peoples all over the world.

It was the law that the building of the Medicine Lodge must always be pledged by a good woman. If a woman had a son or a husband away at war and feared that he was in danger, or if she had a child that was sick and might die, she might pray for the safety of the one she loved, and promise that if he returned or recovered she would build a Medicine Lodge. This pledge was made in a loud voice, publicly, in open air, so that all might know the promise had been made.

At the time appointed all the tribe came together and pitched their lodges in a great circle, and within this circle the Medicine Lodge was built. The ceremony lasted for four days and four nights, during which time the woman who had promised to make the Medicine Lodge neither ate nor drank, except once in sacrifice. Different stories are told of how the first Medicine Lodge came to be built. This is one of those stories:

In the earliest times there was a man who had a very beautiful daughter. Many young men wished to marry her, but whenever she was asked she shook her head and said she did not wish to marry.

"Why is this?" said her father. "Some of these young men are rich, handsome, and brave."

"Why should I marry?" replied the girl. "My father and mother take care of me. Our lodge is good; the parfleches are never empty; there are plenty of tanned robes and soft furs for winter. Why trouble me, then?"

Soon after, the Raven Bearers held a dance. They all painted themselves nicely and wore their finest ornaments and each one tried to dance the best. Afterward some of them asked for this girl, but she said, "No." After that the Bulls, the Kit-Foxes, and others of the All Comrades held their dances, and many men who were rich and some great warriors asked this man for his daughter, but to every one she said, "No."

Then her father was angry, and he said, "Why is this? All the best men have asked for you, and still you say 'No.'" Then the girl said, "Father, listen to me. That Above Person, the Sun, said to me, 'Do not marry any of these men, for you belong to me. Listen to what I say, and you shall be happy and live to a great age.' And again he said to me, 'Take heed, you must not marry; you are mine.'"

"Ah!" replied her father; "it must always be as he says"; and they spoke no more about it.

There was a poor young man. He was very poor. His father, his mother, and all his relations were dead. He had no lodge, no wife to tan his robes or make his moccasins. His clothes were always old and worn. He had no home. To-day he stopped in one lodge; then to-morrow he ate and slept in another. Thus he lived. He had a good face, but on his cheek was a bad scar.

After they had held those dances, some of the young men met this poor Scarface, and they laughed at him and said, "Why do not you ask that girl to marry you? You are so rich and handsome."

Scarface did not laugh. He looked at them

and said, "I will do as you say; I will go and ask her."

All the young men thought this was funny; they laughed a good deal at Scarface as he was walking away.

Scarface went down by the river and waited there, near the place where the women went to get water. By and by the girl came there. Scarface spoke to her, and said, "Girl, stop; I want to speak with you. I do not wish to do anything secretly, but I speak to you here openly, where the Sun looks down and all may see."

"Speak, then," said the girl.

"I have seen the days," said Scarface. "I have seen how you have refused all those men, who are young and rich and brave. To-day some of these young men laughed and said to me, 'Why do not you ask her?' I am poor. I have no lodge, no food, no clothes, no robes. I have no relations. All of them have died. Yet now to-day I say to you, take pity. Be my wife."

The girl hid her face in her robe and brushed the ground with the point of her moccasin, back and forth, back and forth, for she was thinking.

After a time she spoke and said, "It is true I have refused all those rich young men; yet now a poor one asks me, and I am glad. I will be your wife, and my people will be glad. You are poor, but that does not matter. My father will give you dogs; my mother will make us a lodge; my relations will give us robes and furs; you will no longer be poor."

Then the young man was glad, and he started forward to kiss her, but she put out her hand and held him back, and said, "Wait; the Sun has spoken to me. He said I may not marry; that I belong to him; that if I listen to him I shall live to great age. So now I say, go to the Sun; say to him, 'She whom you spoke with has listened to your words; she has never done wrong, but now she wants to marry. I want her for my wife.' Ask him to take that scar from your face; that will be his sign, and I shall know he is pleased. But if he refuses, or if you cannot find his lodge, then do not return to me."

"Oh!" cried Scarface; "at first your words were good. I was glad. But now it is dark. My heart is dead. Where is that far-off lodge? Where is the trail that no one yet has travelled?"

"Take courage, take courage," said the girl softly, and she went on to her lodge.

Scarface was very unhappy. He did not know what to do. He sat down and covered his face with his robe, and tried to think. At length he stood up and went to an old woman who had been kind to him, and said to her, "Pity me. I am very poor. I am going away, on a long journey. Make me some moccasins."

"Where are you going—far from the camp?" asked the old woman.

"I do not know where I am going," he replied; "I am in trouble, but I cannot talk about it."

This old woman had a kind heart. She made him moccasins—seven pairs; and gave him also a sack of food—pemican, dried meat, and back fat.

All alone, and with a sad heart, Scarface climbed the bluff that overlooked the valley, and when he had reached the top, turned to look back at the camp. He wondered if he should ever see it again; if he should return to the girl and to the people.

"Pity me, O Sun!" he prayed; and turning away, he set off to look for the trail to the Sun's lodge.

For many days he went on. He crossed great prairies and followed up timbered rivers, and crossed the mountains. Every day his sack of food grew lighter, but as he went along he looked for berries and roots, and sometimes he killed an animal. These things gave him food.

One night he came to the home of a wolf. "Hah!" said the wolf; "what are you doing so far from your home?"

"I am looking for the place where the Sun lives," replied Scarface. "I have been sent to speak with him."

"I have travelled over much country," said the wolf; "I know all the prairies, the valleys, and the mountains; but I have never seen the Sun's home. But wait a moment. I know a person who is very wise, and who may be able to tell you the road. Ask the bear."

The next day Scarface went on again, stopping now and then to rest and to pick berries, and when night came he was at the bear's lodge.

"Where is your home?" asked the bear. "Why are you travelling so far alone?"

"Ah," replied the man, "I have come to you for help. Pity me. Because of what that girl said to me, I am looking for the Sun. I wish to ask him for her."

"I do not know where he lives," said the bear. "I have travelled by many rivers and I know the mountains, yet I have not seen his lodge. Farther on there is some one—that striped face—who knows a great deal; ask him."

When the young man got there, the badger was in his hole. But Scarface called to him, "Oh, cunning striped face! I wish to speak with you."

The badger put his head out of the hole and said, "What do you want, my brother?"

"I wish to find the Sun's home," said Scarface. "I wish to speak with him."

"I do not know where he lives," answered the badger. "I never travel very far. Over there in the timber is the wolverene. He is always travelling about, and knows many things. Perhaps he can tell you."

Scarface went over to the forest and looked all about for the wolverene, but could not see him; so he sat down on a log to rest. "Alas, alas!" he cried; "wolverene, take pity on me. My food is gone, my moccasins are worn out; I fear I shall die."

Some one close to him said, "What is it, my brother?" and looking around, he saw the wolverene sitting there.

"She whom I wish to marry belongs to the Sun," said Scarface; "I am trying to find where he lives, so that I may ask him for her."

"Ah," said the wolverene, "I know where he lives. It is nearly night now, but to-morrow I will show you the trail to the big water. He lives on the other side of it."

Early in the morning they set out, and the wolverene showed Scarface the trail, and he followed it until he came to the water's edge.

When he looked out over it, his heart almost stopped. Never before had any one seen such a great water. The other side could not be seen and there was no end to it. Scarface sat down on the shore. This seemed the end. His food was gone; his moccasins were worn out; he had no longer strength, no longer courage; his heart was sick. "I cannot cross this great water," he said. "I cannot return to the people. Here by this water I shall die."

Yet, even as he thought this, helpers were near. Two swans came swimming up to the shore and said to him, "Why have you come here? What are you doing? It is very far to the place where your people live."

"I have come here to die," replied Scarface. "Far away in my country is a beautiful girl. I want to marry her, but she belongs to the Sun; so I set out to find him and ask him for her. I have travelled many days. My food is gone. I cannot go back; I cannot cross this great water; so I must die."

"No," said the swans; "it shall not be so. Across this water is the home of that Above

97

Person. Get on our backs, and we will take you there."

Scarface stood up. Now he felt strong and full of courage. He waded out into the water and lay down on the swans' backs, and they swam away. It was a fearful journey, for that water was deep and black, and in it live strange people and great animals which might reach up and seize a person and pull him down under the water; yet the swans carried Scarface safely to the other side. There was seen a broad, hard trail leading back from the water's edge.

"There," said the swans; "you are now close to the Sun's lodge. Follow that trail, and soon you will see it."

Scarface started to walk along the trail, and after he had gone a little way he came to some beautiful things lying in the trail. There was a war shirt, a shield, a bow, and a quiver of arrows. He had never seen such fine weapons. He looked at them, but he did not touch them, and at last walked around them and went on. A little farther along he met a young man, a very handsome person. His hair was long; his clothing was made of strange skins, and his moccasins were sewed with bright feathers.

The young man spoke to him and asked, "Did you see some weapons lying in the trail?"

"Yes," replied Scarface, "I saw them."

"Did you touch them?" said the young man.

"No," said Scarface; "I supposed some one had left them there, and I did not touch them."

"You do not meddle with the property of others," said the young man. "What is your name, and where are you going?" Scarface told him. Then said the young man, "My name is Early Riser (the morning star). The Sun is my father. Come, I will take you to our lodge. My father is not at home now, but he will return at night."

At length they came to the lodge. It was large and handsome, and on it were painted strange medicine animals. On a tripod behind the lodge were the Sun's weapons and his war clothing. Scarface was ashamed to go into the lodge, but Morning Star said, "Friend, do not be afraid; we are glad you have come."

When they went in a woman was sitting

there, the Moon, the Sun's wife and the mother of Morning Star. She spoke to Scarface kindly and gave him food to eat, and when he had eaten she asked, "Why have you come so far from your people?"

So Scarface told her about the beautiful girl that he wished to marry and said, "She belongs to the Sun. I have come to ask him for her."

When it was almost night, and time for the Sun to come home, the Moon hid Scarface under a pile of robes. As soon as the Sun got to the doorway he said, "A strange person is here."

"Yes, father," said Morning Star, "a young man has come to see you. He is a good young man, for he found some of my things in the trail and did not touch them."

Scarface came out from under the robes and the Sun entered the lodge and sat down. He spoke to Scarface and said, "I am glad you have come to our lodge. Stay with us as long as you like. Sometimes my son is lonely. Be his friend."

The next day the two young men were talking about going hunting and the Moon spoke to Scarface and said, "Go with my son where you like, but do not hunt near that big water. Do not let him go there. That is the home of great birds with long, sharp bills. They kill people. I have had many sons, but these birds have killed them all. Only Morning Star is left."

Scarface stayed a long time in the Sun's lodge, and every day went hunting with Morning Star. One day they came near the water and saw the big birds.

"Come on," said Morning Star, "let us go and kill those birds."

"No, no," said Scarface, "we must not go there. Those are terrible birds; they will kill us."

Morning Star would not listen. He ran toward the water and Scarface ran after him, for he knew that he must kill the birds and save the boy's life. He ran ahead of Morning Star and met the birds, which were coming to fight, and killed every one of them with his spear; not one was left. The young men cut off the heads of the birds and carried them home, and when Morning Star's mother heard what

101

they had done, and they showed her the birds' heads, she was glad. She cried over the two young men and called Scarface "My son," and when the Sun came home at night she told him about it, and he too was glad.

"My son," he said to Scarface, "I will not forget what you have this day done for me. Tell me now what I can do for you; what is your trouble?"

"Alas, alas!" replied Scarface, "Pity me. I came here to ask you for that girl. I want to marry her. I asked her and she was glad, but she says that she belongs to you, and that you told her not to marry."

"What you say is true," replied the Sun. "I have seen the days and all that she has done. Now I give her to you. She is yours. I am glad that she has been wise, and I know that she has never done wrong. The Sun takes care of good women; they shall live a long time, and so shall their husbands and children.

"Now, soon you will go home. I wish to tell you something and you must be wise and listen. I am the only chief; everything is mine; I

102

made the earth, the mountains, the prairies, the rivers, and the forests; I made the people and all the animals. This is why I say that I alone am chief. I can never die. It is true the winter makes me old and weak, but every sum-, mer I grow young again.

"What one of all the animals is the smartest?" the Sun went on. "It is the raven, for he always finds food; he is never hungry. Which one of all the animals is the most to be reverenced? It is the buffalo; of all the animals I like him best. He is for the people; he is your food and your shelter. What part of his body is sacred? It is the tongue; that belongs to me. What else is sacred? Berries. They too are mine. Come with me now and see the world."

The Sun took Scarface to the edge of the sky and they looked down and saw the world. It is flat and round, and all around the edge it goes straight down. Then said the Sun, "If any man is sick or in danger his wife may promise to build me a lodge if he recovers. If the woman is good, then I shall be pleased and help the man; but if she is not good, or if she lies, then I

103

shall be angry. You shall build the lodge like the world, round, with walls, but first you must build a sweat-lodge of one hundred sticks. It shall be arched like the sky, and one-half of it shall be painted red for me, the other half you shall paint black for the night." He told Scarface all about making the Medicine Lodge, and when he had finished speaking, he rubbed some medicine on the young man's face and the scar that had been there disappeared. He gave him two raven feathers, saying: "These are a sign for the girl that I give her to you. They must always be worn by the husband of the woman who builds a Medicine Lodge."

Now Scarface was ready to return home. The Sun and Morning Star gave him many good presents; the Moon cried and kissed him and was sorry to see him go. Then the Sun showed him the short trail. It was the Wolf Road— the Milky Way. He followed it and soon reached the ground.

It was a very hot day. All the lodge skins were raised and the people sat in the shade.

104

There was a chief, a very generous man, who all day long was calling out for feasts, and people kept coming to his lodge to eat and smoke with him. Early in the morning this chief saw sitting on a butte near by a person close-wrapped in his robe. All day long this person sat there and did not move. When it was almost night the chief said, "That person has sat there all day in the strong heat, and he has not eaten nor drunk. Perhaps he is a stranger. Go and ask him to come to my lodge."

Some young men ran up to the person and said to him, "Why have you sat here all day in the great heat? Come to the shade of the lodges. The chief asks you to eat with him." The person rose and threw off his robe and the young men were surprised. He wore fine clothing; his bow, shield, and other weapons were of strange make; but they knew his face, although the scar was gone, and they ran ahead, shouting, "The Scarface poor young man has come. He is poor no longer. The scar on his face is gone."

All the people hurried out to see him and to

ask him questions. "Where did you get all these fine things?" He did not answer. There in the crowd stood that young woman, and, taking the two raven feathers from his head, he gave them to her and said, "The trail was long and I nearly died, but by those helpers I found his lodge. He is glad. He sends these feathers to you. They are the sign."

Great was her gladness then. They were married and made the first Medicine Lodge, as the Sun had said. The Sun was glad. He gave them great age. They were never sick. When they were very old, one morning their children called to them, "Awake, rise and eat." They did not move.

In the night, together, in sleep, without pain, their shadows had departed to the Sandhills.

THE BUFFALO–PAINTED LODGES

THE old lodges of the Piegans were made of buffalo skin and were painted with pictures of different kinds—birds, or animals, or trees, or mountains. It is believed that in most cases the first painter of any lodge was taught how he should paint it in a dream, but this was not always the case.

Two of the most important lodges in the Blackfeet camp are known as the Inĭs'kĭm lodges. Both are painted with figures of buffalo, one with black buffalo, and the other with yellow buffalo. Certain of the Inĭs'kĭm are kept in these lodges and can be kept in no others.

This story tells how these two lodges came to be made.

The painters were told what to do long, long ago, "in about the second generation after the first people."

In those days the old Piegans lived in the

north, close to the Red Deer River. The camp moved, and the lodges were pitched on the river. One day two old men who were close friends had gone out from the camp to find some straight cherry shoots with which to make arrows. After they had gathered their shafts, they sat down on a high bank by the river and began to peel the bark from the shoots. The river was high. One of these men was named Weasel Heart and the other Fisher.

As they sat there, Weasel Heart chanced to look down into the water and saw something. He said to his comrade, "Friend, do you not see something down there where the water goes around?"

Fisher said, "No; I see nothing except buffalo," for he was looking across the river to the other side, and not down into the water.

"No," said Weasel Heart; "I do not mean over there on the prairie. Look down into that deep hole in the river, and you will see a lodge there."

Fisher looked as he had been told, and saw the lodge.

Weasel Heart said, "There is a lodge painted

108

with black buffalo." As he spoke thus, Fisher said, "I see another lodge, standing in front of it." Weasel Heart saw that lodge too—the yellow-painted-buffalo lodge.

The two men wondered at this and could not understand how it could be, but they were both men of strong hearts, and presently Weasel Heart said, "Friend, I shall go down to enter that lodge. Do you sit here and tell me when I get to the place." Then Weasel Heart went up the river and found a drift-log to support him and pushed it out into the water, and floated down toward the cut bank. When he had reached the place where the lodge stood Fisher told him, and he let go the log and dived down into the water and entered the lodge.

In it he found two persons who owned the lodge, a man and his wife. The man said to him, "You are welcome," and Weasel Heart sat down. Then spoke the owner of the lodge saying, "My son, this is my lodge, and I give it to you. Look well at it inside and outside; and make your lodge like this. If you do that, it may be a help to you."

109

Fisher sat a long time waiting for his friend, but at last he looked down the stream and saw a man on the shore walking toward him. He came along the bank until he had reached his friend. It was Weasel Heart.

Fisher said to him, "I have been waiting a long time, and I was afraid that something bad had happened to you."

Weasel Heart asked him, "Did you see me?"

"I saw you," said Fisher, "when you went into that lodge. Did you, when you came out of the lodge, see there in the water another lodge painted with yellow buffalo? Is it still there?"

Weasel Heart said, "I saw it; it is there. Go you into the water as I did."

Then Fisher went up the stream as his friend had gone and entered the water at the same place and swam down as Weasel Heart had done, and when Weasel Heart showed him the place he dived down and disappeared as Weasel Heart had disappeared. He entered the yellow-painted-buffalo lodge, and his friend saw him go into it.

In the lodge were two persons, a man and his

110

wife. The man said to him, "You are welcome; sit there." He spoke further, saying, "My son, you have seen this lodge of mine; I give it to you. Look carefully at it, inside and outside, and fix up your lodge in that way. It may be a help to you hereafter." Then Fisher went out.

Weasel Heart waited for his friend as long as Fisher had waited for him, and when Fisher came out of the water it was at the place where Weasel Heart had come out. Then the two friends went home to the camp.

When the two had come to a hill near the camp they met a young man, and by him sent word that the people should make a sweat-house for them. After the sweat-house had been made, word was sent to them, and they entered the camp and went into the sweat-house and took a sweat, and all the time while they were sweating, sand was falling from their bodies.

Some time after that the people moved camp and went out and killed buffalo, and these two men made two lodges, and painted them just as the lodges were painted that they had seen in the river.

111

These two men had strong power which came to them from the Under-water People.

Once the people wished to cross the river, but the stream was deep and it was always hard for them to get across. Often the dogs and the travois were swept away and the people lost many of their things. At this time the tribe wished to cross, and Fisher and Weasel Heart said to each other, "The people want to cross the river, but it is high and they cannot do so. Let us try to make a crossing, so that it will be easier for them." So Weasel Heart alone crossed the river and sat on the bank on the other side, and Fisher sat opposite to him on the bank where the camp was.

Then Fisher said to the people, "Pack up your things now and get ready to cross. I will make a place where you can cross easily."

Weasel Heart and Fisher filled their pipes and smoked, and then each started to cross the river. As each stepped into the water, the river began to go down and the crossing grew more and more shallow. The people with all their dogs followed close behind Fisher, as he

112

had told them to do. Fisher and Weasel Heart met in the middle of the river, and when they met they stepped to one side up the stream and let the people pass them. Ever since that day this has been a shallow crossing.

These lodges came from the Under-water People—Sū'yē-tŭp'pĭ. They were those who had owned them and who had been kind to Weasel Heart and Fisher.

MĬKA'PI—RED OLD MAN

IN Montana, running into the Missouri River from the south, is a little stream that the Blackfeet call "It Fell on Them." Once, long, long ago, while a number of women were digging in a bank near this stream for the red earth that they used as paint, the bank gave way and fell on them, burying and killing them. The white people call this Armell's Creek.

It was on this stream near the mountains that the Piegans were camped when Mĭka'pi went to war. This was long ago.

Early in the morning a herd of buffalo had been seen feeding on the slopes of the mountains, and some hunters went out to kill them. Travelling carefully up the ravines, and keeping out of sight of the herd, they came close to them, near enough to shoot their arrows, and they began to kill fat cows. But while they were doing this a war party of Snakes that had been

114

hidden on the mountainside attacked them, and the Piegans began to run back toward their camp.

One of them, called Fox Eye, was a brave man, and shouted to the others to stop and wait, saying, "Let us fight these people; the Snakes are not brave; we can drive them back." But the other Piegans would not listen to him; they made excuses, saying, "We have no shields; our war medicine is not here; there are many of them; why should **we** stop here to die?" They ran on to the camp, but Fox Eye would not run. Hiding behind a rock he prepared to fight, but as he was looking for some enemy to shoot at, holding his arrow on the string, a Snake had crept up on the bank above him; the Piegan heard the twang of the bowstring, and the long, fine arrow passed through his body. His bow and arrow dropped from his hands, and he fell forward, dead. Now, too late, the warriors came rushing out from the Piegan camp to help him, but the Snakes scalped their enemy, scattered up the mountain, and soon were hidden in the timber.

Fox Eye had two wives, and their father and mother and all their near relations were dead. All Fox Eye's relations had died. So it happened that these poor widows had no one to help them—no one to take vengeance for the killing of their husband.

All day long, and often far into the night, these two sat on a near-by hill and wailed, and their mourning was sad.

There was a young man named Mīka′pi. Every morning when he awoke he heard the mourning of these poor widows, and all through the day he could not forget their sorrow. He pitied them. One day he sent his mother to them, to tell them that he wished to speak with them. When they had come to the lodge they entered and sat down close by the doorway and covered their heads.

"Listen!" said Mīka′pi. "For days and nights I have heard your mourning, and I too have mourned. Your husband was my close friend, and now he is dead, and no relations are left to avenge him. So now I say to you, I will take the load from your hearts; I will go to war and kill enemies and take scalps, and when I return they shall be yours. I will wipe away your tears, and we shall be glad that Fox Eye is avenged."

When the people heard that Mīka'pi was going to war many young men wished to join him, but he refused. "I shall go alone," he said. So when he had taken a medicine sweat and had asked a priest to pray for him in his absence, he left the camp one evening, just as it was growing dark.

It is only the foolish warrior who travels in the day. The wise one knows that war-parties may be out, or that some camp watcher sitting on a hill may see him far off and may try to kill him. Mīka'pi was not one of these foolish persons. He was brave and cautious, and he had powerful helpers. Some have said that he was helped by the ghosts. When he started to war against the Snakes he travelled in low places, and at sunrise he climbed some hill near by and looked carefully over the country in all directions, and during all the long day he lay there and watched, sleeping often, but only for a short time.

When Mïka'pi had come to the Great Place of Falling Water,* it began to rain hard, and, looking about for a place to sleep, he saw a hole in the rocks and crept in and lay down at the farther end. The rain did not stop, and when it grew dark he could not travel because of the darkness and the storm, so he lay down to sleep again; but before he had fallen asleep he heard something at the mouth of the cave, and then something creeping toward him. Then soon something touched his breast, and he put out his hand and felt a person. Then he sat up.

Mïka'pi stretched out his hand and put its palm on the person's breast and moved his hand quickly from side to side, and then touched the person with the point of his finger, which in sign language means, "Who are you?" The stranger took Mïka'pi's hand and made him feel of his own right hand. The thumb and fingers were closed except the forefinger, which was extended. When Mïka'pi's hand was on the stranger's hand the person moved his hand forward with a zigzag motion, meaning Snake.

*The Great Falls of the Missouri.

Mīka'pi was glad. Here had come to him one of the tribe he was seeking, yet he thought it better to wait for a time before fighting him; so when, in signs, the Snake asked Mīka'pi who he was he replied, by making the sign for paddling a canoe, that he was a River person, for he knew that the Snakes and the River people, or Pend d'Oreilles, were at peace. Then the two lay down for the night, but Mīka'pi did not sleep. Through the long night he watched for the first light, so that he might kill his enemy; and just at daybreak Mīka'pi, without noise, strung his bow, fitted an arrow to the string, and sent the thin shaft through his enemy's heart. The Snake half rose up and fell back dead. Mīka'pi scalped him, took his bow and arrows and his bundle of moccasins, and went out of the cave and looked all about. Daylight had come, but no one was in sight. Perhaps, like himself, the Snake had gone to war alone. Mīka'pi did not forget to be careful because he had been fortunate. He travelled only a little way, and then hid himself and waited for night before going on. After drinking from the river he ate and, climbing up on a high rock wall, he slept.

He dreamed that he fought with strange people and was wounded. He felt blood trickling from his wounds, and when he awoke he knew that he had been warned to turn back. Other signs were bad. He saw an eagle rising carrying a snake, which dropped from its claws. The setting sun too was painted, a sure warning that danger was near. In spite of all these things Mīka′pi determined to go on. He thought of the poor widows mourning; he thought of the welcome of the people if he should return with scalps; he thought also of two young sisters whom he wished to marry. If he could return with proof of brave deeds, they would think well of him.

Mīka′pi travelled onward.

The sun had already disappeared behind the sharp pointed dark peaks of the mountains. It was nearly night. As the light grew dim, the far stretching prairie began to be hidden. By a stream in a valley where grew large and small trees were the lodges of a great camp. For a long distance up and down the river rose the smokes of many fires.

On a hill overlooking the valley sat a person alone. His robe was drawn close about him, and he sat there without moving, looking down on the valley and out on the prairie above it. Perhaps he was watching for enemies; perhaps he was praying.

Creeping through the grass behind this person, something was slowly drawing near to him. There was no noise, the watcher heard nothing; still he sat there, looking out over the prairie, and turning his head neither to the right nor the left. This thing behind him kept creeping closer, and presently it was so near it could touch the man. Perhaps then there was some little rustle of the grass, and the watcher turned his head. It was too late. A strong arm around his neck bent his head back, a hand covered his mouth, a long stone knife was thrust into his breast, and he died in silence. The fading light had kept people in the camp from seeing what had happened.

The man who had used the knife scalped his enemy, and slowly, hidden by the grass, crept down the hill that he had just ascended, and when he reached the cover of a low place Mĭka'pi rose to his feet and crept away. He had another Snake scalp tied to his belt. His heart was glad, but he was not satisfied.

Several nights had passed since the signs warned him to turn back, but notwithstanding the warnings, he had succeeded. Perhaps his success had made him too confident. He longed for more of it. "One more scalp I shall take," he said, "and then I will return to the people."

He climbed far up the mountainside and hid among the pines and slept, but when day came he awoke and crept out to a point where he could see the camp. He saw the smoke rising as the women kindled their morning fires; he saw the people going about through the camp, and then presently he saw many people rush up on the hill where he had left the dead enemy. He could not hear their angry cries, nor their mournful wailings, but he knew how badly they felt, and he sung a song, for he was happy.

Once more the sun had disappeared behind the mountains, and as darkness grew Mīka'pi came down from where he had been hiding and carefully approached the camp. Now was a time of danger. Now watchers might be hidden anywhere, looking for the approach of enemies, ready to raise a cry to warn the camp. Each bush or clump of rye grass or willow thicket might hide an enemy. Very slowly, looking and listening, Mīka'pi crept around the outskirts of the camp. He made no noise, he did not show himself. Presently he heard some one clear his throat and then a cough, and a little bush moved. Here was a watcher. Could he kill him and get away? He sat and waited to see what would happen, for he knew where his enemy was, but the enemy knew nothing of him. The great moon rose over the eastern prairie and climbed high and began to travel across the sky. Seven Persons swung around and pointed downward. It was about the middle of the night. At length the person in the bush grew tired of watching; he thought no enemy could be near and he rose and stretched

123

out his arms and yawned, but even as he stood an arrow pierced him through, beneath the arms. He gave a loud cry and tried to run, but another arrow struck him, and he fell.

And now from out the camp rushed the warriors toward the sound, but even as they came Mīka'pi had taken the scalp from his enemy and started to run away into the darkness. The moon was bright, and close behind him were the Snakes. He heard arrows flying by him, and presently one passed through his arm. He pulled it out and threw it from him. Another struck his leg, and he fell, and a great shout arose from the Snakes. Now their enemy was down and revenge for the two lives lately taken was certain.

But Mīka'pi's helpers were not far off. It was at the very verge of a high cut wall overhanging the river that Mīka'pi fell, and even as the Snakes shouted he rolled over the brink into the dark rushing water below. The Snakes ran along the edge of the river, looking into the water, with bent bows watching for the enemy's head or body to appear, but they saw nothing.

Carefully they looked along the shores and sandbars; they did not find him.

Mĭka'pi had sunk deep in the water. The swift current carried him along, and when he rose to the surface he was beyond his enemies. For some time he floated on, but the arrow in his leg pained him and at last he crept out on a sandbar. He managed to draw the arrow from his leg, and finding at the edge of the bar a dry log, he rolled it into the water, and keeping his hands on it, drifted down the river with the current. Cold and stiff from his wounds, he crept out on the bank and lay down in the warm sunshine. Soon he fell asleep.

When he awoke the sun was in the middle of the sky. His leg and arm were swollen and pained him, yet he started to go home, and for a time struggled onward; but at last, tired and discouraged, he sat down.

"Ah," he said to himself, "true were the signs! How crazy I was to go against them! Now my bravery has been useless, for here I must stop and die. The widows will still mourn, and who will care for my father and

125

mother in their old age? Pity me now, O
Sun; help me, O Great Above Person! Give
me life!"

Something was coming through the brush
near him, breaking the sticks as it walked.
Was it the Snakes following his trail? Mīka'pi
strung his bow and drew his arrows from the
quiver. He waited.

No, it was not a Snake; it was a bear, a big
grizzly bear, standing there looking down at
Mīka'pi. "What is my brother doing here?"
said the bear. "Why does he pray for life?"

"Look at my leg," said Mīka'pi; "swollen
and sore. See my wounded arm; I can hardly
hold the bow. Far away is the home of my
people, and my strength is gone. Surely here
I must die, for I cannot walk, and I have no
food."

"Take courage, my brother," said the bear.
"Keep up a strong heart, for I will help you,
and you shall have life."

When he had said this he lifted Mīka'pi in
his arms and took him to a place where there
was thick mud, and there he took great hand-

fuls of the mud and plastered it on the wounds, and while he was putting on the mud he sang a medicine song. Then he carried Mĭka'pi to a place where there were many service berries, and he broke off great branches of the fruit and gave them to him, saying, "Eat, my brother, eat." He kept breaking off branches full of large, ripe berries until Mĭka'pi was full and could eat no more.

Then said the bear, "Now lie down on my back and hold tight by my hair and we will go on"; and when Mĭka'pi had got on his back and was ready the bear started. All through the night he travelled on without stopping, and when morning came they rested for a time and ate more berries, and again the bear put mud upon the man's wounds. In this way they travelled on, until, on the fourth day, they had come close to the lodges of the Piegans and the people saw them coming, and wondered.

"Get off now, my brother, get off," said the bear. "There is the camp of your people. I shall leave you"; and at once he turned and went off up the mountain.

All the people came out to meet Mīka'pi, and they carried him to his father's lodge. He untied the scalps from his belt and gave them to the poor widows, saying, "These are the scalps of your enemies; I wipe away your tears." Then every one rejoiced. All Mīka'pi's women relations went through the camp, shouting out his name and singing songs about him, and all prepared to dance the dance of triumph and rejoicing.

First came the widows. They carried the scalps tied on poles, and their faces were painted black. Then came the medicine men, with their medicine pipes unwrapped, and then the bands of the All Friends dressed in their war costumes; then came the old men; and, last of all, the women and children. They went all through the village, stopping here and there to dance, and Mīka'pi sat outside the lodge and saw all the people dance by him. He forgot his pain and was happy, and although he could not dance, he sung with them.

Soon they made the medicine lodge, and first of all the warriors, Mīka'pi was chosen to cut

the rawhide to bind the poles, and as he cut
the strips he related the coups he had counted.
He told of the enemies he had killed, and all
the people shouted his name and the drummers
struck the drum. The father of those two sisters gave them to him. He was glad to have
such a son-in-law.

Long lived Mīka'pi. Of all the great chiefs
who have lived and died he was the greatest.
He did many other great things. It must be
true, as the old men have said, that he was
helped by the ghosts, for no one can do such
things without help from those fearful and terrible persons.

RED ROBE'S DREAM

LONG, long ago, Red Robe and Talking Rock were young men in the Blackfeet camp. In their childhood days and early youth their life had been hard. Talking Rock was an orphan without a single relation and Red Robe had only his old grandmother.

This old woman, by hard work and sacrifice, had managed to rear the boys. She tanned robes for the hunters, made them moccasins worked with porcupine quills, and did everything she could to get a little food or worn out robes and hide, from which she made clothes for her boys. They never had new, brightly painted calf robes, like other children. They went barefoot in summer, and in winter their toes often showed through the worn out skin of their moccasins. They had no flesh. Their ribs could be counted beneath the skin; their cheeks were hollow; they looked always hungry.

When they grew to be twelve or fifteen years old they began to do better, for now they could do more and more for themselves. They herded horses and performed small services for the wealthy men; then, too, they hunted and killed a little meat. Now, for their work, three or four dogs were given them, so with the two the old woman owned, they were able to pack their small lodge and other possessions when the camp moved, instead of carrying everything on their backs.

Now they began to do their best to make life easier for the good old woman who had worked so hard to keep them from starving and freezing.

Time passed. The boys grew old enough to go out and fast. They had their dreams. Each found his secret helper of mysterious power, and each became a warrior. Still they were very poor, compared with other young men of their age. They had bows, but only a few arrows. They were not able to pay some great medicine man to make shields for them. As yet they went to war only as servants.

About this time Red Robe fell in love.

In the camp was a beautiful girl named
Mā-mĭn'—the Wing—whom all the young men
wished to marry, but perhaps Red Robe loved
her more than all the rest. Her father was a
rich old medicine man who never invited any
except chiefs and great warriors to feast with
him, and Red Robe seldom entered his lodge.
He used to dress as well as he could, to braid
his hair carefully, to paint his face nicely, and to
stand for a long time near the lodge looking
entreatingly at her as she came and went about
her work, or fleshed a robe under the shelter
of some travois over which a hide was spread.
Then whenever they met, he thought the look
she gave him in passing was friendly—perhaps
more than that.

Wherever Mā-mĭn' went her mother or some
woman of the family went with her, so Red
Robe could never speak to her, but he was
often near by. One day, when she was gathering wood for the lodge, and her companion was
out of sight behind some willow bushes some
distance away, Red Robe had a chance to tell
Mā-mĭn' what was in his heart. He walked

up to her and took her hands in his, and she did not try to draw them away. He said to her, "I love you; I cannot remember a time when I saw you that my heart did not beat faster. I am poor, very poor, and it is useless to ask your father to let me marry you, for he will not consent; but there is another way, and if you love me, you will do what I ask. Let us go from here—far away. We will find some tribe that will be kind to us, and even if we fail in that we can live in some way. Now, if you love me, and I hope you do, you will come."

"Ai," replied Mā-mĭn', "I do love you; only you. All the other young men pass before me as shadows. I scarcely see them, but I cannot do what you ask. I cannot go away and leave my mother to mourn; she who loves me so well. Let us wait a little. Go to war. Do something great and brave. Then perhaps you will not uselessly ask my father to give me to you."

In vain Red Robe tried to persuade the girl to do as he wished. She was kind; she threw her arms about him and kissed him and cried, but she would not run away to leave her mother to sorrow, to be beaten by her father, who would blame the poor woman for all the disgrace; and so, too soon, they parted, for they heard her companion coming—the sound of her heavy footsteps.

Three Bulls, chief of the camp, was a great man. He had a fierce temper, and when he spoke, people hurried to do what he ordered, for they feared him. He never talked loud nor called any one by an ill name. When any one displeased him or refused to do what he said he just smiled and then killed the person. He was brave. In battle with enemies he was the equal of twenty men, rushing here, there, into the thickest of the fights, and killing—always with that silent, terrible smile on his face. Because he was such a great warrior, and also because he was generous, helping the poor, feasting any who came to his lodge, he was the head chief of the Blackfeet.

Three Bulls had several wives and many children, some of them grown and married. Gray hairs were now many in his head. His face wrinkles showed that old age was not far distant.

134

No one supposed that he would ever take another wife; so when the news spread through the camp that he had asked the old medicine man for his daughter Mā-mĭn', every one was surprised. When Red Robe heard the news his heart nearly broke. The old medicine man agreed to let the chief have the girl. He dared not refuse, nor did he wish to, for many good presents were to be given him in three days' time. When that was done, he told his daughter, she would be taken to the chief's lodge; let her prepare for the change.

That day Red Robe had planned to start with a party to war; but when he heard this news he asked his friend Talking Rock to take word to the leader that he had changed his mind and would not go. He asked his friend to stay with him, instead of joining the war party, and Talking Rock agreed to do so.

Out in front of the camp was a large spring, and to that place Red Robe went and stood leaning against a large stone and looking sadly down into the blue water. Soon, as he had thought, Mā-mĭn' came to the spring for a skin of water.

He took her hands, as he had done before, and began to beg her to go away with him that very night, before it was too late. The girl cried bitterly, but at first she did not speak.

The two were standing in plain sight of the camp and the people in it, and some one went to the chief's lodge and told him what was taking place.

"Go to the spring," said the chief, "and tell that young man to let the girl go; she is to be my wife."

The person did as he was told, but the two young people paid no attention to him. They did not care what any one said, nor if the whole camp saw them there together. All they could think about was this terrible thing, which would make them unhappy so long as they lived. Red Robe kept asking the girl to go, and at last she consented to do as he wished. They had their arms about each other, not thinking of the crowd that was watching them, and were quickly planning for their meeting and for their going away that night, when Three Bulls quietly walked up to them and stabbed the young man with a flint-

136

pointed lance. Red Robe sank down dying at the young girl's feet, and she, looking down for an instant at her lover, turned and ran to her father's lodge.

"Bring wood," the chief called out; "let every one bring some wood; all you have at your lodges. Those who have none, let them go quickly and bring some from the timber."

All the people hurried to obey. What Three Bulls ordered was soon done, for the people feared him, and soon a great pile of wood was heaped beside the dead man.

The chief lifted the slender young form, placed it on the pile of wood, and told a woman to bring coals and set fire to the pile. When this had been done, all left the place except Three Bulls, who stayed there, tending the fire and poking it here and there, until it was burnt out and no wood or trace of a human body was left. Nothing remained except the little pile of ashes. These he scattered. Still he was not satisfied. His medicine was strong; perhaps his dream had warned him. Now he ordered that the lodges be taken down, that everything be packed up, and that the trail of the moving camp should pass over the heap of ashes.

Some time before this, after Red Robe had made his long fasting, and his dream had come to him and he had returned to his grandmother's lodge, he had told his true friend something of what had been said to him by his dream.

"If I should die," he said, "and you are near, do not desert me. Go to the place where I fell, and if my body should have been destroyed look carefully around the place. If you can find even a shred of my flesh or a bit of my bone, it will be well. So said my dream. Here are four arrows, which the dream told me to make. If you can find a bit of my body, flesh or bone, or even hair, cover it with a robe, and standing over it, shoot three arrows one after another up into the air, crying, as each one leaves the bow, 'Look out!' When you fit the fourth arrow on the bowstring and shoot it upward, cry, 'Look out, Red Robe, the arrow will strike you!' and as you say this, turn and run away from the place, not looking back as you go. If you do

138

this, my friend, just as I have told you, I shall live again."

As the camp moved, Three Bulls stood and watched it filing over the place of the fire, and saw the ashes scattered by the trailing ends of lodge poles and travois, and by the feet of hundreds of people and dogs. Still he was not satisfied, and for a long time after the last of the people had passed he remained there. Then he went on across the flat and up and over a ridge, but presently he returned, once, twice, four times, to the crest of the hill and looked back at the place where the camp had been; but at last he felt sure that no one remained at the place, and went on.

Yet Talking Rock was there. He had been hidden in the brush all the time, watching the chief. Even after Three Bulls had passed over the ridge, he remained crouched in the bushes, and saw him come back again and again to peer over its crest. Still further on there was another higher ridge, and when the young man saw Three Bulls climb that and disappear on the trail of the camp, he came forth.

Going to the place where his friend had lain,
Talking Rock sat down and mourned, wailing
long and loud. Back on the hills the wolves
and coyotes heard him and they too became
sorrowful, adding their cries to his.

The young man had little faith in the power
of the four arrows that he kept so carefully
wrapped in a separate bundle in his quiver. He
looked at the place where Red Robe's body had
been burnt. It was like any other place on the
great trail that had been made, dust and grass
blades mingled together, and scratches made by
the dragging poles. It did not seem possible
that anything of his friend's body remained; yet
he must search, and breaking a green willow
twig he began carefully to work over the dust,
stopping his crying, for the tears blinded his
eyes so that he could not see.

All the long morning and far into the afternoon, Talking Rock swept the dust this way and
that, turning it over and over, in a circle that
grew always wider, and just as he was about to
give up the search, he found a bit of charred and
blackened bone. Was this a part of his friend's

140

frame? Was it not more likely a bit of bone of buffalo or elk, which some dog had carried from one of the fireplaces of the camp and dropped here?

Now for the test. Talking Rock covered the bit of bone with his robe as he had been told to do. He even raised the robe along its middle, making it look as if it really covered a person lying there. Then he shot three of the arrows up in the air, each time crying, "Look out."

Then with a hand that trembled a little, he drew the fourth arrow from the quiver, shot it and cried, "Look out, Red Robe, the arrow will strike you"; and, turning, ran from the place with all his speed.

How he wanted to look back! How he longed to see if his friend was really rising from that bit of blackened bone! But Talking Rock was strong-hearted. He controlled his desires. On and on he ran, and then—behind him the light tread of running feet, a firm hand gripped his shoulder, and a loved voice said, "Why so fast, my friend?" and stopping and turning, Talking Rock found himself face to face with Red Robe.

He could not believe what he saw, and had to pinch himself and to hold his friend hard in his arms to believe that all this was real.

The camp had not moved far, and the lodges were pitched on the next stream to the south. Soon after dark, the two friends entered it and went to their lodge. The poor old grandmother could not believe her eyes when she saw the young man she had reared and loved so dearly; but when he spoke she knew that it was he, and running over to him she held him in her arms and kissed him, crying from joy. After a little time, the young man said to her, "Grandmother, go to the chief's lodge and say to him that I, Red Robe, need some dried meat." The old woman hesitated at this strange request, but Red Robe said: "Go, do not fear him; Three Bulls is now the one to know fear."

When the old woman entered the great lodge and in reply to the chief's look said, "Red Robe sent me here. He wants some dried meat," only Three Bulls of all who were in the lodge, showed no surprise. "It is what I expected," he said; "in spite of all my care he lives again, and

142

I can do nothing." Turning to his wives he said, "Give her meat."

"Did you see Mā-mĭn'?" asked Red Robe, when his grandmother had returned with the meat and had told him what the chief had said.

"No, she was not in the lodge, but two women were approaching as I left it. I think they were the girl and her mother."

"Go back once more," said the young man, "and tell Three Bulls to send me that young woman."

But now the poor old grandmother was afraid. "I dare not tell him that," she exclaimed. "He would kill me, and you. His anger would be fearful."

"Do not fear," said Red Robe, "do not fear, my mother, his anger and his power are no longer to be feared. He is as feeble and as helpless as one of those old bulls one sees on the sunny side of the coulée, spending his last days before the wolves pull him down."

The old woman went to the lodge and told the chief what Red Robe further wished. Mā-mĭn' was there, her head covered with her robe, crying quietly, and Three Bulls told her to arise and go with the messenger. Timidly at first, and then with steps that broke into a run, Mā-mǐn' hurried toward the lodge of her sweetheart and entered it. With a cry of joy she threw herself into his arms, and Talking Rock went out and left them alone.

Great now was the happiness of these young people. Long was their life, full of plenty and of great honor. Red Robe became a chief, respected and loved by all the people. Mā-mǐn' bore him many children, who grew up to be the support of their old age.

THE BLACKFEET CREATION

THE Blackfeet believe that the Sun made the earth—that he is the creator. One of the names by which they call the Sun is Napi —Old Man. This is how they tell of the creation:

In the beginning there was water everywhere; nothing else was to be seen. There was something floating on the water, and on this raft were Old Man and all the animals.

Old Man wished to make land, and he told the beaver to dive down to the bottom of the water and to try to bring up a little mud. The beaver dived and was under water for a long time, but he could not reach the bottom. Then the loon tried, and after him the otter, but the water was too deep for them. At last the muskrat was sent down, and he was gone for a long time; so long that they thought he must be drowned, but at last he came up and floated almost dead on the water, and when they pulled him up on the raft and looked at his paws, they found a little mud in them. When Old Man had dried this mud, he scattered it over the water and land was formed. This is the story told by the Blackfeet. It is very much like one told by some Eastern Indians, who are related to the Blackfeet.

After the land had been made, Old Man travelled about on it, making things and fixing up the earth so as to suit him. First, he marked out places where he wished the rivers to run, sometimes making them run smoothly, and again, in some places, putting falls on them. He made the mountains and the prairie, the timber and the small trees and bushes, and sometimes he carried along with him a lot of rocks, from which he built some of the mountains—as the Sweet Grass Hills—which stand out on the prairie by themselves.

Old Man caused grass to grow on the plains, so that the animals might have something to feed on. He marked off certain pieces of land, where he caused different kinds of roots and berries to grow—a place for camas; and one for wild carrots; one for wild turnips, sweet root and bitter root; one for service berries, bull-berries, cherries, plums, and rosebuds.

He made all kinds of animals that travel on the ground. When he made the big-horn with its great horns, he put it out on the prairie. It did not seem to travel easily there; it was awkward and could not go fast, so he took it by one of its horns and led it up into the rough hills and among the rocks, and let it go there, and it skipped about among the cliffs and easily went up fearful places. So Old Man said to the big-horn, "This is the place for you; this is what you are fitted for; the rough country and the mountains." While he was in the mountains he made the antelope, and turned it loose to see how it travelled. The antelope ran so fast that it fell over some rocks and hurt itself. He saw that this would not do, and took the antelope down on the prairie and set it free there, and it ran away fast and gracefully, and he said to it, "This is the place that suits you."

At last, one day, Old Man decided that he

147

would make a woman and a child, and he mod-
elled some clay in human shape, and after he had
made these shapes and put them on the ground,
he said to the clay, "You shall be people." He
spread his robe over the clay figures and went
away. The next morning he went back to the
place and lifted up the robe, and saw that the
clay shapes had changed a little. When he
looked at them the next morning, they had
changed still more; and when on the fourth day
he went to the place and took off the covering,
he said to the images, "Stand up and walk,"
and they did so. They walked down to the river
with him who had made them, and he told them
his name.

As they were standing there looking at the
water as it flowed by, the woman asked Old
Man, saying, "How is it; shall we live always?
Will there be no end to us?"

Old Man said, "I have not thought of that.
We must decide it. I will take this buffalo chip
and throw it in the river. If it floats, people will
become alive again four days after they have
died; they will die for four days only. But if

148

it sinks, there will be an end to them." He threw the chip into the river, and it floated.

The woman turned and picked up a stone and said, "No, I will throw this stone in the river. If it floats, we shall live always; if it sinks, people must die, so that their friends who are left alive may always remember them." The woman threw the stone in the water, and it sank.

"Well," said Old Man, "you have chosen; there will be an end to them."

Not many nights after that the woman's child died, and she cried a great deal for it. She said to Old Man, "Let us change this. The law that you first made, let that be the law."

He said, "Not so; what is made law must be law. We will undo nothing that we have done. The child is dead, but it cannot be changed. People will have to die."

These first people did not have hands like a person; they had hands like a bear with long claws. They were poor and naked and did not know how to get a living. Old Man showed them the roots and the berries, and showed them how to gather these, and told them how at

149

certain times of the year they should peel the
bark off some trees and eat it; that the little
animals that live in the ground—rats, squirrels,
skunks, and beavers—were good to eat. He also
taught them something about the roots that
were good for medicine to cure sickness.

In those days there were buffalo, and these
black animals were armed, for they had long
horns. Once, as the people were moving about,
the buffalo saw them and rushed upon them
and hooked them and killed them, and then ate
them. One day, as the creator was travelling
about, he came upon some of his children that
he had made lying there dead, torn to pieces and
partly eaten by the buffalo. When he saw this,
he felt badly. He said, "I have not made these
people right. I will change this; from now on
the people shall eat the buffalo."

He went to some of the people who were still
alive, and said to them, "How is it that you people do nothing to these animals that are killing
you?" The people replied, "What can we do?
These animals are armed and can kill us, and
we have no way to kill them."

The creator said, "That is not hard. I will make you something that will kill these animals."

He went out and cut some straight service-berry shoots, and brought them in, and peeled the bark from them. He took a larger piece of wood and flattened it, and tied a string to it, and made a bow. Now he was the master of all birds and he went out and caught one, and took feathers from its wings and tied them to the shaft of wood. He tied four feathers along the shaft and tried the arrow at a mark and found that it did not fly well. He took off these feathers and put on three, and when he again tried it at the mark he found that it went straight. He picked up some hard stones, and broke sharp pieces from them. When he tried them he found that the black flint stones made the best arrow points. He showed them how to use these things.

Then he spoke to the people, and said, "The next time you go out, take these things with you, and use them as I tell you. Do not run from these animals. When they rush at you, and have come pretty close, shoot the arrows at

151

them as I have taught you, and you will see that they will run from you or will run around you in a circle."

He also broke off pieces of stone, and fixed them in a handle, and told them that when they killed the buffalo they should cut up the flesh with these stone knives.

One day after this, some people went on a little hill to look about, and the buffalo saw them and called out to each other, "Ah, there is some more of our food," and rushed upon them. The people did not run. They began to shoot at the buffalo with the bows and arrows that had been given them, and the buffalo began to fall. They say that when the first buffalo hit with an arrow felt it prick him, he called out to his fellows, "Oh, my friends, a great fly is biting me."

With the flint knives that had been given them they cut up the bodies of the dead buffalo. About this time Old Man came up and said to them, "It is not healthful to eat raw flesh. I will show you something better than that." He gathered soft, dry rotten wood and made punk of it, and took a piece of wood and drilled a hole in it with an arrow point, and gave them a pointed piece of hard wood, and showed them how to make a fire with fire sticks, and to cook the flesh of animals.

After this the people found a certain sort of stone in the land, and took another harder stone, and worked one upon the other and hollowed out the softer one, so as to make of it a kettle.

It is told also that the creator made people and animals at another place, and in another way. At the Porcupine Mountains he made other earthen images of people, and blew breath on the images, and they became people. They were men and women. After a time they asked him, "What are we to eat?" Then he took more earth and made many images in the form of buffalo, and when he had blown on them they stood up, and he made signs to them and they started to run. He said to the people, "There is your food."

"Well, now," they replied; "we have those animals, how are we to kill them?"

"I will show you," he said.

He took them to the edge of a cliff and showed them how to heap up piles of stone, running back from the cliff like this :   :   :   :   .   . , with the point of the V toward the cliff. He said to the people, "Now, do you hide behind these piles of stones, and when I lead the buffalo this way, as they get opposite to you, stand up."

Then he went on toward a herd of buffalo and began to call them, and the buffalo started toward him and followed him, until they were inside the arms of the V. Then he ran to one side and hid, and as the people rose up the buffalo ran on in a straight line and jumped over the cliff and some of them were killed by the fall.

"There," he said, "go and take the flesh of those animals." Then the people tried to do so. They tried to tear the limbs apart, but they could not. They tried to bite pieces out of the bodies, but they could not do that. Old Man went to the edge of the cliff and broke some pieces of stone with sharp edges, and showed them how to cut the flesh with these. Of the buffalo that went over the cliff, some were not dead, but were hurt, so they could not run away. The people cut strips of green hide and tied stones in the middle, and with these hammers broke in the skulls of the buffalo and killed them.

When they had taken the skins from these animals, they set up poles and put the hides over them, and so made a shelter to sleep under.

In later times the creator marked off a piece of land for the five tribes, Blackfeet, Bloods, Piegans, Gros Ventres, and Sarsis, and said to these tribes, "When people come to cross this line at the border of your land, take your bows and arrows, your lances and your war clubs and give them battle, and keep them out. If they gain a footing here, trouble for you will follow."

OLD MAN STORIES

UNDER the name Na'pi, Old Man, have been confused two wholly different persons talked of by the Blackfeet. The Sun, the creator of the universe, giver of light, heat, and life, and reverenced by every one, is often called Old Man, but there is another personality who bears the same name, but who is very different in his character. This last Na'pi is a mixture of wisdom and foolishness; he is malicious, selfish, childish, and weak. He delights in tormenting people. Yet the mean things he does are so foolish that he is constantly getting himself into scrapes, and is often obliged to ask the animals to help him out of his troubles. His bad deeds almost always bring their own punishment.

Interpreters commonly translate this word Na'pi as Old Man, but it is also the term for white man; and the Cheyenne and Arapahoe tribes tell just such stories about a similar person whom they also call "white man." Tribes of Dakota stock tell of a similar person whom they call "the spider."

The stories about this Old Man are told by the Blackfeet for entertainment rather than with any serious purpose, and when that part of the story is reached where Old Man is in some difficulty which he cannot get out of, the man who is telling the story, and those who are listening to it, laugh delightedly.

Some stories of this kind are these:

THE WONDERFUL BIRD

ONE day, as Old Man was walking about among the trees, he saw something that seemed very queer.

A little bird was sitting on the branch of a tree. Every little while it would make a strange noise, and every time it made this noise its eyes flew out of its head and fastened on a branch of the tree. Then after a little while the bird would make another sort of noise and its eyes would go back to their places in its head.

157

Old Man called out to the bird, "Little brother, teach me how to do that."

"If I show you how," the bird answered, "you must not send your eyes out of your head more than four times in a day. If you do, you will be sorry."

"It shall be as you say, little brother. It is for you to give, and I will listen to what you say."

When the bird had taught Old Man how to do this, he was glad. He began to do it, and did it four times right away. Then he said, "Why did that bird tell me to do this only four times? He has no sense. I will do it again." So once more he made his eyes go out, but now when he called to them they would not come back.

He shouted out to the bird, "Little brother, come here, and help me to get back my eyes." The little bird did not answer him; it had flown away. Now Old Man felt all over the branches of the tree with his hands, but he could not find his eyes. So he went away and wandered over the prairie for a long time, crying and calling to the animals to help him.

158

As he was blind, he could find nothing to eat, and he began to be very hungry.

A wolf teased him a great deal and had much fun. It had found a dead buffalo, and taking a piece of the meat, it would hold the meat close to Old Man's face. Then Old Man would say, "I smell something dead, I wish I could find it; I am almost starved." He felt all around for it.

Once when the wolf was doing this, Old Man caught him, and plucking out one of the wolf's eyes, he put it in his own head. Then he could see, and was able to find his own eyes, but never again could he do the trick the little bird had taught him.

THE RABBITS' MEDICINE

ONCE, when Old Man was travelling about, he heard some singing that sounded very queer. He had never before heard anything like it, and looked all about to see where it came from. After a time he saw that the cottontail rabbits were singing and making medicine. They had built a fire, and raked out some hot ashes, and they would lie down in these ashes and sing, while one of the others covered them up. They could stay there only for a short time, though, for the ashes were hot.

"Little brothers," said Old Man, "here is something wonderful—that you can lie in those hot ashes and coals without burning. I ask you to teach me how to do this."

"We will show you how to do it, Old Man," said the rabbits. "You must sing our song, and stay in the ashes only a short time." They taught Old Man their song, and he began to sing and lay down, and they covered him with coals and ashes, and the hot ashes did not burn him.

"That is good," he said. "You have strong medicine. Now, so that I may know it all, do you lie down and let me cover you up."

All the rabbits lay down in the ashes, and Old Man covered them up, and then he pulled the whole fire over them. One old rabbit got out, and Old Man was just about to put her back when she said, "Pity me; my children need me."

"It is good," replied Old Man. "You may go, so that there will be more rabbits; but these

I will roast, and have a feast." He put more wood on the fire, and when the rabbits were cooked he got some red willow brush and put the rabbits on it to cool. The grease from their bodies soaked into the branches, so that even to-day if red willow is held over a fire one may see the grease on the bark. Ever since that time, too, the rabbits have a burnt place on the back, where the one that got away was singed.

Old Man sat down by the fire, waiting for the rabbits to get cool, when a coyote came along, limping. He went on three legs. "Pity me, Old Man," he said. "You have plenty of cooked rabbits, give me one of them."

"Go away," said Old Man, very cross; "if you are too lazy to catch food, I will not give you any."

"But my leg is broken," said the coyote; "I cannot run. I cannot catch anything, and I am starving. Give me half a rabbit."

"I don't care what happens to you," said Old Man; "I worked hard to catch and cook these rabbits, and I shall not give any of them away. I'll tell you what I will do, though; I will run a race with you out to that far butte on the prairie, and if you beat me you can have a rabbit."

"Good," said the coyote, and they started.

Old Man ran very fast, and the coyote limped along behind him, but pretty close, until they got near the butte. Then the coyote turned around and ran back very fast, for he was not lame at all. It took Old Man a long time to get back, and just before he reached the fire, the coyote finished eating the last rabbit and ran away.

THE LOST ELK MEAT

OLD MAN had been a long time without food and was very hungry. He was trying to think how he could get something to eat, when he saw a band of elk come up on a ridge. He went over to them and spoke to them and said, "Brothers, I am lonely because I have no one to follow me."

"Go ahead, Old Man," said the elk; "we will follow you." Old Man led them about for a long time, and when it was dark he came near a high, steep cut bank. He ran around to one side, where the hill sloped, and then went back right under the steep cliff and called out, "Come on, that is a nice jump. You will laugh." So all the elk jumped off and were killed, except one cow.

"They have all jumped but you," said Old Man. "Come on, you will like it."

"Take pity on me," said the cow. "I am very heavy, and I am afraid to jump."

"Go away, then," said Old Man; "go and live. Then some day there will be plenty of elk again."

Old Man built a fire and cooked some of the meat, and then he skinned all the elk, and cut up the meat and hung it up to dry. The tongues he hung on a pole.

The next day he started off and was gone all day, and at night, as he was coming home, he was very hungry. He was thinking to himself that he would have some roasted ribs and a tongue and other good things; but when he reached the place, the meat was all gone; the wolves had eaten it.

"It was lucky I hung up those tongues," said

Old Man, "or I should not have had anything to eat." But when he took down the tongues they were all hollow. The mice had eaten out the meat, leaving only the skins.

THE ROLLING ROCK

ONCE when Old Man was travelling about and felt tired, he sat down on a rock to rest. After he was rested he started on his way, and because the sun was hot he threw his robe over the rock and said to it, "Here, I give you my robe because you are poor and have let me rest on you. Keep it always."

He had not gone far when it began to rain, and meeting a coyote, he said to him, "Little brother, run back to that rock and ask him to lend me his robe. We will cover ourselves with it and keep dry."

The coyote ran back to the rock, but presently returned without the robe.

"Where is the robe?" asked Old Man.

"Why," said the coyote, "the rock said that you had given him the robe and he was going to keep it."

This made Old Man angry, and he went back to the rock and snatched the robe off it, saying, "I was only going to borrow this robe until the rain was over, but now that you have acted so mean about it, I will keep it. You don't need a robe, anyhow. You have been out in the rain and snow all your life, and it will not hurt you to live so always."

When he had said this he put the robe about his shoulders, and with the coyote he went off into a ravine and they sat down there. The rain was falling and they covered themselves with the robe, and were warm and dry.

Pretty soon they heard a loud, rumbling noise, and Old Man said to the coyote, "Little brother, go up on the hill and see what that noise is."

The coyote went off, but presently he came back, running as hard as he could, saying, "Run, run, the big rock is coming." They both started, and ran away as fast as they could. The coyote tried to creep into a badger-hole, but it was too small for him and he stuck fast, and before he could get out the rock rolled over him and crushed his hips. Old Man was frightened, and as he ran he threw away his robe and everything that he had on, so that he might run faster. The rock was gaining on him all the time.

Not far away on the prairie a band of buffalo bulls were feeding, and Old Man cried out to them, saying, "Oh, my brothers, help me, help me; stop that rock." The bulls ran and tried to stop it, butting against it, but it crushed their heads. Some deer and antelope tried to help Old Man, but they too were killed. Other animals came to help him, but could not stop the rock; it was now close to Old Man, so close that it began to hit his heels. He was just going to give up when he saw circling over his head a flock of night-hawks.

"Oh, my little brothers," he cried, "help me; I am almost dead." The bull bats flew down one after another against the rock, and every time one of them hit it he chipped off a piece, and at last one hit it fair in the middle and broke it into two pieces.

Then Old Man was glad. He went to where there was a nest of night-hawks and pulled their mouths out wide and pinched off their bills, to make them pretty and queer looking. That is the reason they look so to-day.

BEAR AND BULLBERRIES

SCATTERED over the prairie in northern Montana, close to the mountains, are many great rocks—boulders which thousands of years ago, when the great ice-sheet covered northern North America, were carried from the mountains out over the prairie by the ice and left there when it melted.

Around most of these great boulders the buffalo used to walk from time to time, rubbing against the rough surface of the rock to scratch themselves, as a cow rubs itself against a post or as a horse rolls on the ground—for the pleasant feeling that the rubbing of the skin gives it.

As the buffalo walked around these boulders their hoofs loosened the soil, and this loosened soil—the dust—was blown away by the constant winds of summer. So, around most of these boulders, much of the soil is gone, leaving a deep

167

trench, at the bottom of which are stones and gravel, too large to be moved by the wind.

This story explains how these rocks came to be like that:

Once Old Man was crossing a river and the stream was deep, so that he was carried away by the current, and lost his bow and arrows and other weapons. When he got to the shore he began to look about for something to use in making a bow and arrows, for he was hungry and wanted to kill some food.

He took the first wood he could find and made a bow and arrows and a handle for his knife. When he had finished these things he started on his way.

Presently, as he looked over a hill he saw down below him a bear digging roots. Old Man thought he would have some fun with the bear, and he called out aloud, "He has no tail." Then he dodged back out of sight. The bear looked all about, but saw no one, and again began to dig roots. Then Old Man again peeped over the hill and saw the bear at work, and again called out, "He has no tail." This time the

168

bear looked up more quickly, but Old Man dodged down, and the bear did not see him, and pretty soon went on with his digging.

Four times Old Man did this, calling the bear names, but the fourth time the bear was on the watch and saw Old Man, and started after him.

Old Man ran away as hard as he could, but the bear followed fast. Presently, Old Man tried to shoot the bear with his arrows, but they were made of bad wood and would not fly well, and if they hit the bear, they just broke off. All his weapons failed him, and now the bear was close to him. Just in front was a great rock, and when Old Man came to that, he dodged behind it and ran around to the other side, and the bear followed him. They kept running around the rock for a long time and wore a deep trail about it, and because Old Man could turn more quickly, he kept just ahead of the bear. Old Man kept calling to the animals to help him, but no one came.

He was almost out of breath, and the bear was close to him, when Old Man saw lying on the ground a bull's horn. He picked it up and held

169

it on his head and turned around and bellowed loudly, and the bear was frightened and turned around and ran away as hard as he could. Then Old Man leaned up against the rock, and breathed hard for a long time, but at last he got his wind back. He said to the rock, "This is the way you rocks shall always be after this, with a big hole all around you."

By this time he was pretty tired and thirsty, and he thought he would go down to the river and drink. When he got to the edge of the water he got down on his knees to drink, and there before him in the water he saw bullberries, great bunches of them. He said to himself, "I will dive in and get those bull-berries"; and he took off his moccasins and clothing and dived in, but he could not find the bullberries, and presently he came up. He looked into the water again, and again saw the bullberries. He said to himself, "Those bullberries must be very deep down."

He went along the shore looking for a heavy stone that would take him down into the deep water where the bullberries were, and when he

170

found one he tied the stone to his neck and again dived in. This time he sank to the bottom, for the stone carried him down. He felt about with his hands trying to reach the bullberries, but could feel nothing and began to drown. He tried to get free from the stone, but that was hard to do; yet at last he broke the string and came to the top of the water. He was almost dead, and it took him a long time to get to the shore, and when he got there he crawled up on to the bank and lay down to rest and get his breath. As he lay there on his back, he saw above him the thick growing bullberries whose reflections he had seen in the water. He said to himself, "And I was almost drowned for these." Then he took a stick and with it began to beat the bullberry bushes. He said to the bushes, "After this, the people shall beat you in this way when they want to gather berries."

The Blackfeet women, when gathering bullberries, spread robes under the bushes and beat the branches with sticks, knocking off the berries, which fall on the robes.

THE THEFT FROM THE SUN

ONE time when Old Man was on a journey, he came to the Sun's lodge, and went in and sat down, and the Sun asked him to stay with him for a time. Old Man was glad to do so. One day the meat was all gone, and the Sun said, "Well, Old Man, what do you say if we go out and kill some deer?"

"I like what you say," said Old Man. "Deer meat is good."

The Sun took down a bag that was hanging from a lodge pole and took from it a handsome pair of leggings, embroidered with porcupine quills and pretty feathers.

"These are my hunting leggings," said the Sun; "they have great power. When I want to kill deer, all I have to do is to put them on and walk around a patch of brush, and the leggings set it on fire and drive out the deer, so that I can shoot them."

"Well, well," exclaimed Old Man, "how wonderful that is!" He began to think, "I wish I had such a pair of leggings as that"; and after he

172

had thought about it some more, he made up his mind that he would have those leggings, if he had to steal them.

They went out to hunt, and when they came to a patch of brush, the Sun set it on fire with his hunting leggings. A number of deer ran out, and each shot one.

That night when they were going to bed the Sun pulled off his leggings, and laid them aside. Old Man saw where he had put them, and in the middle of the night, after every one was asleep, he took the leggings and went away. He travelled a long time, until he had gone far and was tired; then making a pillow of the leggings he lay down and slept. After a while he heard some one speaking and woke up and saw that it was day. Some one was talking to him. The Sun was saying, "Old Man, why are my leggings under your head?"

Old Man looked about him and saw that he was in the Sun's lodge. He thought he must have wandered around and got lost and returned there. Again the Sun spoke, and asked, "What are you doing with my leggings?"

"Oh," replied Old Man, "I could not find anything for a pillow, so I put these leggings under my head."

When night came and all had gone to bed, again Old Man stole the leggings and ran off. This time he did not walk at all. He kept running until it was almost morning, and then lay down and slept. When morning came he found himself still in the Sun's lodge.

You see what a fool he was; he did not know that the whole world is the Sun's lodge. He did not know that, no matter how far he ran, he could not get out of the Sun's sight.

This time the Sun said, "Old Man, since you like my leggings so much, I give them to you. Keep them." Then Old Man was glad and he went away.

One day his food was all gone, and he put on the hunting leggings and went out and set fire to a piece of brush. He was just going to kill some deer that were running out, when he saw that the fire was getting close to him. He ran away as fast as he could, but the fire gained on him and began to burn his legs. His leggings were

174

all on fire. He came to a river and jumped in and pulled off the leggings as soon as he could. They were burnt to pieces.

Perhaps the Sun did this because Old Man tried to steal his leggings.

THE SMART WOMAN CHIEF

LONG ago, they tell me, men and women did not know each other. Women were put in one place and men in another. They were not together; they were apart.

He who made us made women first. He did not make them very well. That is why they are not so strong as men. The men he made better; so that they were strong.

The women were the smartest. They knew the most. They were the first to make piskuns, and to know how to tan hides and to make moccasins. At that time men wore moccasins made from the shank of the buffalo's leg, and robes made of wolfskin. This was all their clothing.

One day when Old Man was travelling about, he came to a camp of men, and stayed there

175

with them for a long time. It was after this that he discovered there were such beings as women.

One time, as he was travelling along, he saw two women driving some buffalo over a cliff. When Old Man got near them, the women were very much frightened. They did not know what kind of animal it was that was coming. Too much scared to run away, they lay down to hide. When Old Man came up to them he thought they were dead, and said, "Here are two women who are dead. It is not good for them to lie out here on the prairie. I must take them to a certain place." He looked them all over to see what had killed them, but could find no wound. He picked up one of the women and carried her along with him in his arms. She was wondering how she could get away. She let her arms swing loose as if she were dead, and at every step Old Man took the arm swung and hit him in the nose, and pretty soon his nose began to bleed and to hurt, and at length he put the woman down on the ground and went back to get the other woman; but while he was

176

gone she had run away, and when he came back to get the first one she was gone too; so he lost them both. This made him angry, and he said to himself, "If these two women will lie there again, I will get both of them."

In this way women found out that there were men.

One day Old Man stood on a hill and looked over toward the piskun at Woman's Falls, where the women had driven a band of buffalo over the cliff, and afterward were cutting up the meat. The chief of the women called him down to the camp, and sent word by him to the men, asking if they wanted to get wives. Old Man brought back word that they did, and the chief woman sent a message, calling all the men to a feast in her lodge to be married. The woman asked Old Man, "How many chiefs are there in that tribe?" He answered, "There are four chiefs. But the real chief of all that tribe you will know when you see him by this—he is finely dressed and wears a robe trimmed, and painted red, and carries a lance with a bone head on each end." Old Man wanted to marry the chief

177

of the women, and intended to dress in this way, and that is why he told her that.

Old Man had no moccasins; his were all worn out. The women gave him some for himself, and also some to take back to give to the men, and he went back to the men's camp. When he reached it, word went out that he had returned, and all the men said to each other, "He has got back; Old Man has come again." He gave the men the message that the woman had sent, and soon the men started for the woman's camp to get married. When they came near it, they went up on a bluff and stood there, looking down on the camp. Old Man had dressed himself finely, and had put on a trimmed robe painted red, and in his hand held a lance with a bone head on each end.

When the women saw that the men had come they got ready to go and select their husbands. The chief of the women said, "I am the chief. I will go first and take the man I like. The rest wait here."

The woman chief started up the hill to choose the chief of the men for her husband. She had

178

been making dried meat, and her hands, arms, and clothing were covered with blood and grease. She was dirty, and Old Man did not know her. The woman went up to Old Man to choose him, but he turned his back on her and would not go with her.

She went back to her camp and told the women that she had been refused because her clothes were dirty. She said, "Now, I am going to put on my nice clothes and choose a man. All of you can go up and take men, but let no one take that man with the red robe and the double-headed lance."

After she was nicely dressed the chief woman again went up on the hill. Now, Old Man knew who she was, and he kept getting in front of her and trying hard to have her take him, but she would not notice him and took another man, the one standing next to Old Man. Then the other women began to come, and they kept coming up and choosing men, but no one took Old Man, and at last all the men were taken and he was left standing there alone.

This made him so angry that he wanted to do

179

something, and he went down to the woman's piskun and began to break down its walls, so the chief of the women turned him into a pine-tree.

BOBCAT AND BIRCH TREE

ONCE Old Man was travelling over the prairie, when he saw far off a fire burning, and as he drew near it he saw many prairie-dogs sitting in a circle around the fire. There were so many of them that there was no place for any one to sit down. Old Man stood there behind the circle, and presently he began to cry, and then he said to the prairie-dogs, "Let me, too, sit by that fire." The prairie-dogs said, "All right, Old Man, don't cry; come and sit by the fire." They moved aside so as to make a place for him, and Old Man sat down and looked on at what they were doing.

He saw that they were playing a game, and this was the way they did it: they put one prairie-dog in the fire and covered him up with hot ashes, and then, after he had been there a little while, he would say, "*sk, sk,*" and they pushed the ashes off him and pulled him out.

180

Old Man said, "Little brothers, teach me how to do that." The prairie-dogs told him what to do, and put him in the fire and covered him up with the ashes, and after a little time he said, "*sk, sk*," like a prairie-dog, and they pulled him out again. Then he did it to the prairie-dogs.

At first he put them in one at a time, but there were many of them, and soon he got tired and said, "I will put you all in at once." They said, "Very well, Old Man," and all got in the ashes, but just as Old Man was about to cover them up one of them, a female, said, "Do not cover me up, for I fear the heat will hurt me." Old Man said, "Very well; if you do not wish to be covered up, you may sit over by the fire and watch the rest." Then he covered over all the others.

At length the prairie-dogs said, "*sk, sk*," but Old Man did not sweep off the ashes and pull them out of the fire. He let them stay there and die. The she one that was looking on ran to a hole, and as she went down in it, said, "*sk, sk*." Old Man chased her, but he got to the hole too late to catch her.

"Oh, well, you can go," he said; "there will be more prairie-dogs by and by."

When the prairie-dogs were roasted, Old Man cut some red willow twigs to place them on, and then sat down and began to eat. He ate until he was full, and then felt sleepy.

He said to his nose, "I am going to sleep now; watch out, and in case any bad thing comes about, wake me up." Then Old Man slept.

Pretty soon his nose snored, and Old Man woke up and said, "What is it?" The nose said, "A raven is flying by, over there." Old Man said, "That is nothing," and went to sleep again.

Soon his nose snored again, and Old Man said, "What is it now?" The nose said, "There is a coyote over there, coming this way." Old Man said, "A coyote is nothing," and again went to sleep.

Presently his nose snored again, but Old Man did not wake up. Again it snored, and called out, "Wake up, a bobcat is coming." Old Man paid no attention; he slept on.

The bobcat crept up to the fire and ate all

182

the roasted prairie-dogs, and then went off and
lay down on the flat rock and went to sleep.
All this time the nose kept trying to awaken Old
Man, and at last he awoke, and the nose said,
"A bobcat is over there on that flat rock. He
has eaten all your food." Then Old Man was
so angry that he called out loud.

The tracks of the bobcat were all greasy
from the food it had been eating, and Old Man
followed these tracks. He went softly over to
where the bobcat was sleeping, and seized it
before it could wake up to bite or scratch him.
The bobcat cried out, "Wait, let me speak a
word or two," but Old Man would not listen.

"I will teach you to steal my food," he said.
He pulled off the lynx's tail, pounded his head
against the rock so as to make his face flat,
pulled him out long so as to make him small-
bellied, and then threw him into the brush. As
he went sneaking away, Old Man said, "There,
that is the way you bobcats shall always be."
It is for this reason that the lynxes to-day look
like that.

Old Man went to the fire, and looked at the

red willow sticks where the roasted prairie-dogs had been, and when he saw them, and thought how his food was all gone, it made him angry at his nose. He said, "You fool, why did you not wake me?" He took the willow sticks and thrust them in the coals, and when they had caught fire he burnt his nose. This hurt, and he ran up on a hill and held his nose to the wind, and called to the wind to blow hard and cool him. A hard wind came, so hard that it blew him off the hill and away down to Birch Creek. As he was flying along he caught at the weeds and brush to stop himself, but nothing was strong enough to hold him. At last he grasped a birch tree. He held fast, and it did not give way. Although the wind whipped him about, this way and that, and tumbled him up and down, the tree held him. He kept calling to the wind to blow more softly, and at last it listened to him and went down.

Then he said, "This is a beautiful tree. It has saved me from being blown away and knocked all to pieces. I will make it pretty, and it shall always be like that." So he gashed the

184

bark across with his stone knife, as you see the marks to-day.

THE RED-EYED DUCK

ONCE, long ago, Old Man was travelling north along a river. He carried a great pack on his back. After a time he came to a place where the river spread out and the water was quiet, and here many ducks were swimming about. Old Man did not look at the ducks, and kept travelling along; but presently some of the ducks saw him and looked at him and said to each other, "Who is that going along there with a pack on his back?" One duck said to the others, "That must be Old Man."

The duck that knew him called out, saying, "Hi, Old Man, where are you going?"

"I am going on farther," replied Old Man, "I have been sent for."

"What have you got in your pack?" said the duck.

"Those are my songs," answered Old Man. "Some people have asked me to come and sing for them."

"Stop for a while and sing for us," said the duck, "and we can have a dance."

"No," said Old Man, "I am in a hurry; I cannot stop now."

The duck kept persuading him to stop, and when it had asked him the fourth time, Old Man stopped and said to the ducks, "Well, I will stop for a little while and sing for you, and you can dance."

So the ducks all came out on the bank and stood in a circle, and Old Man began to sing. He sang one song, and then said, "Now, this next song is a medicine song, and while you dance you must keep your eyes shut. No one must look. If any one opens his eyes and looks, his eyes will turn red."

The ducks closed their eyes and Old Man began to sing, and they danced around; but Old Man took a stick, and every time one of them passed him, he knocked it on the head and threw it into the circle.

Presently one of the littlest ducks while dancing could not feel any one on either side of him, and he opened his eyes and looked, and

186

saw what Old Man was doing. He cried out to the rest, "Run, run, Old Man is killing us"; and all the other ducks flew away, but ever since that time that little duck's eyes have been red. It is the horned grebe.

Old Man took the ducks and went off a little way and built a fire and hung some of the ducks up in front of it to roast, and after the fire was burning well, he swept away the ashes and buried some of the ducks in the ground and again swept back the fire over them. Then he lay down to wait for the birds to cook, and while they were cooking he fell asleep.

While he slept a coyote came sneaking along and saw Old Man sleeping there, and the ducks roasting by the fire. Very quietly he crept up to the fire and took the ducks one by one and ate them. Not one was left. Pretty soon he found those that were roasting under the fire, and dug them out, and opening them, ate the meat from the inside of the skin and filled each one with ashes and buried them all again. Then he went away.

Pretty soon Old Man woke up and saw that

his ducks were gone, and when he saw the tracks about the fire, he knew that the coyote had taken them.

"It was lucky," said Old Man, "that I put some of those to roast under the fire." He dug them up from under the ashes, but when he took a big bite from one, his mouth and face were full of ashes.

THE ANCIENT BLACKFEET

LONG, long ago, before our fathers or grandfathers were born, before the white people knew anything about the western half of
North America, the Indians who told these
stories lived on the Western plains. To the west
of their home rose high mountains, black with
pine-trees on their lower slopes and capped with
snow, but their tents were pitched on the rolling prairie. For a little while in spring this
prairie was green and dotted with flowers, but
for most of the year it stretched away brown
and bare, north, east, and south, farther than one
could see.

On these plains were many kinds of wild animals. Sometimes the prairie was crowded with
herds of black buffalo running in fear; or, again,
the herds, unfrightened, fed scattered out; so
that the hills far and near were dotted with their
dark forms. Among the buffalo were yellow

189

and white antelope—many of them—graceful
and swift of foot. Feeding on the high prairie
or going down into the wooded river valleys to
drink were herds of elk, while the willow thick-
ets, the brushy ravines, and the lower timbered
foot-hills sheltered deer. The naked Bad Lands,
the rocky slopes of the mountains, and the tall
buttes that often rise above the level prairie
were the refuge of the mountain sheep, which in
those days, like all the other grass eaters of the
region, grazed on the prairie and sought the more
broken, higher country only when alarmed or
when they wished to rest.

These were the animals which the Blackfeet
killed for food before the white men came, and
of these the buffalo was the chief. Buffalo,
more than any other animals, could be captured
in numbers, and the Blackfeet, like the other
Indians of the plains, had devised a method for
taking them, so that when the buffalo were near
the Blackfeet never suffered from hunger. Yet
sometimes it happened that the buffalo went
away, and that the lonely far travelling scouts
sent out by the tribe could not find them. Then

the people had to turn to the smaller animals—the elk, deer, antelope, and wild sheep.

In those old days, before they had horses, they did not make long marches when they moved. Their only domestic animal was the dog, which was used chiefly as a beast of burden, either carrying loads on its back or hauling a travois, formed by two long sticks crossing above the shoulders and dragging on the ground behind. Behind the dog these two sticks were united by a little platform, on which was lashed some small burden—sometimes a little baby.

In those days, when the people moved from one place to another, all who were large enough to walk and strong enough to carry a burden on the shoulders, were laden. Usually men, women, and children alike bore loads suited to their strength. Yet sometimes the men carried no loads at all, for if journeying through a country where they feared that some enemy might attack them, the men must be ready to fight and to defend their wives and children. A man cannot fight well if he is carrying a burden; he cannot use his arms readily, nor run about

lightly—forward to attack, backward in retreat.
If he is not free to fight well, his family will be
in danger. White men who have seen Indians
journeying in this way, and who have not understood why some women carried heavy loads and
the men carried nothing, have said that Indian
men were idle and lazy, and forced their women
to do all the work. Those who wrote those
things were mistaken in what they said. They
did not understand what they saw. The truth
is that these men were prepared for danger of
attacks by enemies, and were ready to do their
best to save their families from harm.

Carrying on their backs all their property, except the little which the dogs might pack, it is
evident that the Indians in those days could not
make long journeys.

In those days they had no buckets of wood or
tin in which to carry water. Instead, they used
a vessel like a bag or sack, made from the soft
membrane of one of the stomachs of the buffalo.
This, after it had been cleansed and all the open-
ings from it save one had been tied up, the
women filled at the stream with a spoon made of

buffalo horn or with a larger ladle of the horn of the wild sheep. Because this water-skin was soft and flexible, it could not stand on the ground, and they hung it up, sometimes on the limb of a tree, more often on one of the poles of the lodge, or sometimes on a tripod—three sticks coming together at the top and standing spread out at the ground.

Most of the meat cooked for the family was roasted, yet much of it was boiled, sometimes in a bowl of stone, sometimes in a kettle made of a fresh hide or of the paunch of the buffalo. Sometimes these skin or paunch kettles were supported at the sides by stakes stuck in the ground, and sometimes a hole dug in the ground was lined with the hide, which was so arranged as to be water-tight. They were not, as may be imagined, put over a fire, but when filled with cold water this water was heated in quite another way. Near by a fire was built, in which were thrown large stones, and on top of the stones more wood was piled; so that after a time, when the wood had burnt down, the stones were very hot—sometimes red hot. With two rather short-handled forked sticks, the women took from the fire one of the hot stones, and put it in the water in the hide kettle, and as it cooled, took it out and put in another hot stone. Thus the water was soon heated, and boiled and cooked whatever was in the kettle. To be sure, there were some ashes and a little dirt in the soup, but that was not regarded as important.

This was long before the Indians knew of matches, or even of flint and steel. In those days to make a fire was not easy and it took a long time. By his knees or feet a man held in position on the ground a piece of soft, dry wood in which two or three little hollows had been dug out, and taking another slender stick of hard wood, and pressing the point in one of the little hollows in the stick of soft wood, he twirled the stick rapidly between the palms of his hands, so fast and so long that presently the dust ground from the softer stick, falling to one side in a little pile, began to smoke, and at last a faint spark was seen at the top of the pile, which began to glow, and, spreading, became constantly larger. He, or his companion, for often two men twirled the stick, one relieving the other, caught this spark in a bit of tinder—perhaps some dry punk or a little fine grass—and by blowing coaxed it into flame, and there was the fire.

This fire making was hard work, and the people tried to escape this work by keeping a spark of fire always alive. To do this, men sometimes carried, by a thong slung over the shoulder, the hollow tip of a buffalo horn, the opening of which was closed by a wooden plug. When going on a journey, the man lighted a piece of punk, and, placing it in this horn, plugged up the open end, so that no air could get into the horn. There the punk smouldered for a long time, and neither went out nor was wholly consumed. Once in a while during the day the man looked at this punk, and, if he saw that it was almost consumed, he lighted another piece and put it in the horn and replaced the plug. So at night when he reached camp the fire was still in his horn, and he could readily kindle a blaze, and from this blaze other fires were kindled. Often, if the camp was large, the first young men who reached it gathered wood and perhaps kindled four fires, and after the women had reached the camp, unpacked their dogs, and put up their lodges, each woman would go to one of these fires to get a brand or some coals with which to start her own lodge fire.

In warm weather men and boys wore little clothing. They went almost naked; yet in cold weather each man or woman was most of the time wrapped in a warm robe of tanned buffalo skin. Even the little children wore robes, the smallest ones those taken from the little buffalo calves. All their clothing, like their beds and their homes, was made of the skins of animals, Shirts, women's dresses, leggings, and moccasins were made from the tanned skins of buffalo, deer, antelope, and mountain sheep. Often the moccasins were made from the smoked skin cut from the top of an old lodge, for this skin had been smoked so much that it never dried hard and stiff, after it had been wet. The moccasins had a stiff sole of buffalo rawhide; and in the bottom of this sole were cut one or two holes,

in order that the water might run out if a man
had to wade through a stream.

The homes of these Indians were lodges—tents
made of tanned buffalo skin supported on a
cone of long, straight, slender poles. At the top
where the poles crossed was an opening for the
smoke from the fire built in the centre of the
circular lodge floor, while about the fire, and
close under the lodge covering, were the beds
where the people slept or ate during the day.

These homes were warm and comfortable. The
border of the lodge covering did not come down
quite to the ground, but inside the lodge poles,
and tied to them, was a long wide strip of tanned
buffalo skin four or five feet high, and long
enough to reach around the inside of the lodge,
almost from one side of the door to the other.
This strip of tanned skin—made up of several
pieces—was so wide that one edge rested on the
floor, and reached inward under the beds and
seats. Through the open space between the
lodge covering and the lodge lining, fresh air
kept passing into the lodge close to the ground
and up over the lining and down toward the

centre of the lodge, and so furnished draught for the fire. The lodge lining kept this cold air from blowing directly on the occupants of the lodge who sat around the fire. Often the lodge lining was finely painted with pictures of animals, people, and figures of mysterious beings of which one might not speak.

The seats and beds in this home were covered with soft tanned buffalo robes, and at the head and foot of each bed was an inclined back-rest of straight willow twigs, strung together on long lines of sinew and supported in an inclined position by a tripod. Buffalo robes often hung over these back-rests. In the spaces between the back-rests, which though they came together at the top were separated at the ground, were kept many of the possessions of the family; the pipe, sacks of tobacco, of paint, "possible sacks" —parfleches for clothing or food, and many smaller articles.

The outside of the lodge was often painted with mysterious figures which the lodge owner believed to have power to bring good luck to him and to his family. Sometimes these figures

198

represented animals—buffalo, deer, and elk—or rocks, mountains, trees, or the puff-balls that grow on the prairie. Sometimes a procession of ravens, marching one after the other, was painted around the circumference of the lodge. The painting might show the tracks of animals, or a number of water animals, apparently chasing each other around the lodge. On either side of the smoke hole at the top were two flaps, or wings, each one supported by a single pole. These were to regulate the draught of the fire in case of a change of wind, and the poles were moved from side to side, changing as the direction of the wind changed. On such wings were often painted groups of white disks which represented some group of stars. At the back of the lodge, high up, just below the place where the lodge poles cross, was often a large round disk representing the sun, and above that a cross, which was the sign of the butterfly, the power that they believe brings sleep. From the ends of the wings, or tied to the tips of the poles which supported them, hung buffalo tails, and sometimes running down from one of these poles

199

to the ground near the door was a string of tne sheaths of buffalo hooflets, which rattled as it swung to and fro in the breeze.

Their arms were the bow and arrow, a short spear or lance, with a head of sharpened stone or bone, stone hammers with wooden handles, and knives made of bone or stone, and if of stone, lashed by rawhide or sinew to a split wooden handle.

The hammers were of two sorts: one quite heavy, almost like a sledge-hammer or maul, and with a short handle; the other much lighter, and with a longer, more limber handle. This last was used by men in war as a mace or war club, while the heavier hammer was used by women as an axe to break up fallen trees for firewood; as a hammer to drive tent-pins into the ground, to kill disabled animals, or to break up heavy bones for the marrow they contained. These mauls and hammers were usually made by choosing an oval stone and pecking a groove about its shortest diameter. The handles were made by green sticks fitted as closely as possible into the groove, brought together and lashed in position by sinew, the whole being then covered with wet rawhide tightly fitted and sewed. As the rawhide dried, it shrunk and strongly bound together the parts of the weapon.

The Blackfeet bow was about four feet long. Its string was of twisted sinew and it was backed with sinew. This gave the bow great power, so that the arrow went with much force. The arrows were straight shoots of the service berry or cherry, and the manufacture of arrows was the chief employment of many of the men of middle life. Each arrow by the same maker was precisely like every other arrow he made. Each arrowmaker tried hard to make good arrows. It was a fine thing to be known as a maker of good arrows.

The shoots for the arrow shafts were brought into the lodge, peeled, smoothed roughly, tied up in bundles, and hung up to dry. After they were dried, the bundles were taken down and each shaft was smoothed and reduced to a proper thickness by the use of a grooved piece of sandstone, which acted on the arrow like sandpaper. After they were of the right thickness, they were straightened by bending with the hands, and sometimes with the teeth, and were then passed through a circular hole drilled in a rib, or in a mountain sheep's horn, which acted in part as a gauge of the size and also as a smoother, for if in passing through the hole the arrow fitted tightly, the shaft received a good polish. The three grooves which always were found in the Blackfeet arrows were made by pushing the shaft through a round hole drilled in a rib, which, however, had one or more projections left on the inside. These projections pressed into the soft wood and made the grooves, which were in every arrow. The feathers were three in number. They were put on with a glue, made by boiling scraps of dried rawhide, and were held in place by wrappings of sinew. The heads of the arrows were made of stone or bone or horn. The flint points were often highly worked and very beautiful, being broken from larger flints by sharp blows of a stone hammer, and after they had been shaped the edges were worked sharp by flaking with an implement of bone or horn. The points made of horn or bone were ground sharp by rubbing on a stone. A notch was cut in the end of the arrow shaft and the shank of the arrow point set in that. The arrow heads were firmly fixed to the shaft by glue and by sinew wrapping.

Although the Blackfeet lived almost altogether on the flesh of birds or animals, yet they had some vegetable food. This was chiefly berries—of which in summer the women collected great quantities and dried them for winter use—and roots, the gathering of which at the proper season of the year occupied much of the time of women and young girls. These roots were unearthed by a long, sharp-pointed stick, called a root digger. Some of the roots were eaten as soon as collected, while others were dried and stored for use in winter.

After they reached the plains, the main food of the Blackfeet was the buffalo, which they killed in large numbers when everything went right. Many of the streams in the Blackfeet country run through wide, deep valleys bordered on either side by cliffs, or broken precipices, falling sharply from the high prairie above. Long ago the Blackfeet must have learned that it was possible to make the buffalo jump over these cliffs, and that in the fall on the rocks below numbers would be killed or crippled. No doubt after this had been practised for a time, there came to some one the idea of building at the foot of such a cliff where the buffalo were run over, a fence which would form a corral or pound, and which would hold all the buffalo that were jumped over the cliff. This corral they called piskun.

It is often said that the buffalo were driven over these precipices, but this is true only in part. Like most wild animals, buffalo are inquisitive. It was not difficult to excite their curiosity, and when they saw something they did not recognize, they were anxious to find out what it was.

When run into the piskun, the buffalo were really drawn by curiosity almost to the jumping point, and between two long diverging lines of people, who kept hidden until after the buffalo had passed them, and then rose and showed themselves and tried to frighten the animals. Now, to be sure, for the short distance that remained between the place where they were alarmed and the place where they jumped, the buffalo were driven. Any attempt on the open prairie to drive buffalo in one direction or another would be certain to fail. The animals would go where they wished to. They would not be driven, though often they might be led.

To the people the capture of food was the most important thing in life, and they put forth every effort to accomplish it. For this reason it came about that the effort to capture buffalo was preceded usually by religious ceremonies, in which many prayers were offered to the powers of the earth, the sky, and the waters, many sacrifices made, and sacred objects, like the buffalo stone, were displayed.

When the day for the hunt came, the man who was to bring the buffalo left the camp early in the morning, climbed the rocky bluffs to the high prairie, and journeyed toward some near-by herd of buffalo, that had been located the day before by himself or by other young men. He approached the buffalo as nearly as he could without frightening them, and then, attracting the attention of some of the animals by uttering certain calls, tossed into the air his buffalo robe or some smaller object. As soon as the buffalo began to look at him, he retreated slowly in the direction of the piskun, but continued to call and to attract their attention by showing himself and then disappearing. Soon, some of the buffalo began to walk toward him, and others began to look and to follow those that had first started, so that before long the whole herd of fifty or a hundred animals might be walking or sometimes trotting after him. The more rapidly the buffalo came on, the faster the man ran— and sometimes it was a hard matter for him to keep ahead of the herd—until he had got far within the wings and near to the cliff. If there seemed danger that he would be overtaken, he watched his chance and either at some low place quickly dodged out of the line in which the buffalo were running, or hid behind one of the piles of stones of which the wings were formed, or, if he had time, slipped over the rocky wall at the valley's edge, so as to get out of the way of the approaching herd.

As soon as the buffalo had come well within the diverging lines of people who were hidden behind the piles of stones called wings, those whom the buffalo passed rose up from their places of concealment, and by yells and shouts and the waving of their robes frightened the buffalo, so that they quite forgot their curiosity in the terror that now replaced it. When the leaders reached the brink of the cliff, they could not stop. They were pushed over by those behind, and most of the buffalo jumped over the cliff. Many were crippled or injured by the fall, and all were kept within the fence of the piskun below. About this fence the people were collected. The buffalo raced round and round within the pen, the young and weak being injured or killed in the crowding, while above the fence men were shooting them with arrows until presently all in the pen were dead, or so hurt that the women could go into the pen and kill them. The people entered and took the flesh and hides.

Deer, elk, and antelope were shot with arrows, and antelope were often captured in pitfalls roofed with slender poles and covered with grass and earth. Such pitfalls were dug in a region where antelope were plenty, and a long ➤ shaped pair of wings, made of poles or bushes or even rock piles, led to the pit. The antelope is very inquisitive and was easily led within the chute and there frightened, as were the buffalo, by people who had been concealed and who rose up and showed themselves after the antelope had passed. This was done more in order to secure antelope skins for clothing than their flesh for food.

Fish and reptiles were not eaten by the Blackfeet, nor were dogs, although dogs, wolves, and coyotes are eaten by many tribes of plains Indians. Most small animals, and practically all birds, were eaten in case of need. In summer, when the wildfowl which bred on so many of the lakes in the Blackfeet country lost their flight-feathers, during the moult, and again in the late summer, when the young ducks and geese were almost fullgrown but could not yet fly, the Indians often went in large parties to the shallow lakes which here and there dotted the prairie, and, driving the birds to shore, killed them in large numbers.

Earlier in the season, when the fowl had begun to lay their eggs, these were collected in great quantities for food. Sometimes they were roasted in the hot ashes, but a more common way was to dig a deep, narrow hole in the ground in which the eggs were to be cooked. Several little platforms of small sticks or twigs were built in this hole, one above another, and on these platforms they put the eggs. Another much smaller hole was dug to one side of the large hole, slanting down into it. The large hole was partly filled with water, and was then roofed over by small sticks on which was placed grass covered with earth. Stones were heated in a fire built near at hand, and then were rolled down the side hole into the larger hole, heating the water, which at last boiled and steamed, the steam cooking the eggs.

When the Americans first met them on the prairie, the Blackfeet were known as great warriors. But up to the time when they got from the Hudson Bay traders better weapons than they had before known, whether these were metal knives, steel arrow points, or guns, it is probable that they did not do much fighting. There seems to have been no reason why they should have fought, unless they quarrelled about small matters with other tribes. It became quite different when the Indians procured better arms and, above all, when they got horses—a means of swiftly getting about over the country, something that all people wanted to have and which all were so eager to obtain that they would go into danger for them. In the old days of stone arrow heads, when they had to travel on foot and to carry heavy loads on their backs, the whole thought and effort of the tribe must have been devoted to the work of procuring a supply of food.

The tribal and family life of the people was simple and friendly. The man and his wives loved each other and loved their children. Relationship counted for much in an Indian camp, and cousins of remote degree were called brother and sister. Children were not punished; they were trained by persuasion and advice. They were told by older people how they ought to act in order to make their lives happy and successful and to be well thought of by their fellows. Young people had much respect for their elders, listened to what they said, and strove more or less successfully to follow their teachings.

The Blackfeet were very religious. They feared many natural powers and influences whose workings they did not understand, and they were constantly praying to the Sun—regarded as the ruler of the universe—as well as to those other powers which they believe live in the stars, the earth, the mountains, the animals, and the trees. The Blackfoot was constantly afraid that some evil thing might happen to him, and he therefore prayed to all the powers for help—for good fortune in his undertakings, for health, plenty, and long life for himself and all his family.

Among these tribes there are a number of secret societies known as the All Comrades or All Friends—groups of men of different ages, which have been alluded to in the stories. Originally there were about twelve of these

211

societies, but a number have been abandoned of recent years.

The tribe was divided into a number of clans, all the members of which were believed to be related, and in old times no member of a clan was permitted to marry another member of the clan. Relations might not marry.

In olden times, when large numbers of people were together, the lodges of the camp were pitched in a great circle, the opening toward the southeast. In this circle each clan camped in its own particular place with relation to the other clans. Within the circle was often a smaller circle of lodges, each occupied by one or more of the societies of the All Comrades. Sometimes it happened that great numbers of the Blackfeet came together, perhaps even all of the three tribes, Blackfeet, Bloods, and Piegans. When this was the case, each tribe camped by itself with its own circle, no matter how near it might be to one or other of the tribal circles.

We read of some tribes of Indians which believed that after death the spirits of the departed went to a happy hunting ground where game was always plenty and life was full of joy. The Blackfeet knew no such place as this. When they died their spirits were believed to go to a barren, sandy region south of the Saskatchewan, which they called the Sand Hills. Here, as shadows, the ghosts lived a life much like their existence before death, but all was unreal—unsubstantial. Riding on shadow horses they hunted shadow buffalo. They lived in shadow camps and when they moved shadow dogs hauled their travois. There are stories which tell that living people have seen these hunters, their houses, and their implements of the camp, but when the people got close they found that what they thought they had seen was something different. It reminds us a little of the old ballad of Alice Brand, where Urgan tells of the things seen in fairy-land:

> "And gayly shines the Fairy-land—
>   But all is glistening show,
> Like the idle gleam that December's beam
>   Can dart on ice and snow.

> "And fading, like that varied gleam,
>   Is our inconstant shape,

213

BLACKFEET INDIAN STORIES

Who now like knight and lady seem,
And now like dwarf and ape."

Books have been written about the Blackfeet Indians which tell much more about how they lived than can be given here.

END

www.ingramcontent.com/pod-product-compliance
Lightning Source LLC
Chambersburg PA
CBHW070336090426
42733CB00009B/1210